Veloce Classic Reprint Series

PORSCHE 930 to 935
The Turbo Porsches

MARTINI PORSCHE

40

MARTINI
PORSCHE

John Starkey

Other Porsche titles from Veloce Publishing –

Essential Buyer's Guide Series
Porsche 911 (964) (Streather)
Porsche 911 (993) (Streather)
Porsche 911 (996) (Streather)
Porsche 911 (997) – Model years 2004 to 2009 (Streather)
Porsche 911 (997) – Second generation models 2009 to 2012 (Streather)
Porsche 911 Carrera 3.2 (Streather)
Porsche 911SC (Streather)
Porsche 924 – All models 1976 to 1988 (Hodgkins)
Porsche 928 (Hemmings)
Porsche 930 Turbo & 911 (930) Turbo (Streather)
Porsche 944 (Higgins)
Porsche 981 Boxster & Cayman (Streather)
Porsche 986 Boxster (Streather)
Porsche 987 Boxster and Cayman 1st generation
(2005-2009) (Streather)
Porsche 987 Boxster and Cayman 2nd generation (2009-2012) (Streather)

General
Porsche 356 (2nd Edition) (Long)
Porsche 908 (Födisch, Neßhöver, Roßbach, Schwarz & Roßbach)
Porsche 911 Carrera – The Last of the Evolution (Corlett)
Porsche 911R, RS & RSR, 4th Edition (Starkey)
Porsche 911, The Book of the (Long)
Porsche 911 – The Definitive History 2004-2012 (Long)
Porsche – The Racing 914s (Smith)
Porsche 911SC 'Super Carrera' – The Essential Companion (Streather)
Porsche 914 & 914-6: The Definitive History of the Road & Competition Cars (Long)
Porsche 924 (Long)
The Porsche 924 Carreras – evolution to excellence (Smith)
Porsche 928 (Long)
Porsche 944 (Long)
Porsche 964, 993 & 996 Data Plate Code Breaker (Streather)
Porsche 993 'King Of Porsche' – The Essential Companion (Streather)
Porsche 996 'Supreme Porsche' – The Essential Companion (Streather)
Porsche 997 2004-2012 – Porsche Excellence (Streather)
Porsche Boxster – The 986 series 1996-2004 (Long)
Porsche Boxster & Cayman – The 987 series (2004-2013) (Long)
Porsche Racing Cars – 1953 to 1975 (Long)
Porsche Racing Cars – 1976 to 2005 (Long)
Porsche – The Rally Story (Meredith)
Porsche: Three Generations of Genius (Meredith)
Powered by Porsche (Smith)

www.veloce.co.uk

Classic Reprint edition first published in March 2018 by Veloce Publishing Limited, Veloce House, Parkway Farm Business Park, Middle Farm Way, Poundbury, Dorchester DT1 3AR, England. Tel 01305 260068 / Fax 01305 250479 / e-mail info@veloce.co.uk / web www.veloce.co.uk or www.velocebooks.com.
Reprinted July 2018. This paperback edition published March 2021
ISBN 978-1-787117-53-2 / UPC 6-36847-01753-8

Readers with ideas for automotive books, or books on other transport or related hobby subjects, are invited to write to the editorial director of Veloce Publishing at the above address. British Library Cataloguing in Publication Data – A catalogue record for this book is available from the British Library. Typesetting, design and page make-up all by Veloce Publishing Ltd on Apple Mac.
Printed and bound by CPI Group (UK) Ltd, Croydon, CR0 4YY.
Front cover image courtesy of Porsche AG

Veloce *Classic Reprint* Series

PORSCHE 930 to 935
The Turbo Porsches

John Starkey

CONTENTS

ACKNOWLEDGEMENTS

One of the most pleasant aspects of writing a book on motor racing is talking to the people involved when the subject cars were being raced. Naturally, nearly all drivers liked the cars which gave them the most excitement and, in this respect, this book has been more pleasurable to assemble than any previously.

It is no exaggeration to say that drivers' eyes light up when you mention that you are writing a book about the 934s and 935s. Although I carried out a lot of my interviews by telephone, there was no disguising the excitement in their voices as drivers recounted their experiences with the turbocharged beasts.

John Fitzpatrick, Hurley Haywood, John Paul, Jr., Bob Akin, Bob Garretson, Dick Barbour, Preston Henn, Gary Belcher, Chet Vincentz, Nick Faure, Dennis Aase, Bruce Canepa and Milt Minter all loved the cars they drove, and I thank them for their time and trouble. Jürgen Barth at the Porsche factory, now Head of Customer Racing, was kindness personified in providing information on which cars were supplied to the racing teams. My thanks go to Klaus Parr for the factory-supplied photographs and to Achim Stroth (the Kremer Brothers' race team manager) for information regarding the K3s. Also to Reinhold Joest, although having lost his records for this period, he supplied valuable information on the 935s that he modified. I must thank *Autocar* magazine for permission to use Paul Frere's impressions of driving the cars when they were new. His special background of engineering and racing, allied to a keenly analytical mind, gave him a unique insight into how the cars behaved. Ulrich Trispel, Klaus Handemann and Janos Wimpfen for their information on the cars, which ran in the German National Championship, and the FIA's International races. Ulrich proved a tremendous help,

I could not leave these pages without thanking Su, for her patience, enthusiasm and computer design skills, which helped produce this book.

DEDICATION

I dedicate this book to Rolf Stommelen, a great driver, particularly of 935s. Rolf was sadly killed at Riverside in 1983 when part of his car's bodywork became detached. Not only was Rolf a very quick driver, he was loved by all who came into contact with him; a rare attribute.

FOREWORD

Despite the plethora of books on the market which deal with the Porsche 911, it is surprising that there is little written solely about the Porsche race cars which dominated the World and IMSA Championships of 1976–1982, the Porsches 934 and 935.

I was very pleased when John Starkey asked me to write a few words as a foreword to this book. The Porsche 935 provided me with some of the most exciting racing of my career and certainly with more victories than any other car I drove.

Having raced a 911 for the first time in 1967 and continued through the Carreras and RSRs, I was around when Porsche first started development of the Turbo 911. Right from the start, it was obviously a very exciting and brutish car. There was always a surplus of power, particularly in the wet, and lots of things to play with and adjust whilst driving, such as turbo boost, brake balance and sway bar adjustment.

The early cars were modified and lightened production chassis. By the time they came to the end of their useful lifespan in 1983, superseded by the group C and GTP cars, they had developed into custom designed tubular framed monsters, giving anything up to 800 horsepower, depending on who you were talking to at the time. Considering their power and speed, they also had that legendary Porsche reliability.

I was fortunate to drive for most of the leading teams in that era and then went on to run my own team and develop the K4 that Kremer first used in 1981. At the end of its development, I considered that car to have been the ultimate 935. It brought me many victories in IMSA and elsewhere in the world. I have no idea just how much power was on tap when I had the boost turned up for the first lap of a race, but whenever I asked, the only answer I received was "enough". It was difficult to argue with that.

My only regret is that I never won Le Mans in a 935. I came very close with Dick Barbour and Brian Redman in 1980 when we led for many hours, only to develop a misfire which dropped us down to fifth at the finish. The Kremers did win in 1979 with the Whittingtons and quite deservedly so, as they led the 935 development for many years after the factory withdrew. I just happened to be driving for a different team that year. Ah well, that's motor racing.

JOHN FITZPATRICK

PREFACE

I want to tell you a story. Back in 1975 I was thrilled, along with thousands of others, when Porsche introduced the 911 (930) Turbo. Although the U.S. version was still a year away, that didn't stop the buzz or mute the excitement on what would be the car of the decade. I was lucky enough to get to drive one of the first cars to reach these shores and the experience left me flabbergasted. So much power so quickly and I was totally clueless as how to control it. On the racing side, it was the Martini Porsche 935 that was providing all the sights and sounds. The simplicity of Norbert Singer's design was to profoundly influence the aftermarket world for years to come. If the 930 was to make "turbo" an everyday word, it was the 935 that brought us the term "slant nose". If I could only get the chance to drive a 935… Forget it kid, dream on.

Dream I did and finally one day it came true. In 1986, I was the very proud owner of a 1977 935. Not just any 935 but one with a good history and featured on a factory poster. Otis Chandler (publisher of the Los Angeles Times) used to rent Riverside several times a year in order to run his cars in an informal setting. I was fortunate to get invited to such a day. For this occasion, I brought out my 935 for its maiden voyage. Those who remember the old Riverside circuit know how fast and demanding the track could be. The small group that day consisted of Chandler's 917K Gulf-Porsche and 935 Twin Turbo, Dave Morse's 934 with a 935 motor, Dan Gurney's AAR team testing their IMSA GTO Celicas, and Moi.

Watching the Gulf 917 that day reminded me of the myths that surround the 917 and exist to this day. It won everything and couldn't be beaten. Ferrari tried, Alfa tried, Matra tried. Finally the powers that be simply did what they do best: the 917 was written out of existence, a victim of a rules change. I remember caravaning with a group of 30 VWs to a drive-in that was showing the movie Le Mans. Now years later, I was about to go on the same track with one of those cars.

The 935 lit off with a low rumble as I exited pit lane and headed towards turn two. A few laps to warm up the tires and I started to get a good feel for the car. My speeds rapidly increased. Coming out of turn nine, I spotted the 917 coming on the track. I turned up the boost and took off hoping to be able to stay with the Gulf car. For several laps I followed the 917, surprised I was able to stay close. After all, this was a 917, I was driving a 911, right? One lap later, rocketing down Riverside's famous back straight, my 935 blew past the 917. A missed shift perhaps? Nothing that simple, but instead the realization that much progress had been made from 1971 to 1977. A production-bodied 911 six cylinder with a single turbo faster than twelve cylinder tube frame sports prototype? There are still a lot of things I don't understand. But on that particular day, the 935 wasn't one of them.

KERRY MORSE

INTRODUCTION

I was diving down the Craner curves at Donington racecourse in 1987 in a 1974 Porsche RSR Carrera. I was going as fast as I could, with my throttle foot planted to the wall and gripping the steering wheel tightly. I thought I was going quite quickly until a blue "something" shot past me on the outside of the corner, traveling at least thirty miles an hour faster and with orange flame pouring from it's exhaust. Chastened, I attempted to catch "it" under braking at the old hairpin, failed miserably, and watched it rocket up to Maclean's Corner and out of sight.

Such was my first view of a 935 in action. Although I had seen 935s from the trackside, I'd never encountered one on a track before. It was a humbling experience. I was taking part in the modified Porsche Championship at the time and John Greasley, the driver of that 935 K3, simply blasted all opposition out of the way. The only time he had a real struggle was when Rusty French, an Australian 935 owner, brought his ex-Gelo 1980 factory 935 to Europe for a season to race. The resulting duels were exciting and there was no getting away from the fact that the 935 was a mighty and spectacular race car.

In 1987, I wrote a book, "R to RSR, The Racing Porsches", which told the story of the normally aspirated racing 911s. The development story of the RSR Carrera ended in 1974, the year Porsche embarked upon their task to tame the turbocharging principle for the road going 911 (known internally as the Typ 930), and to apply those principles to a new generation of "Silhouette" racers. The most famous of these by far became the Type 935 and I make no apology for claiming it to be one of the most significant racing Porsches (and there have been many) ever made.

This book, however, is not just about the 935 although that car's history occupies a great deal of its content. In these pages, I have attempted to explain that the development which the 934, 935, 959 and 961 underwent was put back into the cars the public were able to buy for the road, the 930 Turbos. It's a fact that, despite the factory's type number of 930, the public have always known the road going sportscar as "the 911 turbo". And why not? That's exactly what they were buying.

The 911 itself has always been cited as "a triumph of development over design". Within these pages, you will read how Porsche took a car introduced to the public in 1963 with a little over 100 horsepower and which, today, copes with up to 500 horsepower! By 1982-83, the fastest of the 935s were powered by engines developing 850 horsepower.

Porsche's engineers have never stood still, using racing as their main tool in the research and development field. Porsche dominated GT racing in the seventies and eighties. Only BMW, of all other manufacturers, came close in terms of effort. If you, at any time, bought a Porsche 911, in both turbocharged and unturbocharged tune, you can rest assured that racing has improved the breed.

FOOTNOTE TO THIS THIRD EDITION:

Since producing the second edition of this book, a lot of detailed history has come my way via the dedicated enthusiasts of the 930 to 935 Porsches, particularly where the racing cars are concerned. Happily, the first and second editions of this book sold out rapidly, which enables me to produce what I hope the reader will judge to be an improved edition.

Most notably, the appendix of the chassis histories has dramatically expanded and improved. It seems everyone wants to be involved where the accuracy of these records is concerned! And understandably so. The Turbocharged 911/930 family of Porsches is a very special family. As anyone who has ever driven one and felt the turbocharger(s) kick in can testify, there's nothing like a turbo on full song!

JOHN STARKEY
November 2017

VISIT VELOCE ON THE WEB – WWW.VELOCE.CO.UK
All current books • New book news • Special offers • Gift vouchers • Forum

9

Chapter 1

THE TURBO'S ARRIVAL

As Norbert Singer had been the engineer in charge of developing the 911 RS and RSR models for Porsche, so it was Dr. Ing. Piech who developed the idea of using the turbocharger, first of all in the 917, and later on in the 911.

International motor racing rules brought about the type 930 turbo series of 911 variants and Porsche found itself in a fortuitous position, able to exploit the turbo-charging technology.

To understand the underlying reasons for the rise of the turbocharger we must, first of all, look at the rule changes instituted by the governing body, the FIA (Federation Internationale Automobiles) in their quest to keep motor racing within safe bounds. During the mid-sixties, cars such as Ferrari's P4 and the Ford GT40 had dominated the 24 Hours of Le Mans, reaching speeds of over 210 mph. The CSI (Commission Sportive Internationale), who were the forerunner of the FIA, had become concerned over these speeds and cut the size of "stock block" engines down to 5-liters and racing engines with overhead camshafts to 3-liters for the 1968 season.

At one stroke, the 7-liter Ford GT40 and the Ferrari P4 were outlawed and the newly-introduced Lola T70 was forced to run with 5-liter Chevrolet V8 power only. Previously, this car had shown great potential with engines of up to 6.4-liters installed.

The CSI left a loophole in their new rules, however; they specified that a pur-pose-built sports racing car with an overhead camshaft engine fitted would have to be manufactured in "not less than fifty units", imag-ining that no manufacturer would take the plunge to make this many cars. The following year, they cut this amount to twenty-five cars.

Porsche saw their opportunity and, after having battled for years for class hon-ors, they came out with twenty-five type 917 sports-prototype cars. These cars could compete for outright victory at all the great venues, such as Le Mans, Daytona, Sebring, the Nürburgring 1000 kilometers, etc, to con-test the World Manufacturers Championship for Sportscars. It was not long before Ferrari followed suit with twenty-five Tipo 512 sports racing cars. Suddenly the CSI was faced with the nightmare of endurance racers that could now achieve some 240 mph down a long enough straight.

The CSI reconsidered their future rule changes. They announced that as of 1972, their policy would be to encourage race cars directly developed from road cars, an attitude that perfectly suited Porsche as they they were, even then, starting to build the 2.7-liter RS Carrera. This was promptly developed further into, first of all the 2.8-liter RSR and then, for 1974, the 3.0-liter RS and its "evolution" car (meant for track use only): the RSR.

In 1970, with the looming disqualifi-cation of the all-conquering 917 in European events, Porsche had adopted turbocharging as a way of increasing the power of the 917 spiders. These were being campaigned in the CanAm series of races in America, where large amounts of prize money were being offered for success.

After an intense period of development, the 917/10 appeared for the sole use of the Roger Penske-led team, which broke the stranglehold of the previously dominant McLarens. With 1,100 bhp available if the boost was used to the full, the big Porsche, in both 917/10 and 917/30 form, dominated the 1972 and 1973 season. George Follmer won the Championship in 1971 and Mark Donohue took the honors in 1972.

Porsche, seeing the way that the rule makers were thinking, realized that by 1973 their 911 engine, in its naturally aspirated form, had reached it's maximum output. The RSR had a claimed 330 bhp from the air and oil-cooled 3-liter flat 6 engine, this figure being achieved at 8,000 rpm by the end of that year. BMW, for their part, had shown a gullwing door-equipped coupe with a turbocharged engine in 1972. Porsche saw this as

The engine with its plumbing as it appeared in 1974.

a direct threat to their hard won sales success with the 911.

Previously, in 1969, Porsche had experimented by building a turbocharged 2-liter flat 6 engine. They now responded to the BMW challenge by building a 2.7-liter version under the direction of Valentin Schaffer. This engine, ready in January 1973, embodied Porsche's previous experience with the 917 turbocars, and immediately proved both powerful and reliable. Once installed in a 911 road car, the engine, although giving in excess of 280 bhp, displayed the turbocharger's "Achilles' heel": throttle lag.

A word here about turbocharging itself. Invented early in the century, (1905 to be precise, by Alfred Buchi), its chief uses had been in ships in the 1920s and then American aircraft engines during World War Two. Briefly, the European nations eschewed turbocharging and used mechanically driven superchargers to pump more oxygen into their (mainly liquid-cooled) aircraft engines.

The Americans realized that turbocharging was an ideal way of using the otherwise wasted exhaust gases. They used their favored air-cooled radial engines, particularly in their Naval aircraft where lightness was most important for carrier aircraft taking off from a short deck. These exhaust gases were used to drive a turbine impeller set into the engine's exhaust pipes. Via a bearing system, the impeller drove a single stage centrifugal compressor that blew air and fuel under pressure into the cylinders of the engine. This resulted in more power being delivered. The casing of the turbine was of cast iron and the turbine itself had to cope with temperatures of up to 900°C. The impeller was mounted in an aluminum housing.

The problem with any form of forced induction is that air, under pressure, becomes heated. This can lead to detonation and subsequent piston destruction. To overcome this, the compression ratio needs to be lowered. Later, it was discovered that if the pressurized, heated air was forced through an intercooler, (essentially, a radiator that extracted the heat), this went further to solve the problem of detonation. The intercooler itself had been invented and then highly developed during the 1920s by the speedway racers of the period, mainly on American Miller racing cars.

Of course, aircraft cruise on set throttle settings for long periods and the throttle lag, which is a feature of turbocharging, was as unimportant in an aircraft application as it had been on the speedways. Throttle lag is caused by the turbocharger's turbine wheel coming to a standstill. This is due to back pressure when the exhaust gases cease as the throttle is cut, thus cutting off the supply of pressurized air to the engine's induction system. When the throttle is opened again, the turbine wheel has to "spool up" (accelerate) to it's previous 80,000-100,000 rpm and the engine thus suffers a time lag to come back up to full power.

After the war, the turbocharger found a new application in lorries with diesel engines. Turbocharging was particularly suited to the thermal properties of diesel fuel. Indianapolis was the first venue to see the turbocharger applied in a serious fashion to a racing engine. Although a turbocharged diesel-powered car had raced there in 1952, it was the demise of the almost perpetual Offenhauser four cylinder engine, itself a descendant of the centrifugally-supercharged

Miller engine of the 1920s, which ushered in the new age.

As we have seen, Indianapolis and other oval racing tracks, are more suited to turbocharger application than road racing tracks. The racing cars keep up a more or less constant throttle opening at Indy, thus minimizing the throttle lag problem. In conjunction with Herb Porter and Stuart Hilborn, Bob De Bischop of the Garrett Company developed the first downsized turbocharged Offenhauser in 1965. It promptly produced over 600 bhp at a time when the rival Ford four camshaft V8 was producing 500 bhp. Capacity of the first "production" turbocharged Offenhausers was just 168 cubic inches (2.8-liters) and it was rated at 625 bhp at 8,000 rpm on 1.6 bar* of boost. After development in 1966, which included 20% more water flow to improve cooling and a reversion from aluminum to iron for the block/head casting, the new turbocharged

Offy proved a winner. It finished seventh at Indianapolis that year and, in 1967, came in first, courtesy of Bobby Unser. Of course, Indianapolis rules allowed the engines to run on Methanol, a much "cooler" fuel than petroleum, which considerably eased cooling headaches. The turbocharged Offenhauser went on to a long and honorable career, its power peaking at 800 bhp at 9,000 rpm using up to 3.0 bar.

*1 bar (barometer) of pressure =14.7 lbs/sq.in. above atmospheric pressure which itself is 14.7 lbs/sq.in. at sea level.

The new "Turbo" (right) alongside a 911 for one of the first Porsche Turbo publicity photographs.

Turbo lag could be ameliorated by the use of a "wastegate". This was basically a trap door, which opened when the throttle was released, dumping exhaust gases to the outside air, thus helping to keep the turbine spinning. This solution to the 917/10's engine was employed early on in that engine's development but turbo lag now reared its head in the new 911 turbo engine.

Whilst Porsche's engineers struggled to match the new technology to the Bosch K-Jetronic fuel injection system, which Dr. Fuhrmann specified (in order to keep costs and emission down), the new road going turbocharged Porsche 911 (known internally by its type number of "930") made a dramatic debut on the Company's stand at the Frankfurt Motor Show in September 1973.

Finished in silver with "Porsche" and flashes outlined in white along its flanks, the new 911 Turbo displayed bodywork that would shortly be adopted for the naturally-aspirated RS 3-liter model. (The display car was taken from the RS 3-liter production line.) This included its flared wheel arches, under which sat 7-inch front and 8-inch rear wide wheels.

Gone now were the dainty bumpers of the previous 911. An enveloping impact-resistant plastic bumper/spoiler wrapped around the front of the car with a large rectangular inlet set beneath the bumper. Behind this bumper was the front-mounted oil cooler, now even more important than before to dissipate the heat of the new engine. On the engine cover was a huge "whaletail", similar in size and shape to that of the RS 3.0. This was needed to give downforce at the rear and to keep the tires in contact with the road, in view of the 150 mph plus performance of the new Model 930. Porsche's engineers claimed that they had tried nine different designs of spoiler before finalizing the design shown, the same as that which would be used on the 1974 RS 3.0 and 2.7 Carrera.

Porsche representatives at the show quoted the capacity of the silver show car as 2.1-liters, with a power output of 280 bhp. This would appear to have been one of the prototype engines which would be seen in the racing RSR Turbo of the 1974 season but this MAY have been a mistake. A 2.7-liter engine was specified as having nestled in the engine bay of the prototype by the factory in later years. Maximum speed of the mocked-up prototype coupe was quoted as 176 mph.

This new engine (Type 930/50) was developed rapidly to a full 3.0-liters for the production car. It employed the aluminum (Al-Si) crankcase of the RS 3.0-liter with 86 mm cylinder head stud spacing, instead of the magnesium one of the RS 2.7, to give greater strength. The bore remained the same as that of the RS 3.0-liter at 95 mm for its Nikasil-coated cylinders. The valve sizes were also identical at 49 and 41.5 mm but the valve included angle was now 2 degrees 15 minutes narrower. The intake port diameter was reduced to 32 mm in the interests of increased medium range torque. The compression ratio was reduced to 6.5:1 and the oil supply to the bottom end was stepped up to cope with the increased stresses, both mechanical and thermal. The cooling fan now rotated at 1.67 times crankshaft speed, as against the previous 1.3 in the normally aspirated car. This gave an air-flow rate of 1,500-liters per second. The new turbocharged engine used the metering unit from the contemporary Mercedes V8 but with two outlets blanked

The Porsche 930 Turbo as it first appeared in factory press literature. Then, it was referred to as the 911 Turbo. Note the extra air intake on the rear wing. The 'G' type bodyshell was essentially the same as that of the 1974 RS 3.0 naturally-aspirated car, the only external differences being the Turbo's more rounded wheel-arches, the sun-roof and the rubber bumper inserts.

off. The boost pressure was 0.8 bar (11 psi) and 260 bhp was achieved at a lowly 5,500 rpm. Torque was quoted as 254 lbs. ft. at 4,000 rpm.

To cope with the increased power and torque, a new gearbox with only four forward speeds was fitted. These gears were wider than those of the previous Type 915 five speed gearbox, which made for extra strength. The Type 915 gearbox had been marginal in this respect. Any loads exceeding the 300 bhp mark (that of the Carrera RSR, for example) put a definite limit on its lifespan. This new gearbox could cope with up to 475 lbs. ft. of torque. A larger clutch of 240 mm diameter (from 225 mm) with an enlarged splined hub was also fitted. The clutch's hub featured a rubber-damped center. A limited-slip differential with a locking factor of up to 80% was used to combat wheelspin. With

the first few 930 Turbos made, a 9/36 or 9/38 final drive ratio was available to suit either 15- or 16-inch diameter wheels. When the wheel size was fixed at 16 inches, the 9/38 ratio became the standard ratio fitted.

The Turbo was most fully equipped and upholstered, even down to the "Turbo" inserts seen here on the rear seat-backs.

In the new 930 Porsche "Turbo" (as the car was immediately dubbed) the exhaust gases went through the turbine before passing through the silencer. The turbine wheel, fitted upon the same shaft that carried the centrifugal compressor, drove this to pull air from the air cleaner. The air, now pressurized and denser, passed to the K-Jetronic's fuel injection. The metering unit governed the amount of fuel sent to the individual injectors. The pressurized air went to the intake manifold and the throttle housing as well as the wastegate and the recirculating valve. Once 0.8 bar was reached, the excess pressure was vented via the wastegate through a separate pipe to the exhaust silencer. A vacuum was caused when the accelerator pedal was released, acting upon the recirculating plunger valve. This then connected the turbine input and output pipes together so that the back pressure, which would normally act upon the turbine, was absent. This allowed the turbine wheel to keep spinning thus reducing throttle lag. At the same time, fuel flow to the cylinders was cut off due to the lack of air reaching the fuel metering unit.

To homologate the new Porsche 930 turbo 3.0-liter and its variants (the types 934/group 4 and 935/group 5) for racing, the factory had to produce 400 road going cars over a two year period. They incorporated many of the lessons learned with the Turbo RSR into the 3.0 Turbo, which went on sale in September 1974. The engine's induction side was now updated from that of the first-seen prototype with a new upside-down airflow metering unit. Overboosted gases were ventilated out of a blow-off valve, in the same way as the racing car.

Unlike the racing car, the road car required a gradual increase in power delivery throughout the rev range, instead of all-out power at the top end. A small inlet scroll was fitted to the turbine wheel, allowing the boost to come in as early as 1,000 rpm. From 2,500 rpm, the boost and power came in strongly, with full boost pressure occurring at 4,500 rpm. The wastegate then opened, not allowing the boost to increase above this figure. European Turbo 930s were rated at 260 bhp, with cars intended for the USA rated at 234 bhp, although capable of running on two-star, 91 octane fuel. Unlike the first prototype, the 917 brakes were not fitted to the early production cars. The brakes used were to the same specification as those fitted to the RS 2.7 Carrera. This omission was cured with the introduction of the 3.3-liter version of the 930, some three years later.

Where the suspension was concerned, the rear trailing arms and hubs of the road going car were made bigger than the previous 911, being closer in size to those of the 917. The suspension movement was altered to disallow positive camber to creep into the movement. At the front, an aluminum cross member carried the suspension mountings and anti-dive under braking was introduced with the raising of the rear torsion bar mountings. The torsion bars, both front and rear, were uprated in diameter to that of the RSR Carrera's 26 mm.

The cockpit of the new 3.0 Turbo had every option available to 911 buyers included as standard fittings. Even the seats were dramatic, having tartan or chequered plaid woven into them if specified!

Paul Frere, the renowned test driver and author of books on Porsche, tested an early 3.0-liter Turbo. He declared it to be

Later on: the 3.3-liter Turbo with its revised whaletail, sixteen-inch diameter wheels and twin exhaust pipes.

easily the fastest production Porsche he had ever tested.

Despite a clutch that did not allow a racing start, Frere still recorded a maximum speed of 155.8 mph, 0-100 mph in 14.2 seconds. Only 25.15 seconds were required for the new 930 to cover the standing kilometer. 60-120 mph could be covered in top gear in just 20 seconds.

Once the road testers started getting their hands on the new Turbo, two things were made apparent to the readers. First was the incredible performance of the car and second was the price, initially £14,822 in the UK, rising within two years to £21,162.

Reading through those tests today, the uniformity of opinion is remarkable.

Though the price seemed jaw dropping in 1975 (when the first deliveries were being made), every road tester agreed that the car was worth every penny.

Autocar wrote, "The Porsche Turbo is an outstandingly exciting motor car, which adds yet another classic car to the achievements of that remarkable German manufacturer."

Denis Jenkinson, writing in *Motor Sport* said, "I never thought the day would come when Ferraris, Maseratis, Lamborghinis and similar exotica would pale into insignificance in my book of motoring, but that day came with the Porsche Turbo. I found it hard to accept that a Porsche could be worth over £20,000. However, when I returned it a week later I had changed my mind completely, convinced that Porsche were offering £20,000 worth of perfor-mance, engineering, quality and, above all else, integrity."

The initial 500 cars were soon sold. Porsche laid down another 500, selling the 1,000th car by May 1976 and then sold still more, the American market's reaction being the same as that of Europe. Porsche, even in those troubled times of oil crisis and economic recession found it difficult to fulfill demand for their Type 930.

In America, the Turbo sold for $28,000 in 1977 and sported some modifications to the wastegate and fuel injection. The car now had power-assisted brakes and face-level air vents in the cabin, together with a boost gauge set into the dashboard. For the US market, with its demand for low exhaust emissions, Porsche developed a turbo engine (Type 930/53), which produced 245 DIN bhp at 5,500 rpm. This engine had air injection

The Turbo in the '90s.

pumps and thermal reactors plus different ignition timing.

Wheel diameter on the 1977 car had now risen to 16 inches. This allowed the use of low-profile Pirelli P7s, a revolution where high-performance tires were concerned. If 15-inch diameter wheels were fitted, an option was 60-series tires to give the same rolling radius.

The 3.0 Turbo lasted in production for three years with subtle on-going modifications being tried out and developed. If they were successful, they were incorporated into the car and, if not, they were discarded. The engine in 1977 became the type 930/52. However, the culmination of all this testing (which went hand in hand with the racing program of the 934 and 935) was the 3.3-liter engined car, introduced in 1978.

Although horsepower and torque had now increased to 300 bhp and 293 lbs. ft. of torque at 5,500 rpm and 4,000 rpm respectively, the weight had also increased by 480 lbs. This was due to the addition of air conditioning and even more trim. The clutch's hub now featured a rubber damped center that helped to damp down low speed chatter. This necessitated a change to steel for the clutch housing. The bell housing was made 30 mm longer, in order to accommodate the clutch hub's thickness.

To counter the increased weight, the 917 brakes were now fitted as standard and the engine sported a large intercooler. This resided inside a newly-designed "whaletail", which had raised lips on the outside to give even more downforce than before.

Top speed, with the fourth gear ratio raised slightly over that used in the 3.0-liter car, now proved to be a genuine 160 mph average of two runs. This was achieved by *Motor* magazine when they took a car to the Ehra-Lessien proving ground, a round trip from London and back of 900 miles. They covered the distance in eighteen hours, complete with all stops and cross-channel ferries.

For many years, until the temporary demise of the road going turbo, the car received periodic updates, such as the one in 1983 when the engine was known as the Type 930/66. This had a new warm-up regulator with an improved fuel distribution system. Coupled with these changes was a new distributor, which featured a temperature-controlled vacuum advance for emission control. Even with a bypassed wastegate exhausting through the silencer, the engine still made 300 bhp at 5,500 rpm.

Mention should be made of one very special Turbo that was built in 1983. Mansour Ojjeh, the boss of TAG Techniques, had arranged with Porsche to supply engines to his Company for use in the Formula One McLarens, which dominated motor racing during this period. As a reward for the association, Porsche built a very special road going car for Ojjeh. According to the data supplied by the factory, this was a 930 Turbo but built at Werk One at Stuttgart on a 934 chassis. The Type 930/66 engine produced some 380 horsepower at 5,500 rpm at 0.8 bar. Bodywise, this "934" resembled a 1978 "customer" 935 with running boards, slope nose and large rear fenders plus a "biplane" tail. Center-locking wheels of 10-inch width at the front and 13-inch width at the rear were fitted and the interior was fitted out in an extremely luxurious fashion, incorporating luggage bins in the rear compartment and a full-house stereo system.

In 1986, the USA, Turbo-less for six years, received a new car. This was based on the old 930 and was in production for just three years, until the new 964 was introduced in Carrera 4 form.

The American 930 had an engine (Type 930/68) with a catalytic converter and an oxygen sensor to meet the very strict US emission laws. This new turbo engine used unleaded fuel and produced 282 bhp at 5,500 rpm, showing a torque factor of 287.4 lbs. ft. at 4,000 rpm.

A new Turbo was introduced in 1990, based upon the design of the new Carreras 2 and 4 (Model Type number 964). As this was a completely new design, using the 911/930's dimensions, it does not, strictly speaking, fall within the parameters of this book. However, as it is the logical successor to the evergreen 911 and 930, and since the very latest racing versions are based upon the 964, a brief description of these cars is in order.

The suspension medium of the 964 eschewed torsion bars and went over completely to coil springs in the interests of serviceability. Whilst retaining the basic layout, the rear suspension adopted a semi-trailing arm layout which, thanks to a clever suspension mounting point and bush design, stopped any tendency of the rear wheels to toe-out, a common by-product of this type of suspension layout under compression. Additionally, the front suspension had to be redesigned to take account of the Carrera 4's front drive shafts.

In the Turbo version, the anti-roll bars are stiffer (21 and 22 mm front and rear respectively), to account for the greater weight, wider track and higher power. Harder springs and Boge dampers recalibrated to a stiffer compression and rebound setting are fitted. A gearbox based on the G50 gearbox of the 964 was introduced in 1989 (Type G50/50), which had a reinforced casing to take the increased stress. The crown wheel and pinion were made larger to take the increased torque. This necessitated the engine and gearbox assembly being mounted 30 mm more to the rear than in the current Carrera. The brake discs all around were of larger diameter than the Carrera's and the front discs were thicker.

This new 964 Turbo was not particularly well received as, although it was based upon the new, better 964 chassis, the engine was still the (now old) 3.3-liter unit. In charge of the Turbo's development was Roland Kussmaul. With the recession biting, he set out with his engineers to do what Porsche does best: develop a car. At Porsche, nothing stands still for long and, for 1992, Porsche introduced the Turbo "S".

The "S" was based upon the 1991 IMSA "Supercar" Championship winner of 1991, which featured larger wheels of 18-inch diameter and 8- and 10-inch width, front and rear respectively. The "S" was also fitted with larger front brake calipers and was lowered by 40 mm. The dampers were uprated to give a firmer, more controlled ride.

The engine benefited from a rise in turbo boost from 0.8 bar to 0.9 bar (13 psi). It had the camshafts from the Carrera 3.6 engine, together with polished intake pipes and ports. A second oil cooler was mounted inside the left front wing.

Brake cooling ducts in the front spoiler were created by moving the sidelights into the main light housings. The "S" also had intakes cut into the rear wings (fenders) to admit more intake air to the engine. Power steering was no longer an option. The "S" had as much weight carved off it as possible, even thinner glass being fitted as on the 1973 RS 2.7 "lightweight" 911s.

Car and Driver tested the Turbo "S" and achieved a time of 3.7 seconds for the 0-60mph dash. Paul Frere tested a Turbo "S" and came up with a more conservative 0-62 mph in 4.7 seconds, 0-99.5 mph in 9.2 seconds and 0-124 mph in 14.2 seconds. Frere remarked that the Turbo "S" was "devastating. A standard Porsche Turbo is fast by any standards but this is just shattering."

In 1995, a totally revamped Turbo was introduced. Based upon the 993 model, this true supercar featured four wheel drive with ABD, (automatic brake differential), Bosch "Motronic" engine management system and twin intercoolers. A compression ratio of 8:1 enabled a power output of a quoted 408 PS at 5,750 rpm. A 6-speed gearbox, suitably strengthened, was taken from the Carrera 4. Additionally, the new Turbo had 8- x 18-inch front and 10- x 18-inch rear wheels. A top speed of 180 mph and an acceleration time of 0-62 mph in 4.5 seconds was quoted.

For the model year 2000, Porsche has produced yet another road going turbo. This is based upon the "new" water-cooled 996 Carrera. It has a water-cooled 3.6-liter engine, which is modeled upon that of the GT1, the car that won Le Mans in 1998. With 4 valves per cylinder, ME 7.8 fuel injection, variable intake valve timing, throttle-by-wire and 12.4 psi of boost, it gives 415 bhp and 413 lbs. ft. of torque. Connected via either a 6-speed manual or 5-speed automatic transmission, the new 911 Turbo has all four wheels driven. Porsche's own figures quote 0-62 mph in 4.2 seconds, 0-100 mph in 9.2 and a top speed of 189 mph. The bodywork is similar to a 996 but the wheel arches are widened by 2.6 inches and a biplane rear wing is fitted. Slots reminiscent of the 959 are cut into the rear skirt and intake air for the intercoolers is drawn in via intakes cut into the front of the rear fenders. Ceramic composite discs will be offered later in 2000. PSM, Porsche's own electronic stability control system looks after any tendency of a wheel to lock-up under braking. One road tester likened this fifth-generation Turbo to a big-capacity motorbike, rather than a 3,400 pound civilized supercar. Price in the USA (at time of writing) is $110,000. ❏

Chapter 2

1974 —
THE RSR TURBO CARRERA

I n October, 1973 Porsche announced that they would cease their own racing activities for 1974, allowing their customers to represent them with the RSR Carrera in races for Group 4 GT cars. However, Martini & Rossi (the drinks company) had offered to pay to sponsor the factory race team with a new turbocharged Group 5 prototype version of the RSR. This offer was greatly appreciated, allowing the racing team to try out some of their ideas for the forthcoming Group 5 "Silhouette" formula, whilst not upsetting their Group 4 customers, as the Group 5 cars would be competing in a separate class.

This was not so surprising as it first sounded. The factory was very aware that the FIA were considering introducing, in 1975, a "Silhouette" formula for the Manufacturer's Championship. If Porsche experimented with the Turbo 911 in 1974, it was very likely, reasoned Norbert Singer (the director of their racing department), that they would be in a strong position to challenge for victory in 1975, using their new technology.

In interpreting the rules of the Group 5 formula, Porsche saw that they had to reduce the capacity of their Turbo engine to 2.14-liters. This was due to the equivalence formula then in use for Group 5. This allowed a maximum unblown limit of 3-liters with the turbo, or supercharging, factor of 1.4:1. This equated to an unblown engine of 4.2-liters. At this time, racing 3-liter engines were producing some 480 bhp. It was not known if a turbocharged 2.14-liter engine could be developed to match this; Porsche was, however, committed to success now, with the forthcoming road going car.

For lightness' sake, the crankcase of the new 2,142 cc engine (Type 911/76) was made of magnesium alloy which, surprisingly,

used a forged crankshaft taken straight from the old 2.0 and 2.2-liter 911. Now fitted with new 83 mm bore cylinders and with the 66 mm stroke of the 2.0 crankshaft, the engine was just one cubic centimeter short of the 2,143 cc size limit. The head-to-cylinder interface, previously a lapped joint, now included an O-ring seal. Polished titanium connecting rods, similar to the ones first used in the 906 were fitted as well as the larger oil pumps from the 908. The camshafts used four instead of three bearings each, as on the RSR, and the camshaft lobes gave a valve lift of 10.5 mm for both inlet and exhaust. Exhaust valves were of nimonic steel and 40.5 mm wide. The inlets were 47 mm across and made of titanium. The inlet valves were sodium-cooled and all the valve adjustment was by shims inserted into small buckets on top of the valve stems.

As in all the Porsche racing engines, twin plugs per cylinder were used, fired by a single distributor that received its energy from a Bosch capacitive discharge electronic ignition system. As in the road car, the compression ratio, aided by flat top pistons, was 6.5:1. The undersides of these pistons were cooled by an oil spray.

The KKK Turbocharger (Kuhnle, Kopp und Kausch AG) was larger than that fitted to the 930 road car. It was centrally mounted at the rear of the engine, upon an aluminum cross member, which had been fabricated to replace the rear cross member of the 911 shell. The previous cross member had been cut out to give space for the engine and its plumbing. A Garrett wastegate was used, mechanically controlled from the cockpit. The engine's inlet manifolds sat atop the cylinder banks, each equipped with an injector and a

The RSR Turbo Carrera of Gijs Van Lennep and Herbert Muller as it pulls away after a pit stop at the Nürburgring.

throttle butterfly. The pressurized intake air was fed to a plenum chamber, which then fed it's equalized air quantity to each intake manifold with a throttle-controlled wastegate incorporated. The gearbox, as in the 3.0 RSR, was the Type 915 oil-cooled 5-speed and reverse unit but with strengthened sideplates fitted. This gearbox was operating at the limit of it's torque-absorbing capacity in the new

25

racing Turbo. This proved to be the car's "Achilles' heel". Fitted at the gear knob's base was an interlock, which stopped the driver from missing a gear. Incidentally, in the bottom three gears, Porsche could never find a tachometer in that period which could match the rise in revs of the turbo racing

The second-placed RSR Turbo Carrera at Le Mans in 1974 before the start of the race. But for a stripped fifth gear, van Lennep and Muller would almost certainly have won the event outright. Sadly, the 915 gearbox was unable to withstand the torque of the turbocharged 2.1-liter engine.

engine. The limited slip ZF differential was, as in the RSR, locked up to 80% and the car was sometimes run with a "spool", or fully locked up rear axle. The drive shafts were in titanium and employed Hooke-type constant-velocity joints.

The suspension followed the experience that had been gained with the RSR. It dispensed completely with the road going car's torsion bar springing and used titanium coil springs all round, to help in changing spring rates and ride height. Bilstein gas-filled dampers were fitted and adjustable

anti-roll bars front and rear were employed, to fine tune the handling (as in the RSR). The lower front wishbones had anti-dive built into the pick-up points, which also had the hub carriers raised on their Macpherson struts. These also benefited by the addition of an aluminum tie bar fitted between the strut mountings, both modifications common to the unblown RSR.

At the rear of the RSR Turbo Carrera, the trailing arms were box-shaped fabrications in aluminum. The coil spring and damper units picked up to a tubular cross member which fitted across the engine bay.

Initially, the wheels and brakes were straight from the RSR which, in turn, had received its brakes from the 917. The brake-balance from front to rear was also adjustable. The new, deeper front "chin" spoiler incorporated newly-shaped front side members in order to duct as much air as possible to the brakes. These were massive, cross-drilled and ventilated discs. The finned calipers were wider than before to take

Mulsanne Corner, 24 Hours of Le Mans on June 16, 1974: Herbert Muller swings the RSR Turbo Carrera into the right hand turn at the end of the Mulsanne straight on his way to second place overall.

thicker, long distance racing pads. Wearing 10.5-inch wide wheels at the front and 15-inch wide wheels at the rear, it seemed as if the Turbo RSR had all the rubber it would need. However, it was not long before the rear wheels had 17-inch wide Dunlop tires to cope with the power the turbocharged engine could deliver.

The cockpit of the RSR Turbo Carrera was not too different from any other 1974 911. The most obvious changes are the addition of the turbo's boost knob (to the right of the steering wheel) and the roll cage.

Inside the car's cockpit, the oil cooler pipes ran through the cabin to the front-mounted oil tank, with it's filler protruding through the GRP bonnet and the cooler in the nose. Of course, a massive aluminum tube rollcage, which also added extra stiffening to the bodyshell, was installed. The driver's seat (the only one fitted) was straight from an RSR as was the dashboard but this had the addition of a turbo boost pressure control. This was situated within easy reach of the driver's right hand. A large aluminum knob,

controlling the amount of boost available via the wastegate, sprouted from the dash. A reserve of fuel was available on demand by a pushbutton mounted on the dashboard, which switched on an electric pump. A nice touch was the fact that it was impossible for the driver to start the car if this was left on as, for instance, straight after a hectic pitstop.

In the front compartment of the Turbo RSR, now devoid of the usual fuel tank, sat the front-mounted oil tank. The Heinzmann fire extinguisher system nestled in the space formerly occupied by the fuel cell.

The bodywork of the Turbo RSR contained a great deal of GRP. Front wings (fenders), chin spoiler, rear wheel arches, doors, bonnet and tail were all made of the lightweight plastic material and all windows (with the exception of the windscreen) were of Plexiglass. Incidentally, the bodyshell itself was a basic "G" type production unit, which had been intended for production as an RS 3.0.

With it's vast rear wheel arches, the Turbo RSR looked, at first glance, similar to a normally aspirated RSR but at the back a huge new rear wing dominated the view. The front spoiler was made deeper and fitted with a splitter lip, to compensate for the increased downforce at the rear. Ernst Fuhrmann insisted that this huge wing be made to look less obtrusive, in order that the car's similarity to a road going 911 could be seen. To this end, the assembly was faired in as much as possible. The rear deck was raised and the Perspex rear window now mounted flush with the bodywork, (a touch the later 935 would be unable to use). The Martini & Rossi paint scheme of red and blue striping over the basic silver was also sculpted in such

a way as to take the eye away from the width of the rear aerofoil. Willy Kauhsen shared the driving of this car (chassis number 911 360 0576) with George Folder in the Nürburgring 1,000 Kilometer race held on May 28. He commented, "The engine was very powerful. It had too much horsepower which made the car very difficult to drive. It was easier to drive a turbocharged 917/10 than the Turbo RSR Carrera!" (*At the limit-Ed.*) "Of course, the car was really too high, not like a racing car. There was understeer when you turned into the corners and oversteer on the way out!"

A second car was built up, again from an RS 3.0 shell, in February 1974. Two more cars were built during the season, chassis numbers 911 460 9101 and 911 460 9102. Both again were taken from the "production" run of the Carrera RS 3.0. These featured the fuel tank, moved from the nose of the car, to the space behind the driver. The passenger side was also used for this purpose. The tank itself was of the bladder type set inside a safety steel casing with the filler caps on each side of the car, just behind the doors. The twin fuel pumps were moved to the right side of the cockpit for easy access and the battery was moved to the nose. The weight distribution of the RSR Turbo Carrera was now 70/30 rear to front which, with the new fuel tank location, did not change as fuel was consumed.

The thermal limit of the engine's head to cylinder joint proved to be 500° Fahrenheit. With the temperature of the incoming pressurized gases at 300° Fahrenheit, Porsche's engineers realized that the engine was hovering on the brink of thermal disaster. An aluminum intercooler was fabricated, after the fashion of the American aircraft engine intercoolers of the Second World War. This was fitted above the engine. The cowling which covered the engine, was modified with a NASA duct to allow incoming air to be directed across the new intercooler. About this intercooler, Hans Metzger, one of the engineers in charge of development noted, "experience from turbocharging had shown that the performance of a turbocharged engine is limited by overheating of the pistons, valves, cylinder head and so forth, rather than by mechanical problems. By providing the engine with an air-to-air intercooler the engine temperatures decreased, and the charge temperature fell from 300° to 150°."

Two cars, one with and one without, an intercooler were brought to the Le Mans test days. The fastest car lapped the circuit eleven seconds quicker than the normally aspirated, Works-entered Group 5 RSR of the previous year. The two cars then participated in the four hour race held on the circuit. Manfred Schurti and Helmuth Koinigg teamed in one car with Gijs van Lennep and Herbert Muller in the other.

The van Lennep/Muller car ran out of fuel in the first heat and blew its turbocharger in the second. The other car retired in the first heat with a broken rocker arm. After this appearance, the intercooler was changed to a alternative design that allowed charged air into the top. This exhausted the cooled air from the underside of the cooler to the plenum chamber, which itself had now been simplified together with the wastegate.

On April 25, the new Carrera RSR Turbo 2.1 (to give the car its full title) took part in the Monza 1,000 Kilometers, the first race in the Manufacturer's Championship. With a boost pressure of 20 psi, the engine was good for 470 bhp at 8,000 rpm in the race itself. For qualifying, the pressure was raised to 22 psi, helping the engine deliver 500 bhp and 400 lbs. ft. of torque.

At Monza, the singleton Turbo RSR came home in fifth place. It finished in third place at Spa-Francorchamps in the 1,000 kilometer race, two weeks later. Two cars were entered in the ADAC 1,000 Kilometers held at the Nürburgring on May 19. They finished in sixth and seventh places, despite some bodywork shredding "incidents".

On June 2, one of the pair of Turbo RSRs entered for Imola displayed what was referred to at the factory as a "Phase Three" engine. This displayed a cooling fan, which was now mounted above and parallel with the cylinder axis, "a la 917". This arrangement gave a more even cooling pattern over the cylinders and, with the turbocharged engine's propensity to run at or near its thermal limit, was seen to be essential for the car's survival in endurance races. The fan was driven, via a vee belt, from the nose of the crankshaft and then via a shaft which, with a bevel drive, turned the drive up to the fan. To make room for the fan's new location, the alternator and injection pump had to be moved.

Despite all the modifications that had gone in to making the Turbo RSR such a bombshell (compared to the purpose-built Group 5 racing cars), the Carrera had its problems. It suffered from an over-large, frontal area (22 square feet), a higher center of gravity and greater weight (1,826 lbs), all liabilities when compared to other purpose-built Group 5 racing cars. The weight had, with the addition of the centrally mounted

Intercooler, plumbing and upright fan dominate this photo of an early 2.1-liter turbocharged engine bay. Later, the engines featured flat fans for cooling the cylinder barrels and heads.

fuel tank, intercooler and various strengthening modifications, risen from an initial 1,660 lbs.

None of the above helped the two cars entered at Imola. One car got stuck in fourth gear as the Type 915 gearbox struggled to cope with the turbocharged engine's torque. The other pitted for replacement of the fan and turbocharger. Neither was classified at the finish.

At Le Mans, the two cars entered featured NASA ducts cut into the rear quarter windows. These had been sheeted over with aluminum panels. From these ducts, the air was led via hoses into the engine compartment for more efficient cooling.

In practice, both cars were on the pace. 189 mph was seen on the Mulsanne straight with the boost wick being turned well and truly up. In the race itself, these practice boost limits were used for the first few laps, to enable the cars to stay well to the fore and harry the Matras and Gulf Mirages. The boost was then turned down so that the engines could survive the long grind ahead of them. For one car, the boost pressure proved too much, resulting in a rare mechanical failure in the form of a broken connecting rod. That ended the six hour run of the Koinigg/Schurti car, which had been in fourth place at the time of the failure. The other Turbo RSR, (driven by van Lennep and Muller) went on to take a tremendous second place overall, despite its gearbox having only third and fourth gears

left by the end of the race. The winning Matra, incidentally, needed a long pitstop to rebuild the gearbox, that also having been designed by Porsche!

At the Watkins Glen 6-Hours, the RSR Turbo posted another second place. It finished fifth at Brands Hatch after the front spoiler had been torn off when the car was being piloted by Herbert Muller. Muller's car, shorn of it's downforce-inducing spoiler, promptly lifted both front wheels under acceleration out of corners!

After the close of the season, in which Porsche had finished in third place in the

Above: One of the 1974 RSR Turbo Carreras seen taking part in the Laguna Seca Historics meeting held in August 1998.

Opposite Page: Two RSR Turbo Carreras, photographed at Weissach while between testing sessions.

Championship again, some chosen journalists were invited to Weissach to experience the Turbo RSR. Paul Frere, of course, was amongst those invited.

He noted that, "As was the case with the turbocharged CanAm car, the Turbo Carrera engine proved beautifully tractable. It would even idle at 1,500 rpm without my blipping the throttle, and the car could be driven gently in first and second gear around the (Weissach) premises with the clutch fully engaged."

"As it was foggy and the track slightly damp, Dunlop intermediate tires had been fitted. For several laps, I tried to find my way through the fog but then decided to stop and wait for the sun to come out. The time was not lost though, because it enabled me to observe at ease how the boost pressure reacted to engine speed and throttle opening."

"When accelerating from low speeds, the boost pressure gauge would start moving at around 4,500 rpm. Full boost was reached at 6,500, the full 20 psi remaining available until the 8,000 rpm limit was reached. Any slight lifting off in the 6,500-8,000 rpm range would not affect the boost materially, but of course it dropped to zero as soon as the accelerator was released. Even if this happened for only a short time, full boost was not restored immediately the pedal was pushed down again. Later in the day, I took the car out again in bright sunshine, though we decided it was not worthwhile changing to slicks, my object being to find out about the car, not to establish any records. The visibility and the track were perfect, so I was able to have a real go, though I had to lift off some 200 yards before the braking point at the end of the main straight, as the Brands Hatch gearing still fitted was too low for the Weissach track."

"Compared with the racing Carrera GT I drove last year, (*the Carrera RSR-Ed*), this one handled infinitely better. The 17-inch

rear rims and appropriate tires have cured any tendency to oversteer, despite the much increased rear weight bias. The typical Porsche tendency to react rather sharply to the throttle opening when cornering fast has also been banished. In this case, the car would just tighten its line gently if the throttle was lifted. For a fast time, though, this is just the thing not to do with the turbo because despite everything that has been done to reduce the blower response time, you are almost sure to come out of the corner with too little power on tap. If some moderation is required, one should always try gently to reduce the throttle opening, rather than to shut off completely, if only for a fraction of a second, for this increases the response time considerably when you open up again."

"Certainly the driver has to adapt to the characteristics of the turbocharged engine. Once there, the power can be very easily and accurately controlled, but it is not always easy to time the throttle opening to obtain full power at just the right moment when coming out of a corner. There's little problem on long, fast bends for even at part throttle, the blower is kept spinning fast and full boost is available almost instantly the throttle is depressed. Short, fast kinks are more difficult, requiring just a little more application of the brakes, followed by full or nearly full acceleration. In those cases, the real power usually comes back later than you would wish and practice is needed by anyone not used to such characteristics to get the best results. Maybe it's a case for left-foot braking, while just easing the throttle with the right one? But as soon as the full boost pressure is reached, the car just rockets away."

"Driving the Turbo Carrera confirmed two things. One is that the apparently almost immediate throttle response I noted when driving the 5-liter, 100 bhp 917/10 was attributable not to the exceptionally quick response of the turbocharging unit, but to the sheer torque of the large engine. Even when the pressure in the intake manifolds is no more than atmospheric. Porsche have done very well to develop a turbocharging installation in which the lag is quite commendably short, but you can't get rid of physical laws."

"The second is that the Porsche's overhung engine is no handicap if you know how to design the running gear accordingly. And they managed it with science to spare, since on most circuits (and it was the case when I drove the car), no front anti-roll bar is used!"

Performance figures for the Turbo RSR were: 0-62 mph in 3.2 seconds and 0-124 mph in 8.8 seconds.

At the end of the 1974 season, the whole project was put "on ice". The factory was unwilling to participate in Group 5 races when the prospect of any better finishes than in 1974 appeared remote. The new Silhouette formula was not now due to take effect until 1976, when Porsche intended to take part with their new 935, of which more anon. In the interim, Porsche found itself supplying three racing teams with 2.14 turbo engines for installation in three old 908/3s of 1970 vintage. The exploits of these three cars are, strictly speaking, beyond the scope of this book but Reinhold Joest did very well with his. He took a second, two thirds and a fourth place in the races which counted towards the Manufacturers Championship and Porsche gained second place overall in the Championship. ❑

Chapter 3

THE 934

Essentially, the 934 was the Group 4 GT race version of the basic 930 Turbo road car. To qualify for Group 4, four hundred 930 Turbos had to be produced in two consecutive model years. Porsche had easily accomplished this.

Introduced in 1976, the 934 was far closer to its production counterpart, the 930 Turbo, than any of its racing predecessors. This was because, running a 3-liter turbocharged engine, it fell into the minimum weight category of a naturally aspirated car of between 4.0 and 4.5-liters. That was 1,120 kilograms (2,470 lbs), only slightly below the weight of the very fully road equipped 930. This allowed weight to be added to ballast the 934, a necessity as the 934 was forced to use the same rear spoiler as the production 930. This allowed the rear of the car to lift at high speeds (a lifting force of 75 kilograms acting upon the rear axle at 187 mph). This rear spoiler carried an air intake, which was used to draw in air for the air conditioning unit on the normal turbo road car. On the 934, it was used to duct air to the transmission oil cooler and the turbocharger.

Taking a standard, galvanized 930 bodyshell, the 934 was built up with a large aluminum rollcage, both for driver protection and to give additional stiffness. No sound

Nürburgring 1000 Kms, 1976: The 934, driven by Gijs van Lennep and Hartwig Bertrams, (930 670 0151), that finished 5th OA. Here it is seen ahead of the Georg Loos-entered 934 of Clemens Schickentanz, who finished 4th OA.

The prototype 934, seen here at the Porsche factory in late 1975.

deadening or mats were fitted to the thirty-one cars built but they did sport electric windows. Inside, no rear or passenger seats were fitted, just the usual sturdy RSR type driver's seat with a six-point safety harness. Three extra gauges, for turbocharger boost, fuel metering and fuel pressure, were fitted to the dashboard. The standard cut-off switch to the electrical system was mounted on the dashboard with an external switch on the scuttle.

The rubber frame pivots for the suspension mountings were all replaced with Delrin nylon bushes and steel balljoints. The rear suspension used the standard production trailing arms. Coil springs supplemented the torsion bar springing of what was a heavy competition car. The anti-roll bars front and rear were adjustable, a tubular bar was used at the rear, a solid one at the front.

The 917's finned calipers and cross-drilled and ventilated disc brakes were in use, together with stronger wheel hubs and center lock wheels. These were now made up in three pieces each by BBS and were of 16-inch diameter. 10.5-inch wide front wheels were fitted, whilst the rear sported only 12.5-inch wide rear wheels. This limit was set, not by the wheel arches extended 1.9-inch width (the wheel's width could have been extended in towards the center of the 934), but by the FIA's rule that rear tire width in Group 4 could not be more than 14 inches total. An increase in wheel diameter to 16 inches was helpful in increasing the rear tires' contact patch, a trick that the 935 would further exploit later.

37

The front compartment was now filled with a 31.7 gallon fuel cell, the front-mounted oil tank, and the battery. It was also strengthened with a large aluminum cross brace in an "X" shape. Inside the main tank was a collector tank, filled by an electrical pump and operating via a one-way valve. Two parallel fuel systems, each one using two Bosch fuel pumps mounted in series, were between this collector tank and the engine. A large air dam/spoiler was fitted at the front, the center of which was cut out to allow incoming air to the huge oil radiator that resided there. On either side were the brake cooling ducts and, alongside them, the intakes to the radiators of the intercooler.

One of the major problems Porsche faced with the 934 was the provision of an intercooler. The rules stated that the rear engine cover had to retain the same dimensions as the road going 930. Because of this, the air-to-air intercooler, which had been fitted to the Turbo RSR, could not be used. Instead, Porsche used a very ingenious method of cooling the charged intake gases. They fitted two water radiators into the front spoiler of the 934. These led the water back to the engine compartment, where each set of pipes ended in a cooler core fitted above each bank of inlet manifolds. On top of each

Dieter Schornstein was a dyed in the wool Porsche racer. He started with an RS 3.0 and was still racing a 956 in the late eighties. He progressed from the RS to a 934 (purchased from the Kremer Brothers), chassis number 930 670 0158. He is pictured here, probably at the Nürburgring, in his car, updated to 934/5 specification with the 935 tail and wider wheels and wheel arches. [Photo—Jeff Fisher.]

The 934 in competition in the USA in 1976. Ted Field drove Vasek Polak's cars in several races.

cooler, the incoming air went through a finned plenum chamber. This was driven around the circuit by a camshaft-driven water pump. The charged gases temperature was lowered from 300° to 120° Fahrenheit. Although the system weighed over 20 kilograms, the 934's weight limit allowed its fitment.

The 934's engine was essentially that of the 930. More rugged pistons were fitted to give greater durability at higher revs. Crankcase, crankshaft, connecting rods and cylinder barrels were identical to the production turbo engine (Type 930/75). The 2,993 cc engine (Type 930/71) had the same type of flat fan location as had been seen on the Turbo RSR. The inlet and exhaust ports were enlarged to 43.5 mm and 36.5 mm respectively and RSR Turbo four bearing camshafts were substituted for the standard three bearing type. With, initially, 10.5 mm of valve lift, these camshafts were replaced later in the season by those giving 11.5 mm. Both types of camshafts gave the following valve timing:

Inlet opens/closes: 45° btdc/90° abdc
Exhaust opens/closes: 95° bbdc/49° atdc
btdc = Before top dead center
abdc = After bottom dead center
bbdc = Before bottom dead center
atdc = After top dead center

The obstacles facing the development of extra power over that of the production 930 were the single ignition system and the K-Jetronic fuel injection system, which had to be used. The 934 used a much larger KKK turbocharger than the 930. The air was first drawn through the metering unit, which was mounted in the rear of the engine bay. Porsche's engineers modified this unit to pass twice as much air as the production 930, and added a spun alloy cone that smoothed out the airflow past the metering disc. This gave a power output of 485 bhp at 7,000 rpm at 18.5 psi (1.4 bar) boost and 434 lbs. ft. of torque

Hurley Haywood in one of the ten 1977 934½s specifically made for the American market.

at 5,400 rpm. Over 500 bhp was possible if the boost limit was set higher (20 psi) but this had a detrimental effect on engine life. By the end of 1976, some teams were seeing as much as 580 bhp!

The single plate clutch was fitted with sintered linings. The 930 transaxle, built to deal with some 440 lbs. ft. of input torque, now had an oil pump fitted (as had the gearbox of the previous Group 4 Carrera). This pump, using oil which was passed through a cooler mounted in the rear spoiler, forced oil around the gearbox, spraying it particularly onto the engaging teeth of each gear. The lim-

ited slip differential used a locking factor of 80%. The external gear linkage was modified to give a shorter shift, and both engine and transaxle were solidly mounted in the bodyshell. This allowed a much crisper and more positive gearchange. Incidentally, Group 4 rules only allowed the use of the production gear ratios plus two alternatives per ratio. Only three final drive ratios were available. Nevertheless, this provided a formidable

One of the Vasek Polak-entered 934½s, this time driven by George Follmer. Note the 935 "double-decker" tail. This gave the 934½s significantly more downforce than the 934, making it much more stable and easier to drive fast.

'... Alan Hamilton, the Melbourne Porsche dealer, bought a brand new 934 from the factory in 1976 and remembered:

"We were very happy to be Porsche dealers and had won thirteen National Championships. When the 934 was announced, I lost no time in obtaining one. I won the Australian Sports Car Championship in 1977 with the car in absolutely stock configuration. In 1980, we re-engined it with a '934 and a half' engine, giving somewhere around 600 horsepower. Again, Alan Moffatt won the championship, some six, one hour races, with it." ...'

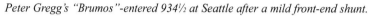

Peter Gregg's "Brumos"-entered 934½ at Seattle after a mild front-end shunt.

'... Nick Faure, the noted Porsche dealer and racer, had dominated British national racing with an RS 3-liter Carrera in 1974. He remembered driving a new 934 at Le Mans in 1976:

"The car came brand new from the factory in white and I painted it red and blue in the paddock at Le Mans for Jean Blaton, the owner. In the race itself, we changed no less than four turbos. It cost Jean (Blaton) a fortune and took 20–30 minutes to change each one. The problem was that the turbo overheated when you switched off in the pits. If only we had realized that and let the engine idle for a minute to cool the turbo... Afterwards Porsche cured the problem with extra oil cooling in 1977. In the end, we just waited in the pits until twenty minutes before the end and then motored around to take the flag."

"The single-turbo cars, whether 934 or 935, were a handful with all that turbo lag. Jackie Ickx told me to commit the car to the corner and saw away at the steering wheel to scrub off the speed whilst not lifting your right foot. I mastered the technique but it took a lot of bottle to start with! Ickx also taught me a lot about wet weather driving, like staying off the standard racing line to get more grip, which is what you see Schumacher doing today in F1." ...'

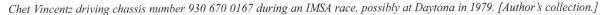

Chet Vincentz driving chassis number 930 670 0167 during an IMSA race, possibly at Daytona in 1979. [Author's collection.]

selection of gearing choices. The 934 sold for DEM97,000, which did not include spare gearbox, or final drive ratios. The differential was sometimes replaced with a spool, as in the Turbo RSR. To support this Group 4 racer, the factory produced an owner's manual and parts list. The manual went into extreme details of operation, even showing new owners how to start their engines by depressing a lever, which operated the fuel enrichment on the fuel injection pump!

The prototype 934 was up and run-ning by September 1975 and the model was announced later that same month. In January 1976, Manfred Schurti tested the 934 at the Nürburgring and lapped fifteen seconds faster than any Carrera RSR had ever managed. At Paul Ricard, the development prototype lapped three seconds faster than that same factory-entered Group 5 Carrera RSR of 1974.

Almost all the racing teams and drivers who had contested the European GT Championships in RSRs bought 934s. They

George Dickinson was a Porsche dealer who supplied a 934 (chassis number 930 670 0173) for Al Holbert to drive in the 1976 TransAm Series. Here, Holbert is pictured driving the car showing his well known race number 14 during that season. [Photo—Jeff Fisher.]

included the Gelo and Kremer teams, Toine Hezemans, Bob Wollek, Helmut Kelleners, Hartwig Bertrams, Jurgen Kannacher, Eberhard Sindel and Reinhard Stenzel. Of course, the 934 dominated the European GT Championship. Bob Wollek, in the Kremer car, dueled fiercely with Toine Hezemans in the Gelo-entered car, with Hezemans finally winning the Championship. These same teams also contested the German National Championship, a series of races growing in stature as the points earned went towards the sought-after "Porsche Cup".

Some of the "European" 934s were upgraded to run in the Group 5 class with the addition of wider wheels and a 935 style twin tail. This gave them more grip and downforce. Effectively, these cars were the

same as the series of 934s sold to American customers for 1977.

In America, IMSA (International Motor Sports Association) forbade the use of turbocharged cars in its Camel GT series in 1976. The many Carrera RSR owners feared the escalation of prices the introduction of the turbocharged cars would bring. They lobbied John Bishop (President of IMSA) successfully to keep the 934 and the 935 out of the Camel GT Championship.

This left Jo Hoppen, CEO of Volkswagen of North America in a quandary. He had already ordered ten cars from the factory in the expectation of them being allowed to run in IMSA. Upon learning of Bishop's refusal, Hoppen cast around for another Championship in which to use his

Ted Field and Danny Ongais of the Interscope team drove 934 and a halfs in the TransAm and IMSA Championships in 1977. Here is Ongais, just ahead of George Follmer in an RSR Turbo, during the Mid-Ohio 6-Hours. [Photo—Author's collection.]

now surplus cars. Hoppen realized that the TransAm was fading away and approached the SCCA (Sports Car Club of America), the sanctioning body of the series. The SCCA admitted the car to its TransAm series and George Follmer won the Championship from Hurley Haywood, both driving Vasek Polak-entered cars. Polak, incidentally, had bought no less than five 934s!

The 934s dominated the 1976 TransAm season and it became apparent that to win, customers had to step up to the expense of buying a turbocharged Porsche. The day of the RSR Carrera was truly over.

In the latter part of 1977, IMSA allowed the 934 and a half to compete, this time with the mechanical fuel injection of the 935. This allowed up to 600 bhp (engine type 930/73), lighter weight, and wider 15-inch wheels. This was, in fact, the same specification as Porsche had used in the TransAm in 1977. The cars were also allowed to use a much bigger rear wing and this, coupled with the wider wheels, made them much more stable to race than their European cousins. When developed still further in American racing, quite a few cars ended up as full-blown 935s. Although retaining single ignition, the 930/73 engine now had the Bosch mechanical twin-row plunger-type fuel injection pump from the 935 engine. In this guise, the 934/77's engine produced 590 bhp. Just one of the ten 934 and a half's produced was sold in Europe, to Coggiola in

Dick Barbour bought a 934 and a half in 1977 and went IMSA racing. Here, he is seen ahead of a modified 911S driven by Renn Tilton of Florida. [Photo—Author's collection.]

'... Gary Belcher began his racing career in 1950s midgets, sprint cars and over two-liter Formula Vees in Central and Southern America before taking to road racing. Soon he decided that this was a better way to go. He bought the ex-Hezemans, ex-Peter Gregg 934. Belcher had it developed steadily into a full 935, which he raced over several seasons besides sharing the driving of other 935s in the endurance events.

He remembered, " I drove for the Vasek Polak Team on a couple of occasions. Vasek was an amazing character and a lovely guy but he wouldn't change a thing about the cars. Springs, gearsets, nothing. He reckoned that was the way the factory made them and that was it! I told him it was just a starting point but he didn't agree. I asked (George) Follmer how he managed as Vasek's driver and he confided that he brought his own springs and gearsets for the mechanics to change!"

"I remember doing 1979 Sebring. We were going well, but the throttle cable broke three times. Each time out of the pits, we'd struggle back to be within reach of the leaders when — ping! Crawl back again. At Riverside that year, we had a problem with a badly fitting wastegate and could only get 1.1 bar maximum. Of course, the engine was well down on power but we still finished OK. In the endurance races, I remember Le Mans in 1979. The Whittingtons shared with Ludwig and he did most of the driving to win the race. Same thing happened with the second-placed 935. There's Paul Newman and Dick Barbour on the podium, fresh as daisies whilst Stommelen looks exhausted. He'd also done most of the driving. I figured out right there that you needed a German driver with you in these long hauls. Engines? Wonderful. I was told to keep the revs down to 7,800 maximum in the longer races but in the short straights, if I was battling with someone else, I'd take it to 8,500 in the gears to stay ahead. Porsche engines never failed!" ...'

Gary Belcher at the 24 Hours of Le Mans.

Italy for Ciro Nappi. The other nine cars were sold to America.

In 1977, Porsche once again won the World Championship of Makes, and Peter Gregg won the TransAm Championship in the USA in a 934 and a half. This car used the titanium half-shafts and brakes from a "customer" 1977 935, which Gregg had purchased at the same time as he had acquired the 934 from Stuttgart. Peter Gregg had modified his 934 and a half too much for IMSA's liking and so he left that series to concentrate on the TransAm where the rule interpretation was more liberal.

As was seen in 1976 with the 934s, the 934 and a half's equally dominated in the TransAm races of 1977.

Skip Gunnel today owns the prototype 934, 930 670 0151. This car was raced by Jurgen Kannacher in 1976, sold to South Africa and then sold to Gunnel in 1983. He described how it had been uprated to 934 and a half specification and how, "The power comes in like a rocketship when that big turbocharger spools up. I've raced powerful cars for years but even a Lola T70 can't accelerate down the straight like that 934 when it's on full boost."

As late as into the 1980s, 934s were still racing in front line competition. Here is chassis number 930 670 0168 during the Daytona 24 Hours. Driven by Jack Refenning, Renn Tilton and Ray Mummery, it failed to last the distance. [Photo—IMSA Collection.]

Dan McLoughlin's AIR Company, based near Los Angeles in California, designed and built new bodywork, which had the oil cooler mounted higher in the nose and the water radiators in the fenders. Thus, if the car had a frontal accident and lost its front spoiler, it could still continue on. This was something the "Eurospec" 934s were unable to do if the same type of racing accident befell them.

In Europe, the 934 went on to compete regularly at Le Mans but there it found itself up against the Ferrari BB 512LM Boxer. The 934 won the Group 4 category in 1977, 1979 (coming in fourth overall) and 1981, and even managed a fine thirteenth overall as late as 1982. In 1977, Ludwig Heimrath and Jim Miller won the Mosport 6-hours, and in 1978, Angelo Pallavicini won the FIA GT cup, in 934s.

The 934 was not an easy car to drive. Heavy, with upwards of 500-600 bhp, and with only relatively small tires, it was always threatening to get away from its drivers. It certainly did not have the nimbleness and featherlight steering of its predecessor, the RSR. Nevertheless, in terms of lap times, horsepower told. The 934 acquitted itself well in the comparatively short period it was extant.

Although the Group 4 934 was effectively dead and gone in European competition by 1982, (except for some honorable exceptions such as Richard Cleare's

car), the 934 had another lease of life in America from 1980 onwards. John Bishop decreed that his "GTO" class would now allow entry to a single-turbo, single-plug version of Porsche's venerable warhorse to bolster the ranks of this class. Effectively, the 935 had been relegated to second division status with the coming of the new generation of GTP cars. Several owners, amongst them Wayne Baker and Chester Vincentz, took 935s and converted them to this specification. With 934-like bodywork and an honest 600 bhp, these "934s" gave good service for several years. Baker won the 1983 GTO Championship and even the Sebring 12-Hours outright. Chet Vincentz was still competing in races with the ex-1980 Daytona winner in 1986.

Dave White, his sometime co-driver, remembered, "That car (*the 934 - Ed*) was a handful. Remember, it had been a 935 and now it still had over six hundred horsepower from the single-plug engine we had to use. It was very, very fast in a straight line but we were limited to 12-inch wide rear wheels, which really hurt us in the handling department. It also got very hot inside. I remember racing at Charlotte in the summer heat. We were wearing cool suits but still almost passed out from heat exhaustion before the end. Still, it was a good car. I remember winning our division in the Lumbermens race at Mid-Ohio with Chet. I still have the plaque on my wall here in the office". ❑

Chapter 4

THE 935

Concurrently with the 934, Porsche had been working hard to get their Group 5 challenger, the 935, ready for the start of the 1976 season. This was the famed 935, a car that surprised Porsche itself by soldiering on into the 1980s, still winning international races as late as 1984. Indeed, even by the 1990s there was still little to touch the final (very developed) variants in some national GT championships.

From the outset, Norbert Singer, the engineer in charge of the 935's development, proposed and installed a 2.8-liter capacity engine, the Type 930/72. It produced up to 600 bhp at 8,000 rpm in its first version.

2.8, when multiplied by 1.4 (to give the unblown equivalent), slotted the 935 into the up to 4-liters capacity category and thus the car's minimum weight had to be 970 kilograms. The substitution of a plunger- type fuel injection for the 934's K-Jetronic type of injection made a dramatic difference to the power of the engine.

The capacity of the 930/72 engine was actually 2,856 cc, the very maximum that the rules allowed. With the 1.4 multiplier then in use, this gave a capacity of 3,999 cc. Stroke was 70.4 mm and the Nikasil cylinder barrels were of 92.8 mm bore. Amazingly, the crankcase and crankshaft were still production units although the latter was minutely checked for hairline cracks. Dual ignition, the aforementioned plunger-type fuel injection, titanium connecting rods and a flat fan, all standard Porsche racing items, were fitted. A 908 type oil pump was utilized plus bush-less forged steel rocker arms. These shafts used a nitrating process, which was the same as that used on the crankshaft and the very special connecting rods. The 935 engine followed Porsche racing practice, using central lubri-

cating camshafts plus spraybar lubrication. This not only kept the cams well supplied with oil but the spraybar also enhanced cooling. An oil mist was used over the finned valve guides and the exhaust valve guides also benefited from a direct supply of oil. Type 917 crankcase studs were also used, enabling the factory to go one size smaller than normal and save a little weight. Fuel consumption, under racing conditions, was 4.38 mpg. The 935 needed a lot of pit stops!

The rules allowed a very free interpretation of the bodywork. Porsche exploited this to the full, developing a car based upon the RSR Turbo of 1974. The new car included the RSR Turbo's coil spring and concentric

Bilstein gas-damper suspension plus a cockpit-adjustable rear anti-roll bar. This device consisted of a "knife blade"-type of bar which, when operated by the Bowden cable from the cockpit lever, would change the anti-roll bar's stiffness dramatically as the blade moved through 90°. This helped the driver to adjust the rear suspension as fuel and tires were used up.

The front wishbones were now tubular fabrications and the rear production-type trailing arms picked up at their ball-joint front mountings. These had been raised to introduce anti-dive. The 4-speed oil-cooled transmission was similar to that of the 934. This was based upon the road going 930 Turbo and featured, as in the 934, a short shift mechanism in the gear change plus a spool for locking the rear drive shafts up permanently. This did away with any sort of limited slip differential. Gear choices were free in Group 5 and gear ratios were plentifully available. Titanium drive shafts

The first 935 during a testing session. Note the 1974 RSR Turbo Carrera tail. The 935 has now received the "slope-nose" treatment, which put the driving lights into the front spoiler and creates a look that became world-famous.

fitted with Hooke constant velocity joints and rubber couplings to dissipate shock, coupled the transaxle's drive to the wheels.

Starting from a standard steel 930 bodyshell and floorpan, and stiffened with the additions and braces used on the 934, Porsche engineers developed a body made almost completely of glass reinforced plastic, (GRP). Only the roof was still made of steel. A safety glass 911-type windscreen was unchanged from the production car but all side and rear windows were in Perspex. At the front, the bodywork was removable in one unit to allow work to be carried out inside the nose bay, which was filled with the safety fuel tank and front-mounted oil tank, all "a la 934".

At the rear, the intercooler was now contained within a box-type cowling, which supported the rear aerofoil. Cool air to feed the intercooler was drawn in through slots in front of the rear wheels which, in the RSR, had been used as brake cooling ducts.

The positioning of the intercooler would cause problems for Porsche later on in the 1976 season. It clashed with the rule which said that the wing support must remain within the 930 outline. The aerofoil design itself was free, and Porsche's engineers took full advantage of this to produce an aerofoil

Below & next page: The rear of the 1976 935 wearing Carrera RSR-type rear fenders.

* 1 bar (barometer) of pressure = 14.7 lbs/sq.in. above atmospheric pressure, which is 14.7 lbs/sq.in. at sea level.

Rear view of the 1976 935 with Carrera RSR-type fenders.

which, although not quite as effective as that of the RSR Turbo's, still gave vastly increased downforce over that of the 934. The weight of the 935 came out 90 kilograms underweight, allowing Porsche to ballast the car as they wished. Some lead went into the nose and the rest into the passenger compartment, to give an ideal 40/60 weight distribution.

The cockpit of the 935 was similar to the RSR Turbo's, a massive aluminum rollcage filling it, which also stiffened the entire structure. The driver was seated on the left hand side of the cockpit. As in the RSR Turbo, a cockpit-adjustable boost knob was mounted in the center of the dashboard. 1.2 bar (17 psi) produced 550 bhp for reliability, at which boost the 935 ran Le Mans, or 1.4-1.5 bar (21.4 psi) giving 630-650 bhp for "sprint" races such as at Watkins Glen and Dijon. Torque was quoted at 438 lbs. ft. at 5,400 rpm.

The restrictions on the wheelrim width that had so bedeviled the 934 were more liberal in Group 5 than Group 4, although there was a maximum wheel and tire width limit of 16 inches. The 935 sported 16-inch

The 935/76 today. 935-001, outside Gunnar Porsche's transporter at the 1998 Monterey Historic Races.

diameter 917-style, five spoked wheels at the front, 10.5 inches wide. At the rear, a revolutionary solution to the ever-widening tires of the time, (which meant more frontal area and thus more drag), were 19-inch diameter wheels, 15 inches wide. The "footprint" of these new   tires, (Goodyear, Michelin and Pirelli were also tested), was thus lengthened, allowing more rubber to make contact with the tarmac. Increasing the diameter of the wheel/tire combination also overcame the Group 5 width limitation. Two degrees of

The works-entered Porsche 935 of Jackie Ickx and Jochen Mass during practice at Watkins Glen in 1976. In this photo, the 935 is ahead of the Vasek Polak entered 934, driven by George Folder and John Morton, which failed to take the start. (Photo courtesy of Porsche).

negative camber could be used on the front wheels but the setting at the rear was just ten minutes. This minimized the rear wheel movement and allowed the giant tires to remain as nearly upright as possible.

At the beginning of 935 development, the wheels were shrouded by RSR Carrera-type wheel arches. These had the maximum allowable wheel arch extensions (5 inches wider than that allowed for the 934). With their characteristic cooling slots in front of and behind the rear wheels, air flowed onto

and from the fitted 917 brakes. These 4-pot calipers had 43 mm front and 38 mm rear pistons to act on the 19 mm thick brake pads. At the front, the air ducting, not so cramped due to the deletion of the water-to-air inter-cooler of the 934, was freer than that car's. The brakes were correspondingly less given to fade. GRP discs with turbine-like blades were fitted to the centers of the front (and sometimes the rear) wheels, which helped to centrifuge hot air away from the brakes.

The new white 935, unadorned with

Watkins Glen, 1976. The Works-entered cars of Ickx/Mass and Stommelen/Schurti pull away from the rest of the pack, composed mainly of 934s, BMWs and Carrera RSRs in the Watkins Glen 6-hour race. [Photo—Ronald C. Miller.]

sponsorship decals, first tested at Paul Ricard in December 1975. With Jackie Ickx and Jochen Mass driving, it covered 2,931 kilometers and showed amazing speed, lapping faster than a Formula One Tyrell testing there at the same time. The 935 was timed at 194 mph on the straight. For Le Mans, it would go still faster. The only problem Ickx and Mass ran into at the Paul Ricard circuit was too much power available(!) This was due to a constricted turbo pressure valve that gave excessive boost. The part was soon re-adjusted. This prototype sported a rear aerofoil which had to be changed before the season started. It did not properly comply with the rules, as it was too large when viewed from the front. It was replaced with a wing on side supports built on the original 930 "burzel's" base. The wheelbase of the first 935 was 89.4 inches; front track was 59.1 inches and rear track 61.3 inches.

In Group 5, Porsche's only competition in 1976 came from BMW who were using a twin turbo version of their 3-liter six cylinder engined car. BMW's car put out some 475 bhp. Schnitzer also developed a 3.2-liter version for which 750 bhp was claimed, although the car weighed a lot more than the 935.

Porsche had built up two 935s,

Manfred Schurti driving the eventual winner of the Watkins Glen 6 Hours, chassis number 930 570 0001. With Rolf Stommelen, the pair completed the six hour race at an average speed of 97.806 mph. Behind Schurti is the Ecurie Escargot RSR Carrera (chassis number 911 560 9117) of John Graves, Dr. David Helmick and John O'Steen, which finished a creditable sixth. This car would go on to win the 1977 Daytona 24 Hours when all the favored turbos dropped by the wayside.
[Photo courtesy of Porsche.]

'... Paul Frere, writing in *Motor* in November 1976, recorded his impressions of the 935. This was after he had been given the chance to try both the 935 and 936 at the Weissach test track. He wrote:

"In my privileged capacity as a Porsche team driver, it has now become a tradition for me to go to Weissach at the end of the racing season to find out for myself how the cars feel on Porsche's own test track. This special session took place just before a press demonstration. Thank you, Dr. Fuhrmann, for accepting the risk! This also gave me a chance to discuss some points with the drivers on the following day."

"Except for cleaning and checking, the cars had not been touched since their last race at Dijon, where they both won (*their respective classes—Ed*). Consequently the gearing was rather too high for Weissach, which was more of a handicap for the 935 (Group 5) which has only four gears than for the 936 which has five."

"The fascia of the Group 5 car still looks vaguely like its production counterpart and the driver has plenty of space. He is surrounded by a full rollcage, which also adds rigidity to the body structure. The view forward was less familiar as the car used the controversial CanAm front end with sloping front wings and the lights incorporated in the front air dam so that the front part of the car is out of sight."

"The finned discs had been fitted to the front wheels only, as the front brakes do most of the work and wear faster. This is why, when a wheel change was made, only the front brakes were checked for wear. At Watkins Glen, the front pads having been found OK, the car was sent back into the race. But after some time, the driver found the brakes had weakened considerably. No wonder! There were no rear pads left and the pistons had made contact with the discs, making a horrible mess which took a long time to rectify."

"Before I started, I was instructed about the various controls and instruments and how they differed from those of the normal car. First was the boost pressure regulating knob (which you leave alone). Next came the boost pressure gauge (with several little lights running around a quadrant, rather than a needle, when the pressure varies). Then came a gear selecting mechanism, which provided a very effective reverse stop by making it mandatory to select first gear before reverse can be engaged. On the floor, a lever controls the adjustable rear anti-roll bar."

"One of the nice things about the turbo engines is that they use much 'softer' timing than atmospheric racing engines. Starter response is immediate and idling is quiet and reliable. The clutch action is by no means light, but over-center springs in the linkage keep the effort required within reasonable limits. This is very reasonable if you remember that a single friction plate is used to transmit a torque of 720 lbs. ft. In order to achieve this, sintered metal linings are used."

"Getting the car off the mark is no problem and in any gear, the acceleration as the turbo starts doing its job is dramatic. Observation of the boost pressure gauge indicates that, on full throttle, the pressure starts rising at just under 5,000 rpm. By that time, the acceleration–especially in one of the lower gears—is almost unbelievable. According to the factory, the car reaches 125 mph from rest in 8.2 seconds–and this with the high Le Mans gearing!"

"But, in spite of the special devices (such as the boost pressure release valve to avoid back pressure on the blower when the throttle is released) used by Porsche to reduce the throttle response time, great care must be taken not to release the throttle unnecessarily or for a longer time than strictly required. Even the quickest of gear changes will drop the boost enough for the recovery time to be just noticeable."

"In this respect, long corners are a lesser problem than short ones. When taking a long bend, it is essential to partly open the throttle as early as possible, nursing the engine so that the car is pushed through the bend smoothly while the blower is kept spinning fast. This allows full acceleration to be obtained when reaching the end of the bend, making optimum use of the solid drive (no differential) to accelerate early. In short corners however, or kinks for which it is necessary to give the brakes a dab, things get more difficult. To enjoy full acceleration coming out of the corner, you must accelerate early and that, in turn, can mean applying the brakes earlier than you would normally do. It is certainly not an easy compromise to find and definitely a handicap, compared with an immediately responding atmospheric (or mechanically supercharged) engine."

"I have now driven four different sorts of Porsches with a solid drive to the rear wheels and still have to discover a disadvantage. At racing or near racing speeds, cornering behavior is certainly not different from what it is with a limited slip differential. While, even when still cornering, a tremendous torque can be put through the driving wheels without any ill effects."

"The springing is hard and there's very little roll. The handling is superb, with magnificent steering response. The car can be powerslid out of corners without fear of unsticking the front. Curiously, the regular drivers say fuel loads have little influence on the car's behavior. But in any case, a means of compensating for weight distribution is provided by an adjustable rear anti-roll bar which is cable-operated from a small central lever which looks like a cheap handbrake. This has the effect of turning the longitudinal arms of the anti-roll bar, made of a flat piece of spring steel, through 90° when they lie flat, their elasticity is added to that of the bar itself. When they are upright, their elasticity is negligible and roll stiffness is increased. Ickx told me that, in fact, he uses the adjustment much more frequently to compensate for tire deterioration than for the weight of the fuel."

"Noise is not objectionable, but I take my hat off to the drivers sharing the 935 over a distance of 1,000 km on the short and winding Dijon circuit, for instance. Steering, brakes, clutch and gear change all call for quite a lot of physical effort. It's really a he-man's car." ..."

(chassis numbers 935.001 and-002 for the Works team for the races of 1976.

The partnership of Jackie Ickx and Jochen Mass started in fine style, winning the first two six-hour races, which were held at Mugello and Vallelunga, in 935-002. The second 935 built featured rear wings (fenders) which were elongated in shape, shrouding the production rear wings. However, they still allowed the wings and lights to be seen from the rear as per the "Silhouette" Group 5 rules.

Whilst scrutinizing the Appendix "J" rulebook, Norbert Singer had spotted a loophole in the regulations for the body shape. He was to spot many more during his long career. Where the shape of the wings (fenders) were concerned, the rules stated that this was "free" . This, of course, referred to the shape of the wheel arches. Singer interpreted this rule in a different way. He introduced another body modification, a sloped nose which did away with the headlight pods and placed the four driving lights behind Perspex covers in the front spoiler. This new front wing design also had slots cut over the front wheels, allowing the pressurized air to escape, as in the 917.

The design helped stability in crosswinds but it was controversial as it added downforce as well. The CSI let it through although this probably was the last straw in Porsche rule bending for 1976. The CSI objected to the intercooler location immediately afterwards.

At Mugello, the scrutineers objected to the reshaped front end. Porsche was only allowed to start after threatening to withdraw from the event. Prior to this, they had wrangled for three hours with the scrutineers and practice was held up until, grudgingly, the 935 (and the rest of the field!) was allowed to take to the track.

Porsche's real problems struck at Imola. The scrutineers there objected to the intercooler location, pointing out that the aerofoil support was meant for that purpose only and not to house the cooler. Furthermore, they decreed that the original 930 rear engine cover should be able to fit the 935, which it palpably could not with the aftercooler being situated where it was. This decision was upheld by the CSI who gave Porsche just seven weeks to come up with a solution.

In the interim, Porsche lost the Silverstone race of the Manufacturer's Championship, when Jackie Ickx burnt out the clutch on the start line. Despite spending almost two hours in the pits, the car still finished tenth, within the time allotted but outside the points.

As a stop-gap measure, Porsche adopted the water-to-air type of intercooling which was in use on their 934, situating the radiators at the front of the rear wheel arches and saving some weight over the 934 installation. Unfortunately, this improvisation did not work properly. The 935 was defeated at the Nürburgring when the engine failed to run properly on partial throttle, leading to a failure of the distributor. The problem had been cured by the time of the next race which was held at Zeltweg on June 27. Much larger radiator cores and a large centrally-mounted plenum chamber, cut-away at the rear to fit under the engine cover, were fitted. This time a throttle shaft, modified from an existing unit and not properly developed, broke and put the cars out of the race.

The Le Mans 24 hour race was run in June, and there the two 935s ran with a slightly smaller aerofoil and a front spoiler of reduced height. These reduced drag and gave the 935 a higher top speed on the Mulsanne straight than with the standard items fitted. The engines also ran reduced boost pressure in the search for 24-hour reliability. One of the cars, driven by Rolf Stommelen and Manfred Schurti, covered 5,378 kilometers and finished fourth overall to win the Group 5 category. A Kremer-entered 934/5 (driven by Heyer, Negrete, Bolanos and Sprowls) was forced to retire in the 24th hour. The BMWs, though fast, did not last the race.

Fortunately for Porsche, their problems for the Championship victory were behind them by the time the Watkins Glen 6-Hour race was run. There, Ickx and Mass lost the race to their team mates, Stommelen and Schurti, due to the rear brake pads wearing down to the backing plates. Porsche kept up their winning record, taking the next round, held at Dijon, where the two cars entered (driven by Stommelen/Schurti and Ickx/Mass) were first and third, amassing enough points to win the FIA World Championship of Makes title.

Manfred Schurti won the Zolder race but from then on it was a battle for the Championship between Stommelen, Schurti and Wollek. No-one else won a race in the ten rounds of the Championship.

At the end of the season, R15, (935-002) had covered a total of 12,800 kilometres whilst R14 (935-001), the development car which had only raced at Le Mans, the Nürburgring and Watkins Glen, had covered 8,950 kilometers.

For a magazine, a 935/76 was timed (with Le Mans gearing fitted) at a maximum speed of 209 mph. It accelerated from 0-125 mph in 8.2 seconds and could generate cornering forces of up to 1.35G.

Road and Track tested a 934 and a 935 and came up with figures such as the 0-60 mph dash as 5.8 and 3.3 for the two cars respectively. 0-100 mph took 10.1 and 6.1 seconds, with the standing quarter mile being covered at the rate of 14.2 and 8.9 seconds respectively. ❏

Chapter 5

FACTORY DEVELOPMENT —
THE 935/77

For 1977, the rules for Group 5 were amended in three significant areas. Whilst the rules were being formulated, BMW had pointed out that they were, in essence, handicapped by running a front-engined car as the exhaust pipes could not exit the outline of the bodywork until past the mid-way point of the wheelbase, thus forcing them to run a "taller" car than could otherwise be designed. With the big-bore exhaust pipes the BMW Turbocar used, this made it impossible to lower the car as much as a mid- or rear-engined car such as the 935.

The CSI thus allowed the floor pan to be raised to the level of the sills, which allowed the exhaust system of a front-engined car to be accommodated. The rear bulkhead could now be moved 200 mm further forward to give more room in the engine bay of the 935, to accommodate the intercooler. The CSI now defined the space between the front and rear bulkhead as the "body structure".

Porsche later took advantage of these amendments with the 935/78. For 1977, they contented themselves by raising the front wishbone pivot points. This limited the camber variations to nil within 30 mm of its static position, allowing the negative camber of the front suspension to be reduced. Additionally, the water-to-air intercooler system was now mounted across the rear of the new engine bay, making use of the rule change that allowed the bulkhead to be moved forward. The front suspension struts were modified, a magnesium hub carrier similar to the 917's being fitted. The cockpit's adjustable anti-rollbar lever now controlled the stiffness of the front suspension, the lightly loaded springs allowing a greater effect than the previously used adjustable rear anti-rollbar. A brake servo was used for the first time on a racing Porsche but discarded after it

was found that pad wear was drastically increased.

The most dramatic differences were to be seen at the rear of the car. The rear window was now cowled in by a coaming. This allowed the airflow to sweep along the raised roof line to the new rear wing, which had the air intakes for the intercooler set into its sides. This rear wing was supported by two fins mounted on top of each rear fender. The new roof line helped to control and direct air more efficiently to the rear wing. A second, Plexiglass, rear window was let into this coaming over the original glass item. This was something not forbidden by the rules, which stated only that the original rear window had to be retained.

To help manage airflow under the car, Porsche's designers also incorporated what appeared to be "running boards", between the rear of the front fenders and the front of the rears, running alongside the sills. Faired-in rear view mirrors were also mounted on top of the front fenders, which contributed towards keeping the airflow on top of the car and helping downforce. The rear wheel arches were elongated to the maximum allowed by the rules and covered the production Turbo's arches. This was a very similar

The factory-entered twin turbo (935/77-005) with Jackie Ickx driving, during the 1977 running of the Nürburgring 1,000 Kilometer race held on May 29. Behind Ickx is 930 770 0911, which was shared by Rolf Stommelen and Tim Schenken. Behind them is the Manfred Schurti/Rolf Kellers Jagermeister-sponsored 930 770 0905. Chassis number 007 0004, the Vaillant-sponsored Kremer Brothers-entered 935 of Bob Wollek and John Fitzpatrick is next, followed by another Georg Loos car (930 770 0908) with the second Works-entered car (935/77-003) briging up the rear. Sadly, Ickx was forced into retirement after just eleven laps. [Photo courtesy of Porsche.]

Jackie Ickx driving 935/77-005 at Silverstone. Partnered by Jochen Mass, the pair won by eight laps from the Bob Wollek and John Fitzpatrick-driven Vaillant-sponsored 007 0004 of the Kremer Brothers.

'... One racing team which used various versions of the 935 over three years of racing was Dick Barbour's. Dick, based in San Diego, had virtually grown up as a racing driver. He had his first half-midget car at the tender age of eight! After this, Dick raced a Porsche 356 whilst still in his teens and started "Automation", a Porsche and Volkswagen race preparation business. In 1968, he raced a Lola T70 in the CanAm series at Riverside in the Los Angeles Times Grand Prix. Dick was then smitten with road racing and bought a Porsche 904 to race, all the time dreaming and scheming of racing at Le Mans. His dream came true in 1978 when he took two 935s to the Sarthe.

Of those times, Dick Barbour said, "I shared my car, a twin-turbo, with Brian Redman and we finished fifth overall, winning the IMSA class. The other car, a single-turbo, had Bob Garretson, Bob Akin and Steve Earle sharing the driving. Bob Garretson wrote it off at the Mulsanne kink. (See Bob Akin's comments.) I can laugh about it now but it was pretty upsetting at the time. It's a coffee table now, a square block with the ignition key sticking up out of it."

"In 1979, I joined forces with Paul Newman and Rolf Stommelen. We were second overall and first in the IMSA class again. If we hadn't lost time with a stuck wheel nut, we would have won outright. Rolf Stommelen, incidentally, took me around the Nürburgring in a hire car to show me the lines. After the second lap, I got out! Back to '79. I had four 935s entered under the Dick Barbour Racing banner and I'm proud of that. We shipped three cars over in our transporter from the States and picked up a brand new 935 from the factory on the way through! Incidentally, the car which was second had a replacement bodyshell onto which we hung the salvageable parts from Bob Garretson's crash of the year before. One of the other cars was fifth. That was a good year for us."

"We used to stay at an old castle at Melahorne. I remember the intensity of the competition at Le Mans. I had some of my best personal drives there. In particular, the Mulsanne straight certainly got your attention when you were flat out in a 935, sometimes at night and with weather that could vary from dry to rain or mist. The cost? Well, I remember that in 1980, we spent around $800,000 to run one car at Le Mans and take part in the IMSA season, a total of sixteen races. The 935 was big in every way. Size, weight, performance and cost, but it captured the imagination of drivers and fans alike." ...⁹

Dick Barbour listens as John Fitzpatrick tells him what it was like out there ...

modification to the one Peter Gregg had used on his Carrera RSR in 1975 for racing in the IMSA Championship. The American rule makers later banned these modifications. (They failed to notice, however, that Gregg's car also had a 3.2-liter engine instead of the more normal 3.0-liter unit!)

At the front, the two driving lights resided behind circular Perspex covers in the forward-raked front spoiler which, again, contained the large oil cooler and the slots to take cool air to the brake discs.

Inside the engine compartment, it could immediately be seen that two turbochargers, each slightly smaller than the single one used the year before, had now been fitted. Each turbocharger and its associated plumbing was now completely separate from the other with each feeding three cylinders per side. This switch to twin, smaller turbochargers almost totally eliminated throttle lag present with the single turbocharger installation, as the inertia of the two smaller turbine compressor units was that much less than one single large unit. This twin-turbo engine was known within the factory as the type 935/78. The improved throttle response made the 1978 customer 935 a much easier car to drive than the 1977 customer version. Power was now increased slightly from the 590 bhp of the 1976 car to 630 bhp at 7,900 rpm.

Two cars were built for the Martini-sponsored Works team of 1977, 935/77-003 and -004. The latter crashed at the Mugello 6 Hour race when Jürgen Barth neglected to pump the brakes after a pad change. As a result, he was left with no alternative but to use John Fitzpatrick's Kremer-entered car as a brake at the first corner! The resulting crash put both cars out of commission and Stommelen and Schurti finished first in the race itself.

Following this incident and for the remainder of the season, 935/77-004 was replaced by -005 and it claimed another three victories: Silverstone, Watkins Glen, and the Brands Hatch 6 Hours, once again, garnering the FIA World Championship of Makes for Porsche. ❏

VISIT VELOCE ON THE WEB – WWW.VELOCE.CO.UK
All current books • New book news • Special offers • Gift vouchers • Forum

69

Chapter 6

1977 —
CUSTOMER 935/77

In 1977, private teams were all queuing up to buy 935s as, with the withdrawal of BMW, the Group 5 category became a Porsche province. The factory built thirteen replicas of its 1976 racer, which were eagerly snapped up by the independent racing teams. They saw a lot of racing.

By now, Porsches were not only eligible for World Championship races but also for National Championships, such as the German one thriving with teams like Gelo (Georg Loos) and the Kremer Brothers running two (sometimes three) cars each. Max Moritz Autohaus of Reutlingen raced a 935/77 as well, whilst bringing a 934 up to that specification.

These customer 935s featured the Type 930/72 engine of 2.8-liters. However, a new engine of 3.0-liters was offered by the factory (Type 930/76), which produced 630 bhp at 7,800 rpm. This engine derived its larger capacity from a bore size of 95 mm. This forced the cars using this larger engine to carry an extra 122 lbs of weight but the increase in torque was thought worth the extra weight. The new twin turbocharger

Dick Barbour took this 1977 "customer" 935 to Sebring where, driven by Bob Akin, Roy Woods and Rob McFarlin, it won the 12 Hour race. [Photo—Author's collection.]

October 9, 1977. Victory. Bob Wollek and John Fitzpatrick have just driven chassis number 007 0004, which was built up on a factory competition 930 bodyshell at Hockenheim. Using a single turbo engine, the 935 K2 of the kremer Brothers was driven to win the Hockenheim six hours, which was composed of two, three hour heats. Already visible are the squared off tops to the rear fenders, which would become such a trademark of the Kremer Brothers' K3 model of 1979. [Photo—Author's collection.]

intercooler system of the 1977 Works-entered cars was employed on these single-turbo 935/77As. Just as with the 934, the factory supplied an owner's manual and a parts list. With each year of production of "customer" cars, the factory updated these.

Jim Busby bought a "customer"' 1977 935 and remembered, "I converted it almost immediately to twin-turbocharger specification and went to Mosport for the international race there with it. It was so hot that, at the finish, I was exhausted and let Jackie Ickx past me for second place. When we got back to the pits, I collapsed on to the floor with heat exhaustion. So did Jackie! He told me afterwards that he almost didn't have the strength to drive past me at the end! I sold that car to Dick Barbour's team. They painted it blue and it won Sebring in 1979."

A kit of parts could also be bought to bring the 934 up to (almost) 935 specification. These were known as 934/5s and three 934s were so converted in 1976. Besides these, the Kremer Brothers (noted tuners of 911 RSRs) built up their own 935 using factory parts on a factory 930 bodyshell and ran it in the German National Championship.

The Kremer Brothers were both enthusiastic racers, Erwin Kremer having raced the very first 911 to be used on the track. Through the 911S, and RSRs in both 1973 and 1974 versions, the Brothers had steadily modified the original Porsche factory product. By 1974, they were building their own race cars with parts purchased from the factory. For 1976, they built what became known as the "K1". Certainly the 935 K3 became their most famous product from 1979 on but "K1" was their first step into turbocharged competition.

7he shape of things to come: The Kremer Brothers' development of the 1977 "customer" 935, the K2. At Le Mans in 1978, chassis number 930 770 0903 was driven by Philippe Gurdjian, Dieter Schornstein and "John Winter" (Louis Krages) but was not classified, having covered insufficient distance due to engine problems. [Photo—Porsche Werk.]

The 1977 customer 935 was an excellent car for a private racing customer in the Group 5 category but (as usual with Porsche) the racing department at Weissach had something even more developed with which to compete in 1977. ❏

'... Brian Redman is a race driver who has driven (and won!) in just about everything he has raced in a long career. Jaguar "E" Type, Lola T70, sundry Formula 5000 Championships and Porsches. From 908s to 917s as a Works driver and then in 935s.

"That's all there was in the late 1970s! Really, the 935 was an incredible car when you consider its road going 911 parentage."

"The handling was acceptable for what was basically a street car but they were hard to balance properly in the handling department. Of course, they had built in understeer as a safety factor and then there was the throttle lag...! They had the usual Porsche reliability built-in and I enjoyed my time in them. Sometimes I would left-foot brake, as at the kink at Road America but by and large, that wasn't necessary."

"I did Le Mans twice in 935s, 1978 and 1980. We were fifth both times, in Dick Barbour-entered cars. 1978 was a steady run but I though we should have won in 1980. If only the engine hadn't gone on to five cylinders ...!"

"In the wet? Well, they had quite a wide power band so you could change up into a higher gear sooner than normal which helped but you still had to deal with the throttle lag. I remember racing with Charles Mendez at Daytona in the finale meeting of 1979. It rained hard. the car was OK on the banking but as soon as I came down into the infield, I saw that some cars were spinning ahead of me. I got off the power and tried to slow down but the 935 just floated along and I was a passenger. I saw John Paul get hit right in the side by a Corvette and then I hit the wall. It really wasn't too bad, I was able to drive it back but the paddock looked like a wrecking yard when they dragged all the cars in afterwards!"

"I suppose I proceeded to destroy the 935's long reign with the Lola T600 but that's really another story!" (See Chapter 11.) ...'

Chapter 7

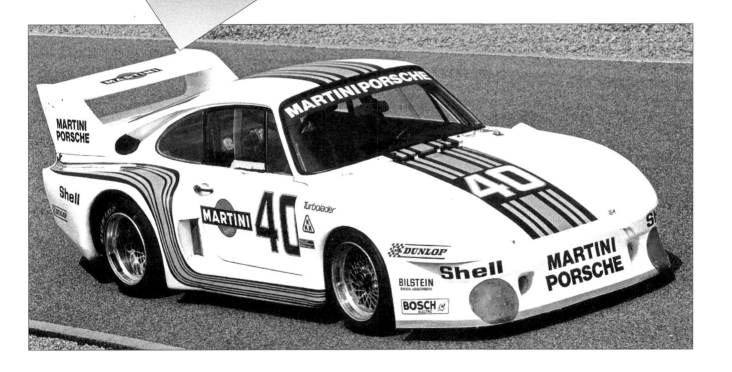

A DIVERSION —
THE 935/2 "BABY"

With the 935 now dominating the World Championship for Makes, BMW withdrew from the series. As we have seen, this left the 935 (run by either the Works or private teams) to take the main honors. The press was quick to point out that Porsche faced only opposition from its customer racing teams.

The two-liter class of the German National Championship races was dominated by rapid variants of Ford Escorts and BMWs. Porsche saw (particularly in view of television coverage of the two-liter heat at the Norisring on July 3) a chance to show that Porsche was just as willing to participate in this class as that of the larger one.

To this end, Porsche developed a "Baby" version of the 935, with a 1.42-liter (equal to 2.0-liters unsupercharged) version of the Type 930/72 (Type 911/79) engine of 71 x 60 mm bore and stroke. With a 6.5:1 compression ratio, this engine produced 370 bhp at 8,000 rpm, using 1.4 bar with an air-to-air intercooler fitted with so-called "jet" cooling.

The "Baby" version of the 935.

Now the 2.0-liter class cars were able to run with a minimum weight limit of 735 kilograms, allowing Porsche to build a radically lightened 935. This car used the 915 five-speed gearbox which did not have to transmit as much power as the "grown-up" 935. Drastic measures were necessary in order to lighten the basic 935/77 structure. The decision was taken to chop off the structures before and behind the cabin structure and to graft on light aluminum tube frames to support the ultra-light GRP bodywork. Missing from the front spoiler was the usual vast oil cooler since the "Baby" did not need as much cooling as its bigger brother. The rear suspension now incorporated newly designed semi-trailing arms built up from fabricated aluminum sheet, copying the original concepts of the Turbo RSR.

An air-to-air intercooler was used since, with the reduction of power, the larger and more bulky water-to-air type was found to be unnecessary. At the end of the exhaust pipe, a venturi was fitted which sucked the air through the aftercooler. The engine and gearbox oil coolers were moved to the spaces previously used by the water radiators of the 935/77, in front of the rear wheels. This saved even more weight. Rear wheels were now reduced to a width of 13.5 inches which allowed narrower rear wings. The fuel tank capacity was reduced to 100 liters.

The "Baby" again. Note the tube frame front structure and the lack of a front-mounted oil cooler.

"Baby" from the rear.

Porsche, after making the decision to go for the 2-liter class on April 5, was forced to rush the design and build of the "Baby". This did not leave enough time to thoroughly test the brand new car which appeared on the grid at the Norisring.

The finished "Baby" weighed 710 kilograms, allowing 20 kilograms to be installed in the nose before the car was sent to Nurnberg for the race. Unfortunately, the lack of testing showed. The gear ratios fitted at the factory were much too high and neces-sitated a change from 19-inch diameter rear wheels to those of 16 inches. The engine also lacked power at the bottom end of the rev range.

The sun blazed down on July 1, and cockpit ventilation of the "Baby" was abysmal. Poor Jackie Ickx stood it as long as possible, running in sixth place before retiring the car on the point of collapse. Doctor Fuhrmann, however, had his revenge. At the following race, at Hockenheim, Ickx, with a now fully-tested car, simply blitzed the opposition and walked the class, finishing half a lap ahead of the second-placed car.

"Baby" never ran again. Porsche had made its point that it could win any class it turned its hand to, and the "Baby" can now be seen in Porsche's museum.

A footnote to the factory-entered "Baby" saga was the car built up by Jan Lundgardh of Sweden in the early 1980s. This was called the "L1" and consisted of a spaceframe-type chassis with Kremer K3-type bodywork. It was also fitted with a 1.4-liter engine to bring it within the 2-liter class rules. It raced at Le Mans in 1981, driven by Lundgardh, Axel Plankenhorn and Mike Wilds but failed to finish. In the German National Championship for which it had been built, it led two races and was demonstrably faster than the Works-entered Lancias. Sadly, a lack of finance put an end to this promising private entrant. ❏

Jackie Ickx during his victorious drive at Hockenheim where he led the 2-litre class from start to finish. Behind his "Baby" 935 are a Max Moritz-entered 934 and a Zakspeed-tuned Ford Anglia.

"Baby" 935.

Chapter 8

FACTORY RACER —
THE 935/78

For 1978, Porsche decided that, as it had now provided many customer racing teams with 935s in both single and double-turbo form, it would leave all national racing championships to them. For international events, including the ever-important 24 Hours of Le Mans, Norbert Singer and his engineers sat down to design the ultimate development of the 935. They would stretch every nook and cranny the rules allowed in order to create a sledgehammer contender of a Group 5 car.

Taking the rulebook at its word, Singer saw that the new, re-defined "body structure" was only that between the front and rear bulkhead. That being the case, he used only those parts of the production 930 bodyshell as a base for the new car, the Type 935/78. In front of and behind these bulkheads, Porsche built lightweight tube frames to support the suspension, ancillaries and bodywork. As the floor could be raised to the height of the sills,

The impressive frontal aspect of 935/78 "Moby Dick".

Porsche did not use the production floorpan but built one out of GRP and mounted it on a level with the sills. This floor now received ground clearance from the 930 (7.5 centimeters), which lowered the whole car by 3 inches and therefore reduced frontal area still more. They now constructed an aluminum tubular frame, which picked up at the bottom of the rollcage feet and had the front and rear tubular frames mount on these also. The effect was of a complete spaceframe with just the roof and door pillars coming from the 930. The opportunity was also taken to make the 935/78 right hand drive, thus placing the driver nearer the apex of the corners on most of Europe's clockwise-running circuits.

The bodywork, all in GRP and carbon-fiber was now extremely sleek and long. The rear wings pulled out several feet past the rear wheels, seeking ultimate maximum speed. Mounted right at the tail end of the body was a wing, which exerted the required down force upon the car.

Scanning the rulebook further, Singer noted that it did not specify how long the front could be. He took advantage of this rule to give the 935/78 an extremely long nose to aid air penetration. A splitter was fitted beneath the nose at its furthest extremity to direct the airflow over, rather than under, the car. The doors were completely faired over, filling in the space between the front and rear wings (fenders) to give a clean line for the air to follow. Singer had also seen that the regulations did not state how far forward the aerodynamic aids of the rear wings could stretch. The original "production"-type doors were underneath and huge NACA ducts were visible in the cowlings over these doors. These led to the air intakes set into the rear

fenders, which then went to the coolant radiators.

One more modification vexed the CSI's scrutineers. The rear window, inset on the normal 930, caused considerable drag and the CSI would not let Porsche replace it with a flush fitted window, which was their preferred solution. Shrugging their shoulders, Porsche's engineers simply built another, flush fitted rear window into the sloped fairing they now used to smooth the airflow to the rear aerofoil. The rules had said that the original bodyshape had to be used. It said nothing about building a superimposed fairing above it!

For some time, Hans Metzger and his team of engine designers had realized that if only they could fit four valve heads to the evergreen flat six-cylindered engine, it would create more power as well as promote a better combustion process, so helpful in a turbocharged engine. To fit four valves in the air-cooled engine was impossible as the cooling would have been marginal at best. So, Metzger and his team designed water-cooled four valve heads to fit to the air-cooled cylinders.

The four overhead camshafts of these new heads were now driven by a train of gears from the nose of the crankshaft. The heads were welded to the cylinder barrels, thus obviating a head gasket problem. The new heads had a narrow valve angle of 30° to allow this welding. (With the two valve heads, welding would have been impossible as the valves could not then have been fitted.) The new camshaft boxes were constructed from magnesium for lightness. Steel buckets, in which shims could be placed for adjustment, were used as tappets. Flat-top pistons were now employed with a compression ratio of 7.0:1. However, the cylinder barrels were still Nikasil-plated and the crankcase was the production 930 unit as the Group 5 regulations specified. Bore and stroke of the new Type 930/71 engine was 95.7 mm x 74.4 mm for a capacity of 3,211 cc. This put the new 935 into the over 4.0 class, which meant a minimum weight of 1,025 kilograms. The design engineers realized that this was worth paying a penalty for, as top speed along the Mulsanne straight was what constituted the most towards a good lap time at Le Mans. 65 kilograms of lead ballast was needed to bring the car up to its minim weight limit. Of course, the engineers were able to place this where they wanted, to bring the weight distribution to an ideal setting.

A separate cooling system was in use for each bank of the engine, the water pump for each being driven by each side's respective exhaust camshaft. The radiators for the coolant were mounted in the engine compartment where, previously, the aftercooler had

been mounted. This was now mounted in the nose of the car, in front of the oil cooler. Also camshaft-driven (intake), was the trigger for the capacitive discharge electronic ignition system. The distributor itself was mounted on the on the left-hand bank of cylinders. Only a single, centrally-mounted sparkplug per cylinder was now necessary, situated right at the top of the pent-roof combustion chambers.

As the cooling fan no longer had to cool the entire engine, its use reverted to the upright type of the production car. However, it was smaller than that of the "standard" 930, and was crankshaft-driven at 1.34 times engine speed. It absorbed only 4 bhp at 8,200 rpm as well as keeping all the cylinders cooler than before since now it did not have the heads to cool also. The alternator was belt-driven from the nose of the crankshaft and mounted on a bracket to the left of the fan.

This 935/71 engine operated with a standard manifold pressure of 1.5 bar and produced 750 bhp at 8,200 rpm. For quali-

Below & opposite page: Two views showing how much lower and longer was the 935/78 compared to its predecessor.

fying, the boost could be raised to 1.7 bar to give 800 bhp at the same revs. The engine was safe to 9,000 rpm. One reason for the increase in boost the engine could sustain was that the head temperatures were now 60° cooler than with the air-cooled two-valve engine.

This engine was mounted in the spaceframe chassis of the 935/78 and the power was transmitted through the 930-type transaxle. This was now mounted upside-down to bring the main gear shaft and spool more in line with the centers of the rear wheels. This reduced the angle the drive shafts had to work through and promoted increased constant velocity joint life. It did force the racing department, however, to make new transmission castings and a new bell housing.

The front track was widened by 122 mm over that of the previous 935 to 1,625 mm. At the rear, the previous semi-trailing arms and trailing arms were gone, replaced by single fabricated aluminum forked semi-trailing arms. The pick-up points were now raised to keep the car level under acceleration.

Whilst the Type 917 brakes had proved satisfactory in the previous 935s, Norbert Singer realized that, with the greater weight and mass of this "ultimate" 935, new brakes would be required. A one-piece light alloy caliper was mounted, floating on the hub. It contained pistons of 43 mm diameter whilst the 332 mm diameter ventilated and radially drilled disc was 32 mm thick.

As in previous years, two cars were built, with chassis numbers 935/78-006 and -007. When the CSI committee came to view the prototype car at Weissach before the start of the season, they were very upset at what they saw. They realized that Norbert Singer and his design team had driven a coach and horses through the rulebook! The committee did save a little face by forcing Singer to remove half of the door's fairing in order to show the original door underneath. They also made the engineers develop another, higher-mounted rear aerofoil to fit within the silhouette of the car when viewed from the front. Porsche's technicians were forced to fit the rear spoiler higher up to find clean air. The new half-faired doors caused too much

turbulence with the previous spoiler setting. Notwithstanding, the CSI's committee must have realized that nobody else would be able to combat the 935/78.

The drivers loved the 935/78. It not only handled much better than the "standard" 935, due to it's weight being concentrated in exactly the right places, but it also went much faster. The engine's quoted power output was probably on the conservative side. The 935 debuted spectacularly, winning the Silverstone 6-hour race which was used as a test for Le Mans.

However, at Le Mans, the Works-entered car failed to live up to expectations. The team of Rolf Stommelen and Manfred Schurti finished only eighth, due to an oil leak which turned out to have been nothing to worry about. Rolf Stommelen went through the speed trap on the Mulsanne with a recorded speed of 227.5 mph. Chassis number 935/78-006 then ran at the Norisring and Vallelunga races It led both races but failed to finish on both occasions. "Moby Dick", as the car was nicknamed, was retired to the Porsche museum.

In later years, two more "Moby Dicks" were built, both by Reinhold Joest Racing. In 1981, the first one, J.R.001, was delivered to one of Joest's best customers, Gianpiero Moretti of "Momo" fame. The car was identical to the factory car (indeed, the chassis looks as if it were built by the factory), with the exception of the engine. This was a "normal" air-cooled unit of 3.2-liters with the characteristic Joest trademark of two separate air-to-air intercoolers fitted, one per bank of cylinders. Moretti had success with his car, winning at Hockenheim in 1981 with Jochen Mass sharing the driving and still achieving top three placings as late as 1983 in America.

The other "Moby Dick" replica, J.R.002, was built to order for John Fitzpatrick Racing and was identical to the Momo car. With this blue and white car, John Fitzpatrick and David Hobbs finished fourth overall at Le Mans in 1982 and won their class. Sadly, Rolf Stommelen was killed in the car a year later at Riverside, when the tail came off and pitched the car head on into the concrete barriers at almost top speed. ❑

Chapter 9

THE 1978 & 1979
CUSTOMER 935s

After the production run of 1976-77 single-turbo customer cars was completed, as we have seen, the factory equipped its own "Works" team with the twin-turbocharged 935 in 1977.

Porsche's customers had been unhappy to see that, once they had acquired (at great expense!) a new single-turbo 1977 935, the factory had put victory beyond their reach with their new cars. At the end of the 1977 season, in response to their customers' demands, fifteen twin-turbocharged cars were built by the factory. Unlike the forthcoming 935/78 of the factory team, these

customer cars were a natural evolution of the Works-run 935/77.

The 1978 935s were essentially the same as the 1977 customer cars but featured the 'running boards' of the Works cars and removable rear fenders to assist maintenance. Most importantly, they had the twin-turbocharger equipped engine, built to the same specifications as that of the Works

The Whittington Brothers, Don and Bill, raced many 935s. Here is one of their 1978 cars with AIR bodywork. This featured rear fenders with fences running along the top, much in the way of the Kremer Brothers' K2.

April 30, 1978. The start of the Eifelrennen, one of the races which counted towards the German National Championship. From the left, in the Jagermeister car: Manfred Schurti in 930 890 0017; Klaus Ludwig in the "Polster Trosse"-sponsored 930 890 0020; Reinhold Joest in 930 890 0016 (Liqui-Moly car); Toine Hezemans in the Gelo-entered 930 890 0020; and behind him, Bob Wollek in the Kremer-entered 930 890 0013. The Konrad-entered car behind Schornstein is driven by Franz Konrad himself and is 930 890 0014. John Fitzpatrick is driving race number 8, another Gelo-entered car, chassis number 930 890 0011. Volkert Merl is driving the Franz Konrad-entered 930 770 0907 (race number 16), whihlst the lone RSR is driven by Jurgen Happel (911 460 9019). [Photo—Racing Car-Bild Studio.]

cars. Their bodywork differed from the Works cars though. They had only one rear window in a "standard" shaped rear body line and a tail (heckfleugel) similar to the 1976 factory cars.

Such was the demand, that at least two more 935s had to be supplied to customers. Dick Barbour took delivery of a curious hybrid, which was effectively a 1978 chassis with a single large turbocharger engine for Daytona in 1978. Bruce Anderson, who worked with Bob Garretson Enterprises in preparing Dick's cars at that time, remembered it as having, "all the same features as a 1977 935. This chassis had bonded-on rear fenders, instead of the later 1978-style removable ones. The engine was essentially a 1978 930/78 but with just one turbocharger. Dick had also bought Ted Field's 934 and a half with which Johnny Rutherford (*in Barbour's 934 and a*

John Fitzpatrick was one of Georg Loos' drivers in 1978. Here he is in action with his regular car 930 890 0011 at Mainz-Finthen in a 935 sandwick. Behind him is the "General-Anzeiger" (Bonn's newspaper) sponsored car of Klaus Ludwig (930 890 0020), with another Gelo-entered car, that of Toine Hezemans (930 890 0015) behind that. The Vaillant-Kremer 935 is 930 890 0013, driven by Bob Wollek. [Photo—Racing Car-Bild Studio.]

By 1978 the German National Championship was vying in popularity with the World Championship of Makes. More 935s entered the German series and it became a happy hunting ground for the teams of Georg Loos and the Kremer Brothers, amongst others. Pictured above is the start of the German National Championship Goodyear 300 kilometer race at the Nürburgring on April 2, 1978. Starting from the left the cars are as follows. Toine Hezemans is in the number 6, Gelo-entered, car (chassis number 930 890 0020). He would finish in second place. Bob Wollek is in the Vaillant-sponsored, Kremer-entered 930 890 0013, which he drove to victory here. Behind Wollek, in the Liqui Moly-sponsored car, is Reinhold Joest in 930 890 0016 with, behind him, Volkert Merl in 930 770 0907. the Jagermeister-sponsored race number 5 car is Manfred Schurti's 930 890 0017 and behind him is Klaus Ludwig in 930 890 0015, who finished third. "Fitz" (John Fitzpatrick) is driving race number 8, the Gelo-entered 930 890 0011 with, behind him, Franz Konrad in 930 890 0014. "John Winter" is driving the Kremer-entered race number 4 (chassis number 930 770 0903). The second Jagermeister car, an RSR driven by Anton Fischaber is chassis number 911 460 9068. Race number 3 (far right) is Dieter Schornstein's 930 890 0012 and Klaus Drees is behind him in the Kremer-built car from 1976, chassis number 006 0004. [Photo—Racing Car-Bild Studio.]

half - Ed) had collided at the end-of-season Daytona Finale race. Dick had the factory supply him with a new chassis and we built the mechanical parts of the wrecked Field car into that. This was the car that we won the 1978 Sebring race with."

The "customer" engines were numbered 930/78. Essentially, this was the Type 1977 works engine, with twin-turbochargers, which now produced some 675 bhp at 8,000 rpm running at 1.45 bar boost. The twin-turbocharger factory water-to-air intercooler installation was also installed. The KKK K-27 turbochargers in use had their casings made of Ni-resist, an alloy able to resist very high temperatures. New head-to-barrel sealing rings were also now made of this material. They were fitted into a groove in the cylinder head and did away with the CE-ring head gasket, which

Danny Ongais was one of the fastest of the American IMSA drivers of 935s. Here he is in his 1978 Interscope-entered 935, chassis number 930 890 0021. He and the team's owner, Ted Field, shared the car in this race at Lime Rock and finished fourth overall. [Photo—Author's collection.]

had previously been used. Two scavenge pumps were used on the turbochargers. These pumped out extra oil to the dry sump's oil tank in the nose of the car. Rolf Stommelen, driving a customer 935, won the German Group 5 Championship, something that the 935 was to make a specialty of.

Jim Busby went to Le Mans in 1978 with a twin-turbo he had hired from the

overjoyed. I remember in the early hours of the morning, I found myself gaining on another 935, driven by Bob Garretson on the Mulsanne straight. We were both doing over 200 mph and, as we came to the kink, I realized that the other 935 was not going to make it. He hit the barrier on the other side and I drove under him as the crash occurred. He must have been over forty feet in the air,

Jim Busby, standing alongside a 1978 Model 935, discusses its handling with the crew. Dan McLaughlin (of AIR), who contributed much to the 935 in IMSA racing, is third from the left.

Kremer Brothers. He thought it a, "beautifully prepared car. I shared the driving with Chris Cord and Steve Knoop. The car went great. No problems. The Mulsanne straight was so long that I would transfer my left foot onto the throttle while I wiggled my right toes to get the feeling back! We won our class and finished in the top ten. Erwin and Manfred, the Kremer Brothers, were

bits flying off all over the place. Of course, the yellow lights came on and the safety car gathered us all up. I was sure Bob must have been killed. Next time around, I saw the roll-cage with the driver still strapped in, his head lolling. Next time around, there was Bob, out of the car and rubbing his sore head! 935s sure were strong!"

Brian Redman, who had been behind

'... Bob Akin, remembering his 935s, said:

"I started Porsche racing with George Dyer's 74 RSR, a great car of which I have fond memories. I did a deal with Dick Barbour to race a single-turbo 935 at Le Mans. We went quite well at Le Mans but Bob Garretson had a huge accident on the Le Mans straight at around 5 a.m. He was very lucky to get away with bruises. Jim Busby had been following him and said that the car went forty feet into the air and he drove underneath it! I went back to the RSR for the rest of the season, but in 1979 I rented another 935 (a 934 and a half with 935 bodywork from Dick Barbour). I could, however, get my own sponsorship which helped to defray the costs. I did the entire IMSA season and some WEC races with this car and did well. For Le Mans, Dick rented us a yellow twin-turbo and we (Woods/McFarlin/Akin) were up with the leaders until the engine broke after some six hours."

"In December of that year, I formed a team of three 935s (with Charles Mendez, a real estate developer from Tampa and Roy Woods) called 'Racing Associates'. Mendez brought two 935s to the party and we had another car with K3 bodywork built on a spare shell by Franz Blam in Atlanta. We obtained a sponsorship deal from Coca Cola, their first involvement in motor racing. At the end of 1980, Charles and Roy decided that they wanted to finish racing, so we sold the assets and I kept the Franz Blam car. I also got race number 5 which had been Charles Mendez's number. It has been mine ever since."

"For 1981, I teamed up with Derek Bell and we were second at the Daytona 24 Hours. Funny thing was, we were second again in 1982! Quite depressing though, after you have done it the year before as well. Bobby Rahal joined us for a very wet Silverstone 6 Hours, where we finished sixth and then we went to the Nürburgring. Bobby had an accident and, although he was OK, the car was immovable, just around a long, sweeping right-hand bend. We implored the marshals to move it but they wouldn't. They even stopped leaving out the yellow flags after an hour. Poor Herbert Muller ran straight into the 935 and was killed. A tragedy."

"After this, I bought Bob Wollek's engine-less "Jagermeister" K3 from the Kremer Brothers and put our spare engine into it. This was a very good car. We took it to Le Mans where we were holding tenth place until the very last lap when the engine failed with an electrical fault. We were gutted. I brought the car back to the US and did well in IMSA races for the rest of that season."

"For 1982, we built the 935 L1. This was a monocoque structure with pannier fuel tanks but it was a big mistake. The weight distribution was all wrong and the handling suffered as a result. It was a white knuckle ride! It did have one compensation, however. It had incredible top speed due to the low frontal area. Other cars would pass us through the corners but we would just accelerate past them on the straights. With Hurley Haywood, I took a fourth place at Mid-Ohio and a seventh at Road Atlanta after Derek Bell had put it on pole. It was wrecked at the Daytona Thanksgiving meeting and I wasn't sorry. I'd had enough of it by then."

"So, for 1983, I brought out the old K3 and it was wonderful! I shared the driving with Derek Bell, John O'Steen, Dennis Aase and Craig Siebert. We were third in the IMSA

Championship that year. At the end of 1983, I had FabCar build me a tube frame car. I had looked at a crashed 935 and decided that this was much safer in an accident than the old 911 shell-based cars. The 956s were not being allowed to run by IMSA and we could not get a delivery date on a 962. I decided to incorporate into this 'last 935' all the lessons I had learned over the years in racing these cars. We debuted the car at the Daytona Finale and it reached 213 mph! We took the pole position and finished second. In 1984, the transmission failed and we DNF'd there. At Sebring, a wheel bearing jammed, necessitating changing the whole front hub assembly. Nevertheless, we finished in fifth place."

"After this, I got my 962 but Jim Mullen drove the 935 in the 1985 Daytona 24 Hours. It came in fifth, right behind us in the 962! It was still being entered in championship races in 1986, prepared by Dave White Racing. Great cars. I remember Jim Busby coming over to ask me my opinion on Porsches when he was thinking of buying a March. I told him, 'There isn't a March owners' club!' He bought a 962." ...⁹

Peter Gregg in his 1979 IMSA Camel GT Championship-winning car,, chassis number 930 990 0029, at Portland on August 5. Gregg won again here, winnining nine races outright to take his sixth IMSA Championship. Gregg was the only driver to race a 935 with a single large turbo instead of the usual two smaller ones. this gave him a weight advantage, which he exploited to the full.
[Photo—Ken Schwoerer/IMSA Collection.]

Busby, remembered that moment well, "I was coming down the Mulsanne straight and catching up to a Chevron. The kink is just over a hill and, until you crest the rise, you can't see it. Something told me that things were not quite right and just as I eased off the throttle, I went straight into a huge cloud of dirt. I couldn't see a thing and the Chevron flashed by, just missing me. I then saw that it was our team car that had crashed. I stopped at our signalling pits and shouted that Bob had had an accident. I was so upset, being sure that Bob must have been killed. I pulled into the pits after just two more laps and received the glad tidings that Bob was OK. I was so relieved".

Dennis Aase of California was driving a Porsche RSR at Le Mans that year. In 1982 and 1983, he shared the driving of Bob Akin's own 935 in many races and loved the car. However, he remembered being on the receiving end of their performance, also at

The founder of the Momo steering wheel company, Dr. Gianpiero Moretti, raced a lot of 934s and 935s. Here he is in the car he raced in 1979, chassis number 930 990 0032. Moretti later had Reinhold Joest t convert the car to a 935J for him. He sold the car in 1980 to Jim Busby, who had Dan McLaughlin of AIR rebody it with his M16 design. The old Joest bodywork was sold to Bruce Leven, who used it on one of his Bayside Disposal 935s. [Photo—Author's collection.]

'... Alwin Springer remembered:

"935s: Randolf Townsend from Reno had one car which is still in Harrah's Museum. This was black, and was driven by Townsend at Le Mans one year. The other drivers were Jean Pierre Jarrier and Harald Grohs. The car was very reliable and Randolf was not fast but rich. Harald was a different story. He was very fast."

"The Howard Meister car (930 890 0013) was a 1978 customer car that we took apart and rebuilt our way and then had Rolf Stommelen, Harald Grohs and Derek Bell drive it in 1981 in the IMSA series. We won three 500-mile races in three consecutive weekends: Mosport; Elkhart Lake; and Mid-Ohio."

"Then we built a new, tube frame car, for Daytona for the following year where it won. Kevin Jeannette still has it now in Florida. This was built from scratch and was based on the factory 'Moby Dick' on the outside. It worked very well."

"We did engines for most of the 934s and 935s that ran in America. When I was with Andial, we refined engines to US market needs, as most racetracks are hotter here than in Europe and torque is more important for getting out of the turns. Intercoolers were no problem. We used the water-cooled ones at first in a 934 and early 935s and then we changed over to the air-cooled variety. Power? About 640–650 bhp and they would run for 24 hours in that state of tune."

"For Le Mans and Daytona, we would pre-test the car and then take the engine back to the shop, go through it one more time and then practice, qualify and run the race. Most of the wear was in the piston rings. The pistons and barrels would wear out but the engine would keep going, it would just use more oil as that blew by the rings. Otherwise, no problems."

In the beginning, we had detonation problems but we worked on the Kugelfischer pump, which had a nozzle in it and which reduced the mixture at the top end of the power band. Kugelfischer and Bosch developed a crude electronic management system which was a major step forward. Fuel consumption? That was low, about three miles per gallon at racing speeds. We made different forms of tails for different courses, a short tail for places like Mid-Ohio, and a long tail for faster circuits." ...'

Le Mans for the first time, "It was the first time I'd been to Le Mans, and it rained for some of the time. Driving the RSR down the Mulsanne straight at it's maximum speed of some 160 mph took some getting used to in the rain, I can tell you! Most of the drivers were very polite - you'd see a flash of head-lights and know that something faster was coming along so you'd move to the right after signalling and the 935s would pass you on the left. The only trouble was, 935s displaced a lot of air and, straight after one of those things had gone by, my RSR would go right, left and right again, without me changing my hands position on the wheel at all. Later, when I drove Bob Akin's 935, I really loved it. All that power and flames out of the exhaust to boot!"

John Greasley, a Rallycross Champion in 911s, and later the campaigner of a GT1 in the British FIA Championship, bought an ex-Joest, Rolf Stommelen-driven 935/78

A pit stop during the Daytona 24 Hour race of 1979. Here is the Interscope car late on in the race. The crowds are gathering to photograph what would turn out to be the winner. The engine was so worn out at the end that the car had to sit at the start-finish line and wait until just before the end of the race to start up and crawl around to finish, such was its lead. Notice how the front spoiler has been literally sandblasted of paint. Whilst the crewmen in the middle and right look after the fuel tank filling, the mechanic on the left is topping up the dry sump's oil tank. [Photo—IMSA collection.]

(930 890 0016) in 1982. John promptly took it to Goodwood to take part in a sprint event and remembered, "I drove it like a hooligan straight away. I was really in over my head but then 935s invited that sort of treatment!

Despite having a slight "off", I set a record, which lasted several years. That was the start of my association with 935s. I raced them right through the 80s and into the 90s, acquiring two K3s in the process. I even raced one of

98

'... Hurley Haywood remembered:

"I started racing the Porsche 934 in the 1976 TransAm, with my team mate in the Vasek Polak team, George Follmer. Of course, George won the series and I was second that year. We thought the 934 was pretty cool at the time. It was pretty skinny, with not very big wheel flares, so it was very fast down the straight. Of course, it was also tricky to drive as it was heavy with full interior trim and instrumentation. In the wet, they were even more tricky so you turned down the boost to cope with that."

"The 934 and a half of 1977 was much easier to drive. It had wider wheels and a wing that actually worked. I don't think the single-plate wing on the 934 did anything! Anyway, the 1977 934 and a half was a lot easier car to handle than the 934."

"The first 935 I drove, as I recollect, was Peter's (*Gregg - Ed*) at Daytona in 1978. I loved it; 700 horsepower, tons of downforce, big wing, a real rocketship. 935s needed a certain technique to get them around corners. You could tell who was driving the 935 ahead of you by watching the driver's technique through the corners. Everyone had their own technique of massaging the throttle to keep the turbocharger spooled up. Some people used left-foot braking but the only car I ever did that in was the Audi in later years."

"In 1979, I won Daytona in the Interscope car with Ted Field and Danny Ongais and then did Sebring too in the same car. After that, Bruce Leven hired me away from Peter's Brumos team to his Bayside Disposal team. We had a good run, except that I had two crashes in two separate Bayside 935s. In the first one, a hub broke at Sears Point and I spun off onto the grass. As the car sat there, the hot turbos ignited the dried grass and by the time the fire fighters arrived, the 935 was history. Bruce went and bought Peter Gregg's last 935, the one with the 6-inch wider track (*chassis number 000 00028 – Ed*). It was not a nice car to drive until developed later. Anyway, at Mosport, it got away from me in turn one and spun before going over the guardrail. I won't tell you Bruce's reaction to that!"

"I drove with the Whittingtons at Le Mans in 1980 in a K3 where, sadly, we had to retire with rear axle failure. Although 935s weren't as comfortable as the sports-prototypes, there were none of those running that year so you didn't have to look in your mirrors too much."

"It was comparatively easy to drive a 935 to 80% of its limit. Then it was quite stable. When you tried to use the extra 20% things got real busy. You had to be aggressive to take the car to its real limit. They had lots of power, lots of downforce in fast corners. In slow corners, there was little downforce and so you had to drift it through the corners and that could be dramatic. Tire management was critical, you could light up the rears in any gears but after a couple of laps when they had gone away, you were in trouble!" ...'

the K3s in the British GT Championship in 1995-6 and won. Wonderful cars."

Porsche's customer 935s of the year before did well in 1977. One of them, entered by the JMS Racing Team, and driven by Claude Ballot-Lena and Peter Gregg, finished third overall at the Le Mans classic and won the Group 5 category. Three other privately-entered 935/76s, two entered by the Gelo Team and one by the Kremer Racing Team, retired as did the Works-entered car, of Stommelen and Schurti. That car retired with engine failure in the fourth hour. Nick Faure remembered sharing a 935 with John

Fitzpatrick and Guy Edwards, "It was the *Penthouse*-sponsored car and was incredibly quick along the Mulsanne straight. The timekeepers were reporting our speed as well over 220 mph. The engine blew in the first hour with "Fitz" driving. It had been well overboosted, I presume."

"Later on, I drove at Brands Hatch with Bob Wollek in a Gelo car and finished third. Still lots of turbo-lag but by now, I'd got the hang of dealing with it." *(See Chapter 3 – Ed.)*

The IMSA Champion in 1978 was, once again, Peter Gregg, driving his own

In 1980 Reinhold Joest came to America to compete in the Daytona 24 Hours, together with Rolf Stommelen and Volkert Merl. He used this car, a 1978 "customer" version, chassis number 930 890 0014 and the team won the race outright. [Photo—Author's collection.]

Brumos Racing 935. He won nine out of the fifteen races in the Championship. Against him were mustered the 935s of the Whittington Brothers, Hurley Haywood, Ted Field's "Interscope" team, etc, and just one BMW 320i Turbo, driven by David Hobbs. 935s competed in the TransAm Championship now and into 1979 also, with excellent results. The SCCA, however, effectively outlawed the cars so that, by 1980, an IROC RSR from 1973 was the overall Champion.

Porsche's European customers did very well in 1978. Jacques Almeras won the European Hill Climb Championship. Apart from the 24 Hours of Daytona, Mugello, Silverstone, Misano and the Vallelunga 6-Hour races, the Nürburgring and Dijon 1,000 kilometer races were all won by various 935s and, once again, the FIA World Championship for Makes fell to the 935/78, plus various 935s run by private racing teams. In truth, international GT racing had now become almost completely Porsche dominated but it did make for some exciting racing between the teams of these fast, relatively heavy, fire-spitting cars.

The German National Championship for Group 5 cars was now drawing enormous crowds. This made it a viable proposition for some 935 owners to contest this series alone. No fewer than twelve 935s appeared for the opening race at Zolder, which Toine Hezemans won in a Gelo-entered car. Georg Loos, the team owner, had bought three of the new 1978 twin-turbos. From then on, Hezemans, Bob Wollek, John Fitzpatrick and Klaus Ludwig dominated the series. No-one else won a race, even though the Kremer Brothers put up a strong resistance with their modified cars.

Some of these 1978 twin-turbo cars went on to have extremely long careers (see Appendix 1), some of them still winning races as late as 1984. Vittorio Coggiola ('Victor') bought 930 890 0017, an ex-Max Moritz car, which had been driven by Manfred Schurti and raced it until 1986. By the time he retired it, the car resembled a 935/77, but with huge air intakes to the intercoolers and a very long, sloped forward nose. 930 890 0014, a car sold first of all to Franz Konrad, was still racing as a "934" in 1985.

Where bodywork was concerned, the customers were always looking for new shapes, to make their car just that much more slippery down the straight. Dan McLoughlin of AIR, based in California, developed and made his own and supplied most of the American teams, either from his shop or via the Vasek Polak Porsche supply truck, which carried parts to all the meetings.

At the end of 1978, as in previous years, Porsche built up a further small batch of seven 935s destined for private customers in the USA. These 935s did not feature the radical developments that had gone into the 935/78. They were based more upon the 1978 935 twin-turbo customer car but with the inverted transmission and bigger Type 935/78 brakes. The engine was fitted with a single, large KKK K-36 turbocharger, to try and cope with new rules that had been introduced by IMSA in an attempt to slow down the 935 and make the opposition credible. They didn't work. It had been thought that a single-turbo 935, even with a favorable weight advantage, would be no match for the older twin-turbo and John Greenwood Corvettes. Peter Gregg was unstoppable again and won most of the IMSA races in 1979, using a single-turbocharged car.

The cockpit of 930 890 0013, the ex-Howard Meister/Andial car. Note the built-up gear change and adjustable boost knob.

The passenger compartment of 930 890 0013, showing the fire extinguisher bottle, plus the extra tubing of the roll cage.

The engine bay of 930 890 0013. Note the waste gate (pop-off valve), the fabricated aluminum-tube engine bay cross member and the out-rigged alternator in front of the flat-fan ducting.

The front compartment of 930 890 0013, with the aluminum crossbrace, the fuel cell on the right and the oil tank (for the dry sump engine) on the left.

The Whittington Brothers owned many 935s. Here is one of their 1978 cars, bodywork removed, at AIR's shop in California.
[Photo—Author's collection.]

A 3-liter air-cooled engine was also made available to customers with 1977 cars. This came from the racing service department at the factory, in conjunction with Mahle, the piston supplier. Sometime later a 3.2-liter version was made available for the 1979 IMSA series but the factory never built another liquid-cooled 935.

The IMSA engine was interesting in that new rules meant that single-turbo cars had their capacity multiplied by 1.5. This gave the capacity class limit and governed the minimum weight they had to comply with. For twin-turbocharged cars, the multiplier was now 1.8. This meant that a single-turbo IMSA car could weigh 88 lbs less than a twin-turbo car. The advances made in turbocharging now led Porsche to believe that they could make a 3.2-liter single-turbo engine as good as, if not better than, the twin-turbocharged 3.0-liter unit.

The new, more efficient and larger single-turbo of the 930/79 engine was matched to a cylinder barrel of 97 mm. This gave a true capacity of 3,122 cc and a power output of 715 bhp at 7,800 rpm. These engines were not favored by the majority of the teams who ran them. Most of them re-converted their engines back to the twin-turbo set-up. Nonetheless, Peter Gregg persevered with his to win races in 1979. John Greasley, owner of a 1978 935 fitted with this engine set-up (chassis number 930 890 0016), commented to the author that he thought the engine was superior to a twin-turbo. It was more powerful and had hardly any turbo-lag.

One of the most interesting cars to appear during the year was Monte Shelton's old 934, which he had converted to a 935 specification mechanically. Seeking an advantage over his competitors, Monte widened the front track by 6 inches, grafting on a spare 917 nose he had in his storeroom. Monte then faired in the gap over the doors "a la Moby Dick" and placed the rear wing higher into the slipstream. "We had everyone come look at it." Monte later recalled, "It was fast, but it wouldn't turn in. We had some small problems, which we got sorted by the time Neil, my son and I ran it at the Glen for the 6-hour race. There, we were doing really well until I stuffed it into the fence. Neil has never let me forget it!"

At least one of the 1977 "customer" cars, chassis number 930 770 0911, was brought up to 1978/9 specification with big brakes, twin-turbo engine and an upside-down gearbox. Charles Mendez bought it from Italy in June 1979. He sent long-time tuner and race-preparer, Franz Blam over from Atlanta to Turin to inspect the car. Franz remembered, "Charles Mendez gave me $30,000 in cash, to use as a deposit if I liked the car, and then I spent an hour in the customs shed at Turin explaining why I had so much money in cash on me! The guy who had come to pick me up nearly left before I got through. Anyway, he drove me to a garage in a small village where I inspected the car. It looked pretty good. The owner told me, 'If you want to test drive the car, go ahead.' I said, 'Where?' He replied, 'We know all the cops around here, just help yourself.' So I did. I drove it about twenty miles and it was great!"

Rick Rothenberger owned a 1978 turbo 935 in later years. He raced it at his "home" track at Moroso Park in Florida. He described the 935 as, "sensational — People in cars with less horsepower simply can't believe just how much faster the 935 is as it blows by on the straight." ❏

VISIT VELOCE ON THE WEB – WWW.VELOCE.CO.UK
All current books • New book news • Special offers • Gift vouchers • Forum

104

Color Dept.

Above and opposite:
The 1976 Porsche 911 Turbo, as it first appeared. The
subject of these photos was the demonstrator, credited with
so many rave review road tests in the 1970s.

This 934 (chassis number 930 670 0162) led a long hard life. First raced by Angelo Pallavicini of Switzerland in World Championship events, together with some German National Championship races, 0162 came to Daytona at the beginning of 1979. After this, she was bought by Werner Frank, who raced her consistently up until 1984. The old 934, now updated to 935 specifications, kept on racing right up until 1986 with Jim Torres, a noted Californian restorer and tuner of all things Porsche. [Photo–Bill Oursler.]

The 934 built for use in Group 4 racing in 1976 proved hard to drive. 930 670 0173 was delivered to George Dickinson (a Porsche dealer in the U.S.A.) and Al Holbert usually drove the car. Here at Mid-Ohio for the 3-hour race in 1977, it was driven by Roy Woods and Doc Bundy into eighth place. Note that the car has already acquired wider wheel arches, wheels and a bi-plane tail. [Photo–Bill Oursler.]

The Turbo's engine as used in the first production cars. The engineers had a hard time making all that plumbing fit within the contours of the engine bay. Over the years, the plumbing has changed dramatically, but the original engine concept has proven sound from its inception.

Below: Remarkable. Monty Shelton took his old 934 and a half and brought it up to 935 twin-turbo specification over the winter of 1978 to 1979. He widened the front track by six inches, fitted a spare nose from a 917 and filled in the gap over the doors, all in the manner of the factory 935/78. The car was fast and competitive. Monty and his son, Neil, ran it in the Watkins Glen 6-Hours where, sadly, Monty crashed the car. [Photo–Bill Oursler.]

Peter Gregg, Hurley Haywood and Bruce Leven shared this 1978 Porsche 935 to place tenth at the 1980 running of the Sebring 12-Hour race. This was Bruce Leven's car, as he had bought it from Gregg at the beginning of the 1979 season. Note that it still wears the Brumos red, white and blue paint scheme. With it, Peter Gregg had won the 1978 Camel GT Championship, winning nine out of the fifteen races entered. [Photo–Bill Oursler.]

The proud victor: John Fitzpatrick, in front of one of the two K3s that he used to win the IMSA Championship.

The great German racer, Rolf Stommelen, driving Howard Meister's 935 at Mid-Ohio in 1981. 930 890 0013 had been a Kremer-entered car in 1978 and 1979. It was raced hard and survived two Le Mans 24 Hours before being sold to Howard Meister. After preparation by Andial, this 935 went on to win three 500 mile races on successive weekends. The bodywork was a further development of the K3 by Dan McLoughlin of AIR (American International Racing) in conjunction with Bernard Pershing. [Photo–Bill Oursler.]

The Turbo in 1996.

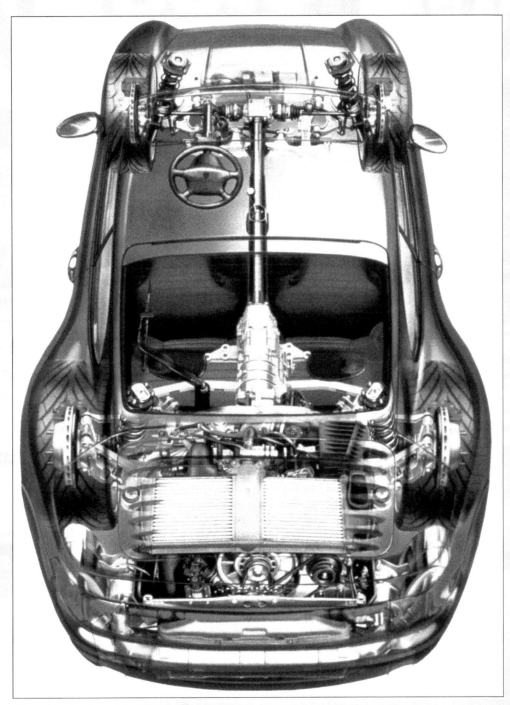

Cut-away drawing of the 1995 Turbo's four-wheel drive system.

The Interscope team of Ted Field and Danny Ongais had a succession of 934s and 935s from 1976 through to 1982. They usually raced in the IMSA Camel GT Series with some World Championship events thrown in. Here is Ted Field at Sebring in 1980 where, using a K3, he and Ongais placed second. [Photo–Bill Oursler.]

The impressive frontal aspect of Jim Busby's ex-Moretti 935J.

The John Pauls (father and son) created a line of 935 Specials. This is JLP-2, effectively a K3 that the father and son drove in 1980 to 1981. They retired in the opening laps of the Sebring 12-Hour race in 1981. [Photo–Bill Oursler.]

The last of the John Paul Specials, the JLP-4. This car featured full ground effects tunnels and gained a reputation as one of the fastest of all the 935s built. [Photo–Mark Leonard.]

The Kremer Brothers built up some very special road going 930 Turbos for their customers. This car, built upon a 934 chassis, was made for Mansour Ojeah of TAG fame.

Paul Weir and Walter Gerber of Seattle are building another 935 from a 1977 930, chassis number 930 780 0718. They are using mostly original spare parts and techniques. This car has a 760 bhp, 3.2-liter 930/81 engine and upside-down transmission. At the time of printing the car is 90% complete. Paul would like to thank many of the owners of 935s featured in this book for helping him on his four year quest for original parts that seemed to be made mostly of "unobtainium"! [Photo–Paul Weir.]

121

The author, John Starkey, racing his single turbo 935 at Snetterton in England in 1990. Despite earning the pole position on its first race, a minor collision with a backmarker after just four laps forced a premature retirement.

At the end of 1982, Wayne Baker bought Bob Garretson's K3 and transformed it into a 934-look alike. This included modifying it for single plug cylinder heads to comply with the new GTO rules for IMSA. In 1983, together with his co-drivers Mullen and Nierop, Wayne Baker scored a spectacular victory at the 12 Hours of Sebring. Even into 1984, the car still placed in the top five at both Daytona and Sebring where the 934 surpassed 215 mph on the straights.

The Kremer Brothers final 935 incarnation: the K4. This is the Interscope Team's car for Ted Field and Danny Ongais for 1982. Note the air intakes at the front of the rear fenders for the turbochargers. To help "clean" air into the turbos, John Fitzpatrick's K4 had the air intakes built into the tops of the front fenders of his Porsche.

John Fitzpatrick's 935 K4 in 1982 at Daytona. The turbocharged engine's characteristic "flame-out" came from unburnt gases combusting as they vented through the hot exhaust via the waste gate (or "pop-off" valve). Note the "first version" NACA air intake ducts in the doors. The car was later modified by AIR with the ducts placed on top of the front fenders.

Above: An early customer for Porsche's GT2 in America was Champion Motorsport, who had their cars driven to success by Bill Adam and Hans Stuck. [Photo–Courtesy of Don Skuta, Champion Motorsport.]

Below: The Champion Racing GT1 was driven in the American Le Mans Series by such notable drivers as Thierry Boutsen, Bob Wollek and Rolf Kelleners. They won the series in 1998 with this car. [Photo–Ulli Upietz.]

Imitation is the sincerest form of flattery. Many copies of the Porsche 934 and 935 have been built in the years following their successes. There are few finer than the example pictured here, owned and driven with enthusiasm in vintage racing events by Eric Derosier. The car is built up on an original 930 Turbo chassis and has a 935-tuned engine delivering more than 600 horsepower. [Photo–Daniel Mainzer.]

126

Arguably, the greatest driver of all the 911-derived competition cars was Peter Gregg, seen here in 1979. He won the IMSA Camel GT and Winston Championships six times and the TransAm twice. Out of 341 starts, he won 152 races, including the Daytona 24 Hours no less than four times. A Porsche dealer from Jacksonville, Florida, Gregg was noted for his car preparation and racing standards. [Photo–Bill Oursler.]

Reinhold Joest built two replicas of the 935/78 "Moby Dick". The one pictured here (the first one) was drive by Jochen Mass and won at Hockenheim in April 1981. It was immediately sold to Dr. Gianpiero Moretti and he raced it for the next three years in the IMSA Camel GT Championship with some good results. It is seen here in 1983 when Moretti drove with the very fast South African driver, Sarel van der Merwe. At Pocono, they finished second overall and placed third at Road Atlanta. [Photo–Author's collection.]

Chapter 10

THE KREMER K3

W

With declining fields in Group 5 and Group 6, and with both being dominated by Porsche, the FIA decreed that the two Groups would be amalgamated for the 1979 season. At the Daytona 24 Hours in February, the Interscope-entered 935 of Danny Ongais/Hurley Haywood/Ted Field won. The car had been suffering severe engine trouble for some time before the finish and just managed to make it to the chequered flag.

As we have seen, the factory built up a batch of cars each year for its private customer racing teams. One of these teams won Le Mans outright in 1979, although in a 935 built following their own ideas. The car that won the 1979 Le Mans 24 Hour race was, strictly speaking, a "K3" model. This denoted that it was the third variant of the basic 935 built up and improved by the Kremer racing team of Cologne.

Erwin and Manfred Kremer had been

The Sachs-sponsored K3 of John Fitzpatrick diving into ...

dealing in and racing Porsche 911s since that car was first produced. Indeed, it could be said that Erwin had raced the first 911 ever to be entered in a race! In 1970, he shared a 911S to finish sixth overall at the Le Mans 24 Hour race. In 1971 he was 10th in another 911S and in 1973, he placed 8th overall and 2nd in the GT class. Achieving success with RS and RSR Carreras (winning the European GT Trophy several times), the brothers' racing team entered Le Mans and German National Championship races for years, all the time developing the basic customer car from Porsche.

With the introduction of the 934, the Kremer Racing Team lost no time in obtaining an example and running that in Group 4 races. They also bought a new bodyshell from the factory and built up a 935, modifying it to their tastes and calling this uprated 1976 935 a "K". It had the flat front of the 935 and very short rear fenders. With this car, the Kremer Brothers contested the World Championship for Makes in Group 5. For 1977, they introduced their K2, again built up on a factory bodyshell but now with much more straight-cut fender edges. Unfortunately, their first try at Le Mans with this car ended in failure. The car did not last past the second hour. This K2 was different

... and through the Karussel at the Nürburgring, 1980.

The typical rolling start of a Deutsche Meisterschaft (German National Championship) race in 1980, here at the Salzburgring for the Bavaria-Rennen on July 13. On the left, Manfred Winkelhock, in pole position, is driving Joest's 935J, chassis number 000 00016 (he finished in fifth place), followed by 000 00022, the Gelo-run factory-built car, here driven by Bob Wollek who finished fourth. Behind him is John Fitzpatrick's ex-Gelo car of 1978 and 1979, chassis number 930 890 0011, here driven by Franz Geschwender. Behind them is Jurgen Lassig in another 935 K3, chassis number 009 0003. On the right, alongside Winkelhock, is John Fitzpatrick in the Kremer Brothers' K3/80, chassis number 000 00011 in which he finished second. Klaus Ludwig, the eventual victor, is in the Zakspeed Ford Capri with Volkert Merl in the "other" 935J, 009 0001. Dieter Schornstein is driving the last 935 visible, his old 1978 factory-built car, 930 890 0012. The Obermeier 934 of Sepp Reiter is visible amongst the seeming hordes of BMW M1s. [Photo—Author's collection.]

from the customer car, having fences along the top of the rear fenders. This prevented the airflow from spilling off and channeled it to a new, more efficient, rear wing.

In 1978 things improved. The team of Jim Busby, Chris Cord and Rick Knoop took a Kremer-prepared 935 into sixth place. This was Dieter Schornstein's car with

which he had been contesting the "Deutsche Rennsport Meisterschaft" (German National Championship). Two other Kremer prepared 935s retired.

The winning car at Le Mans of 1979 was actually built up from a 930 bodyshell and various stock components. This was something the Kremer Racing Team had

John Fitzpatrick at the Flugplatz (literally "Flying Place"), during the Nürburgring 1,000 Kilometers in chassis number 007 0004 in the Kremer Brothers K2. "Fitz" and Bob Wollek finished second overall, beaten by Tim Schenken, Rolf Stommelen and Toine Hezemans in a Gelo-entered 935. [Photo—Author's collection.]

been doing with success since 1974, when they built up their own RSRs. Featuring a carbon-fiber/Kevlar composite body, which was designed in conjunction with Eckerhard Zimmerman's Company, Design Plastics, the K3 also had fences around the tops of the wings to channel the airflow to where it was needed and to increase downforce. At the front of the K3, the number of ventilation slots above the front wheels had been

substantially increased. Only two driving lights were seen behind Perspex covers in the front spoiler. The "running boards", first seen on the 935/77, connected the front with the rear wings, both to help to channel the airflow into the dual brake cooling slots and air intake holes. These were mounted one on top of each other in the front of the rear wings. These "running boards" also helped to keep airflow beneath the car and to promote

Victory!
John Fitzpatrick
& Dick Barbour
celebrate their
1980 12 Hours
of Sebring win.

downforce. At the rear, a 935/77-type roof extension supported a rear aerofoil of the Kremer's own design.

As well as this, the K3 utilized the rollcage, extending its tubing front and rear. This further strengthened the suspension pick-up points and cut out the rear cross member of the original bodyshell. Replacing this with cross-bracing bolt-on tubes facilitated engine changes. The water-to-air aftercooler of the factory 935 was replaced by an air-to-air aftercooler. This was made possible by the forward mounting of the bulkhead. It was not only lighter but also gave a more even temperature drop across the air-cooled cylinders. The engine's cooling fan itself

aspirated some of this hot air which was then expended. This was why the K3's fan rotated slightly faster than the "normal" 935's.

The K3 proved to be very successful. With Klaus Ludwig driving, it won 11 out of 12 German National Championship races in 1979 and claimed the German National Group 5 Championship. None of the other "regulars" (such as Stommelen, Fitzpatrick or Schurti) could get close. Only Bob Wollek managed to push Ludwig into second place at the Nürburgring.

Achim Stroth (the Kremer Brothers' race team manager) remembered, "The secret of the K3 was the air-to-air intercooler and the ducting to the engine bay that the bodywork allowed. At the start of the races, the Georg Loos cars were as quick as our K3 but after a few laps, their engines ran hotter and the power fell off whilst ours kept on producing just as much power as we had at the start. Reinhold Joest realized what he had to do but did not bring out his version of the air-to-air intercooler until 1980."

The K3 featured an engine, the Type 930/80, which had a bore and stroke of 95 mm x 74.4 mm to give a capacity of 3,163 cc. This engine had a Bosch-Kugelfischer fuel injection pump together with an electronically interconnected intercooler and fuel mixture set-up. Now with a compression ratio of 7.2:1 plus 1.7 bar boost, this engine gave 800 bhp at 8,000 rpm. Even with the boost wound down to 1.4 bar, the engine still gave some 740 bhp at 7,800 rpm with outstanding reliability. Most of these 935 engines were good for 30 hours of flat-out running, enough to win Daytona or Le Mans

plus a 6-hour race before needing a rebuild. In 1981, the engine was developed but little, the Type 930/81 having improved oil scavenging (via a new pump with twin scavenge pumps and pick-ups), larger 43 mm intake ports and improved cooling via a higher drive ratio for the flat cooling fan.

Erwin Kremer, in an interview, said, "We started building a special 935 in June 1978 so as to enter it in the Nuremberg 200 miles race. Unfortunately, we didn't finish the car in time but we carried on with it as we wanted to win the German National Championship (something the Kremer Brothers had never before achieved). Taking our standard twin-turbo 1978 model 935 as a base, we built up another 935 with over one hundred modifications to it. We lowered the car four centimeters by turning the gearbox

September 28, 1980. Michael Korton in a K3/80, original chassis number 000 0013, at Hockenheim for the Preis von Baden-Wurttemburg race in which he finished in third place. [Photo—Author's collection.)

upside-down and this also helped to improve the angle of the drive shaft., (Constant velocity joint wear in long-distance races had always been a 935 problem.) By moving the gearbox, we also made it possible to change the gears without taking out the engine. The factory was supplying new brakes but we chose ones that were 40% wider, so we would not have to change them in a 1,000 kilometer race."

"We made the rollcage link up to the suspension mountings to make the chassis stiffer and, using our ideas we had developed since 1977, changed the bodywork dramatically to give the car more speed on the straights and to make it corner in a more stable attitude. We used Kevlar instead of GRP as it is 35% lighter, even though ten times as expensive. Where engine development was concerned, we used an air-to-air intercooler as, with our 3.2-liter engine, we could keep the weight within the 1,025 kg minimum weight limit. I think our competitors' weighed around 60 kilos more. We also changed the instrument panel, the steering wheel and the pedals, and re-positioned the fuel pumps for easier access."

"Once the car was finished, we took it on the autobahn at night for a road test! Manfred, my brother, did the driving with

Bob Wollek in chassis number 000 00011, the Kremer Brothers' K3/80, winning the Nürburgring 300 Kilometer race on March 29, 1981.

Believe it or not, this was once a 934! Chassis number 930 670 0163 was driven by Hartwig Bertrams and later Leo Kinnunen in 1976 before being sold to Tetsu Ikuzawa of Japan. In 1979, the Kremer Brothers converted it to a K3. It raced at Le Mans in 1980, co-driven by Rolf Stommelen and Alex Plankenhorn where it retired just after the halfway mark with engine problems. [Photo—Author's collection.]

Hermann Burvenich, our long-time chief mechanic, in the back. I tried to follow on with my 928 but soon was left behind! After this, we did lots of testing with Klaus Ludwig, our driver, to set the car up to handle as he liked it."

Auto Motor und Sport tested the Le Mans winner, now with a 3.2-liter engine (in place of the 3-liter engine used in the race) and came up with a 0-60 mph time of 3.0 seconds and 0-100 mph in just 5.8 seconds.

Besides the winning K3 of the Whittington Brothers and Klaus Ludwig at Le Mans, there had also been Georg Loos with two of his Gelo Team 935s, plus the ASA Cachia car, the Sekurit Racing 935 and Singleton cars from Claude Haldi and Carlo Pietro Marchi. Six cars were entered in the IMSA class; Dick Barbour entering no less than four cars! One of them, crewed by Barbour himself and the film star Paul Newman, ably assisted by Rolf Stommelen, came in second. This particular car was one of the many "built-up" 935s. Once again, a Porsche had won the FIA World Championship for Makes.

The Kremer Brothers built thirteen copies of their K3 and sold them to eager customers for between DEM350,000-375,000, depending upon the specification requested. They also sold a conversion kit so that racing teams with factory built 935s could bring their cars up to K3 specification. The factory also built more customer cars in 1979-80, in a bid to keep their American racing team clients supplied with the latest technology. Apart from this, it was content to watch the independent teams support the Porsche name.

Reinhold Joest built his own versions of the basic "tub" 935 theme but kept to the bodystyle which the Works-entered 935/77s, with their raised roofs and twin fins supporting the rear wing, had used. Joest used tube-framed engine bays for lightness and strength and employed his own version of air-to-air intercooling, using two separate coolers per bank of cylinders.

For 1980, Reinhold Joest entered one of his own 935s (titled "J") in the Daytona 24 Hours and, with Rolf Stommelen and Volkert Merl partnering him, won by 33 laps. This Joest-modified car had originally been a 1978 factory-built twin-turbo car, which had

The Hudson Wire/Coca Cola-sponsored K3/80, chassis number 000 00013, of Bob Akin on the Daytona banking late on during the 24 Hour race. [Photo—Jeff Fisher.]

After Bob Garretson crashed Dick Barbour's 1978 single turbo 935, chassis number 930 890 0033 at Le Mans in 1978, Dick had it re-shelled with chassis number 009 00030. Bob Garretson bought the car in 1980 and carried on developing it, finally turning it into a K3. Here is the car at the Daytona 24 Hours of 1981 where, driven by Garretson, Bobby Rahal and Brian Redman, it won outright. [Photo—IMSA collection.]

been campaigned by Franz Konrad and then Volkert Merl. So impressed by the car was Gianpiero Moretti that he bought the winning car the next morning, over breakfast with Reinhold Joest! Joest preferred to use the 2.8-liter engine as it gave better fuel mileage than the bigger engines.

The Kremer Team entered the German National Championship again, seeing this as their main objective because it attracted enormous crowds and television coverage which guaranteed sponsorship. Ford Escorts and Capris, BMW 320s and M1s and Lancia Betas all contested this series with the 935s, although there was also a class for the smaller-engined cars. Amongst those taking part in 935s were Bob Wollek in the Gelo car, Rolf Stommelen and Volkert Merl in the Joest car(s), Dieter Schornstein in the Vegla-sponsored 935, plus many others. Klaus Ludwig, as in 1979, won most of the races, this time in a Zakspeed tuned and entered Ford Capri Turbo.

Additionally, the Kremer Team

entered the Silverstone 6 Hours and the Le Mans 24 Hours. The car they used this time was a developed K3 now known as the K3/80. This featured revised rear suspension pick-ups, more developed bodywork with raised fences and a Kugelfischer fuel injection pump. The engine was now developing some 650 bhp (*probably up to 720 bhp - Ed*) at 1.3 bar boost. John Fitzpatrick, driving this car at Silverstone, put it on the pole with a time almost two seconds faster than Jochen Mass had managed in the Works 935/78 of two years before. Sadly, the engine failed when the car was leading by a country mile. The John Pauls had a good result at Silverstone where they finished third in their K3.

The Kremer K3 of Klaus Ludwig in 1979. The nose of one of the Gelo Team cars is barely visible just behind the Kremer K3. The Singleton K3 dominated the German Championship.

Some consolation was available at the Nürburgring, where the Joest car finished second. At Le Mans it was disappointment once more, as the K3/80 retired again. The Kremer Team entered Le Mans in strength, looking after three different 935s but none of them finished. Dick Barbour also entered three 935s at Le Mans and won the IMSA class again, finishing fifth overall. John Fitzpatrick and Brian Redman shared the driving with Barbour himself. Jean Paul, Sr. and Jr. also shared a 935 at Le Mans but clouted a barrier when they were lying eighth, finally managing to finish in ninth position.

Jürgen Barth and Henri Pescarolo drove an ex-Georg Loos 1978 twin-turbo 935, entered by the Sportwagen Team, in the Monza 6 Hours and finished a creditable second. They then won the Dijon round outright. Sadly, Porsche lost the World Championship this year to Lancia. Whilst Porsche dominated the over 2-liter class, the Lancia factory entered a 1.4-liter turbo-charged Beta Monte Carlo. As the points awarded were the same for both classes, Lancia finished the season ahead. Other teams fielding 935s in the World Championship were the Weralit-Elora Team with a K3 and the Vegla-Sekurit Team, which had a 935 dating back to 1978.

A British team running a 935 was that of Charles Ivey who had been entering Porsches at Le Mans for many years. They ran a 1979 car, updated to K3 specification and driven by John Cooper, Dudley Wood

Long life: This is Porsche 935 K3, chassis number 009 0003, driven by John Greasley in 1993 to win a round of the British GT Championship. Originally purchased from the Kremer Brothers by Edgar Doren in 1979, 0003 had a busy life, contesting World Championship and German National Championship races for two years. Sold to Willy Konig, the German tuner, it was then raced for many years in Germany. Eventually, Konig crashed it at the Nürburgring whereupon John Greasley bought the K3 and rebuilt it. For many years, John raced the 935, winning almost everywhere until, in 1993, he retired the K3 to his collection after winning the British Championship outright. [Photo—Mary Harvey.]

and Peter Lovett. They gained a fourth place in the Dijon race and a fifth at Brands Hatch. The 935 was still the car to have in 1980 if you wanted to win the IMSA Series in the USA. Dick Barbour entered John Fitzpatrick in two 935 K3/80s with all the latest modifications. The first car was forced to retire in the Daytona 24 Hours but Barbour and Fitzpatrick won the Sebring 12 Hours. John went on to dominate the season, winning seven races outright plus taking one second place finish at Elkhart Lake. In sec-

ond place in the Championship were the John Pauls (father and son) who drove a 935 K3 built up by their own team, known as JLP-2. They won at Lime Rock in an ex-Interscope, Preston Henn-owned, K3 while their own car was at the Nürburgring for the 1,000 kilometer race. Incidentally, John Paul, Sr. was married at the track before leaving on honeymoon for Le Mans! John Paul, Jr. made his auspicious debut in the second heat and won his first race in a 935.

For once Peter Gregg was not in

the picture. One second place was his only podium result of the year, as he had fallen behind with the development of his 935. The only person to give John Fitzpatrick any real competition was Danny Ongais in one of the two Interscope-entered K3/80s but he failed to finish several races, despite proving as quick as John. Ted Field and Ongais were forever in the top five in their sinister black cars but could not defeat "Fitz".Gianpiero Moretti had bought the 1980 Daytona winning "Liqui Moli" 935J from Reinhold Joest and rapidly acclimatized himself to it, winning the last two races of the season. Bill Whittington won Road Atlanta in the Le Mans-winning K3 of 1979.

Alan Hamilton again, "For 1981, we went to Le Mans with Peter Brock and a 924 GTR but we had gearbox problems, which prevented us from qualifying. At the same time, the factory promised us a 944 LM engine but this was a while coming through and so I bought the very last 935 from Georg Loos that he had bought and I engaged the services of Alan Jones to drive it. He and I had been friends since childhood and he had been 1981 World Champion in F1 with Williams. I doubt that anyone has got a World Champion at such a reasonable price! Anyway, Alan took the 935 and won every race in the Australian Championship. Fabulous car, fabulous year. Afterwards, I sold the car to Rusty French and built up another car, a K4, for him on a spare factory shell. (*Author's note: Rusty French commuted to England every other weekend in the 80s , taking part in the modified Porsche Championship. I was racing an RSR Carrera at the time and remember his battles with John Greasley in a K3 well.*)

1981 was the last year in which the 935 was eligible for the World Endurance Championship. It was now split into two, with six races counting towards the Manufacturers Championship and fifteen making up the Drivers Championship. (Trust the FIA to make matters more complex than they needed to be!) Once again, Lancia won the Manufacturers Championship, beating Porsche by just two and a half points and dominating the under 2-liter class where they had little opposition. In the German National Championship, Bob Wollek in the Kremer entered K3/80 (and, from June, the K4) won most of the races even though he faced stiff opposition from the Ford Capri Turbo and the 3.5-liter BMW M1.

By now, the factory was concentrating on its forthcoming type 956 Group C car but they did bow to the demand for more engine development for the hordes of 935s that were still racing. Rather than a whole new engine, they supplied a set of parts to strengthen the existing engine. This would allow higher boost pressures to be used than before, ie, 1.7 bar instead of 1.45 bar. One other revision to the engine was to the oil scavenging system. A new oil pump with two pick ups was fitted which took out the crankcase oil faster than before, reducing friction and allowing the engine to pick up revolutions faster. Later on, a further pump and pick up was used to make this scavenging of the oil even more efficient. The opportunity was also taken to enlarge the intake ports to 43 mm. All these refinements allowed the 930/81 engine to achieve 760 bhp at 7,800 rpm for long distance races. With the boost turned up to 1.7-1.8 bar for short "sprint" races, the engine now developed well over 800 bhp.

Bob Garretson won the Drivers Championship, sharing the driving with Ralph Kent-Cooke and Roy Woods. He also prepared his own 935 K3 plus that of Cooke Woods Racing also. Garretson won the Daytona 24 Hours to start the season, with Brian Redman and Bobby Rahal driving. At Le Mans, Garretson shared his own K3 with Ralph Kent-Cooke and Annie Charlotte-Verney to take sixth place. After this Bob finished third at Watkins Glen, took seventh place at Mosport and fourth at Elkhart Lake. He then brought his K3 over to Brands Hatch and, partnered again by Rahal, they finished in second place to claim the title. Bob's car was variously known as "The Old Warhorse'" or the "Made in Mountain View Special". The car was a rebuild of the single-turbo 935 that Bob had crashed at Le Mans in 1978. He later bought the car from its owner, Dick Barbour.

In the IMSA Championship, John Fitzpatrick was out of luck. Although he drove a K3/80, other cars (such as those of the John Pauls and Moretti) were equally as fast. John only won one race, at Riverside, even though it was the last of twenty consecutive victories by a 935 in IMSA racing. Ted Field and Danny Ongais each had a K3/80 for Field's Interscope Team but failed to post any useful results. Their best was a third place at Mosport for Field with Don Whittington co-driving. Andial serviced and prepared Howard Meister's 935, originally a factory built car but with Andial modifications. With Harald Grohs and Rolf Stommelen sharing the driving, it won three consecutive 500-mile races at Watkins Glen, Mosport and Mid-Ohio.

The Kremer Brothers built their K4 utilizing the knowledge gained from the factory, which allowed them and Reinhold Joest access to the plans of the 935/78. (See Chapter 8.) Whilst basically following the factory's plans, the Kremers revised the bodywork on their 935/78 replica to incorporate more downforce. The factory had sacrificed some of this in order to capitalize upon the high top speed the long Mulsanne straight at Le Mans allowed. With a K4, Bob Wollek won the Porsche cup in 1981 and Interscope bought another for Ted Field and Danny Ongais but never raced it. They were never able to sort out the cooling problems that the engine suffered with through not being able to "sort" the induction to the intercooling.

John Fitzpatrick purchased the ex-Wollek car from the Kremer Brothers and, using Dan McLoughlin's expertise, Fitzpatrick then campaigned the Kremer K4 but with ground effect skirts. Additionally, the air intakes for the intercooler were re-sited in the tops of the front fenders, to pick up the maximum amount of cooling air. Dan McLoughlin's AIR Company was called in to help sort out the aerodynamics of this car. Dan remembered supplying all the newly-designed bodywork for, "Some $9,000. John called me to tell me his problems and we went testing as usual to see what happened with the airflow. After I determined the problem areas and made new bodywork, the car went out and won the Riverside 6-Hours straight off. Altogether, the Fitzpatrick K4 won four races in America in 1982. After that, it was third at Brands Hatch, beaten only by a 956 and a Lancia LC1."

Gianpiero Moretti shared his Joest replica 935/78 with Mauro Baldi. Their best efforts were seventh places at Spa and Silverstone and an eighth at Mugello.

The driver who won IMSA in 1982 was another Englishman, Brian Redman. Although he started out in a 935 K3 (owned by the Cooke Woods Racing Team), he changed cars mid-way through the season to a Lola T600 (as did John Paul, Jr.), and thereafter dominated the Championship. ❑

Chapter 11

CUSTOMER DEVELOPMENT —
THE 935 "SPECIALS"

A t Le Mans in 1979, and in most other forms of "GT" (Group 5) racing, Porsche dominated. No less than seventeen 934s and 935s ran at the 1979 edition of the Le Mans 24 Hours and twenty entered the 1980 race.

By now, Porsche had released their 3.2-liter engine (Type 930/80) for their customers, which built upon the experience realized by the K3. This had a bore and stroke of 95 mm x 74.4 mm to give 3,160 cc. A big advance on this engine was the use of the Kugelfischer fuel injection pump. It embodied electronic regulation of the fuel mixture. The other secret of the K3's increased power

and reliability was the air-to-air intercooler. 800 bhp at 8,000 rpm was now available, since the engine could run a 7.2:1 compression ratio and boost pressures as high as 1.7 bar with no fear of detonation, thanks to the electronically regulated fuel flow. Even with

Below: "Moby Dick", the John Fitzpatrick version of the 935/78 in chassis form. [Photo—Author's collection.]

The rear of the JLP-4: Easily seen here are the huge plenum chambers atop the two turbochargers, and the outrigged rear wing. The diffusers for the underbody tunnels exit beneath each of the rear lights.

the boost turned down to 1.4, the engine still produced some 740 bhp at 7,800 rpm. For 1981, the Type 930/81 engine with an accelerated fan for improved cooling was also offered from the factory. Porsche turbo race cars (mainly 935-derived specials) now dominated IMSA racing in the USA as well as German National Championship events.

Unlike previous years, Porsche did not build up another batch of 935s at season's end for sale to its racing customers. A strange branch in the history of motor sport had been reached. Quite simply, if a team wanted a 935, it could go to Reinhold Joest,

or to the Kremer Brothers who would buy the necessary parts from the factory, and then build up their own race car, incorporating any modifications the individual team wished to include.

In 1980, the factory built up a car for a special customer, Georg Loos. This incorporated air-to-air intercooling and had 935/77 bodywork fitted. With it Bob Wollek scored

The last 935. Bob Akin's tube frame car, built by Fabcar. This included all the best features of the 935s. [Photo—Author's collection.]

many good results until the car was sold to Australia in 1981. Ex-World Champion Alan Jones used this 935 to win the Australian Championship with a straight nine victories from nine races.

Of these "specials", two tube-frame 935s were built up by the Joest Racing Team. Effectively, they were replicas of the factory's 935/78 "Moby Dick", since the factory had given the plans of the 935/78 to both the Joest and Kremer Brothers' teams. As the air-cooled engines were deemed to give "sufficient" power and the liquid-cooled four-valve engines of the factory were banned in IMSA racing in America, these two cars were fitted with the air-cooled engines. One,

The nose section of the JLP-4: Visible are the dual ducting to the huge front brakes and the rocker arm top suspension with inboard-mounted coil springs and dampers. This suspension design allowed a free air flow to the ground effects tunnels. [Photo—Author's collection.]

driven by John Fitzpatrick and David Hobbs, came in fourth at Le Mans in 1982 with a 2.6-liter Joest-built engine. (The race was run to the new Group "C" fuel consumption formula.) "Fitz" then took it to America where it scored well in the IMSA series.

The other car was that used by Jochen Mass to take part in three races in Germany. Mass scored one victory at Hockenheim in the German National Championship of 1981. Joest then sold the car to Gianpiero Moretti,

who shared the driving at Riverside with Mass until a broken rocker-arm forced their retirement. Moretti drove the car in IMSA races for a further two seasons. Moretti remembered, "Ah, my Moby Dick. You know, looking back, I must have been mad. There I was, surrounded by an aluminum tube-frame structure, doing 200 mph. I wouldn't do it today!" Bobby Rahal drove this car on several occasions and said, "Man, that car was fast! Only trouble (for me) was that it was right hand drive and, therefore, I had to shift with my left hand, which I was not used to but I made myself get accustomed to it!"

In America, many 935 "specials" were built up around 935 components. Dave Klym's Fabcar Company built up several tube frame chassis to take 935 mechanicals, including the John Paul's JLP-4. Bob Akin had what was called the L1 in which he tried to go one step further. This featured an aluminum monocoque chassis for the center section with a widened Lola T600-type nose section. It was reasonably successful despite Akin's crew never being able to totally sort it. The car was damaged when it crashed at over 200 miles per hour at the Daytona Finale race at the end of the season, when a drive shaft let go.

Alwin Springer, the principal of Andial Racing (the Porsche engine builder) built a 935 special in 1982, following the experience of running a 935 K3 in 1981. Nick Soprano owns that K3 today. He remembers seeing it at Daytona, "It was the first time I saw 935s in action. I was watching from the infield where the cars come down to the tight left-hander that leads on to the twisty part. At night, you would see the brake discs glowing orange as the cars braked from over 200 mph on the banking. Then they'd gush fire from the exhausts as the driver changed down the

The Andial-built tube-frame 935 of Preston Henn. This "swap shop" 935 did well, having drivers of the caliber of Mario Andretti and A. J. Foyt guiding it in many long distance races. [Photo—Author's collection.]

gearbox, give a little shuffle as they turned in and then - woosh! Off they would go again with that incredible acceleration of theirs. Fantastic."

One of the principal advantages the Howard Meister-owned car possessed was the aerodynamic aid given by the bodywork. Designed by aerodynamicist Bernard Pershing and made by Dan McLoughlin's AIR Company in Los Angeles, it enabled Meister's car to go faster than other 935s. McLoughlin remembers, "We went to Riverside to test. Pershing painted the K3 with a mixture of white shoe polish and ker-

osene. After a run, Bernard could read which way the airflow was going and from that, I developed the Andial/Meister car's final shape which I called the M16."

AIR developed the M16 body by elevating the rear "cover" window and that allowed the air to flow smoothly down it to meet the rear wing. NACA ducts were built into the the sides of the window strakes to feed air into the engine compartment/inter-

The interior of Preston Henn's 935L, final flowering of the tube-framed cars. Note the huge air intakes to the intercooler and the multiplicity of tubes for the chassis. [Photo—Author's collection.]

cooler and the rear wing had a different end plate design and chord angle from the K3's.

For Andial's next car, Alwin Springer remembered that, in conjunction with Glen Blakely (who had built Don Garlitts' drag racing cars), he drew up the 935s suspension pick up points on a flat plate. He then had the frame constructed from chrome molybdenum steel tubing by Blakely, incorporating all the "tweaks" they could think of. This car had a lowered chassis, wider front track and a long tailed body which, incidentally, was hinged at the top so that it could be easily opened for work to be done upon the engine and gearbox. The car's long-tail bodywork was designed and made by Dan McLoughlin of AIR.

Crouched beside the passenger door, John Paul Senior gives encouragement to Junior as JLP-3 is refueled here in the 1981 Daytona Finale, which Junior went on to win. [Photo—IMSA collection.]

'... Preston Henn: "I started racing with a Ferrari Daytona before buying one of the Interscope 935s from Ted Field. I think it was a 1978 car. To me, the 935 was fine to drive as I only had the Daytona to compare it with. Then I bought John Fitzpatrick's IMSA Championship car (see: 000 0009) and, finally, I had Andial build me a "Moby Dick"-type car".

"I remember racing John Paul's K3 at the Nürburgring. I was sharing the car with John and Brian Redman. Brian was a great driver, never having to drive faster than necessary. I had the luxury of being able to do several day's practice on the old Nürburgring. That and Le Mans are my favorite race circuits in the World, by the way."

"I had A. J. Foyt drive the 'Moby Dick' at Daytona together with Claude Ballot-Lena and they won outright. Foyt called it his most memorable race because his father was dying in the hospital and it was the last Trophy A. J. was ever able to take and show him".

"At Riverside in 1982, A. J. and Mario Andretti were driving the 'Moby Dick' whilst I was driving the K3. In practice, A. J. came in and complained, 'I couldn't even get past Preston!' Little did he know that I had the boost wound right up! I was alongside A. J. at the start and still had the boost turned WAY up. I mean, I didn't care if the engine broke. When the lights changed to green, A. J. was gone! Just like that. I never saw which way he went. He's a different man when it comes to the race." ...'

At the very first IMSA race at Riverside, for which this car was entered, Al Holbert and Harald Grohs were second, despite starting from the back of the grid. After this, Preston Henn bought the car and, with Bob Wollek and A. J. Foyt driving, won the 1983 Daytona 24 Hours. A. J. Foyt drove the fastest lap of Daytona ever recorded with a 935, even though he had never sat in the car before racing it at Daytona, notwithstanding that it also rained a lot during that race! Later that year, this car also won the Paul Revere 250 at Daytona.

By 1982, nearly all the successful 935s had, paradoxically, never seen the inside of the Porsche factory. Although they used Porsche mechanics (engine, gearbox and some suspension parts), they were nearly all built up "tube frame" specials built in independent racing teams' premises. Joest Racing also built up their own car(s) on factory bodyshells with tube frame front and rear ends like the "Baby". Joest used two 908/4 turbo air-to-air intercoolers, which were superior to the factory water-to-air system, allowing a greater heat drop. Joest campaigned one of their own 935 "Js" for Volkert Merl in 1979-81 and then for Dieter Schornstein in 1982. This latter car was very badly damaged at the Le Mans test days when it went out of control at nearly 200 mph. Fortunately, Harald Grohs got away with it, emerging shaken but unhurt from the wreck. Undeterred, Joest set to and built Schornstein another 935 "J" from his old 1978 935, which Joest had acquired from Schornstein in 1980.

Jim Busby bought a Joest-modified 935 "J", "Now that was an interesting car. I had been running BMW M1s but just had no luck with them. At Laguna Seca in 1981, I crashed the M1 in practice, which left me in a quandary as I had to fulfill my sponsorship commitments but had no car! I went straight over to Gianpiero Moretti and bought his "spare" Joest-built car. I had a devil of a time trying to keep the engine cool. Joest had used a 2.8 engine at Daytona and Moretti had been using a 3.0/3.2-liter engine. But when it went…!"

The Kremer Brothers had developed their own C-K5 car using Porsche mechanics, built purely as a Group C car. They shared the running of a K3/80 with Interscope Racing at the Monza 6 Hour event. Rolf Stommelen and Ted Field finished second in this race, which was the best result for any 935 in the World Endurance Championship in 1981.

Where IMSA racing was concerned, 1981 was split between tube frame 935 specials and the Lola T600s. Brian Redman won the IMSA Championship in a Cooke-Woods Lola T600. Brian Redman again, "John Bishop, the head of IMSA, had been trying to break the stranglehold Porsche had on the Championship. He introduced new rules to bring in a Sports-prototype class (GTP), which would favor the good old Chevrolet small-block. I worked with Eric Broadley, of Lola, and the T600 was the result. It was a very good car for the time. No-one really knew much about the science of ground effects but it had good handling and better braking than a 935. 'Course, the 935 had superlative brakes but it was a tad heavy…! I couldn't match the 935s down the straights but I could out-corner them."

In 1982, John Paul, Jr. won the IMSA Camel GT title and his father won the IMSA Camel GT Endurance Championship. They used their JLP-3 and JLP-4 (both cars based on 935 mechanicals), plus a Lola T600. The JLP-3 had been designed by Lee Dykstra and built by Graham "Rabbit" Bartrills of GAACO in Georgia. Its only debt to a standard 911 was the scuttle, windscreen pillars, roof and door frames. The Pauls used JLP-3 for endurance events such as the Riverside 6 Hours and the Daytona 24 Hours where they won.

The JLP-4 was a sprint car variant (again designed by Lee Dykstra) and was built by Dave Klym's Fabcar Company, also in Georgia. This car had a tube-frame chassis and featured inboard front suspension and ground-effects tunnels. The JLP-4 won at Brainerd and Portland. Sadly, the car was then badly damaged at Road Atlanta when the rear wing became detached. This did not deter the John Pauls though. They got back into JLP-3 and won at Road Atlanta, besides coming second at Pocono. Your author shared the driving of JLP-4 at an HSR event at Daytona in 1999 and can report that the acceleration from the infield up on to the banking was truly breathtaking, even when running as low as 1.0 bar boost!

John Fitzpatrick could not repeat the previous year's success, crashing his K3/80 at Sebring when the suspension failed. He did, however, win three races: Mid-Ohio; Lime Rock; and Elkhart Lake. He also took a second at the Daytona finale.

1983 was the swansong for the 935. By now, Lola and March GTP chassis were being used by the majority of the IMSA teams but 935s still managed to score points. John

One of only two 935/78 "Moby Dick" replicas to be built, Gianpiero Moretti's car was very fast, bringing him success during 1982 and 1983. In this picture can be seen how much lower than a "standard" 935, a "Moby Dick" was. [Photo—Jeff Fisher.]

Fitzpatrick had bought the Kremer Brothers' K4, which had been very successful in the German Championship but, "It overheated badly in America. Dan McLoughlin of AIR designed and made new bodywork for it, which placed the air intakes for the turbochargers on the top of the front fenders. That cured the problem and the K4 then became very successful for me."

Bob Akin, after the loss of his L1, brought out his old K3/80. The car went well enough to give him a third place in the Championship. Akin didn't seem to be able

to leave "special" 935s alone. He had another one built by Dave Klym of Fabcar. This became known as the last 935 and it had a Kremer K4-style nose, wider front track and long tail. It came out only for the very last race of the IMSA season, the Daytona Finale. There, Akin and John O'Steen placed second to Al in a Porsche-engined March 83G.

Andial built the tube frame special, later owned by Preston Henn and he proved its efficiency by winning the Daytona 24 Hours with it. He shared the driving with Bob Wollek and Claude Ballot-Lena. A. J. Foyt helped out from the half distance mark. Later in the season, again at Daytona, A. J. Foyt shared the driving of this car with Hurley Haywood, to win outright again. This was its very last victory, entries at Road America and the Daytona 3 Hours ending in retirement.

Sadly, Rolf Stommelen was the only driver to be killed in a 935, dying at Riverside when his Joest-built "Moby Dick" replica 935 lost its rear wing and hit the barriers head on. Ironically, his teammate John Fitzpatrick, teamed with David Hobbs in their K4, won the event but declined to mount the podium as a mark of respect to the great German driver.

By 1984, it appeared that the 935 was completely outclassed but still Preston Henn's 935L finished in second place at the Daytona 24 Hours. It was again driven by A. J. Foyt who was partnered by Bob Wollek and Derek Bell. This car also placed third at the Sebring 12 Hours and took fifth place in the Miami Street Race.

Ironically, Sebring also saw the most surprising result of the season. A Joest-entered 935J, with some five seasons of races behind it, finished in first place driven by Stefan Johansson, Hans Heyer and Mauricio de Narvaez, the owner/leasor. It was a fitting end to one of the most significant racing Porsches in that company's long career.

I cannot leave the subject of "clone" 934/935s without mentioning the fact that they have continued to be created right up to the present day! Of course, there have been many road going "slope nose" 930s built over the years but some people went one step further and re-created the "proper" 935s.

John Greasley built a perfect "Blue Coral" 935 K3 replica in the early 1990s and it was raced very successfully in the British BRDC GT series. Chris Fisher of Powerhaus II has long campaigned a "1978" style twin-turbo 3.5-liter engined car, and Robert Tornello built up a beautiful "customer 1977" style car with no expense spared. This car is today owned, maintained and driven by Eric Desrosiers. It is a testimony to its greatness that the 935 is such a favorite subject for replica builders. ❏

VISIT VELOCE ON THE WEB – WWW.VELOCE.CO.UK
All current books • New book news • Special offers • Gift vouchers • Forum

156

APPENDICES

APPENDIX I – CHASSIS HISTORIES

PREFACE

This is the third edition of "930 to 935 - The Turbo Porsches". Since the first and second editions sold out in just two years, I realized that there was a demand for more information and so this edition has a heavily revised chassis history appendix.

Ulrich Trispel and myself, with help from Klaus Handemann, Janos Wimpfen and too many American sources to name here, totally reviewed and rewrote this section as new information poured in. 934 and 935 owners are nothing if not enthusiastic about their cars! Otherwise, the same caveats apply as to the first edition.

In looking at the sheer amount of race results that apply to these Turbocharged racing Porsches, it becomes apparent just how much racing was done by these cars. Some of them raced for over ten continuous years. Critics of the turbocharged 911-930 Porsches often state that Groups four and five were simply Porsche uber alles; that is true to a certain extent but boy, didn't the drivers get a lot of seat time!

This is the fifth book I've written that has a chassis-by-chassis history appendix. I thought that you, the reader, might like to know how these histories are arrived at and where the aspiring historian's pitfalls lie.

In the case of Porsche, Jürgen Barth (the head of Porsche's Customer Racing) is always very helpful in providing copies of original paperwork, which show who the cars were first delivered to, the date, production, engine and gearbox numbers. From there it is a fairly simple step to obtaining race results of the period (thanks to Ulrich Trispel and Janos Wimpfen) and putting two and two together to make four. Trouble is, where race cars are concerned, it frequently makes five! All race cars are developed, modified, repaired from crashes, have new sponsor's paint schemes applied and all of this can make the tracing of an individual car's history get next to near impossible a couple of years into the car's histories.

There are further complications with these Porsche Turbo race cars. Porsche is a factory with a very high standard of production tolerances. Therefore, unlike the Fifties-era Ferraris where nearly every individual race car was just a little bit different from the next, Porsche race cars of one batch all look (and essentially are) identical to one another. Secondly, not only did the factory supply complete cars, they also supplied replacement bodyshells for crashed cars and also kits of parts to update the older cars. You can suddenly find a 1980 K3 with a replacement bodyshell number, say, 009 00012 (bodyshell of a 1979 model 930), which had started life in 1976 as a 934. Add in the fact that the Kremer Brothers also built their own "customer" K3s on factory replacement bodyshells and you can see the problems any historian of the cars faces! To add a personal touch to it all, I have yet to find a driver of the period who can remember (if he ever knew) the chassis number of the car he drove for a racing team. (The crew chiefs are different, they usually remember everything!) Well ... I think you get the point.

Finally, there is the fact that teams such as GELO (Georg Loos), the Kremer Brothers and Max Moritz all bought two, or sometimes three, of each year's production by the factory; you can see the problem I faced when I assembled the following data. These teams were privately run with the small staff all at full stretch to prepare, transport and, sometimes, repair the cars. There just wasn't anyone to spare to write down just who drove which car at what race.

Today, some of the present owners believe their cars "won Daytona". Some of them did, but quite a few didn't and those were probably the team's other car. Word-of-mouth histories sometimes don't square up with the truth so I'm sorry if some present owners may feel aggrieved at the results I have attributed to their cars. Conversely, some owners will be happy to discover a notable history where they may have known little, if nothing, about their pride and joy's past.

Although this is a reprint of a 2000 edition, where I have received accurate documentation I have managed, in a few cases, to carry the ownership chain to a current conclusion. If you, dear reader, have any information which can add to, or correct, what follows, I should be most grateful to receive it.

Some abbreviations:
DNF: Did not finish.
Acc: Accident.
DNS: Did not start. (usually following a problem in practice/qualifying).
DNA: Did not arrive.
WCM: World Championship for Makes.
EC-GT: European Grand Touring Championship.
DRM: Deutsche Rennsport Meisterschaft. (German National Championship).
EHC: European Hillclimb Championship.
STPO: Sold to present owner.
IC: Italian Championship.
RU: Result unknown.
NC: Not classified.

VISIT VELOCE ON THE WEB – WWW.VELOCE.CO.UK
All current books • New book news • Special offers • Gift vouchers • Forum

159

1974: RSR Turbo Carrera 2.14
The factory drivers were: Gijs van Lennep and
Herbert Muller, Manfred Schurti and Helmuth
Koinigg.

Chassis No: 911 360 0576 R5
Prod. No: 103 4464.
Colour: Colour: Grand Prix White.
Gearbox type: 915/50
Gearbox Number: 783 531.
Built: 3/73 as a 2.8 RSR.

1973: World Championship Races.
25/03: Vallelunga 6-Hours: G. van Lennep/H.Muller;
8th OA.
15/04: Dijon 1000Km: G.van Lennep/H. Muller,
#26; 9th OA.
06/05: Spa-Francorchamps 1000Km: H. Muller/G.
van Lennep; 5th OA.
27/05: Nürburgring 1000Km:G. Follmer/W.
Kauhsen, #66; DNF.

Over the winter of 1973/4, this car was built into the
first of the RSR Turbo Carrera (2.14 Litres) proto-
types for the 1974 World Championship of makes
series of races. 500 B.H.P./7,600 RPM. 56 MKG
Torque/5,400 RPM. 750KG's weight.

1974:
02/06: Imola 1000Km WCM:M. Schurti/H. Koinigg,
#7; NC.
1974-1988: With the Vasek Polak collection, CA.
The car was sold to a collector in West Palm Beach,
Florida in the 1980's and exhibited at the Collier
Museum in Naples, Florida.
Sold to Japan.
Sold to Jeff Hayes.
2002-5: restored back to 1973 RSR Carrera by
Gunnar Porsche.
Turbo parts built into a replica RSR Turbo.
STPO.

Chassis No: 911 460 9016. Factory car R9
Engine: 911/78 (type)
G/Box type: 915/50.
450 B.H.P. /8,000 R.P.M. 46MKG torque/5,500
R.P.M.
Weight: 820 KG.
Colour: Silver.
1974: World Championship Races.
24/03: Le Mans Tests

24/03: Le Mans 4 Hours: G. van Lennep/H. Muller,
#9; DNF.
19/05: Nürburgring 1000Km: H.Koinigg/M.Schurti,
#9; 7th.
02/06: Imola 1000Km: G. van Lennep/H. Muller,
#6; DNF.
30/06: Osterreichring 1000Km: G. van Lennep/H.
Muller, #7; 6th.

1975: September: Sold to Dr Jackson, Colorado.
2000: Sold to Heritage Sportscars, Hollywood.
2003: Sold to Matt Drendel.
2008: STPO.

Chassis No: 911 460 9101. Factory car R12
Engine type: 911/78
Gearbox type: 915/50.
Colour: Silver.

This was the second RSR Turbo 2.14 litre car of 1974. 450 BHP/8,000 rpm and 46 MKG torque/5500 RPM.

1974: World Championship Races.
24/3: Le Mans 4-Hours: H. Koinigg/M. Schurti;. #10; 6th.

25/04: Monza 1000Km: G. van Lennep/H.Muller, #8; 5th.
05/05: Spa 1000Km: G. van Lennep/H. Muller, #14; 3rd.
19/05: Nürburgring 750Km: G. van Lennep/H. Muller, #8; 6th.
16-17/06: Le Mans 24 Hrs: H. Koinigg/M. Schurti, #21; DNF.
30/06: Osterreichring 1000Km: H. Koinigg/M. Schurti, #8; DSQ.

2017: In Factory collection.

Chassis No: 911 460 9102. Factory car R13
Engine: 911/78 (type)
1974 RSR Turbo 2.14 litre car. BHP and Torque as above. All four cars Martini Sponsored and

Coloured. (Silver with red/blue/white stripes).
1974: World Championship Races.

15-16/06: Le Mans 24-Hours: G. van Lennep/H. Muller, #22; 2nd OA.
13/07: Watkins Glen 6-Hours: G. van Lennep/H. Muller, #9; 2nd.
15/08: Paul Ricard 750Km: G. van Lennep/H. Muller, #14; 7th.
29/09: Brands Hatch 1000Km: G. van Lennep/H. Muller, #5; 5th.

1977:
5-6/02: Daytona 24-Hours: D. Ongais/G. Follmer/T. Field, #00; DNF. (Fablon over paint).
28/08: Mid-Ohio 3-Hours: G. Follmer/H. Holmes/J. Ickx, #16; 26thNR.

1998: With the Vasek Polak collection. Silver with Martini stripes.

For sale.
1999: Sold to Jeff Lewis.
Sold to Greg Galdi.
Sold to John Kotts.
STPO.

1976: 934: 31 customer cars built. Chassis numbers run from 930 670 0151 – 0180 plus 930 670 0540

Chassis No: 930 670 0001: (R14)
Production No: 106.?
Prototype.
Colour: Indian red.

Prototype.
1975: Tested at Nürburgring, Paul Ricard, Teldex ABS experimented with.
Windtunnel tests at Volkswagen wind tunnel in Wolfsburg.
Used as the Homologation example for the thirty production 934s to follow.
Rebodied as 935 by factory, again used in wind tunnel tests at VW, Wolfsburg.
1976: Used to wind tunnel test the bodywork for the 937/77.
1978: Reduced to parts.

Chassis No: 930 670 0151
Production No: 106.2821.
Prototype. Options: 165.244.
Colour: Indian red.
Sold to Dieter Marker.

This, the first production 934 built, It's thought that although the car is shown as being sold to Dieter

Marker, it was actually sold to Jurgen Kannacher of Krefeld, Germany. Kannacher raced the car in the German National Championship and then used it for "rent-a-rides". What happened after that is unclear. 0151 was then sold to Skip Gunnel of Florida for many years and has been completely restored. Upon his death, it was bought by another collector/racer in the USA.

Sold to Jurgen Kannacher:
1976: World Championship and German National Championship:
21/03: Zolder: Kannacher, #319; 3rd.
11/04: Hockenheim: Kannacher, #936; 3rd.
25/04: Sylt: (Not DRM): Kannacher; 5th.
02/05: Eifelrennen, Nürburgring: Kannacher, #8; DNF.
23/05: Mainz-Finthen: Kannacher, #19; 14th.
30/05: Nürburgring 1000 Km: Bertrams/Van Lennep, #3; 5th.
07/06: Zeltweg (EC-GT): H. Bertrams; 3rd.
20/06: Hockenheim (DRM): H. Bertrams, #10; 5th.
27/06: Norisring, Nurnberg, (DRM): H. Bertrams, #10:; DNF. (EC-GT): H. Bertrams; DNF.
25/07: Diepholz: (DRM): H. Bertrams, #6; 6th.
01/08: Nürburgring (DRM): H. Bertrams, #5; 3rd.
22/08: Kassel-Calden: Stocks, #17; 6th.

29/08: Hockenheim: (DRM): H. Bertrams, #107; 3rd.
26/09: Hockenheim: Doren; DNS, (Turbo).

1977: Uprated with wider wheels, single-turbo 935 engine, Painted yellow.
24/04: Sylt: "John Winters"; 3rd
19/05: Diepholz: Krages, ("John Winter"); 3rd.
24/07: Syly: "John Winters", #266; 2nd.
17/08: Mainz-Finthen: "John Winters"; 2nd.
21/08: Kassel-Calden: "John Winters", #123; 2nd.
18/09: Ulm-Mengen: "John Winter" RU.
16/10: Zolder: "John Winter", #35; 3rd.
6/11: Hockenheim: "John Winter" 3rd.

1976: Sold to Jurgen Kannacker.
1977: Sold to Louis Krages, ("John Winter")

1979: Painted silver.
10-11/06: Le Mans 24 Hours: A-C. Verney/R. Metge/P. Bardinon, #84; 19th OA.

1980: Sold to Vic Wilson, UK.
1982: Sold to Skip Gunnel of Florida.1999: Completely restored.
2002: STPO.

Chassis No: 930 670 0152
Production No: 106.3330.
Options: 185. 241. 21st car built.
Colour: White.
First Owner: Vasek Polak/agent:

Sold to Vasek Polak and then Paul Miller, a Porsche-Audi dealer, 0152 was raced in the Trans Am and IMSA before being sold to Mike Tillson who raced the 934 at the Watkins Glen 6-Hours of 1977 before selling the car on to Don Whittington soon afterwards.

Don had Dan McLoughlin of AIR clothe the 934 with 935 bodywork and, with a twin-turbocharged engine, the car did many IMSA races before being finally converted to K3 bodywork in 1980. After its competition life was over, 0152 was used at

the Road Atlanta race track as a school car, (The Whittingtons owned the track at the time), before winding up with Paul Reisman in 1989 who raced the car, fitted with a 2.8 liter engine in it in HSR events.

At the Watkins Glen meeting in June, 2000, Paul Reismann swapped 0152 for chassis number 000 00028, the last Peter Gregg car which had been sold to Phil Bagley. In 2005, Tom Hedges owned the car and raced it at Monterey; in 2011, Steve Schmidt, owner of a Porsche shop in California, bought it and has been racing it since.

Sold to Vasek Polak (1).

1976: Sold to Paul Miller.
09/05: Pocono TA: Miller, #36; 6th.
10/07: Watkins Glen 6-Hours WCFM: P.Miller/K. Miller, #36; 13th OA.
29/08: Mid-Ohio 6-Hours IMSA: Miller/; 20th.
19/09: Road Atlanta 1000Km IMSA: Minter/Miller; 5th.

1977:
Sold to Mike Tillson.

09/07: Watkins Glen 6-Hours WCM: Tillson/ Forbes-Robinson, #94; DNF. (engine Mounting).

Sold to the Whittington Brothers. Uprated to 935 specification.

1978: IMSA Championship Races.
18/03: Sebring 12-Hours: D. Whittington/R. Boy, #93; 24th OA.
16/04: Road Atlanta: Don Whittington, #93; 7th.
30/04: Laguna Seca: Don Whittington, #93; 24th OA.
07/05: Hallett: Bill Whittington,#93; 4th OA.
29/05: Lime Rock: Don Whittington,#93; 4th OA.
18/06: Brainerd: Bill Whittington, #93; 3rd OA.
3-4/07: Daytona: Paul Revere 250: Whittington Bros, #93: 3rd OA.
30/07: Sears Point: Don Whittington, #93; 2nd OA.
06/08: Portland. G.I. Joe's GP: Don Whittington, #93; 6th OA.
27/08: Mid-Ohio: Don Whittington, #93; 10th OA.
04/09: Road Atlanta 6-Hours: Don Whittington, #93; 2nd OA.
26/11: Daytona Finale: Don Whittington, #93; 13th OA.

1979: Engine No: 698 0034 (from 930 890 0023) installed.
08/04: Road Atlanta 100 Miles: Don Whittington, #93; 3rd.
29/04: Laguna Seca 100 Miles: Don Whittington, #93; 4th.
13/05: Hallett 100 miles: Don Whittington, #93; 3rd.
28/05: Lime Rock 100 miles: Don Whittington, #93;12th.
17/06: Brainerd 100 miles: Don Whittington, #93; 29th.
04/07: Daytona 250 miles: Don/Bill Whittington, #93;14th.
29/07: Sears Point 100 miles: Don Whittington, #93; 23rd.

1980: Converted to K3 bodywork.
13/04: Road Atlanta: Dale Whittington, #94; 4th.
27/04: Riverside: Dale Whittington/M. Chandler, #94; 4th.
21/09: Road Atlanta: Don Whittington, #93; Heat 1:-22nd NR, Heat 2:-DNS.

1981:
31/1-1/02: Daytona 24-Hours: Dale/Bill/Don Whittington, #94; 57th NR.
21/03: Sebring 12-Hours: Dale/Bill/Don Whittington, #94; 43rd NR.

Used as a school car at Road Atlanta.

1989: Sold to Paul Reisman. Raced in HSR events. Engine number 698 0034 is in the car. This was originally in 1978 935, chassis number 930 890 0016.

2000:
03/06: Watkins Glen: Swapped for 1980 Porsche 935, chassis number: 000 00028.
Sold to Auto Assets, Ohio.
2004: STPO.
2005: Laguna Seca: Tom Hedges, Issaquah, WA. tom@hedgesfamilyestate.com.
2010: For sale with Fantasy Junction.
2011: Sold to Steve Schmidt.
2015: "Rennsport Reunion", Laguna Seca.

Chassis No: 930 670 0153
Production No: 106.3331.
Options: 185. 241. 17th car built.
Colour: Yellow.
First Owner/Agent: Jean Blaton.

This car was delivered straight to the Le Mans race track, just in time for the 1976 race where Jean Blaton, who raced under the pseudonym of "Beurlys" took delivery. He had raced Ferraris at Le Mans and elsewhere for years. One of his co-drivers, Nick Faure of England, painted the car in Blaton's colours in the paddock. Sadly, in the race itself, 0153 went through no less than four turbo-chargers and, although finishing the race, was not classified due to insufficient distance being covered.

0153 was advertised for sale in a Swiss racing magazine in 1989. It has since changed hands to another Belgian owner.

1976:
8-9/6: Le Mans 24-Hours: Beurlys/Faure/Goss, #70; Not classified. (actually 27th OA/11th in the Group 4 class).

1977:
11-12/6: Le Mans 24-Hours: Ortega/Koob/Braillard, #57; DNF. (Engine).
04/09: Zolder: W, Braillard, #81; 2nd.
24/09: Zolder: W. Braillard; 2nd.

1978:
10-11/6: Le Mans 24-Hours: W.Braillard/J-L/J. Ravenel/P. Dagoreau, #69; DNF. (Engine).
23/04: Zolder: W. Braillard, @72; 1st.
07/05: Spa 600Kms: W. Braillard; 1st.
09/07: Novellas: M. Duez; 2nd.
13/08: Nivelles: M. Duez; 3rd.
15/10: Zolder: W. Braillard; 15th.

1977: Sold to J-P Gaban.
1980: Sold to Schaerer.
1989: Sor sale in Switzerland.
1997: For sale in Belgium.

Chassis No: 930 670 0154
Production No: 106.3332.
Engine number: 676 002

Gearbox number: 77620/8.
4th car built.
Colour: Arrow Blue.
First Owner/Agent: Eugen Kiemele

Eugen Kiemele raced this car enthusiastically before having an accident with it at the Krahberg hill-climb in May, 1976 when the throttle jammed open. Fortunately, Kiemele escaped but the car was very badly damaged and was sold to Jurgen Kannacher who removed the engine and gearbox and sold the damaged shell to Josh Sadler of Autofarm.

Josh restored the car, re-engining it with an RSR 2.8 litre engine and in this form, the 934 was sold to Mark Niblett and raced at Brands Hatch and Silverstone in two World Championship events.

After this, the 934 was sold to John Bell of England who had Neil Bainbridge re-engine it again, this time with a 3.3 litre 930 engine with a 934 metering unit to increase horsepower. In this form, John raced the car in British club events until having an accident at Silverstone with it in 1988, (right in front of your author!), which necessitated another complete rebuild, this time by Neil Bainbridge.

After this was completed, the car was sold at

Auction to noted Italian Porsche racer, Mauro Borella, who raced it once, at Misano, before selling to to Mario Illien.

In 1995, your author inspected the car in England and shortly thereafter, it was sold to noted Porsche collector, Dick Gundeck of New Jersey. He sold it on to paolo Faldini of Italy in 2010 and it has been sold on since.

1976: Sold to Eugen Kiemele on 31/3/76. (Invoice date).
21/02: Hockenheim: Kiemele; 1st.
21/03: Zolder: Kiemele; 6th.
28/03: Taunus, (Hillclimb): Kiemele, ; 4th.
11/04: Hockenheim: Kiemele; 7th.
25/04: Heilbronn (hillclimb): Kiemele; 1st.
02/05: Krahberg: (Hillclimb): Kiemele, #243; DNF (Throttle jammed open, accident).
Sold to Jurgen Kannacher.

Sold to Mark Niblett; prepared by Charles Ivey Racing.

1979:
06/05: Silverstone 6-Hours: T. Dron/M.Niblett, #19; NC.
05/08: Brands Hatch 6-Hours: T.Dron/Niblett, #20; 15th.
Sold to ? Road registered and used as daily transport, featured in "Car and car conversions" in an article entitled: "Silver dream racer".
UK registration document, V5, was issued on 05/10/1980
Sold to John Bell, raced in the 1980's Modified Porsche and Intermarque Championship.

1988: Crashed at Silverstone, rebuilt by Neil Bainbridge.
1993: Sold to Mauro Borella. Raced at Misano.
Sold to Mario Illien.
1995: Sold to Dick Gundeck, USA.
2006: Sold to Paolo Faldini, Italy.
2015: STPO.

Chassis No: 930 670 0155
Production No: 106.3333.
Options: 185.245. 2nd car built.
Colour: Orange.
First Owner/Agent: Max Moritz.

Egon Evertz was a German Industrialist who was another dedicated Porsche customer, having previously raced an RSR Carrera, chassis number 911 460 9111. He bought two 934's of which this one was used in order to compete in the Group 4 class of World Championship events. After just three rounds, he had the factory uprate the car to 935 specifications. For a co-driver, he had hired Leo Kinnunen, the Finnish ex-Porsche works driver who had driven the 917 in its heyday. Evertz and Kinnunen placed third a couple of times and Evertz won a couple of minor races.

Evertz sold this 934 to Kenneth Leim of Sweden for the 1977 season and he raced it in World Championship events during 1977, 78 and 1979. In 1980, Richard Cleare of England bought the car and uprated the engine to 935 type fuel injection. Cleare, partnered by Tony Dron campaigned the car in World Championship events for the next few years, either winning or placing second in their class in all the races competed in in 1982.

In 1995, Dave Morse of Morspeed bought the car and raced it in club events in the USA until "retiring" the 934 and giving it a total restoration during 1995. Sold then to Matt Drendel, sold on since.

Sold through Max Moritz to Egon Evertz.

1976: World Championship Races.
31/01-1/02: Daytona 24-Hours: Greger/Evertz/Lassig, #11; DNF.
21/03: Mugello 6-Hours: Kinnunen/Evertz, #7; 3rd.
04/04: Vallelunga 6-Hours: Kinnunen/Evertz, #7; DNF. (engine).
09/05: Silverstone 6-Hours: Kinnunen/Evertz, #16; 3rd. 935 specification.
30/05: Nürburgring 1000Km: Kinnunen/Evertz, #4; DNF. (Transaxle).
27/06: Osterreichring: Kinnunen/Evertz/Schurti, #3; DNF. (Disq).
10/07: Watkins Glen 6-Hours: Kinnunen/Hezemans/Evertz, #6; 2nd.
25/07: Diepholz DRM: Evertz; DNS. (Brakes).
01/08: Misano: Kinnunen; NC.
05/09: Dijon 6-Hours: Kinnunen/Evertz, #9; 4th. G5
19/09: Salzburgring: Evertz, #34; 1st.
26/09: Preis von Baden: Evertz, DNS; (Engine).
17/10: Zolder: Evertz; 1st.
31/10: Hockenheim: Evertz, #52; DNF.

Sold to Kenneth Leim.

1978: World Championship Races.
16/04: Dijon 6-Hours: Simonsen/Leim, #36; 9th OA. 2nd in Group 4 class.
14/05: Silverstone 6-Hours: Leim/Lombardi, #22; 15th OA.
28/05: Nürburgring 1000Km: Leim/Lombardi/Kohler, #40; DNF.
25/06: Misano 6-Hours: Leim/Simonsen, #24; DNF.

1979: World Championship Races.
18/03: Mugello 6-Hours WCM: Leim/Simonsen, #57; DNF.
22/04: Dijon 6-Hours WCM: Leim/Simonsen, #50; 14th.
06/05: Silverstone 6-Hours WCM: Leim/Simonsen, #14; 8th.
05/08: Brands Hatch 6-Hours WCM: Leim/Lombardi, #10; 16th.

Sold to Richard Cleare. Returned to factory to have engine overhauled and fitted with 935 fuel injection system.

1980: World Championship Races.
16/03: Brands Hatch 6-Hours: Dron/Cleare, #27; DNF.
11/05: Silverstone 6-Hours: Cleare/Dron, #29; 8th.
25/05: Nürburgring:1000 Km: Dron/Cleare, #72; DNA.
07/09: Vallelunga 6-Hours: Dron/Cleare, #14; 10th OA.
28/09: Dijon 6-Hours: Cleare/Dron, #44; 11th OA.

1981: World Championship Races.
10/05: Silverstone 6-Hours: Rouse/Cleare, #30: DNF.
24/05: Nürburgring 1000Km: Cleare/Kennedy, #34; 49th OA.
27/09: Brands Hatch1000Km: Cleare/Kennedy, #43; 12th.

1982: World Championship Races.
18/04: Monza 1000Km: Cleare/Dron, #94; 9th OA. 1st in Group 4 class.
16/05: Silverstone 6-Hours: Cleare/Dron, ; 19th OA. 2nd in Group 4 class.
19-20/06: Le Mans: Cleare/Dron/Jones, #90; 13th OA. 1st in Group 4 class. R. Cleare entry.
05/09: Spa 1000Km: Cleare/Dron, #90; 17th OA. 2nd in Group 4 class.
19/09: Mugello 1000Km: Cleare/Dron, #90; DNF. (driveshaft).
17/10: Brands Hatch 6-Hours; Cleare/Dron, #36; 14th OA. 1st in Group 4 class.
12/82: Track tested for "Thoroughbred and Classic Cars" magazine by Roger Bell.

167

1983: Sold to Mark Shmar? South Carolina, USA.

1995: Sold to Dave Morse, USA.
Raced in club events.

1998: Under restoration in the USA.
Monterey Historics, Laguna Seca: Mark Morse.
1999: Restored.
12/99: Featured in Porsche magazine, "Excellence".
2001? Sold to Matt Drendel, USA.
2015: STPO.

Chassis No: 930 670 0156
Production No: 106.3322.
Options: 185.243. 10th car built.
Colour: White.
First Owner/Agent: the Almeras Brothers, France.

The Almeras brothers ran their old RS 3.0 Carrera, 911 460 9034 in that race. This car was delivered straight to the Le Mans race track, just in time for the race where Jean Blaton, who raced under the pseudonym of "Beurlys" took delivery. He had raced Ferraris at Le Mans and elsewhere for many years. His co-driver, Nick Faure of England, painted the car in Blaton's colours in the paddock. Sadly, in the race itself, 0152 went through four turbochargers! (see Chapter 4) and, although finishing the race, was not classified due to insufficient distance being covered.

The Almeras Brothers competed with this 934, mainly in hillclimbs, for many years. Jacques Almeras won his class in the European Hillclimb Championship with a 934 in 1978. In 2001, it sold on.

26/06: Mont Ventoux: J. Almeras, #39; 7th OA, 1st in class.
08/8: Mont Dore: J. Almeras; 13th OA/1st in class.
17-24/09: Tour de France: Almeras/Tilber, #438; 3rd. (Slant nose-probably a converted RSR).

1977:
27/03: Ampus: Jacques Almeras; 12th OA/1st in class.
22/05: Montseny: J. Almeras; 1st in class.
03/07: Bolzano-Mendola: Almeras: 1st in class.
10/07: Trento Bondone, (EHC): J. Almeras; 4th in class.
17/07: Dobratsch: J. Almeras; 1st in class.
31/07: Borella Hillclimb: J. Almeras; DNQ.
07/08: Mont Dore: J. Almeras; 1st in class.
21/08: St. Ursanne; J. Almeras; 2nd in class.
28/08: Trofeo Scarfiotti: J. Almeras; 1st in class.
15-23/09: Tour de France: Almeras/"Tilber"; DNF.

1978:
Note: In 1978, Jacques Almeras won the European Hillclimb Championship in a 934, (Group 4).
09/04: Ampus: J. Almeras; 1st in class A4, (Group 4).
14/05: Sierra da Estrella, (EHC): 1st in class.
21/05: Montseny: J. Almeras; 1st in class.
18/06: Coppa Sila: J. Almeras; 1st in class A4, (Group 4).
09/7: Dobratsch Villach, (EHC): J. Almeras;1st.
23/07: Ascoli: J. Almeras; 1st in class A4, (Group 4).
29/07: Dobratsch: J. Almeras; 1st.
30/07: Rieti: J. Almeras; 1st in class A4, (Group 4).
13/08: Mont Dore: J. Almeras; 1st in class A4, (Group 4).
20/08: St. Ursannes, (EHC): J. Almeras; 1st.
17/09: Cefalu: J. Almeras; 1st in class A4, (Group 4).
1979;

01/04: Ampus: J. Almeras; 1st in class A4, (Group 4).

01/05: Alpl-Krieglach: J. Almeras; 1st in class.

20/05: Montseny: J. Almeras' 1st in class.

27/05: Estrella: J. Almeras; 1st in class.

20/05: Montseny: J. Almeras; 1st in class A4, (Group 4).

09/06: Dobratsch: Almeras; 1st in class.

24/06: Bolzano-Mendola; J. Almeras; 2nd in class.

15/07: Trofeo Scarfiotti: J. Almeras; 1st in class.

22/07: Potenza: J. Almeras; 1st in class.

19/08: St. Ursannes: J. Almeras; 1st in class.

02/09: Mont Dore; J. Almeras; 2nd in class.

23/09: Puigmajor: J. Almeras; 1st in class.

1980:

30/03: Ampus: J. Almeras; 1st in Group 4.

04/05: Alpl-Kreiglach: J. Almeras; 1st in class.

18/05: Montseny: J. Almeras; 1st in class.

23/05: Estrella: J. Almeras; 1st in class.

14-15/06: Le Mans 24-Hours: Almeras entry. Almeras Bros/Hopfner.#94; NRF. (Acc).

29/06: Rieti: J. Almeras; 1st in class.

06/07: Trento Bondone: J. Almeras; 1st in class.

20/07: Freiburg: J. Almeras; 6th in Group 5. 2nd in class

27/07: Ascoli: J. Almeras; 1st in Group 4 class.

24/08: St. Ursannes: J. Ameras; 1st in class.

02/09: Mont Dore: J. Almeras; 3rd in Group 4.

07/09: Turckheim: J. Almeras; 1st in class.

14/09: Cefalu: J. Almeras; 1st in class.

28/09: Puigmajor: J. Almeras; 1st in class.

30/10-6/11: Giro d'Italia: J. Almeras; DNF, (Acc.)

1982:

09/5: J.M. Almeras had a heavy accident with a "600 bhp 935."

Later in the season, Jacques Almeras raced a 935.

PERHAPS: Sold to Roland Biancone: Hillclimbed.

2000: The car was located in Japan.

Chassis No: 930 670 0157

Production No: 106.3523.

Options: 185.240. 15th car built.

Colour: White.

First Owner/Agent: Bianco.

The first 934 to be sold to Italy. 0157 was campaigned in World Championship events, entered by the Jolly Club. Its best result came at the Monza 6 Hours in September where it placed fourth in the European GT round held there. At Mugello, in 1977, 0157 was driven by the ex-Ferrari driver Arturo Merzario to place fourth in a World Championship race.

1976: Jolly Club entered. White/Blue/orange spoiler.

21/3: Mugello 6-Hours WCM: Schon/Bianco/Gargano, #14; DNF.

04/4: Vallelunga 6-Hours WCM: Schon/Tommasi/Bianco, #12; 5th.

02/5: Trofeo Ufficiali, Monza: G. Schon; #5; 1st.

16/5: Targa Florio: G. Bianco/L Tommasi; 4th.

30/5: Trofeo Ranz, Varano: G. Bianco; 1st.

27/6: Osterreichring 6-Hours WCM: Frisori/Mocini, #9; 10th.

01/8: Misano (EC-GT): L. Tambauto; 1st.

05/9: Monza 6-Hours, (EC-GT): L.Tambauto/L. Tomasi; 4th.

1977:
20/3: Mugello 6-Hours WCM: A. Merzario/G.
Bianco, #18; 4th OA/1st in G.T. class.
12-16/6: Giro d'Italia: G. Biancho/L. Tommasi,
#499; 2nd.
27/6: Osterreichring 6-Hours WCM: Frisori/Macini;
10th.
10/7: Misano: G. Bianco; 4th.
27/9: Magione: G. Bianco; 1st.
20/10: Giro d'Italia: G. Bianco/"Tambauto", #499;
2nd OA/1st Group 4.

Chassis No: 930 670 0158
Production No: 106.3524.
Options: 185.246. 4th car built.
Colour: White.
First Owner/Agent: the Kremer Brothers.

First of all sold to Gerhard Holup by the well known
German tuners and race team, the Kremer Brothers
of Cologne, 0158 raced in the Deutsche Rennsport
Meisterschaft in 1976 before being sold to Dieter
Schornstein who had previously raced a Porsche RS
3.0 Carrera, (chassis number 911 460 9023), in 1975
and 76.

　　Schornstein had the car brought up to 934/5
specification and won three races in 1977, at
Hockenheim, the Nürburgring and at the Mainz-
Finthen airfield.

　　At the end of 1977, Dieter Schornstein sold
0158 to Edgar Doren, who raced it until the end of
1979, with success. Doren then sold 0158 to Jack
Refenning of America and, in 1980, Refenning raced
the car at Daytona, Sebring and Riverside, placing a
creditable 4th in the Paul Revere race at Daytona in
1981. Refenning then sold the car to a pilot in the
U.S.A.F. but later bought it back. He later on sold
the restored car to France

1976: German National Championship unless otherwise noted.
21/03: Zolder: Holup; 4th.
04/04: Nürburgring: Holup, #8; DNF.
11/04: Hockenheim: Holup; 4th.

25/04: Sembach: Holup; DNF.
02/05: Nürburgring Eifelrennen: Holup, #7; DNF.
23/05: Mainz-Finthen: Holup, #10; 8th.
20/06: Rheinpokal Hockenheim: Holup; 7th.
27/06: Norisring, (EC-GT): Wollek, #6; DNF.
25/07: Diepholz: Holup, #12; 7th.
30/07: GP von Deutschland, Nürburgring: Holup;
DNS. (Acc).
29/08: Preis der Nationen, Hockenheim:Holup; 4th.
19/09: Imola, (EC-GT): Heyer; 2nd.
26/09: Preis von Hessen, Hockenheim: Bertrams;
7th.
10/10: Nürburgring: Holup; 3rd.

17/10: Zolder: Holup; 5th
23/10: Nürburgring: Schornstein; 1st.
31/10: Hockenheim, (EC-GT):Heyer, #7; 4th.

Sold to Dieter Schornstein.
Track tested at Dijon by Pierre Francois Rousselot,
published in the Belgian Magazine: "Auto hebdo"
#38. (18/11/76).

1977:
13/03: Bergischer Lowe, Zolder DRM: Schornstein,
#61; 7th.
27/03: Nürburgring DRM: Schornstein, #61; 6th.
(National); 4th.

17/04: Hockenheim:Schornstein; 4th.

24/04: Sylt: Schornstein; 1st in Group 4.

Converted to 934/5 specification.

01/05: Eifelrennen, Nürburgring DRM: Schornstein, #61; 6th.

08/05: Kassel-Calden DRM: Schornstein, #61; DNF, gearbox.

15/05: Hockenheim: Schornstein, #224; 1st.

22/05: Mainz-Finthen DRM: Schornstein, #61; 8th.

29/05: Nürburgring 1000Km WCM: Schornstein/von Tschirnhaus; 5th OA.

12/06: Nürburgring: Schornstein; 1st.

26/06: Zolder: Schornstein; 2nd.

03/07: Norisring: Schornstein, #61; NC, (DRM/200 Miles) and 10th, (Money-race).

24/07: Diepholz DRM: Schornstein, #61; 5th.

31/07: GP von Deutschland, Hockenheim DRM: Schornstein, #61; DNF.

07/8: Mainz-Finthen: Schornstein, #5; 1st.

14/8: Westfalen-Pokal, Zolder DRM: Schornstein, #61; 6th.

28/8: Nürburgring: Schornstein; DNS. (Engine).

25/9: Brands Hatch WCM: Schornstein/Peltier, #4; 10th OA.

02/10: Supersprint Nürburgring: Schornstein, #61; 8th.

09/10: Hockenheim 6-Hours WCM: Schornstein/Peltier, #61; 8th OA.

1978: Weralit-sponsored. Green stripes. Sold to Edgar Doren.

19/03: Mugello 6-Hours WCM: Doren/Holup, #27; 12th.

02/04: Nürburgring 300 Km DRM: Doren, #20; 8th.

16/04: Dijon 4-Hours WCM: Doren/Holup, #38; 16th.

14/05: Silverstone 6-Hours WCM: Doren/Holup; DNF.

28/05: Nürburgring 1000Km: Doren/Holup, #46; DNF. (Max Moritz-entry).

10-11/06: Le Mans 24-Hours: Holup/Doren/Poulain/Feitler, #68; DNF. Poulain entry. Jaegermeister sponsored. Painted Orange.

25/06: Misano 6-Hours WCM: Doren/Holup/Schimpf; 8th. Re-painted white.

20/08: Westfalen-Pokal, Zolder DRM: Holup, #31; 8th.

03/09: Vallelunga 6-hours WCM: Doren/Holup, #24; 8th.

17/09: Norisring: Doren, #20; 6th.

1/10: Supersprint Nürburgring: Doren, #41; (DRM); 8th. (Group 4 race): 1st.

14/10: Zolder; Holup; 11th, 1st in Group 4 class in G5 race, 2nd in G4 race.

1979: German National Championship, Group 4:

11/03: Bergischer Lowe Zolder: Doren,#79;10th.

25/03: Luxembourg Trophy: Doren; 2nd.

08/04: Jim Clark Rennen, Hockenheim: Doren;9th.

29/04: Eifelrennen Nürburgring: Doren;12th.

20/05: Bavaria Salzburgring: Doren; 9th.

17/6: Mainz-Finthen: Doren; 7th.

24/06: Norisring Nurnberg: Doren; 11th.

01/07: Zandvoort Trophy: Doren; 8th.

22/07: Diepholz: Doren; 11th.

19/08: Westfalen Zolder:Doren; 10th.

02/09: Hessen-Cup Hockenheim: Doren; 12th.

23/9: Supersprint Nürburgring: Doren; 14th.

7/10: Hessenpreis Kassel-Calden, Interseries:Glatz; 6th.

14/10: Zolder: Holup; 10th (group 2/4/5). 1st, (group 4 race).

4/11: Hockenheim: Doren; 2nd in G3/4 +2000 class. Edgar Doren won the Group 4 Division of the German National Championship.

Sold to Jack Refenning in the USA.

1980:

2-3/2: Daytona 24-Hours: Refenning/Mummery/Tilton, #24; 37thNR

1981:

21/3: Sebring 12-Hours: Refenning/Tilton/Welter, #24; 37thNR.

04/7: Daytona: Tilton, #24; 4th.

20/11: Daytona:Refenning/Tilton, #24; 42nd.

1982:
30-31/1: Daytona 24-Hours: Refenning/Tilton/Bond, #24; 9th OA.
1984:
29/4: Riverside 6-Hours: Griffin/Allen/Schwarz, #24; 12th.

Sold to a USAF Pilot.
Sold back to J. Refenning.
Sold to M. Ratel.
1991. Dec: Sold to Jean Paul Richard, France.
1994: Featured in "Auto Retro" in Jaegermeister colours.
2004: Sold to Manfred Freisinger.
2012: Private collector in USA.
2013: Sold to John Minshaw, UK.
2014: Sold to John Rothenberger, USA.
2017: STPO.

Chassis No: 930 670 0159
Production No: 106. 3525.
Options: 185.240. 7th car built.
Colour: White with blue stripes.
First owner/Agent:Tebernum Racing.

Clemens Schickentanz was a noted German racer, winning the 1973 European GT Championship in a 2.8 RSR Carrerar, chassis number 911 360 0885, which today resides in Britain. After carrying on racing with less success with RSR's in 1974 and 75, Schickentanz bought 0159 and had it run by Jurgen Kannacher of Krefeld for the Tebernum team of Edith Tebernum, occasionally running as a Gelo entry also. Major success with the 934 eluded Schickentanz, however, as he only managed to win at Sylt, the Nürburgring and Hockenheim.

What happened to the car in 1977 is not known but Peter Zbinden bought the car at some point. Peter Zbinden carried on racing the 934/5, in conjunction with his co-driver, Edi Kofel from 1978 to 1980 and sold the car in 1982.

After this, the trail goes cold but the car is alive and well in Germany today.

Sold to Clemens Schickentanz: 'Tebernum Racing Team Georg Loos KG, Cologne'.

1976: German National Championship unless otherwise noted.
21/03: Mugello 6-Hours WCM: Hezemans/Schickentanz, #19; DNF..
04/04: Nürburgring (EC-GT): Schenken, #52; 3rd.
25/04: Sylt, (Not DRM): Schickentanz, #110; 1st.
02/05: Eifelrennen, Nürburgring: Schickentanz, #5; 14th.
23/05: Mainz-Finthen: Hezemans, #6; 10th.
30/05: Nürburgring 1000Km: Schickentanz/Muller/Schenken, #22; DNF.
20/06: Rheinpokal Hockenheim: Schickentanz; DNF, (turbo).
27/06: Norisring Nurnberg: Schenken; (DRM); DNF. (EC-GT): #2; DNF. Oil pipe.
25/07: Diepholz:Schenken, #3; 2nd.
01/8: Misano (EC-GT):Schenken, #18; RU.
15/8: Zolder: Schickentanz; 3rd.
29/08: Preis der Nationen, Hockenheim: Schenken, #101; 1st.
05/09: Monza 6-Hours, EC-GT: Ludwig/Schenken/Hezemans, #2; 2nd.

12/09: Supersprint, Nürburgring: Schenken; 1st/
19/09: Imola (EC-GT): Schenken, #1; 4th.
26/09: Preis von Hessen Hockenheim: Schenken; 4th.
31/10: Hockenheim (EC-GT): Schenken, #3; 2nd.

Sold to Peter Zbinden, Switzerland.

1978:
28/05: Nürburgring 1000Km WCM: Zbinden/Kofel, #41; 18th.
16/07: Hockenheim, Swiss Championship: Kofel; 1st.
29/07: GP von Deutschland, Hockenheim DRM: Kofel, #39; 11th.
5/11: Rheintal-Rennen, Hockenheim: Kofel; 1st.

1979:
01/04: Paul Ricard: Kofel; 1st.
15/04: Dijon: Kofel; 1st in class.
22/04: Dijon 6-Hours, WCM: Zbinden/Kofel, #48; 7th.
29/04: Hockenheim: Kofel; 2nd in class.
06/05: Silverstone 6-Hours WCM: Zbinden/Kofel, #24; 6th.
03/06: Nürburgring 1000Km WCM: Zbinden/Kofel, #41; DNF.
16/09: Vallelunga 6-Hours: Zbinden/Kofel. #5; 11th.
14/10: Hockenheim 3-Hours: Zbinden/Kofel, #133; 1st.

1980:
06/04: Dijon: Kofel; 1st. in Group 4.
27/04: Hockenheim: Kofel; 1st in Group 4.
04/05: Dijon: Kofel; 2nd in Group 4.
11/05: Silverstone 6-Hours: Zbinden/Kofel, #30; DNF. (engine)
18/05: Monza: Kofel; 1st in Group 4.
13/07: Hockenheim: Kofel; 1st in Group 4.
03/08: Ayent-Azerre: Kofel, 1st in class.
17/08: Oberhallau: Kofel; 2nd in class.
24/08: St. Ursannes: Kofel; 2nd in class.
07/09: Gurnigel: Kofel; DNF. (transmission).
28/09: Hemberg: Kofel; 1st in class.

1982: Advertised in "*Auto Motor und Sport*" for sale: Peter Zbinden
2000: In Europe. Alain Pfefferle?

Chassis No: 930 670 0160
Production No: 106. 3526.
Options: 196.414. 5th car built.
Colour: White.
First Owner/Agent: E. Sindel.

Eberhard Sindel was another German racer who had specialised in RSR Carreras, having raced a 1974 RSR Carrera, chassis number 911 460 9078 in 1974 and 75. For 1976, Sindel bought 0160 and commenced racing it, with Group 5 modifications, in the German Championship. With sponsorship from Valvoline, Sindel did quite well, scoring two victories in 1976 and three in 1977.

At the end of 1978, Sindel sold the car to Johannes Forster who only did two races with the car, perhaps hiring it out for two more in 1979. 0160 was then sold to Hans Obermaier, who had it raced by Joseph ("Sepp") Reiter. Herr Obermaier has now had the 934 completely restored.

Sold to Eberhard Sindel. White w/red stripe and fenders. Blue Front spoiler. Maintained by J. Kannacher.
1976: "Valvoline Deutschland" sponsored; German National Championship unless otherwise noted.
04/4: Nürburgring 300Km(EC-GT): Sindel, #55; 11th OA.
11/4: Hockenheim: Sindel; DNF.
25/4: Sembach, (Not DRM): Sindel; 1st.
02/5: Eifelrennen: Nürburgring: Sindel, #10; 6th.
09/5: Kassel-Calden: Sindel; DNF.
30/5: Nürburgring 1000Km WCM: Bross/Sindel, #26; 6th.
20/6: Rheinpokal, Hockenheim: Sindel; DNS.
27/6: Osterreichring 6-Hours WCM: Sindel/ Steckkonig; #6: 9th.
04/7: Salzburgring: Sindel; 2nd. (G2/4/5 +2000 cc).
25/7: Diepholz: Sindel, #11; 6th. (National race). DRM: 8th.

01/8: G.P. von Deutschland: Sindel, #20; DNF, (acc.)
15/8: Zandvoort: Sindel; 1st. Int. Race; 3rd.
21/8: Nürburgring: Sindel/Kannacher; 1st.
04/9: Dijon 6-Hours WCM: Sindel/Steckkonig, #41; 10th.
12/9: Ulm-Mengen: Sindel; DNF.
19/9: Salzburgring: Sindel; 3rd.
31/10: Hockenheim: Sindel; 12th OA/2nd in class. (Group 5 modifications).

1977:
27/3: 300Km Nürburgring: Sindel, #67; DNF.
17/4: Hockenheim: Sindel; 2nd. (Valvoline-sponsored).
22/5: Avus: Sindel; 2nd.
29/5: Nürburgring 1000Km WCM: Sindel/Steckonig, #33; DNF.
05/6: Salzburgring: Sindel, #15; 1st. (Valvoline-entered).
12/6: Nürburgring: Sindel; 2nd.
26/6: Zolder: Sindel, DNF.
03/7: Nürburgring: Sindel, #172; 1st.
23/7: Bilstein Cup, Nürburgring: Sindel/Steckonig; DNF.
20/8: Nürburgring 4-Hours: Sindel/Steckonig; 1st OA.
28/8: Nürburgring: Sindel; 3rd.
18/9: Ulm-Mengen: Sindel; 1st.
25/9: Brands Hatch 6-Hours WCM: Sindel/Steckonig, #14; 5th.
2/10: Supersprint, Nürburgring: Sindel, #56; 6th.
9/10: Hockenheim 6-Hours: Sindel/Steckonig, #14; 6th. (Perhaps a rented 935?)

1978: Sold to Hans Forster of Donauwoerth.
19/3: Mugello 6-Hours WCM: Forster/Gschwender, #42; 14th.
02/4: Nürburgring 300 Km DRM: Forster; DNS. (Acc.)
1/10: Erding: Gschwender; 1st.
Sold to Hans Obermaier of Halsbach, Germany.

1979:
26/8: Ulm-Mengen: Reiter; 7th (group 2/4). 3rd, (group 3/4).

1980: Driven by Joseph ("Sepp") Reiter.
11/5: Avus-Rennen Berlin: Reiter; 2nd.
22/6: Norisring DRM: Reiter; 9th.
13/7: Bavaria Salzburgring DRM: Reiter; DNF.
27/7: Diepholz DRM: Reiter; 11th.
07/9: Hessen-Cup, Hockenheim DRM: Lassig; DNS.
21/9: Supersprint Nürburgring DRM: Reiter; DNF.
18/10: Nürburgring 4-Hours: Lassig/Duge; 1st.

1981:
24/10: Nürburgring 4-Hours: Lassig/Duge; 1st OA.

1982:
25/4: Eifelrennen; Nürburgring: Reiter; 19th. 6th in Group 4 class.
02/5: Avus-Rennen, Berlin: Reiter; DNF.
12/9: Salzburgring: Reiter; DNF.

1983:
29/5: Nürburgring 1000Km WCM: Reiter/Friebel/Duge; DNC. (as a 930).
04/9: Spa 1000Km WCM: Reiter/Hutwelker/Beilke; 16th.

The sales only took place on paper, for tax reasons. The car always remained the property of Sindel. On Sindel's death, the car, still very original, was put up for sale.

2007: Sold to Jurgen Brodessor.

Chassis No: 930 670 0161
Production No: 106. 3716.
Options: 185.248. 28th car built.
Colour: Yellow.
First Owner/Agent: Losch.(Koob).

Nicholas Koob only raced this 934 once, at Zolder, before selling it, at the end of 1976, to Hans Christian Jurgensen who promptly started enjoying a three year long campaign with the 934 which netted him many first and second places.
In the winter of 1979/80, Armando Gonzales of

Puerto Rico bought the car and gave it to Chuck Gaa of Atlanta to update with increased rollcage stiffness, a raised gearbox, (to reduce drive-shaft travel), 935-style nose and tail and an airscoop on the rear window to funnel air into the air to air intercooler. Thus equipped, Gonzales also raced the 934 for the next three seasons before selling it to Kikos Fonseca. Fonseca raced the car in IMSA and South American events before selling it at a Christie's auction as he had built a tube frame 935 by this time from a 911RSR run by Luis Mendez, which was numbered as 930 670 0161R.

1994 saw the 934 being exchanged for a Ferrari 275 GTB and the 934 was stripped with a rebuild in mind by the new owner but never finished. Jim Torres of Burbank Coach Works bought the project and restored it back to its 1980 configuration in 1999. 0161 has been demonstrated by Torres at Daytona and Willow Springs and is remarkably fast!

1976:
27/06: Zolder: Koob; 4th.

Sold to Hans Christian Jurgensen of Flensburg, Germany.

1977:
17/04: Hockenheim: Jurgensen; 5th.
08/05: Kassel-Calden: Jugensen, #77; 5th.
19/05: Diepholz: Jurgensen, #267; 1st.
22/05: Avus (G4/5 + 3000 cc): Jurgensen;DNF. (driveshaft).m
12/06: Wunstorf: Jurgensen, #422; 1st.
26/06: Zolder: Jurgensen; 1st.
24/07: Diepholz: Jurgensen, #77, DRM; DNS. National race: 1st.
21/08: Kassel-Calden: Jurgensen, #125; 1st.
18/09: Ulm-Mengen: Jurgensen; 2nd.
9/10: Hockenheim 6-Hours WCM: Jurgensen/Sell, #12; DNF.
16/10: Zolder: Jurgensen; 2nd.
29/10: Nürburgring 4 Hours: Jurgensen; DNF. (rear axle).

27/11: Hockenheim: Jurgensen; 7th.

1978:
16/04: Fassberg: Jurgensen, #140; 1st.
15/05: Saarlouis: Jurgensen; 1st.
11/06: Wunstorf: Jurgensen; 1st.
16/07: Kassel-Calden: Jurgensen, #25; 10th.
13/08: Zandvoort: Jurgensen; 5th.
03/09: Kassel-Calden: Jurgensen; 2nd.
15/10: Zolder: Jurgensen; 1st in G4 race.

1979:
11/03: Bergischer Lowe Zolder DRM: Jurgensen; DNF. (engine).

24/03: Hockenheim: Jurgensen; 1st in Group 4 class.
08/04: Jim Clark-Rennen, Hockenheim DRM: Jurgensen, #83; DNF. 3rd in G4 race.
06/05: Fassberg: Jurgensen; 2nd in class.
27/05: Wunstorf: Jurgensen; 1st in Group 4 class.
24/06: Norisring Nurnberg, (DRM): Jurgensen; 12th.
22/07: Diepholz: Jurgensen; DNF. 1st in group 4 race.
20/10: Hockenheim: Jurgensen; 1st in Group 4 class.
4/11: Hockenheim: Jurgensen; 3rd in G3/4 race.
Some races with Edgar Doren?

175

1980:
15th January: Sold to Armando Gonzales in Puerto
Rico. DM25,710.00.

Uprated to 935 specification by Chuck Gaa of
Atlanta with raised gearbox mountings and other
modifications.

1980: IMSA Championship Races.
22/03: Sebring 12-Hours: Gonzales/Febles/
Soldevilla, #58; 42nd/17th in GTO class.
13/04: Road Atlanta: Gonzales, #35; 26th/12th.
14-15/06: Le Mans 24-Hours: Febles entry.
Gonzales/Romero/Febles; #:80. DNF. (Acc.)
04/07: Daytona: "Jamsal"/Barrientos, #32;17th/6th.
21/09: Road Atlanta (1): Gonzales, #35; 23rdNR.
(2): 10th/4th.
30/11: Daytona Finale: Gonzales, #35; 48thNR.

1981: IMSA Championship Races.
21/03: Sebring 12-Hours: Gonzales/B. Fernandez/
Cochesa, #35; 14th/7th.
26/04: Riverside 6-Hours: Gonzales/B. Fernandez,
#35; DNS.
25/05: Lime Rock: Gonzales/Febles, #35; 19th/10th
in GTO NR.

1982:
Raced in South America?

1983:
27/02: Miami GP: H. Cruz, #69; 17th.
19/3: Sebring 12-Hours: Gonzales/Cruz, #69;
20th/77th in GTO.

1984: This MAY have been the #24 car in IMSA.
(rental).
4-5/02: Daytona 24 Hours: B. Hefner/J. Griffin/H.
Gralia, #24; 19th OA.
26/02: Miami GP: J. Fangio/H. Gralia, #24; 12th
OA.
24/03: Sebring 12 Hours: M.L. Speer/J. Griffin, #24;
50thNR.

Sold to Kikos Fonseca, Puerto Rico.
1985:
24/02: Miami GP: Fonseca, #33; 4th.(GTO race).

1986:IMSA Championship Races.
2-3/02: Daytona 24 Hours:K. Fonseca/L.
Mendez/"Jamsal", #34; 13th OA/3rd GTO.
02/03: Miami GP: K. Fonseca, #34; 6th GTO race.
22/03: Sebring 12 Hours: K. Fonseca/L.
Mendez/"Jamsal", #34; 25th OA/7th GTO.
05/04: Road Atlanta: K. Fonseca, #34; th GTO Race.
27/04: Riverside: K. Fonseca/"Jamsal", #34;
33rdNR.
04/05: Laguna Seca IMSA: K. Fonseca, #34; 7th
OA.
22/06: W. Palm Beach: K. Fonseca, #34; 3rd GTO
Race.
06/07: Watkins Glen1: K. Fonseca/R. Valverde, #34;
26th OA/7th GTO.

1988: Sold at Christie's Auction, Monte Carlo.

Fonseca then drove a tube-frame 934. (with the
same chassis number - This was sold into America
in 1992). This car had been raced in 1980 in IMSA
and by Luis Mendez from 1986-1988.

With this 935;
1988:
21/03: Sebring 12 Hours: L. Mendez/K. Fonseca,
#68; DNF.

1989:
05/3: Miami GP: K. Fonseca, #34; 10th.
19/03: Sebring 12 Hours: L. Mendez/T. Ferrar/M.
Gonzales, #68; DNF.

1989-1999: Raced by Fonseca in South America.

1994: Original 934 traded for a Ferrari 275 GTB/4.
1999: Belonged to Dale Kennet, sold to and restored
by Jim Torres, effectively a 934/5GTO spec.
9/99: Restored. 1978 935 front, 1980 934 "GTO"
bodywork. Red and has single turbo engine with

962 intakes plus an air intake over the roof.

2000:
06/02: Daytona 24 Minutes: J. Torres.
06/03: Willow Springs: J. Torres. Demonstration.

2002: Sold to Rick Davies, Naples, FL. 239 572 0161
2008: Sold to Monte Shelton.
2013: Sold to Mauro Borella, restored by Kremer Racing.
2014: Sold to Bill Kincaid, USA.
2015: "Rennsport Reunion", Laguna Seca.
2017: Monterey Reunion.

Chassis No: 930 670 0162
Production No: 106. 3717.
Options: 200. 190 19th car built.
Colour: Yellow.
First Owner/Agent: Pallavicini.

Angelo Pallavicini of Zurich has long been a collector/dealer specializing in Porsche racing cars. He bought 0162 new and, with co-driver Bernhard, won the Group 4 class of the World Championship for Makes in 1978.

In 1979, Pallavicini took the 934 to Daytona where, with co-driver Werner Frank, he placed tenth overall and fourth in the GTO class. Pallavicini sold 0162 to Frank after the race and returned home to carry on racing another 934, chassis number 930 670 0178. Werner Frank then raced 0162 until 1983, selling it to Rick Borlase. Borlase raced 0162 until 1986, its swansong being a fine 10th overall at the Daytona 24-Hours with Jim Torres co-driving.

In 1988, Borlase sold the 934 to Sid Ho who in turn, sold it to Jim Torres in 1990. Jim restored 0162 and he sold it at the RM Auction at Monterey in 1999.

1976:
10/04: Dijon (Swiss Championship race): Pallavicini; 1st.
07/06: Zeltweg (EC-GT): Pallavicini; 8th.

27/06: Norisring Nurnberg (EC-GT): Pallavicini;5th. (DRM); 9th.
01/08: Misano: Pallavicini; 2nd.
05/09: Monza 6-Hours (EC-GT): Pallavicini/Keller; 5th.
19/09: Imola (EC-GT): Pallavicini; 8th.
26/09: Hemberg (hillclimb): Pallavicini, 2nd in class
31/10: Hockenheim: (EC-GT) Pallavicini; 8th. (National); 1st.

1977: World and German/Swiss National Championship:
26/02: Hockenheim: Pallavicini; 1st.
27/03: Ampus, (EHC): Pallavicini; 5th /3rd in class.
03/04 Le Castellet: Pallavicini, 2nd in class
17/04 Monza: Pallavicini, #58, 1st in class
15/5: Hockenheim: Pallavicini; 2nd.
29/05 Österreichring: Pallavicini, 1st in class
10/7: Trento Bondone: Pallavicini, (EHC); 1st in class.
17/07 Hockenheim: Pallavicini, 1st in class
30/7: G.P. von Deutschland, Hockenheim: Pallavicini, #57; 9th.
07/08 Ayent-Anzère (hillclimb): Pallavicini, 2nd in class
21/8: St. Ursanne: Pallavicini, (EHC); 6th in class.
04/09 Dijon: Pallavicini, 1st in class
11/09 Gurnigel (hillclimb): Pallavicini, 4th in class

15/10 Hockenheim 3-Hours: Pallavicini, DNF (brakes)

1978:
19/03: Mugello 6-Hours WCM: Pallavicini/Bernhard, #18; DNF.
16/04: Dijon 1000Km WCM: Pallavicini/Bernhard, #31; 8th.
14/05: Silverstone 6-Hours WCM: Pallavicini/Bernhard, #24; 8th.
28/05: Nürburgring 1000Km WCM: Pallavicini/Vanoli/Bernhard, #55; 28th.
25/06: Misano 6-Hours WCM: Pallivicini/Kofel/Vanoli, #18; 7th.
08/07: Watkins Glen 6-Hours WCM: Pallavicini/Calderari, #17; 18th.
29/07: GP von Deutschland, Hockenheim DRM: Pallavicini, #44; DNF.
03/09: Vallelunga 6-Hours WCM: Pallavicini/Vanoli, #12; 9th.
24/09: Hemberg: Pallavicini; 1st.
Pallavicini won the World Championship for manufacturers, Group 4 class in 1978.

1979: Red.
3-4/02: Daytona 24-Hours: Pallavicini/Calderari/Vanoli, #03; 10th OA/4th in GTO.

Sold to Werner Frank:
08/04: Road Atlanta: Frank, #03; 24th/12th in GTO class.
17/06: Brainerd: Frank, #03; 16th OA/6th in GTO class.
04/07: Daytona: Frank, #03; 15th/6th in GTO class
21/07: Road America, Elkhart Lake, (TA): Frank; 6th.
26/08: Mid-Ohio 500-Miles: W. Frank/R. Bartling; 11th.
02/09: Road America: Frank/Bartling, #03; 16th/6th in GTO class.
23/09: Road Atlanta: Frank, #03; 27th/14th in GTO class.
25/11: Daytona Finale: Frank, #03; 9th/3rd in GTO class.

1980:
2-3/02: Daytona 24-Hours: Frank/Pallavicini/Crang, #03; 63rd/24thNR in GTO class.
22/03: Sebring 12-Hours: Frank/Brolin, #03; 12th/3rd in GTO class.
13/04: Road Atlanta: Frank, #03: 16th/5th in GTO class.
27/04: Riverside 5-Hours: Frank/Schramm, #03; 12th/5th in GTO class.
04/05: Laguna Seca: Frank,#83; 12th/4th in GTO class.
15/06: Brainerd, W. Frank, #03; 13th in GTO class.

1981:
31/01-1/02: Daytona 24-Hours: A. Pallavicini/N. Crang/J. Sheldon, #03; 38th NR.
21/03: Sebring 12-Hours: A. Pallavicini; 69thNR.
26/07: Road America: W. Frank;TA; ?
09/08: Brainerd: W. Frank, TA;?
23/08: Road America: Frank/Bartling, #03;38th/14th in GTO class.
30/08: Mid-Ohio: Frank/Bartling, #03; 19th/12th in GTO class.
06/09: Trois Rivieres: W. Frank TA; ?
12/9: Mosport: W. Frank, TA; ?

1982:
20/03: Sebring 12-Hours: Frank/Madren; DNS.
22/08: Road America: Frank/Bartels; 24th/10th in GTO class.
05/09: Mid-Ohio: Frank/Bartels; 30th/10th in GTO class.
26/09: Pocono: Frank/Bartels, #22; 6th/3rd in GTO class.
28/11: Daytona Finale: Frank/Bartels, #82; 60th/30th in GTO class NR.

1983: Sold to Rick Borlase.
19/06: Mid-Ohio: Frank/Borlase, #83; 12th/4th.
21/08: Road America: Frank/Borlase, #83; 36th/12th.
25/09: Riverside, TA: Borlase; ?
8/10: Caesers Palace, Las Vegas, TA: Borlase; ?

1984:
24/03: Sebring 12-Hours: Borlase/Hammond, #56; 77th/27th in GTO class, NR.
29/04: Riverside 6-Hours: Borlase/Kravig/ Hammond; 14th/.2nd.
06/05: Laguna Seca: Borlase; 32ndin GTO/GTU.
29/07: Portland: Hammond; 30th/13th in GTO NR. Willow Springs: Lap record.

1985:
2-3/02: Daytona 24-Hours: Hammond/Kravig/ Torres, #58; 64th/24th in GTO class, (as a 934).
25/03: Sebring 12-Hours: Borlase/Hammond/Torres, #58; 20th OA/8th in GTO class.
28/04: Riverside: Borlase, #58; 53rd NR/15th in GTO class.
28/07: Portland: Torres; 33rd in GTO/GTU.

1986:
22/03: Sebring 12-Hours: Borlase/Torres, #58; 11th/5th in GTO class.
27/04: Riverside 6-Hours: Borlase/Torres, #58; DNF. (as 930).
NOTE: Jim Torres then drove in the Trans Am series until March 1988 with this car.

1988:Sold to Sid Ho in Switzerland
1990: Sold back to Jim Torres.
Restored by Jim Torres of Burbank
1999: RM Auction, Monterey.
Sold to Stuart Coleman.
2007: (Michael Schafer). Yellow.
2008: Sold to Monte Shelton.
2009: STPO, USA.

Chassis No: 930 670 0163
Production No: 106.3718.
Options: 196.408. 26th car built.
Colour: Orange.
First Owner/Agent: Evertz.

The second 934 sold to German industrialist Egon Evertz, 0163 was driven in 1976 by Hartwig Bertrams who had won the European GT Championship in

1975 in a 1974 RSR Carrera, chassis number 911 460 9067, run by the Tebernum Team of Krefeld.

Bertrams raced this 934, run by the Loos/ Tebernum team, with moderate success until falling out with Evertz; thereafter, his place was taken by Leo Kinnunen.

In 1977, the car was sold to Tetsu Ikuzawa of Japan who raced it to many victories in Japan. In 1979, 0163 was returned to Germany, to the Kremer Brothers in Cologne who transformed the 934 into a K3. Ikuzawa raced the K3 at Le Mans in 1980 but it retired. At the Suzuka 1000Kms of 1981, Bob Wollek and Henri Pescarolo won outright with this K3 after which it was "pensioned off" in Yoshiko Matsuda's collection.

In 1999, 0163 was sold to the Symbolic Motor Car Company in La Jolla, California and it has since been sold. In 2015, it raced at "Rennsport" at Laguna Seca.

Sold to Egon Evertz.

1976: Red w/yellow stripe on roof. Maintained by J. Kannacher.
04/04: Nürburgring 300 Km (EC-GT): Bertrams; #56; 9th OA, 5th in GT.
02/05: Eifelrennen, Nürburgring DRM:Bertrams, #2; DNF.
09/05: Silverstone 6-Hours: Lombardi/Martin, #26; 5th.
23/05: Mainz-Finthen DRM: Bertrams, #23; 6th.
30/05: Nürburgring 1000Km WCM: Lombardi/ Martin/Evertz, #23; DNF. (Acc.)
07/06: Osterreichring: Bertrams; 3rd.
20/06: Rheinpokal Hockenheim DRM Bertrams; 5th.
27/06: Osterreichring 1000 Km: Schmid/ Oppitzhauser, #4; 11th.
25/07: Diepholz DRM: Bertrams, #6; 6th.
01/08: GP von Deutschland, Nürburgring DRM: Bertrams; 3rd.
15/08: Zolder, (not DRM): Schenken; 2nd.
29/08: Preis der Nationen, Hockenheim DRM: Bertrams; 3rd.
12/09: Supersprint Nürburgring DRM: Kinnunen,

#9; 2nd.
26/09: Hockenheim; Kinnunen; 6th.
1977:
20/03: Mugello 6-Hours WCM: Evertz/Kinnunen;
DNA.

1978: Sold to Tetsu Ikuzawa.
29/10: Fuji 500 Miles: Takahara/Ikuzawa, #3; 4th.

Many races and victories in Japan.

1979: Converted to 935 K3 Specification by Kremer
Bros. 930/78-1 engine. 693-0079

1980:
14-15/06: Le Mans 24-Hours: Stommelen/Ikuzawa/
Plankenhorn, #42; DNF.
06/7: Donington: Edwards, #2; 2nd.

1981:
30/08: Suzuka 1000Km: Wollek/Pescarolo, #6; 1st.

Sold to the Matsuda Collection.
1999: For sale in U.S.A. by Symbolic Motor Car Co.
White.
2000: Sold.
2005: For sale: Phil Bagley.
2007: Reno Historic Races: Ransom Webster: 2nd in
Group 3 race.
2015: "Rennsport", Laguna Seca.
2017: Monterey Reunion.

Chassis No: 930 670 0164
Production No: 106.3719.

Options: 196.406. 6th car built.
Colour: Indian Red.
First Owner/Agent: Hubert Striebig.

Raced in three World Championship events in 1976,
this French-entered 934 retired in each race until
coming in a surprise second in class at the Le Mans
24-Hours in June. It bears an "Eminence" sticker in
one window which was the Almeras Brothers sponsor.

 After this, the trail goes hazy until the car was
brought by Matsuda in 1980 and placed in his
museum. Another 934 bought by Symbolic Motors
of La Jolla, 0164 was then sold to RM classics
of Canada. Harry Bytzek, long time owner and
Aficianado of Porsche RSR Carreras, bought the car
in June, 2000 and told the author that it was: "Very
original, seemed to have hardly been used." In 2008,
Your author sold th car to a customer of Manfred
Freisinger and it has since been sold to the UK, in
2011.

Louis Meznarie entered.

1976:
04/04: Vallelunga 6-Hours WCM: Striebig/Verney,

#8; DNF.
09/05: Silverstone 6-Hours WCM: Striebig/ Chasseuil/Verney, #15; DNF.
13-14/06: Le Mans 24-Hours 24-Hours: Race No: 54. Striebig/Verney/Kirschoffer; 11th OA//1st in 4-5 liter/5th in Group 5 Class.

Sold to the Matsuda collection, Japan.
1999: Sold to Symbolic Car Co.
2000: R.M. Auctions. Not sold.
Sold to Harry Bytzek, Canada.
2007: Sold to USA.
2008: Sold by John Starkey to Manfred Freisinger.
2011: Sold to UK.

Chassis No: 930 670 0165
Production No: 106.3720.
Options: 200. 175. 8th car built.
Engine No: 676 2011.
Colour: Indian Red.
First Owner/Agent: Hamilton.

The first Porsche turbocharged 930 to be sold into Australia, this 934 won the Australian Sports Car Championship with it in 1977, 1978 and in 1980, this time uprated with a 934 and a 1/2 engine.

Sold to Norman Hamilton. (Australia).

1977: Allan Hamilton won the Australian Sports Car Championship, (6 x 1 hour races), with this car.
1978: Australian Sports car Champion.
Sold to Allan Moffat

1980: Alan Moffat won the Australian Sports car Championship in the car, this time engined with a 934.5 engine. Engines numbered: 676 2021, (540 bhp) 676 2078 (620 bhp) and 676 2011 are currently with the car.

1981: Sold to Martin Sampson.
1982: Sold to George Parlby.
1983: Sold to Bruce Harris.
2001: Sold to Ian Henderson.

2009: Sold to Larry McFarlane

Chassis No: 930 670 0166
Production No: 106.4445.
Options: 196.418. 9th car built.
Colour: Vaillent Green.
First Owner/Agent: The Kremer Brothers.

Raced by Bob Wollek for the Kremer Brothers in 1976 and 1977, 0166 scored many victories and places. During the second half of 1977, the 934 was used as a "rent a ride" for drivers such as "John Winter" (Louis Krages) of Bremen, Germany who won two second and three third places with it.

After this, 0166 was sold to "Harry Hirsch" (Fritz Engelhardt). "Harry Hirsch" raced the 934 until 1980, mainly in the German Championship, when he sold it to Walter Pauwels of Belgium.

Sold to the Kremer Brothers. Vaillent Sponsored.
1976: German National/European GT Championship:
11/04: Hockenheim: Wollek, #938; 1st.
020/5: Eifelrennen, Nürburgring: Wollek, #6; 3rd.
23/05: Mainz-Finthen: Wollek, #9; 1st.
07/06: Zeltweg (EC-GT): Wollek; 2nd.
20/06: Rheinpokal Hockenheim: Wollek, #6; 2nd.
27/06: Norisring, Nurnberg: Wollek, #6, DRM; 1st.
25/07: Diepholz: Wollek, #1; DNF, Acc.
01/08: GP von Deutschland: Nürburgring: Wollek;

DNF, Acc.

290/8: Preis der Nationen, Hockenheim: Wollek, #103; 2nd.

04/09: Dijon 6-Hours WCM: Joest/Barth/Wollek; 8th/1st class.

12/09: Supersprint, Nürburgring: Wollek; 3rd.

19/09: Imola (EC-GT): Wollek, #9; 1st.

26/09: Preis von Hessen: Wollek, #4; 1st.

10/10: Nürburgring: Wollek; 1st.

31/10: Hockenheim: (EC-GT):Wollek, #6; 4th.

1977:

0/1: Track tested by Bernd Renneisen for German magazine: "Rallye and Racing".

German National Championship.

17/04: Jim Clark Rennen, Hockenheim: Wollek, #491; 1st.

08/05: Kassel-Calden, (DRM); Renneisen, #75; DNF.

22/05: Mainz-Finthen, (DRM): Haehnlein, #70; DNF.

11-12/06: Le Mans 24-Hours 24-Hours: Wollek/'Steve'/Gurdjian, #58; 7th OA/1st in G.T. Class.

24/07: Diepholz: (National race): Krages, ('John Winter'); 2nd.

07/08: Mainz-Finthen: Krages; 2nd.

21/08: Kassel-Calden: Krages, #123; 2nd.

18/09: Ulm-Mengen: Krages; 3rd.

2/10: Supersprint Nürburgring: Schaefer, #71; 9th.

16/10: Zolder: Krages; 3rd.

06/11: Rheintalrennen Hockenheim; Krages; 3rd.

1978: Sold to Raymond Raus of Belgium.

09/07 Nivelles: Raymond Raus, #70, 4th OA

13/08 Nivelles: Raymond Raus, 2nd OA

10/09 Coupes d'avenir, Zolder: Raymond Raus, 2nd OA

17/09 Zandvoort: Raymond Raus, 4th OA
Dakar 6-Hours?

1979

01/04 Zolder: Raymond Raus, 3rd OA

10-11/6: Le Mans 24 Hours: A-C. Verney/R.

Metge/P. Bardinon, #84; 19th OA/3rd Gr.4.
Perhaps:

1979:

22/04: Dijon 1000Km: Ennequin/Bourdillat; DNF. Alain Michel Bernard entry.

9-10/06: Le Mans 24-Hours: Bourdillat/Ennequin/ Bernard, #86; 16th OA/2nd in Group 4.

05/08: Brands Hatch 6-Hours: Bourdillat/Ennequin, #11; 19th.

16/09: Vallelunga 6-Hours: Bourdillat/Ennequin/ Roland, #56; DNF.

1980:

14-15/06: Le Mans 24-Hours: Bourdillat/Ennequin/ Bernard, #90; 24th.

28/09: Dijon 1000Kms: R. Ennequin /G. Bourdillat/P. Alliot, #27; 14th OA/3rd Gr.4.

Sold to Belgian "Alex" (= Paul De Kock)
Note: "Alex" raced a Turbo-Porsche in 1979, which is described as a 930. Maybe it was this 934. "Alex" was killed in an accident and the car was later sold by his widow to Walter Pauwels.

Chassis No: 930 670 0167
Production No: 106. 4446.
Options: 200.176. 11th car built.
Colour: Orange.
First Owner/Agent: Max Moritz.

Painted in the well known "Jaegermeister" colours, 0167 was driven by Rheinhard Stenzel in 1976 after he had campaigned a 1974 RSR Carrera, chassis number 911 460 9060 during 1974 and 1975.

Stenzel gained several second, third and fourth places before selling the car to Gianpiero Moretti who won the Italian GT Championship with it and took in just three World Championship events in 1977 with it before selling it on in 1978 as he had now acquired a 935.

In 1978, 0167 appears to have done only one race, that at the Nürburgring 1000Kms, with Edgar Doren and Gerhard Holup. They failed to finish.

After this, 0167 was one of the many 934's sold

to Chet Vincentz who raced it in IMSA events in
1979 through 1981.
Sold to Max Moritz. (No:2).
Jaegermeister sponsored car.

1976: German National and European GT
Championship:
04/04: Nürburgring 300Km: Stenzel, #54; 6th OA/
4th in EC-GT race.
11/04: Hockenheim: Stenzel, #932: DNF (off road).
02/05: Eifelrennen, Nürburgring: Stenzel, #14; 2nd.
23/05: Mainz-Finthen: Stenzel, #2; 3rd.
30/05: Nürburgring 1000Km: Bell/Steckonig/
Stenzel, #24; 10th.
20/06: Rheinpokal, Hockenheim: Stenzel; 4th.
27/06: Norisring, Nurnberg EC-GT: Stenzel, #4;
2nd.
25/07: Diepholz: Stenzel, #7; 3rd.
01/08: Nürburgring: Stenzel, #2; DNF (driveshaft).
29/08: Preis der Nationen, Hockenheim: Stenzel;
DNF.(turbo).
05/09: Monza 6-Hours EC-GT: Bell/Kelleners/
Stenzel; DNF. (Turbo).
12/09: S/sprint, Nürburgring: Stenzel, #5; DNF.
(drivebelt).
19/09: Imola, (EC-GT): Stenzel; DNF. (Turbo).
26/09: Preis von Hessen: Stenzel, #9; 3rd
31/10: Hockenheim (EC-GT): Stenzel, #4; 15th.

1977: Sold to G. Moretti.
15/05: Silverstone 6-Hours WCM: Moretti/
Brambilla, #9; 7th.
12-16/6: Giro d'Italia:
24/07: Paul Ricard 500Km WCM: Moretti/Schoen,
#46; 14th.
05/09: Monza, Coppa Intereuropa:
23/10: Vallelunga 6-Hours WCM: Moretti/Schoen,
#5; DNF.

1979: Sold to C. Vincentz.
26/08: Mid-Ohio: Vincentz/White; 20thNR.
23/09: Road Atlanta 100 Miles: Vincentz, #32;
26th/13th in GTO class, NR.
1980: IMSA Championship Races.

13/04: Road Atlanta: Vincentz, #32; 29th/14th in
GTO class, NR.
04/07: Daytona:Jamsal/Barrientos, #32; 17th
Rented??
06/07: Watkins Glen 6-Hours WCM: Vincentz; 18th
OA,1st in Gp 4.
21/09: Road Atlanta 50 Miles, Heat One: #32;
27th/13th in GTO class.

1981:
31/05: Mid-Ohio: C. Vincentz/L. Van Every, #91;
22nd/6th in GTO class.
16/08: Mosport: C. Vincenz/D. Bell, #91; 21st/8th in
GTO class.
30/08: Mid-Ohio: C. Vincentz/J. Wood, #91; 7th/3rd
in GTO Class.
27/09: Pocono: C. Vincentz, #91; 34th/ /7th GTO,
NR.

Restored.
2001: Still with Chester Vincentz.
2006: Sold to Jim Edwards, USA.

Chassis No: 930 670 0168
Production No: 106. 4447.
Options: 196.412. 12th car built.
Colour: Orange

First Owner: Max Moritz. (No:3).

Both this car and 0167 were first of all sold through the Max Moritz dealership of Reutlingen, Germany. Whatever, 0168, (or 0167), was driven by Helmut Kelleners to win the Eifelrennen at the Nürburgring in 1976 before being uprated to 934/5 specification and being driven in the German Championship by Edgar Doren in 1977. Edgar Doren, (another previous Porsche Carrera racer in 1976, racing the Kremer built 005 0005), attracted Jaegermeister sponsorship and had the 934/5 brought up to full 935 specification. Doren then raced the car for the next two seasons, sometimes co-driving with original owner, Gerhard Holup. Edgar Doren won the 1979 Group 4 Class of the German Championship.

1976: Jagermeister sponsored.
04/04: Nürburgring 300Km: Kelleners, 53; 3rd. (EC-GT): Kelleners, #53; 2nd.
11/04: Hockenheim: Kelleners, #931; 2nd.
02/05: Eifelrennen Nürburgring DRM: Kelleners, #12; 1st..
23/05: Mainz-Finthen DRM: Kelleners, #1; DNS (acc).
30/05: Nürburgring 1000Km WCM: Bell/Kelleners/Stenzel, #25; 3rd OA.
20/06: Hockenheim: Kelleners; 3rd.
27/06: Norisring Nurnberg, (EC-GT): Kelleners, #5; 3rd. DRM: 7th.
04/07: Trento Bondone EHC: Kelleners; 2nd in class B.
25/07: Diepholz: Kelleners; 5th
01/08: GP Deutschland, Nürburgring DRM: Kelleners, #3; 2nd.
29/08: Hockenheim: Kelleners; DNF.
05/09: Monza 6-Hours (EC-GT): Kelleners/Stenzel/Bell; 3rd.
12/09: Supersprint, Nürburgring DRM: Kelleners; 4th.
19/09: Imola (EC-GT): Kelleners; 3rd.
26/09: Preis von Hessen, Hockenheim, DRM: Kelleners; 5th.
31/10: Hockenheim: (EC-GT): Kelleners; 6th.

1977: German National Championship. Uprated to 934/5 specification. Valvoline/Romulus Sponsored. Entered by Max Moritz Racing.
13/03: Bergischer Lowe Zolder: Doren, #53; 6th.
27/03: 300Km Nürburgring: Doren, #53; 5th.
01/05: Eifelrennen, Nürburgring: Doren, #53; 5th.
08/05: Kassel-Calden: Doren, #53; 4th.
22/05: Mainz-Finthen: Doren, #53; 7th.
29/05: Nürburgring 1000Km WCFM: Doren/Barth, #8; 13th.
03/07: Norisring, Nurnberg: Doren, #53; (Trophy Race); 6th. DRM: 6th.
24/07: Diepholz: Doren,#53; DNF.
30/07: G.P. von Deutschland, Hockenheim: Doren, #53; DNF, (Turbo).
14/08: Westfalen-Pokal, Zolder: Doren, #53; 4th.
11/09: Schwabische Alb, (hillclimb): Doren, #230; 2nd.
18/09: Ulm-Mengen G4: Doren; 1st.
2/10: Superprint, Nürburgring: Doren, #53; DNF, (turbo).
9/10: Hockenheim 6 Hours: (2 x 3-Hours): Doren/Schimpf/Holup; 7th.

Sold to Arabia.

184

Chassis No: 930 670 0169
Production No: 106. 3959.
Options: 200.177. 14th car built.
Colour: Indian Red.
First Owner/Agent: Girolamo Capra/Boldrin.

Sold to Girolama Capra and run by the Scuderia Brescia Corse, 0169 took part in World and Italian Championship races in 1976, 77 and 78.

1976: Scuderia Brescia Corse car.
21/03: Mugello 6-Hours WCM: Lepri/Gottifredi/ Capra, #9; 7th.
04/04: Vallelunga 6-Hours WCM: Gottifredi/Capra/ Parpinelli, #9; 7th.
02/05: Trofeo Ufficiall Gara; Capra.
09/05: Coppa Aci Verona: Capra.
16/05: Targa Florio: Capra.
30/05: Nürburgring 1000Km WCM: Capra/ Gottifredi/Parpinelli, #11; 17th.
27/06: Osterreichring: Capra/Gottifredi, #10; 5th.
01/08: Misano (EC-GT): Capra; 5th.
22/08: Coppa aci Padova: Capra.
04/09: Dijon 6-Hours WCM: Lepri/Capra/Gottifredi, #49; DNF.
19/09: Imola (EC-GT): Capra; 6th.

1977:
20/03: Mugello 6-Hours WCM: Capra/Gottifredi, #11; DNF.
15/05: Silverstone 6-Hours WCM: Capra/Gottifredi/ Cogato, #14;12th.
29/05: Nürburgring 1000Km WCM: Capra/ Gottifredi/Cogato, #14; 19th. Citta dei Mille entry.
10/07: Trofeo Mare Pulito, Misano: Capra; RU.
17/07: Coppa aci Padova: Capra; RU.
06/08: Nürburgring: Capra/Gottifredi; 2nd OA, 1st in class.
20/08: Misano by night: Capra RU.
04/09: Coppa Intereuropa, Monza: Capra; RU.
25/09: Brands Hatch 6-Hours WCM: Gottifredi/ Capra/"Archimede"; 13th. Citta dei Mille entry.
23/10: Vallelunga 6-Hours WCM: Haldi/Capra/ Gottifredi; DNF.

1978:
19/03: Mugello 6-Hours WCM; Gioia/Capra, #5; DNF.
25/06: Misano 6-Hours WCM: Capra/Gottifredi/ Gioia, #25; 9th.
03/09: Vallelunga 6-Hours WCM: Gottifredi/Capra/ Gioia, #23; 13th.

1980? Sold to Loris Ruggi.

1981: Possibly:
26/04: Monza 1000Kms: G. Gottifredi/G. Galimberti/G. Rebai, #7; 9th OA. 4th Gr.5.

Chassis Number: 930 670 0170
Production Number: 106. 4261.
Options: 196. 413. 13th car built.
Colour: Black.
First Owner/Agent: Sold to Auct-Porsche, Madrid.

Little is known about this 934 apart from the fact that it was owned for many years by Dr Lazcano.

1978: Sold through Giuseppi Risi to the USA.
1997: Featured in the Japanese magazine: "Rennsport"

Chassis No: 930 670 0171
Production No: 106. 3958. 27th car built.
Colour: Indian Red.
First Owner/Agent: Georg Loos.

Jürgen Barth at the factory has confirmed that this car had first been sold to Georg Loos of "GELO" race team fame. Jürgen Barth further confirmed that the car had placed second in class at the 24 Hours of Le Mans, after which it had been sold to the noted Swiss privateer, Claude Haldi.
    Haldi raced 0171 in World Championship and European Championship races and European Hillclimb events in 1976 and 1977, keeping it in "standard" 934 form, as it is listed as being in the GT class, rather than in the uprated Group 5 class.
    Afterwards, in 1978, Claude Haldi sold it to

"Jamsal", (Enrique Molins), of San Salvador, as Haldi had by then bought himself a 935. "Jamsal" had the car converted to 935 twin-turbo form immediately and raced it in North America in IMSA and South America until 1981. In 1978, it won the 6 Hours of El Salvador, which gave Don Whittington a World Champion title.

Later, in around 1980, Molins had the car rebodied in it's current form with K3/M13 bodywork by Chuck Gaa in Florida and fitted with the Andial built flat fan twin plug engine it now has. It was later on sold, via Dick Fritz, in 1989 to the USA and it passed through several owners until, in 2005, yours author found it and brokered it to the current owner, who undertook a no-holds-barred complete strip down and restoration, which included:

3.2 litre engine rebuilt by Dick Elverude with Carillo rods, new bearings, pistons, barrels.

New air-to-air Intercooler system.

Upside down gearbox rebuilt with all new bearings.

Chassis blasted and re painted.

Fuel cell rebuilt.

All suspension dis-assembled, crack tested, new wheel bearings fitted.

Brakes stripped, inspected, new caliper seals fitted.

Wiring completely renewed.

All re-assembled, re-painted as the car last ran in 1981.

New Ti axles and Guibo joints.

By 2006, the car was in superb condition and ready to race. It was exhibited and practiced at that year's Monterey Historics at Laguna Seca. Since then it has changed hands twice more in the USA.

1976: Red.
21/3: Mugello 6 Hours: T. Schenken/R. Stommelen, #18; 6th/2nd GT-FQ.
30/5: Nürburgring 1000Km WCM: T. Schenken/T. Hezemans, #6; 2nd OA.
12-13/6: Le Mans 24 Hours: T.Hezemans/T. Schenken, #57; 16th/2nd in GT class.

Sold to Claude Haldi.
27/06: Zeltweg 1000Km WCM: Haldi/Zbinden, #5; 3rd OA/1st in GT. GVEA-entered.
04/07: Trento Bondone: (EHC): Haldi; DNS.
25/07: Diepholz DRM: Haldi; 4th.
08/08: Mont Dore, (EHC): Haldi; DNF. (Acc.)
29/08: Andorra-Botella (EHC): Haldi; 1st in class.
04/09: Dijon 6-Hours WCM: Haldi/Muller, #11; 5th OA.
12/09: Nürburgring DRM: Haldi; DNF.
19/09: Imola, (EC-GT): Haldi; 5th.
26/09: Preis von Hessen Hockenheim (DRM): Haldi; 8th.
31/10: Hockenheim: Haldi; 5th.

1977:
20/03: Mugello 6 Hours WCM: Haldi / Ferrier / Mueller, # 7; 7th/4th GT
27/03: Ampus-Draguignan (EHC): Hldi; 2nd.
17/05: Silverstone 6 Hours WCM: Haldi / Joest / Ferrier, # 10; 8th 2nd GT
22/05: Montseny EHC: Haldi; 2nd
29/05: Nürburgring 1000 KM WCM: Haldi / Joest, #32; 7th/1st GT
11-12/06: Le Mans 24 Hours: F.Servanin/ F. Hummel/ L. Ferrier, # 59; DNF. (Gear Box).
03/07: Norisring DRM: Haldi, # 80; 7th
03/07: Norisring Trophae: Haldi, # 80; 18th

10/07: Trento Bondone EHC: Haldi ; 3rd
24/07: Paul Ricard WCM: Haldi/Ferrier, #42; 10th.
31/07: Coll de la Botella EHC: Haldi; ?
07/08: Mont Dore EHC: Haldi ; 2nd
25/09: Brands Hatch 6 Hours WCM: Haldi / Pallavicini, # 9; 6th/1st GT
8-9/10: Hockemheim 2x3 Hours: Haldi / Pallavicini /Calderari , #10; 10th 3rd GT
23/10: Vallelunga 6 Hours WCM: Haldi / Pallavicini , #9; GT DNS
27/10: Ampus-Draguignan EHC: Haldi; 2nd.

1978:
21-28/01: Monte-Carlo Rallye: C.Haldi / B. Sandoz, # 9; Grp 4 DNF (Clutch).
16/04: Dijon 4 Hours: Gehard Vial / Antoine Salamin, # 30; 14th/ 7th GT
14/05: Silverstone 6 Hours: Haldi/Bleynie/ Delaunay / Guerin, # 28; DNF
28/05: Nürburgring 1000 KMS: Haldi / Gehard Vial, # 61; GT DNA
10-11/06: Le Mans 24-Hours: De Latour/Bleiny/ Ennequin, #60; DNQ.

Sold to Enrique Molins, Salvador. Scorpio Racing. Raced in South America. By now converted to 934/5 spec.

Round 6: Central American Championship of Makes Guatemala "Jamsal" 1st
500 kms of Viceroy "Jamsal" 1st.
500Kms of Rio Hato "Jamsal" 1st.
500KMs of Panama "Jamsal" 1st.

5/11: Trans-Am Mexico City: "Jamsal" 181 10th/6th

1979
1979: National Championship of Motoring El Jababli: "Jamsal" 1st Modified Tourism
?/02: Great Delta Prize, El Jabali Jamsal: 2nd J.Paul 1st Modified Tourism
?/07: National Championship of Motoring: "Jamsal"; DNA Modified Tourism
21/10: El Salvador 6 Hour:t "Jamsal" / Bill

Whittington / Don Whittington, # 81; 1st Grp 5+3.0 Don Whitting. World Endurance Drivers Championship
1980:
04/07: Daytona 250 Mile "Paul Revere": "Jamsal" Barrientos,#32; 17th /6th GTX

1981:
31/1-1/02: Daytona 24 Hours: "Jamsal" / Barrientos / Valiente# 84 8th 4th GTX
21/03: Sebring 12 Hours: "Jamsal" / Barrientos 84 26th 8th GTX
26/04: Riverside 6 Hours: "Jamsal" / Barrientos 84 35th 12th GTX DNF
05/07: Daytona 250 Mile: "Jamsal" / Barrientos 84 23rd 8th GTX NR
16/08: Mosport 6 Hours: "Jamsal" / Galdamez 84 10th 7th GTX
23/08: Road America 500 Mile: "Jamsal" / Erstad / Galdamez 84 32nd 11th GTX

1989: Sold to Dick Fritz from Scorpio Racing, Salvador. Red/Yellow.
Sold to Jan Jablowski.
1991: Sold to Frank Gallogly. Kerry Morse had it painted White.
1992: Sold to Gunnar Racing.
1994: Sold to Bill Ferran. White. $125,000. Needs restoration.
2005: Sold to John Starkey.
2006: Sold to Van Zannis.
Sold to present owner, completely restored.

Chassis No: 930 670 0172
Production No: 106. 4258.
Options: 185-251. 16th car built.
Colour: White.
First Owner/Agent: R. Leder.

Richard Leder was a German driver who had raced both 1973, (chassis number 911 360 0791), and 1974 RSR Carreras, (chassis number 911 460 9095), before buying 0172 for 1976 and winning at Kassel Calden and the Avus. Sadly, shortly after the Nürburgring 1000 kilometre race in May, he was killed in a road accident and 0172 was then sold to Volkert Merl who won with it at Ulm.

Merl had 0172 brought up to 934/5 specification over the winter of 1976/77 and was always up with the leaders, except when the car failed. Merl joined with Franz Konrad for 1978 and 0172 was sold, in 1979, to Pierre Schaerer for him and Peter Zbinden to drive.

1976 German National Championship.
11/04: Hockenheim, (not DRM): Leder; 6th.
25/04: Sylt, (not DRM): Leder; 3rd.
02/05: Eifelrennen, Nürburgring: Leder, #11; 9th.
09/05: Kassel Calden: Leder; 1st.
23/05: Avus, (not DRM): Leder; 1st.
30/05: Nürburgring 1000Km WCM: Zanuso/Leder, #10; DNF. (Acc.)
Sold to Volkert Merl.

15/08: Zandvoort: Merl; 2nd. Int. Race; 4th.
22/08: Kassel-Calden: Merl, #6; 5th.
29/08: Preis der Nationen, Hockenheim: Merl; DNF.
12/09: Ulm: Merl; 1st.
26/09: Preis von Hessen, Hockenheim: Merl; DNF.

1977: 934/5 specification.
13/03: Bergischer Lowe, Zolder: Merl, #60; DNF.
17/04: Hockenheim: Merl; 3rd in G4 race.
24/04: Sylt: Merl; 2nd in G4 race.
08/05: Kassel-Calden, (DRM): Merl; DNS.
22/05: Avus: Merl; 1st.
12/06: Wunstorf: (G4 + 3000 cc): Merl; DNF. (Tyre).
03/07: Norisring Nurnberg: Merl, (DRM), #60; DNF.
24/07: Diepholz: Merl, #60; 4th.
30/07: GP von Deutschland, Hockenheim: Merl, #60; 7th.
21/08: Kassel-Calden: Merl; DNF.
18/09: Ulm-Mengen; Merl; 2nd.
25/09: Brands Hatch 6-Hours WCM: Merl/Hahnlein, #5; DNF. Kremer entry.
1978: Uprated to 935 specification.

4-5/02: Daytona 24-Hours WCM: Konrad/Joest/Merl, #21; 13th.
12/03: Bergischer Lowe Zolder: Merl, #16; 7th.
02/04: 300 km Nürburgring: Merl, #16; 7th.
30/04: Eifelrennen Nürburgring: Merl, #16; 6th.
21/05: Avus-Rennen Berlin: Merl, #16; DNF. (engine).
30/05: Nürburgring 1000Km WCM: Merl/Konrad/Schreiber, #12; 4th.
18/06: Mainz-Finthen: Merl, #16; DNF. Acc.
02/07: Zandvoort-Trophy: Merl, #16; 5th.

Sold to P. Schaerer.

1980:
16/03: Hockenheim: Zbinden; 1st.
13/07: Bavaria-Rennen Salzburgring: P. Schaerer; 15th.
03/08: Ayent-Azerre: Zbinden; 2nd.
17/08: Nordzee-Cup Zandvoort: P. Schaerer; 2nd.
19/10: Hockenheim 3-Hours: Wiili/Zbinden; 1st.

1981: 934/5.
22/03: Hockenheim: P. Schaerer; 2nd.
19/04: Dijon, (Swiss Championship): P. Schaerer; 8th/4th in class.
10/05: Dijon, (Swiss Championship): P. Schaerer;

6th/4th in class.
07/06: Misano: (Swiss Championship): P. Schaerer; 5th/3rd in class.
12/07: Hockenheim: (Swiss Championship): P. Schaerer; 8th/5th in class.
01/08: AvD Gold-Pokal, Hockenheim, (DRM): P. Schaerer, #68; DNF.
09/08: Ayent-Azerre: (Swiss Championship): P. Schaerer; 11th/4th in class.
23/08: St. Ursannes: P. Schaerer; 4th.
06/09: La Roche La Berra: (Swiss Championship): P. Schaerer; 7th/5th.
13/09: Gurnigel: (Swiss Championship): P. Schaerer; 10th/6th.

1982: Sold to Peter Baumann, Switzerland.

Chassis No: 930 670 0173
Production No: 106. 4259.
Options: 196. 409. 19th car built.
Colour: Sunoco Blue.
First Owner/Agent: George Dickinson/Al Holbert.

George Dickinson had owned a 1974 RSR Carrera, chassis number 911 460 9056, with which Al Holbert had won the 1976 Sebring 12-Hour race. Dickinson bought 0173 for Holbert to race in the Trans Am series as the turbocharged Porsches were not allowed to race in IMSA events until late 1976. Although Holbert had quite a good year, George Follmer was unstoppable in Vasek Polak's 934, winning the series. Although this 934 did not race much, it was driven on the road (with a dealer plate!) by Doc Bundy. It was then sold to someone in Pennsylvania, but never raced.

In 1979, the 934 was sold to R.D Whittington, father of Don and Bill, and then stored.

1976: Trans-Am series.
09/05: Pocono: Holbert, #14; 2nd.
30/05: Nelson Ledges: Holbert; 32nd NR, (engine).
10/07: Watkins Glen 6-Hours: Holbert/Busby, #14; 16th.
24/07: Road America: Holbert; 4th.

15/08: Brainerd: Bundy; DNS.
21/08: Mosport: Holbert; 2nd.
29/08: Mid-Ohio: (IMSA Race):G. Follmer/Bundy, #6; 14th OA.
05/09: Trois Rivieres TA: Holbert; 2nd.

1977: Brought up to 934 1/2 specification.
28/08: Mid-Ohio 3-Hours: Bundy/Woods, #44; 8th OA.
Sold to Pennsylvania.
Sold to R.D. Whittington.

1978:
02/04: Talladega 6-Hours: R.D. Whittington; DNS.

1979:
04/02: Daytona 24 Hours WCM: R.D./Dale Whittington/Henn, #93; 29th.
17/03: Sebring 12-Hours: Dale & R.D. Whittington/M. Minter, #92; 44thNR.

2017: In Arizona, USA.

Chassis No: 930 670 0174
Production No: 106. 4260.

Options: 185. 242. 22nd car built.
Colour: White.

First Owner/Agent: Vasek Polak.
Sold to Vasek Polak, the Californian Porsche dealer in Hermosa Beach, California, 0174, "First National City Travellers Cheques"-sponsored, was the car driven by George Follmer to win the 1976 TransAm Championship.

After just a few more races, the 934 was stored in Vasek Polak's fantastic collection of racing Porsches until his death, after which it was sold to the Austrian enthusiast, Ottokar von Jacobs.
.

1976: Trans Am.
09/05: Pocono:G. Follmer, #16; 3rd.
30/05: Nelson Ledges:G. Follmer, #16; 1st.
13/06: Rose Cup, Portland:G. Follmer, #16; 32nd NR.
10/07: Watkins Glen 6-Hours:G. Follmer/Morton, #16; Crash in practice; T car; 11th.
24/07: Road America:G. Follmer, #16; 2nd.
15/08: Brainerd:G. Follmer, #16; 2nd.
21/08: Mosport:G. Follmer, #16; 3rd.
05/09: Trois Rivieres:G. Follmer, #16; 1st.
9/10: Laguna Seca: IMSA:G. Follmer, #16; 9th.

1977:
01/05: Laguna Seca: Follmer, #16; 3rd.
Uprated to 935 Spec?

IMSA Camel GT:
29/08: Mid-Ohio 6-Hour:G. Follmer/Bundy; 14th.
3/10: Laguna Seca:Follmer #3 ; 37th.

1998: Sold to Austria.
2000: Daytona HSR race: O. von Jacobs.

Chassis No: 930 670 0175
Production No: 106. 3960.
Options: 200. 186. 20th car built.
Colour: Indian Red.
First Owner/Agent: Georg Loos.

The second Georg Loos' owned 934, 0175 was driven in the European GT Championship by Toine Hezemans who won the series outright for the Loos/Tebernum team. After this, Peter Gregg, head of the Brumos Racing Team of Jacksonville, Florida, bought it and, with Jim Busby, raced it at the Daytona 24-Hour race of 1977 where they placed tenth after being well up at the beginning of the race. After this, 1t was sold to Gary Belcher who ran it in 1977 and 1978 before it was sold to Colombia. Today, the car is back in the U.S. with 935 K3 style bodywork.

1976: Sold to Sold to Gelo-Racing Team. Guards Red.
21/03: Mugello 6-Hours WCM: Stommelen/Schenken, #18; 6th.
04/04: Nürburgring 300 Km: (EC-GT) Hezemans, #51; 1st.
25/04: Sylt, (Not DRM): Stommelen, #111; 2nd.
02/05: Eifelrennen, Nürburgring DRM: Hezemans, #3; 4th.
23/05: Mainz-Finthen: Schenken, #5; 2nd.
30/05: Nürburgring 1000Km WCM: Schenken/Hezemans, #6; 2nd OA.
07/06: Osterreichring, (EC-GT): Hezemans; 1st.
13-14/06: Le Mans 24-Hours: Gelo entered: Hezemans/Schenken; #57; 16th OA.
20/06: Hockenheim DRM: Hezemans, #7; 1st.
27/06: Norisring (EC-GT): Hezemans; 1st.(DRM); 11th.

25/07: Diepholz: Hezemans, #2; 1st.
01/08: GP von Deutschland, Nürburgring DRM: #24; Hezemans; 1st.
05/09: Monza 6-Hours EC-GT: Hezemans/ Schenken/Ludwig, #1; 1st.
12/09: Nürburgring DRM: T. Schenken/T. Hezemans. #21; DNF.
19/09: Imola (EC-GT): Hezemans, #2; 20th.
26/09: Preis von Hessen, Hockenheim DRM: Hezemans, #7; 2nd.
31/10: Hockenheim: (EC-GT) Hezemans, #1; 1st.

Hezemans' European GT Championship winning car, Race No: 1 at the Norisring.

Sold to Jim Busby.
28/11: Daytona: Busby, #61; 37th NR.

1977:
5-6/02: Daytona 24-Hours: J. Busby/P. Gregg, #61; 10th OA.

Sold to Gary Belcher.

19/03: Sebring 12-Hours: Belcher/J. Gunn, #09; 4th OA.
17/04: Road Atlanta: Belcher, #09; 27th NR.
01/05: Laguna Seca: Becher, #09; 40th NR.
15/05: Mid-America: Belcher, #09; 5th.
30/05: Lime Rock: Belcher, #09; 31st NR.
04/07: Daytona: Belcher, #09; 3rd.
10/07: Watkins Glen: Belcher/Woods, #09; 15th.
14/08: Pocono: Belcher, #09; 6th.
28/08: Mid-Ohio: Belcher, #09;31st NR.
05/09: Road Atlanta: Belcher, #09; 10th.
9/10: Laguna Seca: Belcher, #09; 20th.
5/11: Mexico City TA: Belcher, #09; DNS.
28/11: Daytona Finale: J. Busby, #09; 37th NR. (Flywheel came off).

1978:
3-4/02: Daytona 24-Hours: Bundy/Belcher/Holbert, #09; 6th NR.
18/03: Sebring 12-Hours: Belcher/Bundy, #09; 40th

NR.
26/11: Daytona: Belcher, #09; 46th NR. Acc.
NOTE: The car was repaired, using the front from a 911.(911 620 0385).

1979: Converted to 935 spec.
17/03: Sebring 12-Hours: R. Londono/G. Garces/J. Gunn, #97; 50th NR.
25/11: Daytona: R. Londono, #92; 18th NR.

Sold to Colombia.
2000: Seized by U.S. Customs.
2001: Sold to Tod Ziebko.
2004: Ebay; $1.5M.

Chassis No: 930 670 0176
Production No: 106. 4448.
Options: ? 23rd car built.
Colour: White.
First Owner/Agent: Vasek Polak, (3).

The third car delivered to Vasek Polak, this 934 was raced very little. It was sold through the well known Ferrari dealer, Ron Spangler. It has changed hands very few times since then.

1976: Sold to a Porsche dealer, Paul Miller,
Pocono TA: Miller; 6th.
Nelson Ledges TA: Miller; 6th.
03/07: Watkins Glen 6-Hours: K./P. Miller; 13th
OA/3rd in class.

Sold to Ron Spangler.

1981: Sold to a collector in Connecticut
Sold to Chuck Kendall.
Sold To Jamie Mazotta.
Sold to Joe Wong.
Sold to the Blackhawk collection.
Sold to Byron Madsen.
STPO.

Chassis No: 930 670 0177
Production No: 106.4619. 24th car built.
Colour: White.
First Owner/Agent: Sonauto.

Sold to ASA Cachia, this 934 raced at Le Mans
in 1976 after which it went through the hands of
several French owners and then went to Germany.
Along the way, it was entered into several World
Championship races.

1976: Red/Blue/White.
12-13/6: Le Mans 24-Hours: J-C Andruet/H.
Cachia/J.Borras, #61; 26th OA, N.C.
04/9: Dijon 6-Hours WCM: C. Ballot-Lena/J.
Borras, #61; 11th OA/2nd Group 4.

1977:
15/5: Silverstone 6-Hours: C. Ballot-Lena/J-L
Laffose/P.Dagoreau, #12; 13th OA/4th in Group 4.
11-12/6: Le Mans 24-Hours: C.Grandet/J-L.
Bousquet/P. Dagoreau, #56; 19th OA/4th in Group
4. JMS entry. (Painted Black/Red).

1978: Sold to Daniel Urcun. Painted black/white.
10-11/6: Le Mans 24-Hours: G. Chasseuil/J-C
Lefevre, #61; DNF.

1979:
18/3: Mugello 6 Hours: G. Bourdillat/A-M. Bernard,
#58; DNF. (Acc.)
22/4: Dijon 1000Km: R. Ennequin/G.Bourdillat;
DNF. Alain Michel Bernard entry.
9-10/6: Le Mans 24-Hours: G.Bourdillat/R.Ennequin/
A-M.Bernard, #86; 16th OA/2nd in Group 4.
05/8: Brands Hatch 6-Hours: G.Bourdillat/R.
Ennequin, #11; 19th.
16/9: Vallelunga 6-Hours: G.Bourdillat/R.Ennequin,
#56; DNF.

1980:
14-15/6: Le Mans 24-Hours: G. Bourdillat/R.
Ennequin/Bernard, #90; 24th.
29/9: Dijon 1000Kms: R. Ennequin/P. Alliot/A-M
Bernard, #27; 14th.

1981: Sold to Valentin Bertapelle.
14-15/6: 24 Hrs Le Mans: V. Bertapelle/T. Perrier/B.
Salam, #70; 17th.
Rallye du Rhin: Valentin Bertapelle (F).
Rallye des Vosges: Valentin Bertapelle (F).
Course de cote de Fouchy #517: Valentin Bertapelle
(F).

1984: Sold to Manfred Freisinger.
2008: 24h of Le Mans Classic #24, finished 30th in plateau 6.
Drivers: Manfred Freisinger (G), Stephane Ortelli (F).

2010: Sold to Gerald Harrison, UK.
2012: Sold to Dr. U. Schumacher, Germany.
2016: Sold to Kobus Cantrane.

Chassis No: 930 670 0178
Production No: 106.4620. 25th car built.
Colour: White.
First Owner/Agent: Schiller.

0178 was sold to Gerd Schiller who had it raced by Claude Haldi and Florian Vetsch at Le Mans and Dijon. In 1977, the 934 was raced in several World Championship events and crashed in practice at the end of the season.

Sold to Angelo Pallavicini, this car then succeeded in winning its class outright at Le Mans in 1979, coming in fourth overall.

Rented to Vittorio Coggiola in 1982, it was driven to second overall in the Italian GT Championship.

1976:
Possibly some hillclimbs.

13-14/06: Le Mans 24-Hours: Schiller racing entered. Haldi/Vetsch. DNF. Race No: 69.
04/09: Dijon 6-Hours WCM: Vetsch/Cheneviere, #15; 13th.

1977: DeLaunay?
03/04 Le Castellet: Schiller, 1st in class
11-12/06: Le Mans 24-Hours; Schiller entry: Haldi/Vetsch/Pallavicini, #60; DNF.
24/07: Paul Ricard 500 Kms: Haldi/Ferrier, #42; 19th OA/2nd in Group 5?
04/09 Dijon: Schiller, 2nd in class

Sold to Angelo Pallavicini.

1978:
18/03: Mugello 6-Hours: Pallavicini/Vanoli/R. Cescato, #52; DNS.
22/04: Dijon 1000Km WCM: Pallavicini/Vanoli, #51; 11th.

1979:
06/05: Silverstone 6-Hours WCM: Pallavicini/Vanoli, #22; DNF.
9-10/06: Le Mans 24-Hours: Muller/Pallavicini/Vanoli, #82; 4th OA, 1st in Group 4 class.
29/07: GP von Deutschland, Hockenheim: Pallavicini; 7th.
23/09: Supersprint, Nürburgring: Pallavicini, #80; 12th.

1980:
16/03: Brands Hatch 6-Hours WCM: Pallavacini/Muller, #26; 8th OA.
11/05: Avus-Rennen, Berlin: Pallavicini; 1st in class.
18/05: Mainz-Finthen DRM: Pallavicini; 6th.
25/05: Nürburgring 1000Km WCM: Pallavacini/Muller, #74; 12th OA.

01/06: Kreutzritter-Rennen Spa, DRM: Pallavicini; DNF.
07/09: Vallelunga 6-Hours WCM: Pallavacini/ Bernard, #9; 11th OA.
28/09: Dijon 6-Hours WCM: Pallavacini/ Crang, #28; 12th OA.

1981
21/03: Sebring 12-Hours: Pallavicini/N. Crang/D. Simpson, #51; DNF.
10/05: Silverstone 6-Hours WCM: Pallavacini/ Crang, #31; 14th OA.
28/06: Enna-Pergusa 6-Hours WCM: Pallavacini/ Kofel; 4th OA.
27/09: Brands Hatch 6-Hours WCM: Pallavacini/ Crang, #42; 14th OA.
11/10: Hockenheim 3-Hours: Pallavicini/Buehrer; 1st.
14/11: Hockenheim: Pallavicini; 1st.

Chassis No: 930 670 0179
Production No: 106.4621? 29th car built?
Colour: Yellow.
First Owner/Agent: Vasek Polak (4).

This 934 was sold to Vasek Polak and driven by Hurley Haywood in the 1976 Trans Am Championship where Haywood took it to second behind George Follmer in the standings at the end of the season.

After just a few more races, it was put into storage in Polak's collection until being sold in 1999.

1976 TransAm Championship.
09/05: Pocono: Haywood, #0; 1st.
30/05: Nelson Ledges: Haywood, #0; 2nd.
13/06: Portland TA: Haywood, #0; 30thNR.
15/08: Brainerd: Haywood, #0; 4th.
21/08: Mosport, TA: Haywood, #0; DNS.
05/09: Trois Rivieres: Haywood, #0; 10th.
3/10: Laguna Seca IMSA: Haywood, #0; 3rd.
28/11: Daytona Finale IMSA: Haywood, #0; 21st?
28/11: Daytona: Ongais, #0; 3rd.

Hurley Haywood finished second in the Trans Am Championship.

1977: Uprated to 934 1/2 specification.
01/05: Laguna Seca: R. Wood, #20; 15th.
30/05: Seattle TA: Roy Woods, #0; 10th.

Sold/leased to Ted Field? If so:
09/07: Watkins Glen 6-Hours, #0; Field/Ongais;5th.
20/08: Mosport 6-Hours: Shelton/McKitterick, #0; DNC.
28/08: Mid-Ohio: D. Bundy/R. Woods, #44; 8th.

Remained in the Vasek Polak collection.
Sold to Roman Hurtado, USA.
Sold to Bruce Canepa, USA.
STPO in California. Restored.

Chassis No: 930 670 0180
Production No: 106.4622.
Colour: White.
First Owner/Agent: Polak (5)

With bigger wheels and wheel arches, 935 tail and an uprated engine, 0180 was sold to Ted Field for his Interscope team. He and Danny Ongais raced it

a lot in 1977 in the Trans Am and IMSA.
The prototype of the 934 and a 1/2.
1976: Sold to Interscope

1977: IMSA Championship Races. Painted black.
19/03: Sebring 12 Hours: Ongais/Field/Haywood,
#0; 5th.
17/04: Road Atlanta 100 Miles: Field; #00; 9th.
01/05: Laguna Seca 100 Miles: Field; #00; 10th.
05/06: Mid-Ohio 100-Miles: Field; #00; 8th.
19/06; Brainerd 100 Miles: Ongais; #00; 1st.
04/07; Daytona 250 miles: Ongais; #00; 40th.
10/07: Watkins Glen 6-Hours: Guthrie/Lewis; 10th.
14/08: Pocono 100-Miles: Field; #00; 22nd.
28/08; Mid-Ohio 3-Hours: Ongais; #00; 5th.
05/09: Road Atlanta 100-Miles: Ongais; #00; 4th.
27/11: Daytona Finale: Ongais; #00; 47th.

Sold through Andial to Hal Shaw. Shaw had Jim
Busby Racing bring the car up to 1978 Twin-turbo
935 specification. With this:

1978.
4-5/02: Daytona 24-Hours: Shaw/Busby/Meister,
#13; 10th OA.
18/03: Sebring 12-Hours: Shaw/Spalding, #13; 3rd,
02/04: Talladega 6-Hours: Shaw/Spalding, #13;
23rd.
30/04: Laguna Seca: Shaw, #13; 13th.
21/05: Sears Point TA: Shaw; #13; 5th.
04/06: Coquitlam TA: Shaw; 2nd.
08/07: Watkins Glen 6-Hours: Shaw/Shelton, #13;
4th.
13/08: Brainerd TA: Shaw; DNS.
20/8: Mosport, TA: H. Shaw Jr.; 6th in class.
04/09: Road America, Elkhart Lake TA: Shaw, #13;
4th.
8/10: Laguna Seca TA: Shaw; DNF.
5/11: Ricardo Rodriguez Autodrome, Mexico City
TA: Shaw, #13; 11th.

1979:
3-4/2: Daytona 24-Hours: Shaw/Spalding/Ridgely,
#13; 40thNR.

17/3: Sebring 12-Hours: Shaw/Ridgely, #13; 6th.
22/4: LA Times GP, Riverside: Shaw, #13; 53rdNR:
07/7: Watkins Glen 6-Hours: H. Shaw Jr./G. Belcher,
#13; 23rd NR. Fire.
Shaw fourth in Trans Am, Category 2,
Championship.

1982: Sold to Tom McIntyre.
2009: Sold to Bruce Canepa. Restored.
2011: STPO.

Chassis No: 930 670 0540
Colour: Orange.
First Owner/Agent: Kauwertz.

Appearing in mainly World Championship races,
and driven by Klaus Drees, and Wolfgang Kauwertz,
(Both having previously shared RSR Carrera number
911 460 9061), 0540 was a steady, if unspectacular
performer.
    Sold to Wolfgang Kauwertz.

1976:
30/05: Nürburgring 1000Km WCM: Drees/
Kauwertz, #28; 16th.
05/06: Nürburgring: Drees/Kauwertz, #1; 1st OA.
27/06: Norisring EGTC: J. Kannacher, #8; 4th.

27/06: Norisring DRM: #8; DNF.
18/07: Zandvoort G.P.: C. Sierertsen, #97; 1st.
15/08: Zandvoort: C. Sievertsen, #8; DNF.
29/08: GP Holland, Zandvoort: C. Sievertsen, #70; 2nd.

1977:
13/3: Bergischer Lowe Zolder: Zirkel, #59; 10th.
27/3: 300 Km Nürburgring: Neuhaus, #57; DNF, (gearbox).
17/4: Hockenheim: Zirkel; 6th.
24/07: Sylt: A. Zirkel; 1st.
01/05: Nürburgring: K. Drees, #58; 9th.
15/05: Zandvoort: A. Zirkel; 1st.
29/5: Nürburgring 1000Km WCM: Drees/Kauwertz, #10; 25th. Schultz entry.

1978: Full 935, blue, w/red/white stripes
12/3: Zolder: (DRM): K. Drees, #18; 10th OA.
19/3: Mugello 6 Hours: W. Kauwertz/K. Drees, #29; 16th OA.
02/4: Nürburgring 300Kms: (DRM): K. Drees, #25; DNF.
16/4: Dijon 6 Hours, (WCM): K. Drees/W. Kauwertz, #12; 10th OA.
30/4: Nürburgring Eifelrennen: K. Drees, #18; 9th OA.
14/5: Silverstone 6 Hours: K. Drees/M. Franey, #17; 14th OA.

28/5: Nürburgring 1000KMs; K. Drees/P. Hahnlein, #19; 17th OA.

1979: Stored by Kauwertz in Germany and later in Austria.

1991: Sold to a private consortium of Japanese collectors who displayed the car in their personal museum outside Tokyo

2011: Sold to Matt Drendel, USA.

2012: Amelia Island Concours.
05/12: RM Auction, Monaco: Sold at $616,420.00.

Chassis No: 930 770 0951
Production No: 107.3472.
Engine No: 677 2807.
Gearbox No: 777 2814
Colour: White.

From the time that he and Hurley Haywood had won the Daytona 24-Hours of 1973, Peter Gregg had dominated the IMSA Camel GT and the Trans Am series from 1973 to 1975, always driving RSR Carreras. He was, effectively, Mark Donohue's replacement as Porsche's Works driver in the U.S.A., always receiving preferential treatment from the factory. 0951 was his first 934 although he passed it on almost immediately to Jim Busby as Gregg had taken delivery of another 934, (see 930 770 0952).

Jim Busby, who had previously raced RSR Carreras, had good placings with the car before selling it to Monte Shelton of Portland, Oregon in 1978. Monte had been racing many cars since the 1960's, including a Lola T70 and he raced this car until 1980 before selling it on.

Sold to Peter Gregg/Jim Busby.

1977: Mitcom-Sponsored
19/03: Sebring 12-Hours WCM: Busby/Gregg, #61; 3rd.

17/04: Road Atlanta 100 miles IMSA: Busby, #61; 35th.
01/05: Laguna Seca IMSA: Busby, #61; 2nd.
15/05: Mid-America 100 Miles IMSA: Busby, #61; 25th.
05/06: Westwood TA: Busby/O'Steen; #61; 3rd.
09/07: Watkins Glen 6-Hours WCM: Busby/Frank, #61; 12th.
27/11: Daytona Finale IMSA: Busby, #09; 65thNR.

1978:
Sold to Monte Shelton. Painted blue.
11/06: Portland TA: Shelton, #57; 19th.
25/06: St. Jovite: Shelton, #57; 1st.
13/08: Brainerd: TA Shelton, #57; 3rd.
20/08: Mosport: Shelton; 4th.
04/09: Road America, Elkhart Lake: Shelton; DNS.
08/10: Laguna Seca: Shelton; 30th NR.

1979: Trans Am: Brought up to 935 specifications.
03/06: Westwood TA: Shelton, #57; 8th.
10/06: Portland: Shelton, #57; 11h.
07/07: Watkins Glen 6-Hours WCM: N. Shelton/M. Shelton, #57;23rd.

1980:
04/05: Laguna Seca: Shelton, #57; 6th.

Sold to a Porsche dealer in Bend, Oregon.
Sold to a customer.
1995: Sold to Florida.
1996: Sold to David Aase.
2001: STPO, USA.

Chassis No: 930 770 0952
Production No: 107.3473.
Engine No: 677 2801
Gearbox No: 777 2812
Colour: White.

The second 934 to be sold to Peter Gregg. Always seeking the fastest car, Gregg had his Crew Chief, Jack Atkinson, modify the 934 with the 935-type rear fenders, wing and titanium axles from his first 935, chassis number 930 770 0909. When Gregg turned up for the first IMSA race, he was protested for this infringement and left to take part in the Trans Am Championship. Jack Atkinson also modified the fuel injection, cutting down the turbo-lag considerably. Gregg won the 1977 Trans Am Championship, winning no less than seven races and carrying on where he had left off with the RSR.

For 1978, Peter Gregg took delivery of his first twin-turbo 935 and sold his "old" 934 to Bruce Leven of Bayside Disposal. Leven raced 0952 in the Trans Am to receive the title of: "Most improved rookie of the year" before selling the car to Les Lindley. In turn, Lindley sold the car to another long time Porsche devotee, David Aase in 1987 who looked after it with care until 2003, when he sold it to Bob Weber.

1977: Sold to Brumos for Peter Gregg. Fitted with the axles and gearbox from 930 770 0909.
Collected from New York on 27/4/77. Race #59.
30/05: Seattle TA: Gregg; DNS. (Acc. With Greg Pickett).
05/06: Westwood TA: Gregg; 1st.
26/06: Nelson Ledges TA: Gregg; 1st. (First race with modified injection).
09/07: Watkins Glen 6-Hours WCM: Gregg/Ballot-Lena, #59; 6th OA.

24/07: Hallett TA: Gregg; 1st.
13/08: Brainerd TA: Gregg; 1st.
20/08: Mosport 6-Hours WCM: Gregg/Wollek, #59; DQ.
28/08: Mid-Ohio 3-Hours WCM: Gregg, #59; 1st. (with nose from 935).
03/09: Road America, Elkhart Lake TA: Gregg (1); 2nd. (2); 1st.
11/09: St. Jovite: Gregg; 1st.

1977: Second in the Trans Am Championship.
Sold to Bruce Leven.

1978: Trans Am races:
04/06: Coquitlam: Leven, #85; 7th.
11/06: Portland: Leven, #85; 4th.
13/08: Brainerd: Leven, #85; 7th.
20/08: Mosport: Leven; 16th.
08/10: Laguna Seca: Leven, #85; 6th.
5/11: Mexico City: Leven, #85; 7th.
Leven voted 'Rookie of the year.'

1978 sold to Les Lindley--motor and transmission rebuilt by Andial in Santa
Ana. documentation for this including engine #6772872, Andial 141;

transmission #25/11/7772812 as being in the car and rebuilt by Andial.
1987 sold to Dave Aase in California.
2003 sold to Bob Weber in California with engine #6772872, Andial 141;
transmission #25/11/7772812. All verified with vehicle inspection with
Andial and their records.

Chassis No: 930 770 0953
Production No: 107.3474.
Engine No: 677 2804
Gearbox No: 777 2815
Colour: White.

This 934 and a 1/2 was sold to the Interscope Team and was later on painted in their Black with orange, brown and pink pinstripes. Ted Field and Danny Ongais raced it in the 1977 TransAm and IMSA series, Ongais winning at Laguna Seca.

At the last IMSA race of the season, the Daytona Finale, Ted Field was driving the car when he hit Johnny Rutherford, driving one of Dick Barbour's 935s when the race was black flagged, both cars being very badly damaged. Dick Barbour bought 0953 and used some of the parts in a new bodyshell he bought from the factory, probably 930 890 0037. With this, the Dick Barbour team won the 1978 Sebring 12-Hours. (see 930 890 0037).

NOTE: In May, 2007, the remains of 930 770 0953 were sold by Dick Barbour to a new owner in the U.S. who is rebuilding the Interscope 934 1/2 back to it's original specification.

1977: Black with pinstriping.
17/04: Road Atlanta 100 Miles: Ongais, #0; 32nd.
01/05: Laguna Seca 100 Miles: Ongais; #0; 1st.
05/06: Mid-Ohio 100-Miles: Ongais,#0; 36th.
19/06; Brainerd 100 Miles: Field,#0; 13th.
04/07; Daytona 250 miles: Field; #0; 28th.
10/07: Watkins Glen 6-Hours: Field/Ongais; 5th.
14/08: Pocono 100-Miles: Ongais; #0; 21st.
28/08; Mid-Ohio 3-Hours: Field; #0; 23rd.
05/09: Road Atlanta 100-Miles: Field, #0; 17th.

27/11; Daytona Finale; Field; #0; 52nd. Crash with
J.Rutherford.
Damaged car sold to Dick Barbour.

2007:
May: Parts and identity sold in America. Car being
rebuilt.

2008:
November 18-21: PIR, Phoenix, AZ: J.Starkey; #0;
9th.

See: 930 890 0037.

Chassis No: 930 770 0954
Production No: 107.3475.
Engine No: 677 2803
Gearbox No: 777 2816
Colour: White.

First sold to George Dyer, who had campaigned
a 1974 RSR Carrera, chassis number 911 460
9040, very successfully, 0954 raced in the IMSA
Championship in 1977, Dyer winning the Paul
Revere race at Daytona in July.
    At the end of the season, Dyer sold the car to
Bruce Canepa of California who raced it just three
times, placing third at the 1979 Daytona 24 Hours.

Sold to George Dyer.

1977: IMSA Championship Races. Painted blue and
yellow.
17/04: Road Atlanta: Dyer, #30; 3rd.

01/05: Laguna Seca: Dyer, #30; 37thNR.
19/06: Brainerd: Dyer, #30; 4th.
04/07: Daytona 3-Hours: Dyer, #30; 1st.
14/08: Pocono: Dyer, #30; 25thNR.
28/08: Mid-Ohio: Dyer, #30; 37thNR,
05/09: Road Atlanta: Dyer, #30; 25thNR.
9/10: Laguna Seca: Dyer, #30: 6th.
27/11: Daytona Finale: Dyer, #30; 19thNR.

Sold to Bruce Canepa.

1978:
30/07: Sears Point IMSA: Canepa, #71; 7th.
8/10: Laguna Seca TA: Canepa;4th.

1979:
3-4/02: Daytona 24-Hours: Canepa/Mears/Shelton,
#11; 3rd.

Chassis No: 930 770 0955
Production No: 107.3476.
Engine No: 677 2802
Gearbox No: 777 2819.
Colour: White.

    Sold to Vasek Polak for George Follmer to

drive in the 1977 TransAm Championship, 0955 gave a good account of itself but everyone else was overshadowed by Peter Gregg's dominance. Then uprated to 935 specification in 1979 for a few races, 0955 was put into storage at Vasek Polak's shop until being sold in 1998.

1977:
01/05: Laguna Seca TA:G. Follmer, #16; 3rd.
30/05: Kent TA:G. Follmer, #16; 2nd.
12/06: Portland IMSA: G. Follmer; 1st.
9/10: Laguna Seca: G. Follmer, #16; 9th.
1978:
21/05: Sears Point TA:G. Follmer, #16; 15th.
Possibly:-
08/07: Watkins Glen 6-Hours:J. Guthrie/B. Redman/H.Haywood, #3; 8th.
Perhaps:
5/11: Mexico City TA:J. Guthrie, #8; 4th.
1979: As a 935.
29/07: Sears Point IMSA: Minter, #17; 4th.
05/08: Portland IMSA: Minter, #17; 4th.

14/10: Laguna Seca TA,: Minter, #17; 2nd.
In storage at Vasek Polak's race shop.
1998: Sold to Brazil.
2008: Sold to Official Porsche importer, Brazil.
2012: Sold to Dener Pires, Sao Paolo, Brazil.
2015: At Rennsport Reunion, Laguna Seca, USA.

Chassis No: 930 770 0956
Production No: 107.4140
Engine No: 677 2808
Gearbox No: 777 2813
Colour: White.

Listed by the factory as an "extra" 935/77, 0956 was sold to Italian industrialist Martino Finotto tand then to Ciro Nappi of Naples.

Nappi teamed up with Turizio(?) to take part in the Giro d'Italia, an Italian version of the "Tour de France", but a death in Nappi's family caused him to cut the event short. After this, the car was sold to Dino Male who raced under the pseudonym: "Dino". "Dino" and co-driver Moreschi did just one race with the almost new 935 and won the Vallelunga 6 Hours, a round of the World Championship for Makes.

After this, the car was sold to the Sportwagen Team of Sassiolo, near Modena and it is this car that was raced by Jurgen Lassig in 1979. ("Came from Italy, painted in silver").

The car was then sold to Australia where it competed in the 1980 and 1981 Australian Sports Car Championship, winning every race and the Championship in 1981. After this, the car was sold to Jeff Dutton and then Peter McNamara who had the car converted to right hand drive and registered for the road! The car is still in Australia.

Sold to Martino Finotto.

1977: Sold new to Ciro Nappi of Naples.

12-16/06: Giro d'Italia: Nappi/Turizio; DNF. (Death in Nappi's family).
Sold to Dino Male.
10/07: Misano: "Dino", 2nd.

17/07: Enna-Pergusa: "Dino"; 2nd.
20/8: Misano Night race: "Dino"; 3rd.
04/9: Coppa Intereuropa, Monza: "Dino"; 6th.
18/9: Coppa Enna: "Dino"; 1st.
23/10: Vallelunga 6 Hours, WCM: "Dino"/L. Moreschi; 1st. (935/76A).

1978: Sold to Sportwagen of Sassuolo in Modena.

Probably:-
19/3: Mugello 6-Hours WCM: Casoni/Manfredini; 17th.
16/4: Dijon 4-Hours WCM: Casoni; DNF.
Entered at Silverstone 6-Hours. DNA.

Sold to Max Moritz.
Sold to Jurgen Lassig.
1979: German National Championship Races. Silver with black centerstripe and nose, plus red front spoiler. BOSS-Sponsored.
11/3: Bergischer Lowe, Zolder: Lassig, #72; 12th.
08/4: Jim Clark-Rennen, Hockenheim: Lassig, #72; 10th (DRM) and 1st (group 4 race).
29/4: Eifelrennen, Nürburgring: Lassig; 13th.
20/5: Bavaria-Rennen, Salzburgring: Lassig; 8th.
30/5: Nürburgring 300Km DRM: Lassig; 7th.
03/6: Nürburgring 1000Km WCM: Lassig/Holup/Duge, #44; 7th.

17/6: Mainz-Finthen DRM: Lassig, #72; 11th.
24/6: Norisring, Nurnberg DRM: Lassig, #72; 16th.
01/7: Zandvoort Trophy DRM: Lassig; 9th.
22/7: Diepholz: Lassig DRM; DNF.
19/8: Westfalenpokal, Zolder DRM: Lassig; 12th.
26/8: Ulm-Mengen: Lassig; 2nd (group 2/4) 1st (group3/4).
02/9: Hessen-Cup, Hockenheim DRM: Lassig; DNF.
16/9: Schwabische Alb (hillclimb): Lassig; 1st in class.
23/9: Supersprint, Nürburgring DRM: Lassig; DNF.
14/10: Zolder: Lassig, #34; 8th (group 2/4/5) 3rd (group 4).

Rebuilt for Max Moritz by the factory.

Sold to Bruce Spicer in Australia.

1980:
?/02: Sandown Park: J. Latham; DNF. (eng.).
Rebuilt by Bruce Spicer.
Baskerville: J. Latham; 5th.
Amaroo Park. J. Latham; 1st.
Won all the next races.

1981:
Won every race from pole. J. Latham.
Australian Sports Car Champion.

1982: Sold to Jeff Dutton.
Sold to Peter McNamara. Converted to RHD. Road registered.
Sold to Ian Kenny.
Sold to Bowden Co.
STPO. Restored by Marc de Siebenthal.

Chassis No: 930 770 0957
Production No: 107.6663
Engine No: 677 2805
Gearbox No: 777 2817
Colour: White.

Sold to Bob Hagestad, who had previously raced

two 1973 RSR's, (911 360 0782 and 0997), and a 1974 Carrera, (chassis number 911 460 9057), 0957 was driven by Hurley Haywood in IMSA and Trans Am races in 1977, winning at Nelson ledges and the Daytona Finale.

In 1978, Hagestad had the car brought up to 935 specification and he and Haywood shared the car, placing second in the Sebring 12 Hours with Haywood taking another second at Laguna Seca.

In November, Bob Hagestad sold his 934/5 to Charles Mendez, a real estate developer from Florida who placed fifth with it at Watkins Glen and Portland. After this, Mendez used the 935 as a "rent a ride" car as he had bought chassis number 930 770 0911, a 1977 "customer" 935 that had been uprated to 1978 twin-turbo specification by the factory.

Retiring 0957 in 1980, Mendez had it turned into a street car (!) describing it to the author as: "A real road rocket!"

In 1988, Mendez sold 0957 to Kevin Jeannette of Gunnar Racing who restored it back to its original configuration. The car was sold at auction in 1998. In 2006, it was sold again.

1977: IMSA Championship Races unless otherwise noted.
17/04: Road Atlanta: Haywood, #95; 31st.
01/05: Laguna Seca: Haywood, #95; 7th OA.
15/05: Mid-America: Haywood; #95; 3rd.
30/05; Lime Rock: Haywood; #95; 2nd.
05/06: Mid-Ohio: Haywood, #95; 38th NR.
19/06: Brainerd: Haywood, #95; 2nd
26/06: Nelson Ledges TA: Hagestad; 1st.
04/07: Daytona: Paul Revere 250: Haywood, #95; 2nd OA.
31/07: Sears Point: Haywood, #95; 16th OA, NR.
14/08; Pocono: Haywood/Hagestad,#95; 3rd.
28/08: Mid-Ohio: Haywood/Hagestad,#95; 4th OA.
05/09: Road Atlanta: Haywood, #95; 3rd OA.
9/10: Laguna Seca: Haywood, #95; 39th NR.
27/11: Daytona Finale: Haywood, #95; 1st.

1978: Uprated to 935 specification.

4-5/02: Daytona 24-Hours: Hagestad/Haywood, #95; 40th NR.
18/03: Sebring 12-Hours: Hagestad/Haywood, #95; 2nd.
02/04: Talladega: Hagestad/Haywood, #95; 26thNR.
16/04: Road Atlanta: Haywood, #95; 23rdNR.
30/04: Laguna Seca: Haywood, #95; 2nd.

11/78: Sold to Charles Mendez, Florida.

1979: IMSA Championship Races.
08/04: Road Atlanta: Miller/Mendez, #5; 8th
22/04: Riverside 6-Hours: Mendez/Miller, #5; 37th NR.
13/05: Hallett, Mendez, #5; 6th.
28/05: Lime Rock: Mendez, #5; 3rd.
17/06: Brainerd: Mendez, #5; 4th.
07/07: Watkins Glen 6-Hours: P. Miller/C. Mendez, #6; 5th NR.
29/07: Sears Point: R. McFarlin, #95; 13th.
05/08: Portland: Mendez, #5; 5th.
25/11: Daytona: Akin/Woods, #05; 6th.

1980: Used as a "Rent a ride" car. Engine number: 698 0056 installed.
2-3/02: Daytona 24-Hours: R.Kent-Cooke/G. Bleynie/C. Ballot-Lena, #55; 48th NR.
22/03: Sebring 12 Hours WCM: R. Kent-Cooke/L.

St. James, #55; 49th NR.
27/04: Riverside, L.A. Times G.P: H. Meister/J. Morton, #55; 44th NR.
04/05: Laguna Seca: Meister, #55; 15th NR.

1983: Made into a street car.
1988: Sold to Kevin Jeannette.
Restored to 934 1/2 specification.
1998: STPO. Raced in vintage events.
2006: STPO.

Chassis No: 930 770 0958
Production No: 107 6664
Engine No: 677 2806
Gearbox No: 777 2820

Sold to Ludwig Heimrath, the noted Canadian Porsche racer, who had been a mechanic at Stuttgart, and raced many Porsches, including the very last RSR Carrera built by the factory, 0958 had a long career. She was first raced by Heimrath in the 1977 Trans Am which finished in a bitter wrangle over whether Heimrath or Gregg had won the series. Heimrath took two victories and protested Gregg's 'unfair advantage' of using parts from his 935.

After 1977, Heimrath uprated the car to 935 specification and raced it until 1980 when he built up a new car on a used 930 chassis from Dan McLaughlin at AIR. Andre Gaudet had Jacques Rivard of Canada restore the 935 back to it's original 934 1/2 specification as it had a 962 specification engine and Kremer K3 bodywork.

1977:
30/05: Kent TA: Heimrath, #7; 1st.
05/06: Westwood TA: Heimrath; 18th.
12/06: Portland: TA: L. Heimrath; 6th.
26/06: Nelson Ledges TA: Heimrath; 2nd.
10/07: Watkins Glen 6-Hours WCM: Heimrath/Miller, #7; 9th.
31/07: Hallet TA: Heimrath; 2nd.
13/08: Brainerd TA: Heimrath, #7; 2nd.
20/08: Mosport 6-Hours WCM: Heimrath/Miller, #7;

1st in Trans Am. 1st OA.
28/08: Mid-Ohio TA: Heimrath/Miller; 35th NR.
03/09: Road America, Elkhart Lake TA: Heimrath; 1st.
04/09: Road America, Elkhart Lake TA: Heimrath; 19th.
11/09: St. Jovite TA: Heimrath; 2nd.
27/11: Daytona IMSA: Heimrath/Ridgely; 28th NR.
Heimrath Winner of Trans Am Championship.

1978: Race No: 7. Brought up to 935 specification. Painted yellow.
04-05/02: Daytona 24-Hours: Heimrath/Bienvenue/Ridgeley; DNF. (Acc.)

18/03: Sebring 12-Hours: Heimrath/Ridgeley; DNF. (Eng.)
08/07: Watkins Glen 6-Hours: Heimrath/Miller; 15th OA.
21/05: Sears Point TA: Heimrath, #7: 19th.
04/06: Coquitlam TA: Heimrath, #7; 1st.
11/06: Portland TA: Heimrath, #7; 2nd.
25/06: St. Jovite TA: Heimrath, #7; 2nd.
13/08: Brainerd TA: Heimrath; 32nd NR.
20/08: Mosport TA: Heimrath; 2nd.
04/09: Road America, Elkhart Lake TA: Heimrath, #07; DNF.
8/10: Laguna Seca: Heimrath, #7; 3rd.
5/11: Mexico City TA: Heimrath, #7; 1st.
26/11: Daytona Finale IMSA: Heimrath/Moran; 5th.
Third in Trans Am Championship. Category 2.

1979:
17/03: Sebring 12-Hours WCM: Heimrath/Molins/Moran #7; DNF.
09/05: Mexico City TA: Heimrath; 6th.
03/06: Westwood TA: Heimrath; 2nd.
10/06: Portland TA: Heimrath; 9th.
17/06: Brainerd 100 Miles TA: Heimrath, #77; 31st.
07/07: Watkins Glen 6-Hours: Heimrath/Moran; DNF. (Eng.)
21/07: Road America, Elkhart Lake: Heimrath; 2nd.
05/08: Watkins Glen: Heimrath TA; 4th.
19/08: Mosport TA: Heimrath; 8th.
26/08: Mid-Ohio: Heimrath; 25th NR.
02/09: Road America, Elkhart Lake: Heimrath/Lunger; DNF.
Third in Trans Am Championship, Category 2.
NOTE: This MAY have been the 935 that Kathy Rude crashed in 1983/4.
1996: Sold to Jacques Rivard.
1996: Restored by Jacques Rivard.
Sold to A. Gaudet.
2004: Totally restored with 934.5 engine and bodywork.

NOTE: For 1980, Ludwig Heimrath swapped his old RSR, 911 560 9123, for a 1976 Turbo bodyshell, with built-up 935 gearchange tower and rollcage from Dan McLaughlin.

1980: IMSA Championship Races unless otherwise noted.
02-03/02: Daytona 24-Hours WCM: Heimrath/Moran/Rutherford, #07; DNF.
22/03: Sebring 12-Hours WCM: Heimrath/Rutherford/Moran, #07; 8th OA.
13/04: Road Atlanta: Heimrath; 27th.
26/05: Lime Rock: Heimrath; 6th.
05/07: Watkins Glen 6-Hours: Heimrath/Rutherford/Moran, #7; 11th OA.
17/08: Mosport 6-Hours: Heimrath/Rutherford; 21st NR.
31/08: Road America, Elkhart Lake: Heimrath; 47th NR.

21/09: Road Atlanta: Heimrath: Heimrath; Heat 1: 24th NR.
30/11: Daytona: Heimrath; 59th NR.
1982: Sold to Enrique Molins, ("Jamsal"). Scorpio Racing.
30-31/01: Daytona 24-Hours WCM: Jamsal/Barrientos, #84; 29th NR.
20/03: Sebring 12-Hours WCM: Jamsal/Barrientos, #84; 43rd NR.
25/04: Riverside 6-Hours WCM: Jamsal/Galdamez, #84; 41st NR.

1985:
31/1-1/02: Daytona 24-Hours WCM: Jamsal/Galdamez/Anbagua, #89; 43rd NR.
24/02: Miami GP: Jamsal, #89; 9th GTO.
25/03: Sebring 12-Hours WCM: Jamsal/Fonseca/Mena, #89; 12th.

Stolen. Recovered.
2015: With Steven Lawrence, USA.
2015: "Rennsport Reunion", Laguna Seca.

Chassis No: 930 770 0959
Production No: 107 6665
Engine No: 677 2809
Gearbox No: 777 2818

Sold to Dick Barbour of San Diego in 1977 for his use in the IMSA series, 0959 acquitted itself well until being badly damaged at the Daytona Finale in a collision with An Interscope car. Over the winter of 1977-1978, 0959 was re-chassised and used in 1978 and 1979 as a "rent a ride" car, finishing a creditable nineth at Le Mans in 1979.

In 1980, the car was sold to Japan and stayed there until being sold to the noted English dealer of racing and classic cars, Brian Classic. The car was offered at Coy's auction in May, 2000 but did not sell. It was offered again at the July, Silverstone, Coy's auction.

1977: IMSA Championship Races.
01/05: Laguna Seca: Barbour, #06; 31st NR.
15/05: Mid-America 100-miles: Barbour, #6; 11th.

30/05: Lime Rock 100 miles;Barbour, #6; 5th.
05/06: Mid-Ohio 100 miles: Barbour; #6; 9th.
19/06: Brainerd: Barbour, #6; 14th NR.
10/07: Watkins Glen 6-Hours: Barbour/Rutherford, #66; 4th.
31/07: Sears Point: Bondurant, #92; 22nd NR. (perhaps!)
05/09: Road Atlanta; #6; 7th.
9/10: Laguna Seca: Barbour, #6; 40th.
27/11:Daytona Finale: Rutherford, #6;51st NR. (collision with Field-badly damaged).

1978: Re-chassised. Original chassis with Gunnar Racing in 1988. (Gary Quast).
30/04: Laguna Seca: Bondurant, #6; 17th.
04/07: Daytona: Hinze/Yarosh, #9; 52nd NR.
05/11: Mexico City, Trans Am: J. Guthrie, #8; 4th.
.
1979:
17/03: Sebring 12-Hours WCM: Garretson/Belcher/Bondurant, #3; 3rd.
22/04: Riverside 6-Hours WCM: Garretson /Belcher/McKitterick, #4; 9th.
9-10/06: Le Mans 24-Hours: Kirby/Hotchkiss, #73; 9th OA, 4th in IMSA class.
07/07: Watkins Glen 6-Hours WCM:T.Thomas/N.Ridgely, #66; 13th.
29/07: Sears Point IMSA: Harmon, #66; 23rd NR.
05/08: Portland IMSA: Nierop, #66; 10th.
26/08: Mid-Ohio IMSA: T.Bagley/B. Akin, #66; 16th NR.

02/09: Road America, Elkhart Lake IMSA: Nierop/Ridgely, #66; 17th.

1980: White with red and blue flashes. Engine number 677 2912 installed.

Sold to Matsuda, Japan.
1999: Sold to Brian Classic.
2000: Coy's Auction.

Chassis No: 930 770 0960
Production No: 107. 6666
Engine No: 677 2810
Gearbox No: 777 2811
Colour: White.

Sold to Clifford Kearns in 1977, this 934 was raced by him in the IMSA Camel GT Championship until it was crashed at Daytona in 1978.
Returned to AIR in California, 0960 was re-chassised with another bodyshell. This one is marked: "State of California DMV 470 12CA". It was then run as the number 28 car of Desperado Racing by Clifford Kearns.
At one point, Marty Hinze bought the car. He later sold it to Preston Henn who, in 1986, sold it to Kevin Jeannette of Gunnar Racing. He sold the car to Phil Bagley of Klub Sport and Mike Gammino bought it from him and raced it in HSR. Some time afterwards the car was sold but, whilst being transported, it suffered another accident and has been rebuilt again on another bodyshell.
The original tub was bought by Kevin Jeannette and he rebuilt 0960 back to its original configuration.

1977:
30/05: Kent TA: Brown, #12; 36th NR.
05/06: Westwood TA: Brown, #12; 22nd NR.
12/06: Portland TA: Brown, #12; 7th.
04/07: Daytona 250 miles: Kearns/Mendez; #28; 36th NR.
31/07: Sears Point: Kearns, #28; 9th OA.
14/08: Pocono 100-Miles; Kearns, #28; 8th.
05/09: Road Atlanta: Kearns, #28; 23rd NR.

9/10: Laguna Seca 100 Miles: #28; 24th.
27/11: Daytona Finale: Kearns/Minter, #28; 3rd OA.

1978: IMSA Championship Races.
18/03: Sebring 12-Hours; Kearns/Hinze/Behr, #28;49th NR.
02/04: Talladega 6-Hours: Kearns/Minter, #28;33rd NR.
16/04: Road Atlanta: Kearns, #28; 30th NR.
30/04: Laguna Seca: Kearns, #28; 20th.
29/05: Lime Rock: Kearns, #28; 8th.
18/06: Brainerd: Kearns, #28; 6th.
04/07: Daytona Paul Revere 6-Hours, #28: Kearns/Minter; 2nd.
30/07: Sears Point: Kearns, #28; 8th.
06/08: Portland: Kearns, #28; 5th.
27/08: Mid-Ohio: Kearns/Minter, #28; 3rd.
04/09: Road Atlanta: Kearns, #28; 26th NR.
26/11: Daytona Finale: Kearns/Minter, #28; 16th NR. Crashed. Rebuilt by AIR.

1979:
17/03: Sebring 12-Hours WCM: Kearns/Moretti, #28;63rd NR.
08/04: Road Atlanta 100 Miles IMSA: Kearns, #32;32nd NR.
10/06: Portland TA: Kearns, #28; 3rd.

1980: Sold to Dave Dopke. Raced.
Sold to Marty Hinze.
21/9: Road Atlanta: Hinze, #2; 26th NR

1981:

20-21/3: Sebring 12-Hours WCM: Hinze/Minter/Whittington, #2; 3rd.

1982:
20/3: Sebring 12-Hours: Hinze/D.Whittington/B. Whittington, #16; 27th NR
Sold back to Clifford Kearns.

1986: Sold to Kevin Jeannette.
Sold to Phil Bagley.
Sold to Mike Gammino.
See: Note above for information on the original bodyshell.

Chassis No: 006 0022
Production No: 107.3472.
Engine type: 930/72.
Gearbox Type: 930/25.
Colour: White.

This 934/5 was built up by the Kremer Brothers Racing Team in Cologne.

1976:
8-9/06: Le Mans 24-Hours: Beaumont/Wollek/Pironi, #65; 19th OA/4th in GT Class.

1977: Possibly:-
7-8/06: Le Mans 24-Hours:Fernandez/Baturone/Tarredas, #55; DNF. Engine.

1978: Sold to Preben Kristoffersen of Denmark.
16/04: Dijon 4 Hours WCM: Sindel/Kristoffersen, #32; DNF. Turbo.
14/05: Silverstone 6 Hours WCM: Sindel/Kristoffersen, #25; 7th OA, 1st in GT class.
28/05: Nürburgring 1000Km WCM: Sindel/Kristoffersen, #47; DNF.
10-11/06: Le Mans 24-Hours: Bourdillat/Favresse/Bernard, #64; NC.
25/06: Misano 6 Hours: Sindel/Kristoffersen, #11; DNF. Accident.

Sold to Manfred Freisinger.

Sold to Fritz Englehardt. ("Harry Hirsch").
16/07: Kassel-Calden: "Harry Hirsch" (Fritz
Englehardt), #27; DNF.

1979: German National Championship.
11/03: Bergischer Lowe Zolder: "Harry Hirsch" ;
13th.
08/04: Jim Clark Rennen, Hockenheim: "Harry
Hirsch"; NC.
29/04: Eifelrennen Nürburgring: "Harry Hirsch";
14th.
20/05: Bavaria Salzburgring: "Harry Hirsch"; 12th.
27/05: Wunstorf: "Harry Hirsch"; 2nd in Group 4
class.
17/06: Mainz-Finthen: "Harry Hirsch"; 10th.
24/06: Norisring Nurnberg, (DRM): "Harry Hirsch";
13th.
01/07: Zandvoort Trophy: "Harry Hirsch"; 10th.
22/07: Diepholz: "Harry Hirsch"; 12th.
23/09: Supersprint Nürburgring: "Harry Hirsch",
#73; 10th.
14/10: Zolder: "Harry Hirsch"; 2nd in Group 3/4
race. 9th in G2/4/5 race.

1980:
23/03: Bergischer Lowe Zolder: "Harry Hirsch"; 10th.

Sold to Peter Pospieszczyk:
18/05: Mainz-Finthen: Pospiesczyk; 7th.
22/06: Rundstreckrennen Duren, Zolder:
Pospiesczyk; 1st in class.
27/07: Diepholz: Pospiesczyk; 12th.
14/09: Siegerland: Pospiesczyk; 1st in class.
12/10: H.P. Joisten-Trophy, Zolder: Pospiesczyk; 1st
in class.

Sold to Japan.

2005: For sale. $260,000.
2007: Sold at auction.

1976: Porsche 935. Works cars
Chassis No: 935 001: R15
Engine Type: 930/72.
Gearbox Type: 930/25
Colour: White with red and blue stripes.

Built with upright headlamps, this prototype was
swiftly transformed with a slope nose and longer
rear wings, (fenders). 0001 was the principal test car
of the works team in 1976.

Testing:
December, 1975: Paul Ricard: 2931 Km. ? 750 Km.
February: Paul Ricard: 3158 Km.
Nürburgring: practice car, (768 Km).

1976: World Championship for Makes.
10/7: Watkins Glen 6 Hours; Stommelen/Schurti, #4;
1st OA. (1360 Km).
04/9: Dijon 6-Hours: Stommelen/Schurti;#3 3rd.

Sold to Vasek Polak.

1979:
29/07: Sears Point: H. Haywood, #7; 3rd.
05/08: Portland: H. Haywood, #7; 2nd.

1999: Sold to Kevin Jeannette.
2009: Sold to Matt Drendel.
STPO.

Chassis No: 935.002: R16
Engine Type: 930/72.
Gearbox Type: 930/25
Colour: White with red and blue stripes.

Built with upright headlamps, this second prototype
was swiftly transformed with a slope nose and longer rear wings, (fenders). 002 was the principal test
car of the works team in 1976. It won the Group 5
class of the World Championship for Makes. After a
brief, unsuccessful foray at Daytona in 1977, it was
pensioned off to the factory's museum.

1976: World Championship for Makes.
21/3: Mugello 6 hours:J. Ickx/Mass; Race No: 4. 1st
OA.
04/4: Vallelunga 6-Hours:J. Ickx/Mass, #1; 1st OA.
09/5: Silverstone 6-Hours,J. Ickx/ Mass, #9; 10th OA.
30/5: Nürburgring 1000Km:J. Ickx/Mass, #1; DNF.
12-13/6: Le Mans 24-Hours 24 hours: Stommelen/
Schurti, #40; 4th OA, 1st Group 5.
27/6: Zeltweg 6-Hours:J. Ickx/Schurti, #1; DNF.
10/7: Watkins Glen 6-Hours:J. Ickx/Mass, #2; 3rd OA.
04/9: Dijon 6 Hours;J. Ickx/Mass, #1; 1st OA.

1977:
05-06/2: Daytona 24 Hours WCM:J. Ickx/Mass, #1;
DNF. Badly damaged.
20/93: Mugello 6 Hours: M. Schurti/R. Stommelen,
#2; 1st.

In the Porsche Museum, Stuttgart.

Chassis No: 935-003: R17
Engine type: 930/72.
Gearbox: 930/25.
Color: White.

Used just once to win the first round of the 1977 World Championship for Makes, 003 was "pensioned off" and used as a Renntaxi to give visiting VIP's occasional rides around Weissach. Equipped with a huge wind cheating "Barn door" type of rear fairing, it tried to help Jean-Claude Rude to obtain a World speed record for cyclists, which ended when the cycle had a puncture.

1977:
03/7: Norisring, Nurnberg 200 miles: B. Wollek/J. Ickx, #50; 2nd.

Chassis No: 935-004: R18
Engine type: 930/72.
Gearbox: 930/25.
Color: White.

Again used just once in a race in the World Championship in 1977, 004 was leading when it came in for a pit stop and for Jürgen Barth to take over from Jochen Mass at Mugello. Exiting the pitlane and headed for the first corner, Barth suddenly discovered he had no brakes and used John Fitzpatrick, ahead of him in the Kremer 935, to stop, having little alternative!

The remains were in California since 1994. Today, the car has been completely restored in Germany.

1977:
20/3: Mugello 6-Hours; Mass/Barth, #1; DNF. (Acc.)

1994: Sold to Kerry Morse, USA.
2014: Sold to and restored by Freinger's in Germany.

Chassis No: 935-005: R19
Engine type: 930/72.
Gearbox: 930/25.
Color: White.

The 935/77 which did the rest of the 1977 season as a replacement for 003 and 004, 935/77-005 was retired to the Porsche museum at the end of the year.

1977:
15/5: Silverstone 6-Hours, #1:J. Ickx/Mass; 1st OA.
29/5: Nürburgring 1000Km:J. Ickx/Mass, #1; DNF.
09/7: Watkins Glen 6-Hours:J. Ickx/Mass, #1; 1st O.A.
21/8: Mosport 6-Hours:J. Ickx/Schurti, #1; DNF.
25/9: Brands Hatch 6-Hours:J. Ickx/Mass, #31; 1st OA.
9/10: Hockenheim 6 Hours: M. Schurti/J. Ickx, #1; DNF. (Engine).

In the Porsche Museum.

935/77 "Baby":
Chassis No: 935/ 2 001

Developed to take part in the two litre class of the German National Championship, the "Baby" had a 1.4 litre engine and was raced just thrice by Jackie Ickx.

"Baby" failed in it's first race, poor Ickx being almost roasted alive in it's cockpit heat but after cooling holes had been made, the "Baby" performed well in it's next race heat.

"Baby" dominated the next race at Hockenheim and was retired to the Porsche museum, having made Porsche's point that they could succeed in any class.

1977:
04/07: 200 miles of Nurnberg, Norisring(DRM/2: J. Ickx, #40; DNF. (Heat exhaustion).
04/07: Norisring Trophy, Nurnberg 200:J. Ickx: #40;); DNF. Trophy; 7th.
30/7: Hockenheim:J. Ickx, (DRM/2), #40; 1st.
In the Porsche Museum.

1978: 935/78
Chassis No: 935-006: R20
Colour: White.

The "Moby Dick" which so astonished and con-founded the FIA rulemakers when they inspected it. Although a spectacular performer, 006 only won one race in 1978, despite leading the Silverstone 6-Hours by miles at the end.

At Le Mans, for the 24-Hours, the car was slowed by the Porsche team management as they had observed a slight oil leak. At the end of the race, it was found to be insignificant.

1978: World Championship Races.
14/5: Silverstone 6-Hours: J.Ickx/J.Mass, #1; 1st OA.
10-11/6: Le Mans 24-Hours 24 Hours: R.Stommelen/M.Schurti, #43; 8th OA
03/9: Vallelunga 6-Hours: J. Ickx/Schurt, #1; DNF after leading.
17/9: Norisring 200-Miles:J. Ickx, #40; 21st.

In the Porsche Museum.

Chassis No: 935-007: R21
Colour: White.

A factory built chassis only, 935.007 was sold to Kerry Morse in 1988, who kept it in his Californian shop for many years. Finally sold to Manfred Freisinger in 2007. Freisinger's shop completed the car and it was first raced at Spa in a CER race in 2010 by Stephane Ortelli.

1976-1977: 13 replicas of the single-turbo 1976 works-entered cars built and sold to private customers: 930 770 0901 to 930 770 0913

Chassis No: 930 770 0901
Production No: 107.2193.
Engine No: 677 2909
Gearbox No: 777 2909
Colour: White.
Sold to: Hamilton, Australia.

Sold to the Australian enthusiast, L. C. O'Neil, 0901 received Laurex sponsorship and was painted blue with red, green and white stripes. The car was the subject of a 1978 feature in the "Australian Sports Car World" magazine. It was raced in Australia just once by Ian Geoghegan at Phillip Island, Sydney where it won.

In 1988, the Australian customs were demanding extra import duties from Mr O'Neil and so he sent the 935 to the Kremer brothers of Cologne for storage.

In 1989, it was sold on to France.

1977:
13/11:Tourist Trophy, Phillip Island: Geoghegan, #10; 1st.

1988: Stored at the Kremer Bros; Cologne.
1989: Sold to M. Miloe, France.

Chassis No: 930 770 0902
Production No: 107.2385.
Engine No: 677 2901
Gearbox No: 777 2901
Colour: White.

Sold to Martino Finotto of Italy, 0902 immediately started racing in early 1977, Finotto, Facetti and Camathias finishing a good second at the Daytona Twenty Four Hours and then coming second again at the Mugello 6-Hours. Another second place was taken in the Giro d'Italia but outright success with the car eluded the Italians and after Facetti crashed the car in August, 1978, it's history becomes vague.

Finotto sold this 935 to Massimo Sordi in 1999. and, apart from a couple of races, 0902 has disappeared from sight.

1977:
05-06/02: Daytona 24-Hours WCM: Facetti/Finotto/ Camathias, #3; 2nd OA. Jolly Club Entry.
20/03: Mugello 6-Hours WCM; Finotto/Facetti/ Camathias, #5; 2nd OA.
17/04: Trofeo Morelli, Varano: Finotto, #244; 1st.
15/05: Silverstone 6-Hours WCM: Facetti/Finotto, #8; 6th OA.
12-16/06: Giro d'Italia: Finotto/Mohr, #537; DNF. (Transmission).
17/07: Corsa dell' Etna, Pergusa: Finotto; 4th OA, 1st in class.
24/07: Paul Ricard 500Km WCM: Finotto/ Camathias, #50; 8th OA.
20/08: Misano by Night: Finotto; 1st.
04/09: Coppa Intereuropa, Monza: Finotto; 1st.
23/10: Vallelunga 6-Hours WCM: Facetti/Finotto, #1; DNF.
13/11: Trofeo Natale Nappi, Vallelunga: Finotto; 3rd.

1978:
04-05/02: Daytona 24-Hours WCM: Facetti, #3;66th NR.
20/03: Mugello 6-Hours WCM: Finotto/Facetti, #3; 5th OA.
14/05: Silverstone 6-Hours WCM: Facetti/Finotto, #14; DNF.
25/06: Misano 6-Hours WCM: Facetti/Finotto/ Grano, #9; DNF. (Acc).
30/08: NOTE: Finotto crashed a 935 turbo in testing.

1980: Perhaps the car sold to Nourri?

1981:
22/03: Zolder: Doren; DNS.
29/03: Nürburgring 300Km: Gall, #72; 12th.

1999: Sold to M. Sordi.

Chassis No: 930 770 0903
Production No: 107.2386.
Engine No: 677 2902
Gearbox No: 777 2902
Colour: White.

The first factory built 935 to be supplied to the Kremer Brothers, this 935, was mainly driven by Bob Wollek who had previously raced the Kremer Brother's RSR Carrera, chassis number 911 560 9017. Wollek did well with the car, despite it not winning any major victories but there were some good placings.

In 1978, the 935 was sold to Claude Bourgoigne of Belgium, who had two excellent seasons of racing with it. It was then sold to Stafania Cohen in 1982. Steve Southard, of Auto Assets, bought the car in 2002. It was then bought and is raced by an enthusiastic collector who had it restored in 2007 and then sold it.

1977: Sold to: The Kremer Bros. Kremer entered.
5-6/02: Daytona 24-Hours WCM: Wollek/Joest/Krebs, #8; 3rd .
20/03: Mugello 6-Hours WCM: Wollek/Fitzpatrick, #3; DNF, (collision with Barth's 935).
15/05: Silverstone 6-Hours: Wollek/Fitzpatrick, #3; 2nd OA.

14-15/06: Le Mans 24-Hours: Fitzpatrick/Edwards/Faure, #42; DNF.
03/07: Norisring: P. Gregg, #70 (DRM); 3rd. Trophy race: P. Gregg; 15th.
30/07: G.P. von Deutschland Hockenheim DRM: Fitzpatrick, #30; 4th.
25/09: Brands Hatch 6-Hours WCM: Wollek/Faure, #2; 4th OA. "Rivet Supply Co.Ltd"
2/10: Nürburgring: Christmann, #70;7th.
9/10: Hockenheim 2 x 3 Hours:Haldi/Christmann/Wollek, #5; 4th.
16/10: Zolder: Schornstein, #59; 7th.
6/11: Rheintalrennen Hockenheim: Brambring; 2nd.

1978:
Sold to Team Willeme, Racing City 7, Brussels, Belgium. Driven by Claude Bourgoignie.
12/03: Bergische Lowe, Zolder DRM: Bourgoignie, #33; 4th.
27/03: Paasraces, Zandvoort: Bourgoignie; 1st.
02/04: Bekers van Belgie, Zolder: Bourgoignie, #73; 1st.
16/04: Zolder: Bourgoignie, #73; 1st.
15/05: Pinsterraces, Zandvoort: Bourgoignie: 1st.
18/06: Promotieraces, Zandvoort: Bourgoignie, #73; DNS.
02/07: Zandvoort Trophy: Bourgoignie, #33; 4th.
09/07: Nivelles: Bourgoignie, #73; 1st.
29/07: GP von Deutschland, Hockenheim DRM: Bourgoignie, #33; 10th.
13/08: Nivelles: Bourgoignie, #73; 1st.
10/09: Bekers der Toekomst, Zolder: Bourgoignie, #73; 1st.
17/09: Zandvoort: Bourgoignie, #73; 1st.
30/09: E.G. Trophy, Zolder: Bourgoignie; 1st.
1/10: Zolder: Bourgoignie, #73; 1st.
8/10: Finale Races, Zandvoort: Bourgoignie; 1st.
14/10: Zolder; "Davit"; 5th.
15/10: Zolder: Bourgoignie, #8; 1st.
Bourgoignie was Benelux Champion, Group 2-5.

1979:
11/03: Bergischer Lowe Zolder DRM: Bourgoigne, #58; 4th.

25/03: Zandvoort: Bourgoignie; 1st.
01/04: Zolder: Bourgoignie; 1st.
22/04: Zolder: Bourgoignie; 1st.
29/04: Coupe d'Ixelles: Bourgoignie; 1st.
20/05: Colmar-Berg: Bourgoignie; 1st.
10/06: Zolder: Bourgoignie; 1st.
24/06: Nivelles: Bourgoignie, #57; 1st.
12/08: Nivelles: Bourgoignie; 1st.
09/09: Coupes de l'Avenir; Bourgoignie;1st.
Bourgoignie was Benelux Champion, Group 2-5. He won the Benelux Championship.

1980: Re-engined with twin-turbo engine #698 0070 by Kremer.
Bourgoigne won the Benelux Championship:.

1981:
23/10: Sold to Philippe Bervoets, Brussells, Belgium.("Davit").
Spa 1000Km: G. Trigaux; 1st?
Won the Belgian Championship Int. Racing Trophy.

1982:
23/05: Sold to Stefania Cohen (stefania@ix.netcom.com).

2002: Sold to Auto Assets, USA.
2003: Sold by John Starkey to Bill Cotter. Restored.
2005: Monterey Historics.
Restored.
2007: Rennsport Reunion. Concours winner. As K2.
2008: STPO.

Chassis No: 930 770 0904
Production No: 107. 2387
Engine No: 677 2903.
Gearbox No: 777 2908.
Colour: Indian Red

Jurgen Kannacher raced 0904 only a few times before selling it to the Swiss enthusiast, Claude Haldi. Haldi, together with Herbert Muller, raced 0904 in World Championship events in 1977 and 1978.

In 1979, Haldi, together with Jacques Rey, the previous owner of a Lola T70, took in an assortment of races in 1979 before Haldi sold the car, probably to Herve Poulain who, after just three races, sold it, to whom we do not know. It was exhibited at the Le Mans museum until 2016, when it was auctioned.

Sold to: Reiner Kamphausen (Jurgen Kannacher's team manager).

1977: German National Championship:
13/03: Bergischer Lowe Zolder: Kannacher, #56; 5th.
20/03: Mugello 6-hours WCM: Haldi/Ferrier, #7; 7th./4th.
27/03: 300Km Nürburgring: Kannacher, #56(DRM); 7th.(National); 5th. ????

1977: Sold to Claude Haldi. Prepared by Haberthur.
27/03: Ampus-Draguignan, (EHC): Haldi; 2nd.
17/05: Silverstone 6-Hours WCM: Haldi/Joest/Ferrier, #10; 8th./2nd.
22/05: Montseny, (EHC): Haldi; 2nd.
29/05: Nürburgring 1000Km WCM: Haldi/Joest, #32; 7th./1st.

11-12/06: Le Mans 24-Hours: Servanin/Hummel/
Ferrier, #59; DNF.
03/07: Norisring: Haldi, #80, (DRM); 7th. Trophy
Race: 18th.
10/07: Trento Bondone, (EHC): Haldi; 3rd.
24/07: Paul Ricard WCM: Haldi/Ferrier, #42; 10th.
/2nd.
07/08: Mont Dore, (EHC): Haldi; 2nd.
25/09: Brands Hatch 6-Hours WCM: Haldi/
Pallavicini, #9; 6th./1st.
9/10: Hockenheim 6-Hours :Pallavicini/Calderari;
10th/3rd.
23/10: Vallelunga 6 Hours WCM: Haldi, #9; DNS.
(Accident).

1978:
19/03: Mugello 6-Hours WCM: Haldi/Muller, #22;
4th.
16/04: Dijon 4-Hours WCM: Haldi/Haldi/Muller,
#4; DNF (engine).
30/04: Eifelrennen Nürburgring: DRM: Haldi, #19;
7th.
14/05: Silverstone 6-Hours WCM: Haldi/Muller,
#15; DNF.
28/05: Nürburgring 1000Km WCM: Haldi/Muller,
#18; 36th. (driveshaft).
10-11/06: Le Mans 24-Hours. Mecarillos entered.
Haldi/Muller/Nico, #48; DNF.
29/07: G.P. von Deutschland DRM: Haldi, #11; 5th.
03/09: Vallelunga 6-Hours WCM: Haldi, Muller, #7;
DNF.
17/09: Norisring: Haldi, #15; (DRM); 5th. Trophy
race: 6th.
22/10: Hockenheim 3-Hours: Haldi/Muller; 1st..

1979: Red.
01/04: Ampus EHC: Rey; 4th in class.
22/04: Dijon 6-Hours WCM: Haldi, Lowe, #4; 4th
OA.
29/04: Eifelrennen, Nürburgring DRM: Haldi, #70;
DNF.
27/05: Estrella EHC: Rey; 2nd in class A5.
 9-10/06: Le Mans 24-Hours: Haldi entered. Haldi/
Lowe/Teran, #43;11th OA.

24/06: Bolzano-Mendola EHC: Rey; 2nd in class.
15/07: Trofeo Scarfiotti EHC: Rey; 4th in class.
22/07: Potenza: Rey; 5th in class.
05/08: Brands Hatch 6-Hours WCM: Haldi, Lowe;
DNA.
14/08: St. Ursannes EHC: Rey; 1st in class.
02/09: Mont Dore EHC: Rey; 2nd in class.
23/09: Supersprint, Nürburgring DRM: Haldi, #58;
5th.
23/09: Puigmajor: Rey; 2nd in class.

Sold to Herve Poulain. White with blue stripes.

1980:
13/04: Mugello 6-Hours WCM: Snobeck/Destic,
#28; 8th.
14-15/06: Le Mans 24-Hours 24-Hours: Poulain/
Snobeck/Destic, #89; 20th OA.

1982: Sold to France.
2016: Sold at Auction. $1.42M.

Chassis No: 930 770 0905
Production No: 107 2388.
Engine No: 677 2904
Gearbox No: 777 2903
Colour: Orange.

Driven by ex-Porsche works driver, Manfred Schurti, 0905 was adorned with the spectacular orange paintwork of its "Jagermeister" sponsor. This 935 achieved four wins in the 1977 German Championship, Schurti sometimes having Edgar Doren as a co-driver.

For 1978, 0905 was sold to Gianpiero Moretti of "Momo" fame. Moretti took the car to America to race in the IMSA series and, at the end of 1978, he sold this car to Randolph Townsend of Reno, Nevada. Townsend started racing the car in the IMSA Championship besides taking in Le Mans where, with Touroul and Jean-Pierre Jarier, he was forced to retire.

Townsend raced the car in the long-distance American races of 1979 before donating it to a museum.

Sold to: Max Moritz. "Jaegermeister" sponsorship.

1977: German National Championship Races, Race #52 except where otherwise noted.
13/03: Bergischer Lowe Zolder: Schurti, #52; 1st. (Pole)
27/03: 300Km Nürburgring: Schurti; 2nd.(DRM and National races).
01/05: Eifelrennen Nürburgring; Schurti; 10th.
08/05: Kassel-Calden: Schurti; DNF.
22/05: Mainz-Finthen: Schurti; 4th.
29/05: Nürburgring 1000Km WCM: Schurti/ Kelleners, #7; 6th OA.
03/07: Norisring Nurnberg: Schurti; (DRM); 2nd. Trophy; 1st.
17/07: Dobratsch: (EHC): Kelleners, #94; 3rd OA, 1st in class.
24/07: Diepholz: Schurti; DNF. (oil cooler).
30/07: GP von Deutschland Hockenheim: Schurti; 5th. (Pole).
14/08: Westfalen-Pokal Zolder: Schurti; DNF.
21/08: St. Ursanne-Les Rangiers, (EHC): Kelleners; 2nd in class.
11/09: Schwabische Alb, (hillclimb); Schurti; #231; 1st.
25/09: Brands Hatch 6-Hours WCM: Schurti/Doren, #7:2nd OA.

2/10: Supersprint Nürburgring: Schurti; 3rd. (Pole)
9/10: Hockenheim 6-Hours WCM: Ertl/Barth/Doren, #11; DNF.

Sold to Dr. G. Moretti.

1978: IMSA series by Gianpiero Moretti. Race No: 30.
02/04: Talladega 6-Hours; Moretti/Mendez, #30; 32nd NR.
16/04: Road Atlanta 100 Miles: Moretti, #30; 4th.
30/04: Laguna Seca 100 Miles: Moretti, #30; 7th OA.
07/05: Hallett 100 Miles: Moretti, #30; 3rd OA.
29/05: Lime Rock 100 Miles: Moretti, #30; 12th OA.
18/06: Brainerd 100 Miles: Moretti, #30; 2nd OA.
04/07: Daytona, Paul Revere 250: Moretti, #30; 48th, (DNF).
30/07: Sears Point 100 Miles: Moretti, #30; 3rd OA.
06/08: Portland, G.I. Joe's GP: Moretti, #30; 2nd OA.
27/08: Mid-Ohio 250 Miles: Moretti, #30; 4th OA.
04/09: Road Atlanta 100 Miles: Moretti, #30; 4th OA.
26/11:Daytona Finale: Moretti/Haywood, #30; 4th OA.

Sold to Randolph Townsend.

1979: IMSA Championship Races except where otherwise noted. Black with red and yellow flashes.
9-10/06: Le Mans 24-Hours: Jarier/Townsend/ Touroul, #74; DNF (engine).
07/07: Watkins Glen 6-Hours WCM: Forbes-Robinson/Townsend/Lunger, #20; 4th OA.
29/07: Sears Point 100 Miles: Townsend, #13; 27th
05/08: Portland 100 Miles: Townsend, #13; 9th.
26/08: Mid-Ohio: Townsend/Forbes-Robinson/ Lunger, #13; 3rd.
01/09: Trois Rivieres TA: Townsend; 11th. Acc.
23/09: Road Atlanta 100 Miles: Townsend, #13; 35th NR.

14/10: Laguna Seca TA: Townsend, #13; 7th.

1980: Engine number 699 0062 installed.
2-3/02: Daytona 24-Hours WCM: Townsend/
Meister/Forbes-Robinson, #13; 45th NR.
22/03: Sebring 12-Hours WCM: Townsend/Morton,
#13; 61st NR.
27/04: Riverside 5-Hours WCM: Townsend/Jenner,
#13; 6th OA.
04/05: Laguna Seca: Townsend, #13; 11th.
07/07: Watkins Glen: Jenner/Townsend/Grohs; 8th.

Donated to a museum in Reno, NV.

Chassis No: 930 770 0906
Production No: 107. 2389.
Engine No: 677 2906
Gearbox No: 777 2904
Colour: Silver.

This 935 was sold to Vittorio Coggiola, ("Victor")
of Italy for the Scuderia Vesuvio to run. "Victor",
usually accompanied by co-driver Monticone, did
very well with it as the results below testify.
    In 1981, "Victor" rented the car to Gianni Mussato
to take part in the Italian GT Championship.

1977:
20/3: Mugello 6-Hours: Coggiola/Monticone, #26;
3rd OA.
12-16/06: Giro d'Italia: Coggiola/Monticone, #536;
1st OA.
05/09: Monza, Coppa Intereuropa: Coggiola; 2nd
OA.
23/10: Vallelunga 6-Hours: Coggiola/Monticone;
2nd OA.

1978:
19/03: Mugello 6-Hours: Monticone/Coggiola, #26;
DNF.
28/05: Misano, Coppa AC Torino, (IC): Coggiola;
1st OA.
25/06: Misano 6-Hours WCM: Coggiola/Monticone,
#23; 2nd OA.

15/08: Misano, Trofeo Mare Pulito (IC): Coggiola;
1st OA.
20/08: Magione (IC): Coggiola; 1st OA.
25/08: Misano (IC): Coggiola; 2nd OA.
03/09: Vallelunga 6-Hours (WCM): Coggiola/
Monticone, #4: 11th OA.
13-18/10: Giro d'Italia: Coggiola/Monticone, #512;
DNF. Acc.

Winner of Italian Group 5 Championship.

1979-1980: In storage as "Victor" was racing his
1978 Porsche 935, 930 890 0017.

1981: Rented to Gianni Mussato.

31/05: Vallelunga (IC): Mussato; 3rd in class.
14/06: Varano, Trofeo Cariplo (IC): Mussato; 3rd in
class.
13/07: Cesana-Sestriere: Mussato; 2nd in class.
25/08: Magione, Trofeo Urat (IC): Mussato, #808;
2nd in class.
20/09: Pergusa, Coppa Citta di Enna (IC): Mussato;
2nd in class.
27/09: Varano (IC): Mussato; 4th in class.
11/10: Magione (IC): Mussato; 2nd in class.

217

1/11: Vallelunga, Trofeo Natale Nappi (IC):
Mussato; 2nd in class.

Chassis No: 930 770 0907
Production No: 107. 3870.
Engine No: 677 2905
Gearbox No: 777 2910.
Colour: White.

Sold to Josef Brambring, another previous driver of
RSR Carreras, 0907 was "Mobel-Franz" sponsored
and took part in the German National Championship
of 1977, with creditable results. Usually driven by
Franz Neuhaus (and once for a victory by Jochen
Mass), 0907 was then sold mid-season to Franz
Konrad, that long-time Porsche privateer.

For 1978, Konrad sold the 935 to Klaus Drees
who raced it several times before selling the 935 to
Mahlke, a tyre dealer.

Mahlke employed several drivers, amongst them
Ralf-Dieter Schreiber, Franz Gschwender and Klaus
Bohm to drive the car but for 1980, only Bohm was
still racing it. NOTE: This 935 was re-chassised with
a 1971 911S body shell and engine number: 698
0074 after a pit fire at Monza in 1981. The original
bodyshell is still in Europe and was repaired. Both
cars are now, (2018), with the same owner and the
original parts of both cars have been combined to
result in just one 930 770 0907.

1977:
Race #54 except where otherwise noted.
13/3: Bergischer Lowe, Zolder: F. Neuhaus; 3rd.
27/3: 300Km, Nürburgring DRM: J. Mass; 1st.
0 1/5: Eifelrennen, Nürburgring: F. Neuhaus, #54; 3rd.
08/5: Kassel-Calden: F. Neuhaus; 3rd.
22/5: Mainz-Finthen: F. Neuhaus, #54; 5th.
27/5: Nürburgring 1000Km WCM: F. Neuhaus/L.
Kinnunen;#9; DNF.

Sold to Franz Konrad.
24/7: Diepholz: F. Konrad, #58; 6th.
31/7: GP von Deutschland, Hockenheim: F. Konrad,
#55; 6th.

14/8: Westfalen-Pokal, Zolder: F. Konrad, #58; 3rd.
28/8: Nürburgring: F. Konrad, #94; 1st.
25/9: Brands Hatch 6-Hours WCM: F. Konrad/B.
Wollek, #3; 3rd.
2/10: Supersprint, Nürburgring: F. Konrad, #58; 6th.
9/10: Hockenheim 6-Hours, (2 x 3-Hours): F.
Konrad/R. Joest/B. Wollek; DNF.
16/10: Zolder: F. Konrad; #54; 2nd.(Int. Race).
Sold to Klaus Drees.

1978:
12/3: Bergischer Lowe Zolder DRM: Drees, #18; 10th.
19/3: Mugello 6-Hours WCM: K. Drees/W.
Kauwertz, #29; 16th.
02/4: 300 Km Nürburgring DRM: K. Drees, #25;
DNF.
16/4: Dijon 6-Hours WCM: W. Kauwertz/K.
Drees/M. Haehnlein, #12; 10th OA.
30/4: Eifelrennen Nürburgring DRM: K. Drees, #18;
9th.
14/5: Silverstone 6-Hours WCM: M. Franey/K.
Drees, #17; 14th OA.
28/5: Nürburgring 1000Km WCM: K. Drees/M.
Haehnlein/M. Franey, #19; 17th OA.
Sold to Mahlke, a Tyre dealer in Cologne.

1979:
11/3: Bergischer Lowe Zolder DRM: Ralf-Dieter
Schreiber, #68; 11th.
08/4: Jim Clark-Rennen Hockenheim DRM: R-D
Schreiber, #80; DNF.
22/4: Dijon 1000Km WCM: M. Hahnlein/F.
Gschwender/M. Bohm; 5th.
29/4: Eifelrennen Nürburgring DRM : R-D

Schreiber; 11th.
20/5: Bavaria Salzburgring DRM: R-D Schreiber; 13th.
09/6: Nürburgring 1000Km WCM: R-D Schreiber/M Hahnlein/ Lagodny, #10; DNS. (fire)
17/6: Mainz-Finthen DRM: M. Hahnlein; 12th.
24/6: Norisring Nurnberg: M. Bohm; 15th (DRM) 8th (200 Miles).
22/7: Diepholz DRM:F. Gschwender; 6th.
28/7: Hockenheim: P. Hahnlein; 6th.
13/8: Mugello 6-Hours WCM:F. Gschwender/ Feuerlein/R-D Schreiber; DNF (engine).
19/8: Westfalenpokal Zolder DRM: M. Bohm, # 59; 8th.
7/10: Hessenpreis Kassel-Calden Interseries: "Harry Hirsch"; 8th.
14/10: Zolder:M. Bohm; 6th.

1980:
01/6: Schwanbergrennen: M. Bohm; 3rd.
22/6: Norisring, Nurnberg: M. Bohm; 6th.
13/7: Bavaria-Rennen Salzburgring:M. Bohm; 11th.
27/7: Diepholz: M. Bohm, #12; DNF.
24/8: Westfalen-Pokal Zolder: M. Bohm; 9th.

1981:
26/4: Monza 1000Km WCM: Feuerlain/P. Hahnlein, #2; DNF. (Fire).

1982: Original car dismantled, in Germany.
Parts and papers sold to Jurgen Kannacher. A "new" car was built up, using a 1971 911S body shell.

1983: Car with 911S chassis advertised in "Auto Motor und Sport" by Jurgen Kannacher as "The last original 935 in Germany".

2000: Sold to Max Blees.
2012: Sold to Italy.
2017: Sold to owner of the original chassis of 0907.
2006: Original chassis with Racine Feustel, being rebuilt.
2014: Car with original chassis sold to present owner.
2017: The car built on a 911S body shell has also been sold to owner of the car with the original

chassis. Parts reunited, car restored to original specification.
2017: Sold to Porsche A.G.

Chassis No: 930 770 0908
Production No: 107. 3871.
Engine No: 677 2907
Gearbox No: 777 2905
Colour: Indian Red.

The first of Georg Loos' 1977 935's, 0908 was usually driven by Rolf Stommelen who scored four victories with it, Schenken taking another and Henry van Oorschott taking a couple more at the end of the season.

Van Oorschott bought the 935 from Loos for the 1978 season and scored four more victories with it before selling the car.

After this, the car was sold to the well known Porsche race car collectors, Jeff Lewis, Kerry Morse and then Frank Gallogly, who had the factory restore the car.
930 770 0908 was sold at the R.M. Auction at Monterey to Mr Escobar in Brazil in 1997.

Sold to: Georg Loos (1).

1977: German National Championship except where otherwise stated. Gelo entered:
27/03: 300Km Nürburgring: Stommelen, #66; 1st.
01/05: Eifelrennen Nürburgring: Stommelen, #66; 2nd.
08/05: Kassel-Calden: Stommelen, #66; 2nd.

15/05: Silverstone 1000Km: Stommelen/Hezemans, #6; 3rd. (or 930 770 0911?).
22/05: Mainz-Finthen: Stommelen, #66; 1st.
29/05: Nürburgring 1000Km WCM: Stommelen/Hezemans/Schenken, #3; 1st.
14-15/06: Le Mans 24-Hours: Hezemans, Schenken, Heyer, Ludwig, #38; DNF.
03/07: Norisring Nurnberg: Stommelen, #66; (DRM); 1st. National Race; 3rd.
24/07: Diepholz: Stommelen, #66; 1st.
30/07: G.P. von Deutschland, Hockenheim: Stommelen, #66; 2nd.
14/08: Westfalen-Pokal Zolder: Stommelen, #66; 2nd.
02/10: Supersprint Nürburgring:Schenken, #66;DNF.
09/10: Hockenheim 6-Hours:Van Oorschott, #2; DNF.
16/10: Zolder: van Oorschott; G5; 6th, G4; 1st.
06/11: Hockenheim: van Oorschott; G5, #169; 1st.

1978: Sold to Henry van Oorschott. Auto Nijmegen sponsored, red/white.
12/03: Bergischer Lowe Zolder DRM: van Oorschott, #31; 5th.
27/3: Paasraces, Zandvoort: Van Oorschott; 1st.
02/04: Bekers van Belgie, Zolder: Van Oorschott; 2nd.
16/04: Zandvoort: Van Oorschott, #74; 6th.
15/05: Pinksterraces, Zandvoort: Van Oorschott; 2nd.
18/06: Promotieraces, Zandvoort: Van Oorschott; 1st.
02/07: Zandvoort-Trophy: Van Oorschott, #31:DNF. (Acc.)
29/07: G.P. von Deutschland, Hockenheim DRM: van Oorschott, #45: 7th.
13/08: Zandvoort: van Oorschott, (G4); 1st. (Division 1); 1st.
20/08: Westfalen-Pokal Zolder DRM: van Oorschott, #19; 3rd.
27/08: GP van Nederland: Van Oorschott; 1st.
10/09: Zolder: Van Oorschott, DNS. (engine).
17/09: Zandvoort: Van Oorschott; 2nd.
08/10: Finale race, Zandvoort: Van Oorschott, #74; DNF. (engine).

1980: Restored by the factory.
1982: Sold to Gerry Sutterfield
1982: Sold to Jeff Lewis
1985: Sold to Kerry Morse. Of interest , while owned by Kerry Morse, 930 770 908 was featured on a postage stamp in the Loos colors of the German Championship.
1992: Sold to Frank Gallogly
1997: 16/8: Sold through Monterey auction to a buyer in Brazil.

Chassis No: 930 770 0909
Production No: 107. 3872.
Engine No: 677 2908
Gearbox No: 777 2906
Colour: White.

Although noted in the factory records as being sold to Vasek Polak, this car went straight to Peter Gregg's Jacksonville-based "Brumos" distributorship. There, it was stripped of parts for use in Gregg's 934 and a half, which he drove in the 1977 Trans Am Championship, (see: 930 770 0952). 0909 did nothing in 1977 until, at the end of the year, Jack Atkinson rebuilt the car and Peter Gregg used it to establish speed records during the Finale meeting at Daytona.

In 1978, Gregg shared the car with Brad Friselle

at the 24-Hour race at Daytona, placing ninth and
then had an uncharacteristic accident in it at Sebring,
putting the car on its roof. Jack Atkinson and his
crew took the car back to Jacksonville, repaired
it and Gregg won the next two IMSA races at
Talladega, (with Brad Friselle), and Road Atlanta.

After this, Peter Gregg sold the 935 to Bruce
Leven as he had taken delivery of his 1978 twin-
turbo car and Leven raced the 935 for the rest of the
season before retiring it and using it as a road car!

Sold to Dave Morse in California, 0909 was
fastidiously restored and sometimes vintage raced.
Christopher Stahl bought her in 2006 but then, in
2008, she was sold, via Franco Lembo, back to
Bruce Leven!

Sold to: Vasek Polak.
Delivered to Peter Gregg. The axles and gearbox
were used in Gregg's 934 before April,
1977.

27/11: Daytona speed records with Peter Gregg: 190
mph for 10 miles from a standing start.

1978:
4-5/02: Daytona 24-Hours WCM: Gregg/Ballot-
Lena/Frisselle, #59; 9th. (JMS-Brumos entered).
18/03: Sebring 12-Hours WCM: Gregg, #59;
69thNR. (Acc).
02/04: Talladega 6-Hours IMSA: Gregg/Frisselle,
#59; 1st.
16/04: Road Atlanta IMSA: Gregg, #59; 1st.

Sold to Bruce Leven.

1979:
30/04: Laguna Seca IMSA: Haywood; 2nd.
06/05: Mexico City TA: Leven, #85; 3rd.
03/06: Westwood TA: Leven, #85; 4th.
10/06: Portland: Leven, #85; 4th.
07/07: Watkins Glen 6 Hours WCM: Leven/Gregg/
Haywood, #85; DNF.
21/07: Road America, Elkhart Lake TA: Leven, #85;
5th.

29/07: Sears Point IMSA: Leven, #85;11th.
05/08: Portland 100 Miles IMSA: Leven, #85; DNF.
26/08: Mid-Ohio: Gregg/Haywood IMSA, #85; 14th.
23/09: Road Atlanta: Haywood, #85; 4th.
14/10: Laguna Seca TA: Leven, #85; 6th.

1980:
13/04: Road Atlanta: Leven, #85; 25th NR
27/04: Riverside: Leven; Spare car.
04/05: Laguna Seca: Leven, #85; 7th.
03/08: Portland: Leven, #88; 7th.

Used as a road car. White.

1984: July: Advertised in "Panorama" from Bruce
Leven.

Sold to Dave Morse, restored.
1998: Displayed and driven at the Monterey
Historics.
2003: Sold to David Mohlman.
2004: Sold to Christopher Stahl.
For sale on Franco Lembo's site. Automobilia.
2007: STPO, USA.
2015: "Rennsport Reunion", Laguna Seca. Bruce
Leven.

Chassis No: 930 770 0910
Production No: 107.3873.
Engine No: 677 2912
Gearbox No: 777 2907
Colour: White.

Sold to Jo Hoppen of Volkswagen of America for
Peter Gregg, 0910 was almost immediately sold to
Jim Busby of California. He converted the car to
twin-turbo configuration, obtained "Mitcom" sponsorship and raced 0910 in World Championship
events where his best result was a third place at
Mid-Ohio.

At the end of the season, Busby re-converted the
935 to single-turbocharger specification and sold
the car to Otis Chandler, the publisher of the Los
Angeles Times.

Chandler raced the 935 just once, together with John Thomas, at the Watkins Glen 6-Hours race of 1978 where the pair finished in sixth place. After this, Chandler sold the 935 to fellow Californian, Dick Barbour. Barbour painted the car blue and used the car as a "rent a ride" and it did very well, winning the 1979 Sebring Twelve Hour race.

In 1980, the car was sold to the Matsuda collection in Japan and, in 1999, it was bought by the Symbolic Motor Car Company of La Jolla, California. In turn, they sold it to Dave Mohlmann of Miami who employed your author to seek out it's history.

In 1999, the 935 was sold to Mike Smith, who had Gunnar Racing go through the car and re-paint it in it's 1979 Sebring 12-Hour colors.

In February, 2001, 0910 was sold to Hugh Fuller, and then to Matt Drendel. Upon Drendel's death, It was sold to Christopher Stahl and then in 2009, to Jean-Marc Merlin.

1977: Converted to twin-turbo specification.
09/07: Watkins Glen 6-Hours WCM: J.Busby/Tom Frank, #61; 12th.
20/08: Mosport 6-Hours WCM: J.Busby/Wietzes, #61; 19th.

28/08: Mid-Ohio 3-Hours: J.Busby, #61; 3rd. Converted back to single turbo configuration. Sold to Otis Chandler.

1978:
09/07: Watkins Glen 6-Hours WCM: J.Thomas/O. Chandler, #71; 6th.

1979: Sold to Dick Barbour.
3-4/02: Daytona 24-Hours WCM: Akin/McFarlin/ Woods, #9; DNF. (engine).
18/03: Sebring 12-Hours WCM: Akin/McFarlin/ Woods. #9; 1st.
22/04: Riverside 6-Hours WCM: McFarlin/Woods/ Akin, #9; 4th.
10-11/06: Le Mans 24-Hours: Garretson/ McKitterick/Abate, #72; 8th.
07/07: Watkins Glen 6-Hours WCM: Garretson/ McKitterick/Marcus, #72; 9th OA.
02/09: Road America, Elkhart Lake IMSA: Garretson/McKitterick, #4; 19th OA.

1980: Engine number 698 0121 installed.
Sold to the Matsuda collection.

1999: Sold to D. Mohlman.
2000: Sold to Mike Smith. Completely restored and repainted by Gunnar Racing, Florida.
2000: June: For sale.
2001: Feb: Sold to Hugh Fuller.
2001: Sold to Matt Drendel.
2008: Sold to Christopher Stahl.
2009: STPO.

Chassis No: 930 770 0911
Production No: 107. 6077.
Engine No: 677 2910
Gearbox No:
Colour: Indian Red.

Chassis number 930 770 0911 has had a long career! The second 935 to be sold to Georg Loos' team in 1977, it was driven by all the team's 1977 drivers including Rolf Stommelen, Toine Hezemans

and Tim Schenken. It won at Diepholz and the Nürburgring "Supersprint" DRM race.

At the end of 1977, the car was sold to italy and raced there until 1979 when it was sent to the factory and updated with a twin-turbo engine, bigger brakes and an upside down gearbox.

0911 was then sold to Charles Mendez who raced it with success in IMSA races, winning at the July Daytona meeting and coming second at Road America in September. In November, the 935 was involved in the big crash at the Daytona Finale and was re-chassised with chassis number 009 0005.

Sold to: Georg Loos (2)

1977: German National Championship:
01/05: Eifelrennen Nürburgring: Schenken, #74; 4th.
15/05: Silverstone 6-Hours WCM: Bell/Schenken, #5; DNF (engine).
22/05: Mainz-Finthen: Schenken, #67; 3rd.
29/05: Nürburgring 1000Km WCM: Stommelen/Schenken, #2; DNF.
03/07: Norisring Nurnberg: Schenken;(DRM) 4th. Hezemans, #67; Trophy; 13th.
24/07: Diepholz: Hezemans, #67; 1st.
30/07: GP von Deutschland, Hockenheim: Schenken, #67; 3rd.
14/08: Westfalen-Pokal, Zolder: Schenken, #67; 8th.
2/10: Supersprint Nürburgring:Stommelen, #67;1st.
9/10: Hockenheim 6-Hours: Heyer/ Stommelen, #67; 11th.

Sold to Carlo Noce, "Sportwagen" race team of Sassuolo, Italy.

1978:
19/03: Mugello 6 Hours, WCM: M. Casoni/C. Manfredini, #7; 17th
16/04: Dijon 4 Hours WCM: M. Casoni/D. Mallet, #11; DNF. (Turbocharger).

Probably sold to Carlo Facetti. If so:

03/09: Vallelunga 6-Hours WCM: Facetti/Ghinzani/Moreschi, #5; 5th.

1979:
3-4/02: Daytona 24-Hours WCM: Facetti/Finotto/Moretti; 45th NR. (accident).
18/03: Mugello 6 Hours WCM: Facetti/Finotto, #3; 3rd.

Returned to the factory and brought up to 1979 specification with twin turbo engine, big brakes and upside-down gearbox at a cost of DM120,000.

06/05: Silverstone 6 Hours WCM: Facetti/Finotto, #11; DNA.
1979: June: Sold to Charles Mendez. Engine number 677 2910.

1979: IMSA Championship Races.
04/07: Daytona 250 Miles: Mendez/Haywood, #5; 1st.
15/07: Mid-Ohio 250 Miles: Mendez/Miller, #5; 5th.
29/07: Sears Point 100 Miles: Mendez, #5; 7th. Acc. Hit by Bob Akin.
02/09: Road America 500 Miles: Mendez/Miller, #5; 2nd.
23/09: Road Atlanta: Mendez/Akin; 8th.
25/11: Daytona Finale: Mendez; 3rd. Acc.

Uprated to K3 specification. See 009 0005.

Chassis No: 930 770 0912
Production No: 107.6078.

Engine No: 677 2911.
Gearbox No: 777 2912.
Colour: Black.

Sold to Henri Cachia, 0912 was raced in World Championship events and took a second place at Brands Hatch and a class victory and third overall at Le Mans in 1977. In 1978, at the same race, it came in seventh overall.

In later years, the car came to America, (Ash Tisdelle), before being sold to Kevin Jeannette, who sold it back to Germany. It has since returned to the USA.

1977: ASA Cachia entered.
15/05: Silverstone 6-Hours WCM: Ballot-Lena/Lafosse, #12; 13th OA.
11-12/06: Le Mans: Ballot-Lena/Gregg, #60; 3rd OA/1st in Group 5. JMS Racing entry.
25/09: Brands Hatch 6-Hours WCM: Ballot-Lena/Leclerc; DNA. J.M. Smadja entry.
9/10: Hockenheim:Lafosse/Ballot-Lena, #7; 2nd. J.M. Smadja entry, (JMS).

1978:
19/03: Mugello 6-Hours WCM: Ballot-Lena/Lafosse, #16; 15th OA.
16/04: Dijon 4-Hours WCM: Lafosse/Ballot-Lena, #9; 5th OA.
14/05: Silverstone 6-Hours WCM: Lafosse/Leclerc, #16; DNF.
10-11/06: Le Mans 24-Hours: Guarana/Gomes/Amaral, #41; 7th OA. 2nd in class.
17/09: Norisring 200 Miles WCM: Lafosse, #29; 5th.

1979:
22/04: Dijon 6-Hours WCM: Lafosse/Leclerc, #11; 8th.
10-11/06: Le Mans 24-Hours: Guerin/Alliot/Goujon, #39; 15th OA. Kores entry

Sold to Christian Bussi.

1980:
16/03: Brands Hatch 6-Hours WCM: Bussi/Salam/Schlesser, #10;DNF.
13/04: Mugello 6-Hours WCM: Salam/Bussi; #27; DNF. (accident).
11/05: Silverstone 6-Hours WCM: Bussi/Salam, #15; DNA.
28/09: Dijon 6-Hours WCM: Bussi/Salam, #37; 10th OA.

1981:
12/04: Mugello 6-Hours WCM: Bussi/Guerin, #6, 4th OA.
26/04: Monza 1000Km WCM: Barth/Guerin/Bussy, #6; DNF.
10/05: Silverstone 6-Hours WCM: Guerin/Bussi/Delaunay, #25; 10th OA.
27/09: Brands Hatch 1000Km WCM: Guerin/Bussi, #30; 17th.
Perhaps:
20/03: Sebring 12-Hours: Pallavicini/Sheldon/Crang, #03; 37th NR. (935).
Sold to Ash Tisdelle. Painted blue.

1985:
2-3/02: Daytona 24-Hours WCM: Van Every/
Tisdelle/Refenning, #95; 53rdNR.
23/03: Sebring 12-Hours WCM: Van Every/Tisdelle,
#95; 63rdNR.

1986: Sold to Kevin Jeannette, Gunnar Racing,
Florida.
1987: Sold to Burkhard von Schenk, Germany.
STPO.

Chassis No: 930 770 0913
Production No: 107. 6079.
Engine No: 677 2913
Gearbox No: 777 2913
Colour: White.

   Sold to Vasek Polak for the IMSA series, this
935 saw comparatively little racing, but was rented
to Ted Field's Interscope team for 1978. It MAY
have raced in 1977.

1977:
09/07: Watkins Glen 6 Hours: B. Lunger/G. Folder,
#16; 2nd.
14/08: Pocono: M. Minter, #4; 4th.
20/08: Mosport 6 Hours: B. Lunger/G. Follmer, #16;
17th.
28/08: Mid Ohio 3 Hours: J. Ickx/S. McKitterick,
#15; 2nd.

1978: Rented to Ted Field.
3-4/02: Daytona 24 Hours: Ongais/Field/Minter, #0;
DNF.
08/07: Watkins Glen 6 Hours: G. Follmer/J. Ickx,
#1; 26th.

1980: With Vasek Polak. Engine number 677 2913
installed.

1998: Sold at Brooks Auction, Nürburgring to
Walter Pauwels of Belgium.
2007: In Brazil.

**1978-1979: 24 Customer twin-turbo 935 cars
built:**

Chassis No: 930 890 0011
Engine No: 698 0021.
Gearbox No: 798 0000
Colour: Red.

Sharing the driving with Georg Loos' drivers, Toine
Hezemans and Rolf Stommelen, Peter Gregg won
the 1978 Daytona 24 Hours in this car, painted in
Brumos colours. After this auspicious debut, the
first twin-turbo customer 935 was driven to victory
at Zandvoort by John Fitzpatrick and in the Watkins
Glen 6-Hours, partnered by Gregg and Hezemans.
In 1979, Fitzpatrick drove it to victory again at the
Silverstone 6-Hours and in the Nürburgring 1000
kilometre race also.
   At the end of 1979, Loos sold his three 1978 cars
and this one went to Franz Gschwender, who raced
it until 1981 when he sold it to German restorer/
racer, Siggi Brunn. He, in turn, sold to South
Africa where it has resided until being sold back to
Germany and restored.
 1978: Sold to Gelo Racing.
04-05/02: Daytona 24 Hours WCM: Gregg/
Hezemans/Stommelen, #99: 1st OA. (In Brumos
Colours).

12/03: Bergischer Lowe Zolder DRM:Fitzpatrick, #8; 3rd.

19/03: Mugello 6-Hours WCM: Fitzpatrick/ Hezemans/Ludwig, #11; 9th.

02/04: 300Km Nürburgring DRM: Fitzpatrick, #8; 6th.

16/04: Dijon 1000Km WCM: Fitzpatrick/Heyer/ Hezemans, #5; 2nd.

30/04: Eifelrennen Nürburgring DRM: Fitzpatrick, #8; 2nd.

14/05: Silverstone 6-Hours WCM: Hezemans/Heyer/ Fitzpatrick, #5; DNF.

21/05: Avus-Rennen DRM: Fitzpatrick, #8: 3rd.

28/05: Nürburgring 1000Km WCM: Hezemans/ Heyer /Fitzpatrick. #2; DNF. (head gasket).

10-11/06: Le Mans 24-Hours, WCM: Fitzpatrick/ Hezemans, #47; DNF. (engine).

18/06: Mainz-Finthen DRM: Fitzpatrick, #8; 2nd.

25/06: Misano 6-Hours WCM: Fitzpatrick/Heyer, #8; DNF. (no fuel).

02/07: Zandvoort Trophy DRM: Fitzpatrick, #8; 1st.

09/07: Watkins Glen 6-Hours WCM: Gregg/ Hezemans/Fitzpatrick, #30; 1st OA.

16/07: Kassel-Calden DRM: Fitzpatrick, #8; 3rd.

29/07: G.P. von Deutschland; Hockenheim DRM:Fitzpatrick, #8; 4th.

20/08: Westfalen-Pokal Zolder DRM: Fitzpatrick, #8; 2nd.

03/09: Vallelunga 6-Hours WCM: Fitzpatrick/ Hezemans/Ludwig, #8; 2nd.

17/09: Norisring Nurnberg: Fitzpatrick, #8; (DRM); DNF, (Temperature). 200 Miles; 4th.

Track tested in German magazine: "Sport Auto" 8/78

1979: Race #53.

11/03: Bergischer Lowe Zolder DRM: Fitzpatrick, #53; 9th.

08/04: Jim Clark-Rennen, Hockenheim DRM: Fitzpatrick, #53; 2nd.

29/04: Eifelrennen, Nürburgring DRM: Fitzpatrick; 4th.

06/05: Silverstone 6-Hours WCM: Fitzpatrick/ Heyer/Schurti/Wollek, #3; 1st.

20/05: Bavaria Salzurgring DRM: Fitzpatrick; 4th.

03/06: Nürburgring 1000Km WCM: Fitzpatrick/ Schurti/Wollek, #6; 1st.

9-10/06: Le Mans 24-Hours: Gelo entry. Fitzpatrick/ Grohs/Lafosse,#37; DNF. Seiko-sponsored.

17/06: Mainz-Finthen DRM: Fitzpatrick; 4th.

24/06: Norisring Nurnberg: Fitzpatrick, 53; (DRM) 2nd, (200 Miles) 2nd.

01/07: Zandvoort Trophy DRM: Fitzpatrick, #53; 3rd.

22/07: Diepholz DRM: Fitzpatrick, #53; DNF.

19/08: Westfalenpokal Zolder DRM: Fitzpatrick, #53; 3rd.

Sold to FG Werbe-Racing GMBH, Munich. Franz Gschwender

02/09: ADAC Hessen-Cup Hockenheim DRM: Gschwender, #53; 9th.

23/09: Nürburgring Supersprint DRM: Gschwender, #53; 9th.

30/09: Samerberg, (hillclimb): Gschwender; 1st.

7/10: Int. ADAC Hessen-Preis,Kassel-Calden: Gschwender; 2nd.

14/10: Zolder: Gschwender; 2nd.

1980:

23/03: Bergischer Lowe, Zolder DRM: Gschwender; DNS. Crash.

13/04: Mugello 6 Hours: E. Schiebler/F. Muller, #29; DNF. (engine) Gold w/Black/Red stripes, Warsteiner sponsored.

22/06: Norisring DRM: Gschwender; 8th.

29/06: Int.ADAC Flugplatz Erding: Gschwender; 1st

13/07: Salzburgring DRM: Gschwender; DNF.

27/07: Diepholz DRM: Gschwender; DNS.

07/09: Hessen-Cup, Hockenheim: Gschwender; 9th.

1981:

26/04: Monza 1000Kms: P. Hahnlein/W-D. Furerlein, #2; DNF. (Fire).

24/05: Nürburgring 1000Km WCM: F. Gschwender/ Feuerlein, #21;12th in class. (Valvoline entry).

28/06: Norisring:Gschwender, (DRM); DNF. (Trophy), #59; 10th.

05/07: Erding: Gschwender; 2nd.

12/07: Bavaria Rennen, Salzburgring DRM:
Gschwender, #59; 5th.
06/09: Hessen-Cup, Hockenheim DRM:
Gschwender, #54; 9th.

1983: Sold to Siggy Brunn.
10/07: Erding: S.Brun; DNF.

1985: Sold to Andre Bezuidenhout, South Africa.
1996: February. Featured in 'Classic Cars" article,
driven by Derek Bell at the Bugatti circuit, Le Mans.

1999: Sold to a racer in South Africa.
2000: Repainted in Martini colours.
13/02: Killarney, Capetown: G. Rook; 1st heat; 4th,
2nd Heat, 1st.
2003: Sold to Stephen Reutmayer.
2005: Sold to Stefan Mayer, Belgium.

Chassis No: 930 890 0012
Engine No: 698 0022.
Gearbox No: 798 0000.
Colour: White.
Sold to the Kremer Bros.

After racing an RS 3.0 Carrera and a 934, Dieter
Schornstein bought 0012 new from the Kremer
Brothers and had them maintain it for him.
Paradoxically, the car's only victory in 1978 was at
Le Mans where it was "rented" to Jim Busby, Chris
Cord and Steve Knoop, who came in sixth overall
and won the Group five class.

Schornstein carried on racing this 935 right
through until the end of 1980, placing well and
winning his class at Le Mans in 1980 with Gotz von
Tschirnaus and the very fast Harald Grohs.

At the end of 1980, Schornstein sold this 935
to the Joest Racing Team. After this, the car was
converted to a 935J with factory "works" 1977 bodywork and air to air intercooling. In 1981, De Narvaez
rented it for Le Mans but it retired. In 1982, Dieter
Schornstein rented the car back from Joest Racing for
a few races after his 935J, chassis number 000 0016,
had been very badly damaged at Le Mans. In 1983,

the car was rented to Mauricio de Narvaez who,
together with Hans Heyer and Stefan Johansson, won
the last international victory for a 935, the Sebring 12
Hours. Today, the car is in Europe.

Sold to Dieter Schornstein.

1978: White with blue stripes, Sekurit-sponsored.
12/03: Zolder DRM: Schornstein, #3; 8th.
19/03: Mugello 6-Hours WCM: Schornstein/Winter/
Wollek, #8; 7th.
02/04: Nürburgring 300 Km DRM: Schornstein, #3;
11th. (Acc.)
16/04: Dijon 1000Km WCM: Schornstein/"Winter",
#3; 6th OA.
30/04: Eifelrennen, Nürburgring DRM: Schornstein,
#3; 10th OA.
14/05: Silverstone 6-Hours WCM:
Schornstein/"Winter"/Wollek, #9; 5th OA.
21/05: Avus DRM: Schornstein, #3; 7th.
28/05: Nürburgring 1000Km WCM: Schornstein/
Winter/Wollek, #5; DNF, engine.
10-11/06: Le Mans 24-Hours: Busby/Cord/Knoop,
#44; 6th OA. 1st in Group 5.
18/06: Mainz-Finthen DRM: Schornstein, #3; 7th.
02/07: Zandvoor DRM: Schornstein, #3: DNF.
16/07: Kassel-Calden DRM: Schornstein, #3; 9th.

29/07: GP von Deutschland, Hockenheim DRM: Schornstein, #3; 9th.
20/08: Westfalen-Pokal, Zolder DRM: Schornstein, #3; 5th.
03/09: Vallelunga 6-Hours WCM: Schornstein/"Winter"/Wollek, #6; 6th OA.
17/09: Norisring: Schornstein, #3; (DRM); 4th.200 Miles; 11th.
01/10: Supersprint, Nürburgring DRM: Schornstein, #3; 6th.
15/10: Zolder: Schornstein; 2nd.

1979: Sekurit-Racing Team.
11/03: Zolder: Schornstein DRM, #57; 8th.
08/04: Jim Clark-Rennen, Hockenheim DRM: Schornstein, #57; DNF.(driveshaft)
22/04: Dijon 6-Hours WCM: Schornstein/Doren, #5; 3rd OA.
29/04: Eifelrennen, Nürburgring DRM: Schornstein, #57; 10th.
06/05: Silverstone 6-Hours WCM: Doren/Schornstein, #26; 3rd OA.
20/05: Bavaria-Rennen, Salzburgring DRM: Schornstein, #57; 7th.
03/06: Nürburgring 1000Km WCM: Schornstein/Doren/von Tschirnhaus, #7; 4th OA.
09-10/06: Le Mans 24-Hours: Sekurit entered. Schornstein/Doren/von Tschirnhaus, #42; 7th OA/3rd in Group 5 class.
24/06: Norisring: Schornstein; 7th (DRM) 11th, (Money race 200 miles).
01/07: Zandvoort Trophy DRM: Schornstein; 7th.
22/07: Diepholz DRM: Schornstein; 10th.
05/08: Brands Hatch 6-Hours: Schornstein/Doren, #24; 4th OA.
19/08: Westfalen-Pokal, Zolder DRM: Schornstein, #57;7th.
26/08: Ulm-Mengen: Schornstein; 1st OA.
16/09: Vallelunga 6-Hours WCM: Schornstein/Doren, #44; 8th OA.
23/09: Supersprint, Nürburgring DRM: Schornstein, #57; 8th.
14/10: Zolder: Schornstein; 4th.

1980: Light blue with white centre stripe; Sekurit/Vegla sponsored.
16/03: Brands Hatch 6-Hours WCM: Schornstein/Grohs, #15; 7th OA.
23/03: Bergischer Lowe Zolder DRM: Schornstein;#5; 5th.
30/03: Nürburgring 300Km DRM: Schornstein, #5; 6th.
13/04: Jim Clark-Rennen, Hockenheim DRM: Schornstein, #5; 5th.
27/04: Monza 6-Hours WCM: Schornstein/Grohs, #18; 4th OA.
11/05: Silverstone 6-Hours WCM: Schornstein/Grohs, #16; 5th OA.
25/5: Nürburgring 1000Km WCM: Schornstein/Grohs, #5; 7th OA.
14-15/06: Le Mans 24-Hours: Vegla entry. Schornstein/ Grohs/Tschirnhaus. 8th OA. 1st in Gr 5. Race No: 49.
22/06: Norisring DRM: Schornstein, #5; 5th.
13/07: Bavaria Salzburgring DRM: Schornstein, #5; 7th.
27/07: Diepholz DRM: Schornstein, #10; 4th.
24/08: Westfalenpokal Zolder DRM: Schornstein, #10;15th NR.
07/09: Hessen-Cup Hockenheim DRM: Schornstein, #10; 6th.
21/09: Supersprint Nürburgring DRM: Schornstein, #10; 7th.
28/09: Preis von Baden-Wurttemburg Hockenheim DRM: Schornstein, #10; 4th.
12/10: Zolder; Schornstein; 1st.
Sold to Joest Racing in part-exchange for 000 0016.

1981:
13-14/06: Le Mans 24-Hours 24-Hours: De Narvaez/Miller/Stekkonig, #40; DNF. (Fire).
1982: Rented/leased to Schornstein.
07/08: GP von Deutschland, Hockenheim: Schornstein, #7; DNF.
29/08: Int. ADAC Hessen-Cup, Hockenheim: Schornstein, #7; 7th. (2.8 Turbo).
19/09: Mugello 1000Km: Schornstein/Merl/Wollek, #2; 6th.

26/09: Supersprint, Nürburgring: Schornstein, #7; 8th. (2.8 Turbo).

1983:
24/03: Sebring 12-Hours: De Narvaez/Johansson/ Heyer, #48; 1st OA. (Joest entry).

2001: For sale in Europe.
2004: STPO.

Chassis No: 930 890 0013
Engine No: 698 0025.
Gearbox No: 798 0000.
Colour: Green.
Sold to the Kremer Racing Team.

Raced by Bob Wollek in the German National Championship, 0013 was very successful in 1978. The car was taken over by Axel Plankenhorn for 1979 in the DRM.

In 1980, the car was sold to Howard Meister who had Andial in California rebuild it with new bodywork and uprated engine. In 1981, the car won three IMSA long-distance races on three consecutive weekends, albeit with Grohs and Stommelen co-driving!

After a few more races, the 935 was "pensioned off", passing through various hands until finding a home with noted racing and Classic car dealer, Nick Soprano of White Plains, USA.

1978: German National Championship. One of the Kremer entries, driven by Wollek.
12/03: Bergischer Lowe, Zolder DRM: Wollek, #2; 2nd.
02/04: 300Km, Nürburgring DRM: Wollek, #2; 1st.
30/04: Eifelrennen, Nürburgring DRM: Wollek, #2; 4th.
21/05: Avus-Rennen DRM: Wollek, #2; 5th.
18/06: Mainz-Finthen DRM; Wollek, #2; 1st.
02/07: Zandvoort Trophy DRM: Wollek, #2; DNF.
16/07: Kassel-Calden DRM: Wollek, #2; 1st.
29/07: G.P. von Deutschland, Hockenheim DRM: Wollek, #2; 6th.

20/08: Westfalen-Pokal, Zolder DRM: Wollek, #2; DNF.
17/09: Norisring, Nurnberg: Wollek, #2;(DRM); 3rd. 200 Miles; 1st.
01/10: Supersprint Nürburgring DRM: Wollek, #2; 1st.
15/10: Zolder: Brambring; DNF.

1979:
11/03: Bergischer Lowe Zolder DRM: Plankenhorn, #55; 5th.
08/04: Jim Clark-Rennen, Hockenheim DRM: Plankenhorn, #55; 6th.
29/04: Eifelrennen Nürburgring DRM: Plankenhorn, #55;5th.
20/05: Bavaria Salzburgring DRM: Plankenhorn, #55; 6th. Rebodied as a K3.
9-10/06: Le Mans 24 Hours: L. Ferrier/F.Servanin/F. Trisconi, #40; 3rd OA.
17/06: Mainz-Finthen DRM: Plankenhorn, #55; 6th. White/Blue stripes.
24/06: Norisring, Nurnberg DRM: Plankenhorn, #55; 5th. Trophy; 4th. (white with blue stripes).
01/07: Zandvoort Trophy DRM: Plankenhorn, #55; 5th.
22/07: Diepholz DRM: Plankenhorn, #55; 5th.
28/07: GP von Deutschland, Hockenheim DRM:

Plankenhorn, #55; 1st. White, orange and red stripes.
05/08: Brands Hatch 6-Hours WCM: Bourgoigne/
Winter/Ludwig, #28; DNF. (Engine).
19/08: Westfalenpokal Zolder DRM: Plankenhorn,
#55; 4th.
02/09: Hessen-Cup Hockenheim (Kleiner Kurs)
DRM: Ludwig, #54; 1st.
17/09: Norisring Nurnberg: Plankenhorn, #55:
(DRM); 5th. (200 Miles); 4th.
23/09: Supersprint Nürburgring DRM: Plankenhorn,
#55; (DRM); 3rd. G5 race; 4th.

Sold to Howard Meister in USA. Andial-built 3.2
litre engine installed. Bodywork modified by Dan
McLoughlin of AIR to M16 body.

1980: IMSA.
27/04: Riverside 6-Hours: Meister/Morton, #55;
DNF. Suspension damage.
04/05: Laguna Seca: Meister, #55; DNF.

Rebuilt by Andial of California.

1981: IMSA.
31/1-1/02: Daytona 24-Hours: Stommelen/Meister/
Grohs, #51;24thNR.
21/03: Sebring 12-Hours: Meister/Stommelen/
Grohs,#3; 4th OA.
26/04: Riverside 6-Hours: Meister/Stommelen,#3;
DNF.
03/05: Laguna Seca: Stommelen, #3; DNF.
25/05: Lime Rock: Stommelen, #3; 3rd.
31/05: Mid-Ohio: Stommelen, #3; DNF.
16/08: Mosport Park 6 Hours: Stommelen/Grohs,
#3; 1st.
23/08: Road America, Elkhart Lake 500 miles:
Stommelen/Grohs, #3; 1st.
30/08: Mid Ohio 500 miles, Stommelen/Bell, #3;1st.

Traded by Andial to Preston Henn in exchange for
930 890 0021 with engine number: 698 0029.

Sold to Marty Yacobian
1987: STPO.

Chassis No: 930 890 0014
Engine No: 698 0027.
Gearbox No: 798 0000.
Colour: White.

This 935 was first of all sold to Franz Konrad who
campaigned it heavily in 1978 and then sold it on to
Volkert Merl for 1979. The car was then converted
by Reinhold Joest into a 935J and ran in the German
Championship as a "Liqui Moli" sponsored car.

In 1980, with a 2.8 litre engine fitted, for fuel
economy, it won the 1980 Daytona 24-Hours race
with Joest, Stommelen and Merl sharing the driving.

The morning after the race, Gianpiero Moretti
bought the car from Joest and raced it in IMSA
events until the early part of 1981, selling it then
to Chet Vincentz. Chet gave the car another "life",
converting it into a single-plug "934" to run in the
IMSA GTO class but keeping all the original parts.

Vincentz raced the "934" until 1985 when it was
damaged in a fire. The car was then sold to Jacques
Rivard who undertook a complete restoration before
selling it to its present owner, a noted historic
Porsche collector/restorer. The restoration was completed by Dennis Brioda in 2001 and the owner ran
the 935 in the 24 minutes of Daytona in February,
that year. It has since been sold on.

Sold to Franz Konrad.

1978: German National and World Championship
for Makes.
3-4/02: Daytona 24-Hours: Konrad/Joest/Merl, #21;
13th OA.
12/03: Bergischer Lowe Zolder DRM: Konrad, #10;
12th.
19/03: Mugello 6-Hours WCM: Konrad/Joest/Merl,
#15; 2nd OA.
02/04: 300 Km Nürburgring DRM: Konrad, #10;
5th.
16/04: Dijon 1000Km WCM: Konrad/Merl, #8;
DNF. (engine)
30/04: Eifelrennen Nürburgring DRM: Konrad, #10;
5th.

21/05: Avus-Rennen DRM: Konrad, #10; DNF. (engine)
14/05: Silverstone 6-Hours WCM: Konrad/Lloyd; 6th OA.
28/05: Nürburgring 6-Hours WCM: Merl/ Schickentanz /Konrad, #11; 8th OA.
18/06: Mainz-Finthen DRM: Konrad, #10; 6th.

25/06: Misano 6-Hours WCM; Konrad/Merl, #12; 3rd OA. Note: This may have been another 935.
02/07: Zandvoort DRM: Konrad; DNS.
16/07: Kassel-CaldenDRM: Merl, #16; 7th.
29/07: GP von DeutschlandDRM, Hockenheim: Merl, #16; 8th.
13/08: Zandvoort: Schreiber; 2nd.
20/08: Westfalen-Pokal, Zolder DRM; Merl, #16; DNF.
03/09: Vallelunga 6-Hours WCM: Konrad/Merl, #19; 7th OA.
17/09: Norisring 200 Miles DRM: Konrad, 200 mile race; 3rd. Merl, (DRM); DNF.
01/10: Supersprint Nürburgring (Start-Ziel-Schleife): Merl, #16; DNF.

Converted by R. Joest into a 935J.

1979:
05-06/02: Daytona 24-Hours: Joest/Stommelen/ Merl, #4; DNF.
11/03: Bergischer Lowe Zolder DRM: Merl, #67; 3rd,
08/04: Jim Clark-Rennen, Hockenheim DRM: Merl, #67; 7th.
29/04: Eifelrennen, Nürburgring DRM: Merl, #67; 7th.
20/05: Bavaria Salzburgring DRM: Merl, #67; 10th.
22/07: Diepholz DRM: Merl, #67; 7th. (with modified rear tail section)
26/08: Ulm-Mengen G5 + 2000: Merl; 2nd.
02/09: Hessen-Cup Hockenheim (Kleiner Kurs) DRM: Merl, #67; 6th.
23/09: Supersprint Nürburgring DRM: Merl, #67; DNF.

1980: IMSA season:
02-03/02: Daytona 24-Hours; Joest/Merl/Stommelen, #4; 1st OA. 2.8 liter engine.

04/02: Sold to Dr. G. Moretti. IMSA Races. Race #30.

22/03: Sebring 12-Hours: Moretti/Pianta/Zorzi, #30; 27th NR.
13/04: Road Atlanta: Moretti; 7th.
27/04: Riverside, Los Angeles Times: Moretti/M. Minter, #30; 33rd NR.
04/05: Laguna Seca: Moretti/Busby; DNS. Accident in practice.
26/05: Lime Rock: Moretti; 10th.
04/07: Daytona 250Miles: Moretti/Mendez; 5th.
27/07: Sonoma: Moretti; 19th.
03/08: Portland: Moretti, #30; 2nd.
24/08: Mid-Ohio Lumbermens 500: Moretti/Busby, #30; 3rd OA, 1st in Group 5 class.
31/08: Road America 500 Miles: Moretti/Busby; 15th.
21/09: Road Atlanta 50 Miles, two heats: (1): 5th. (2): 1st.
30/11: Daytona 250 Miles: Moretti/Joest; 1st.

231

1981: IMSA Races.
31/1-1/02: Daytona 24-Hours: Moretti/Mendez/De Narvaez, #30; 34th, 339 laps.
21/03: Sebring 12-Hours: Moretti/Mendez/De Narvaez, #30; 6th OA.
12/04: 100 Miles Road Atlanta: Moretti, #30; 9th.

Sold to Chet Vincentz. Original bodywork kept. Raced as a Porsche 934 (GTO car) in IMSA till 1985. IMSA Races.

31/05: 200 Miles Mid-Ohio: Vincentz/van Every, #91; 22nd OA, 6th in GTO class.
12/07: Watkins Glen 6-Hours WCM: Vincentz/van Every, #91; 7th.
16/08: 1000Km Mosport WCM: Vincentz/Bell, #91; 21st OA/8th.
30/08: Mid-Ohio: Vincentz/Wood; 7th.
27/09: Pocono: Vincentz: 34th OA/ 9th.
1982: IMSA Races.
23/05: 100 Miles Mid-Ohio: Vincentz: 15th OA, 7th.
15/08: 6 Hours Mosport: Vincentz/Baker; 8th OA, 1st.
22/08: 500Miles Road America: Vincentz/Hutchins; 11th OA, 2nd.
05/09: 6 Hours Mid-Ohio: Vincentz/Baker; 9th OA, 2nd.
12/09: 500Km Road Atlanta: Vincentz/Baker; 35th OA, 12th.
26/09: 500Km Pocono: Vincentz/Baker; 3rd OA, 1st.
28/11:3 Hours of Daytona: Vincentz/Baker; 8th OA, 4th.

1983: IMSA Races.
27/02: Miami GP: Vincentz; 12th.
10/04: 500Km Road Atlanta: Vincentz; 57th OA, 22nd.
15/05: 500Km Charlotte: Vincentz/White; 8th OA, 4th.
19/06: Mid-Ohio: Vincentz/White; 4th,2nd.
14/08: 6 Hours Mosport: Vincentz; 29th OA, 11th.
11/09: 500Km Pocono: Vincentz/Mullen;10th OA, 4th.

1984: IMSA Races.
08/04: Road Atlanta: Vincentz/Hutchins;15th/3rd.
20/05: 500Km Charlotte: Vincentz/White; 7th OA, 3rd.
10/06: 500Km Mid-Ohio: Vincentz/White; 9th OA, 1st.
08/07: Watkins Glen; Vincentz/Mullen; 6th/1st.
26/08: 500 Miles Road America: Vincentz/Mullen/Nierop; 10th OA, 1st.
09/09: Pocono: Vincentz/Mullen; 11th, 2nd.
16/09: 500Km Michigan: Vincentz/Mullen; 5th/1st.
30/09: Watkins Glen: Vincentz/Mullen; 8th, 1st.

1985: IMSA Races.
24/02: Miami GP: Vincentz; 18th. GTO race.
14/04: Road Atlanta: Vincentz/Nierop, #91; 12th/2nd.
28/04: 600Km of Riverside: Vincentz; DNF, acc. Fire.
1988: Sold to Jacques Rivard.
Sold to Lloyd Hawkins. Completely restored.
2010: STPO.

Chassis No: 930 890 0015
Engine No: 698 0026.
Gearbox No: 798 0000.
Colour: Red.

The second car sold to Georg Loos in 1978, 0015 was driven in German and World Championship events by, (principally), Klaus Ludwig in 1978. 0015 was the Polster-Trosser-sponsored car with "General Anziger" (A Bonn newspaper) on the windscreen strip. Manfred Schurti drove it in 1979.

At the end of 1979, Loos sold this car to Claude Haldi who added many more races to its tally. In 1981, it was converted to K3 specification.

After its front line career was over, 0015 passed through several hands before being restored and vintage raced in Europe.

Sold to Gelo Racing

1978:
02/04: 300Km Nürburgring DRM: Ludwig, #9; 3rd.

29/04: Eifelrennen, Nürburgring DRM: Ludwig, #9; 3rd. Polster Trosser sponsored.
14/05: Silverstone 6-Hours WCM: Ludwig/Hezemans/Fitzpatrick, #6; 16th.
21/05: Avus-Rennen DRM: Ludwig, #9; 4th.
28/05: Nürburgring 1000Km WCM: Ludwig/Heyer/Hezemans, #3: 1st.

18/06: Mainz-Finthen DRM: Ludwig, #9; 3rd.
25/06: Misano 6-Hours WCM: Ludwig/Hezemans, #6; DNF.
02/07: Zandvoort Trophy DRM: Ludwig, #9; 3rd.
16/07: Kassel-Calden DRM: Ludwig, #9; 4th.
29/07: G.P. von Deutschland, Hockenheim DRM; Ludwig, #9; 1st.
20/08: Westfalen-Pokal Zolder DRM: Ludwig, #9; 9th.
17/09: Norisring Nurnberg: Ludwig, #9; (DRM); 2nd. 200 Miles; 17th.
01/10: Supersprint Nürburgring DRM; Ludwig, #9; 3rd.

1979:
03-04/02: Daytona 24-Hours WCM: Wollek/Ickx/Gregg, #1; DNF.
11/03: Bergischer Lowe Zolder DRM: Schurti, #52; 6th.
18/03: Mugello 6-Hours WCM: Wollek/Schurti/Fitzpatrick, #12; 1st.
08/04: Jim Clark-Rennen, Hockenheim DRM:Schurti, #52.; 3rd.
22/04: Dijon 6-Hours WCM: Schurti/Ickx /Wollek, #1; 2nd OA, 1st in Group 5.
29/04: Eifelrennen, Nürburgring DRM:Schurti, #52.; 6th.
06/05: Silverstone 6-Hours WCM: Wollek/Schurti/Fitzpatrick, #2; 5th.
20/05: Bavaria Salzburgring DRM: Schurti, #52.; 3rd.
03/06: Nürburgring 1000Km WCM: Schurti/Fitzpatrick/Wollek,#3; DNF.
9-10/06: Le Mans 24-Hours: Heyer/Schurti, #36; DNF.
17/06: Mainz-Finthen DRM:Schurti, #52.; 5th.
24/06: Norisring Nurnberg:Schurti, #52.; 3rd (DRM) 5th (200 Miles)
01/07: Zandvoort Trophy DRM: Schurti, #52; 4th.
22/07: Diepholz DRM: Schurti, #52.;.4th.
19/08: Westfalenpokal Zolder DRM: Schurti, #52.; DNF
02/09: Hessen Cup, Hockenheim DRM: Schurti, #52.; 4th.
23/09: Nürburgring Supersprint DRM: Schurti, #52.; DNF 5th (Money race)

Sold to Claude Haldi.

1980: Sponsored by Rinsoz-Ormond (Meccarillos).
11/05: Silverstone 6-Hours WCM; Haldi/Beguin, #17; DNS.
18/05: Mainz-Finthen DRM: Haldi; DNS. (Engine).
25/05: Nürburgring 1000Km WCM: Haldi/Bell/Beguin, #8; DNF.
14-15/06: Le Mans 24-Hours: Meccarillos entry. Haldi/Beguin/Merl, #46; DNF.
22/06: Norisring, Nurnberg DRM: Haldi, #14; DNF. (Turbo).
24/08: Westfalenpokal Zolder DRM: Haldi; 6th.
07/09: Hessen-Cup, Hockenheim DRM: Haldi, #11; DNF.
21/09: Supersprint Nürburgring DRM: Haldi, #5; DNF.

28/09: Dijon 6-Hours WCM: Haldi/Beguin, #3; 2nd OA.

1981:
24/05: Nürburgring 1000Km WCM: Haldi/Mendez, #22; 12th OA.
13-14/06: Le Mans 24-Hours: Haldi, Thatcher, Poulain, #57; DNF. (gearbox)
01/08: Gold-Pokal Hockenheim DRM: Haldi, #65; DNF. (wheel bearing).
27/09: Brands Hatch 6-Hours WCM: Haldi/Teran, #28; DNF.

1982: Uprated to K3 specification.
25/04: Eifelrennen, Nürburgring DRM: Haldi, #24; 13th. (K3).
09/05: Mainz-Finthen DRM: Haldi, #24; 4th.
31/05: Nürburgring 1000Km WCM: Haldi/Beguin/ Grohs, #36; DNF.
19-20/06: Le Mans 24-Hours: Haldi/Teran/Hesnault, #75; DNF. (Transmission).
27/06: Nurnberg 200, Norisring DRM: Haldi, #24; 14th.
07/08: G.P. von Deutschland, Hockenheim DRM: Haldi, #24; 11th.
29/08: Int. ADAC Hessen Cup, Hockenheim DRM: Haldi, #22; 5th.
26/09: Supersprint, Nürburgring DRM; Haldi; 9th.

1983-1989: In storage with Claude Haldi. At some time, 3.0 litre engine number 677 2904 installed.

1989: Sold.
For sale at GTC, Marseilles.
1999: Sold to Switzerland.
Fully restored, races in club events in France.

2001: For sale in France
2006: For sale again in France.
2007: STPO.

Chassis No: 930 890 0016
Engine No: 698 0024.
Gearbox No: 798 0000.
Colour: White.

This 935 was sold to Reinhold Joest who campaigned it heavily in the German Championship in 1978. At the end of the year, Joest crashed the car at Hockenheim in a practice session.

In 1979, the car was stripped of parts and the bodyshell sold, via Jurgen Kannacher, to John Lagodny who rebuilt his ex-Kremer Brothers 935, chassis number 006 0019 around it. After he raced the car up to the end of 1981, the car was sold, via Jurgen Kannacher, to Heinz-Jurgen Dahmen. It was then sold to Bo Strandell and raced in 1983 in the Swedish GT Championship by Anders Olofsson.

Shortly thereafter, the car was sold to English arch-enthusiast, (he had four 935s!), John Greasley who had it for many years.

The car has a 1979 IMSA-spec. single-turbo engine, water to air Intercooler and upright gearbox. It was painted In Jagermeister colours. The original engine is in a 934, uprated with 935 K3 bodywork, chassis number: 930 670 0152, which resides in the USA. In 2007, the car was sold to a German racer, who had it repainted back to it's original colors and restored.

Sold to Joest Racing.

1978: German National Championship driven by Reinhold Joest.
White with blue and red centre stripe . Liqui Moly sponsorship.
12/03: Bergischer Lowe Zolder DRM: Joest, #7; 6th.
02/04: 300Km Nürburgring DRM: Joest, #11; 4th.
30/04: Eifelrennen Nürburgring DRM: Joest, #11; DNF, (engine).
21/05: Avus-Rennen DRM: Joest, #11; 6th.
28/05: Nürburgring 1000Km WCM: Joest/Barth, #7; 5th.
13-14/06: Le Mans 24-Hours: D./B. Whittington/ Konrad, #94; DNF. Accident. Note: Whittington entered.
16/07: Kassel-Calden DRM: Joest, #11; 6th. (Rebuilt car).
29/07: GP von Deutschland, Hockenheim DRM: Joest; DNS. (accident in practice, Joest injured, car

badly damaged.) Rebuilt on a different bodyshell. (Perhaps 000 0012?) With this car:
1/10: Supersprint Nürburgring DRM: Joest, #11; 4th.

1979:
03/06: Nürburgring 1000 Km WCM: Merl/ Stommelen/Bell #1; 5th.
17/06: Mainz-Finthen DRM: Merl, #67; DNF.
24/06: Norisring Nurnberg: Merl, #67; (DRM) 4th. (200 Miles) 6th.

Bodyshell of 930 890 0016 sold to Jurgen Kannacher.
Bodyshell then sold to John Lagodny. Rebuilt with parts from Lagodny's K1. Painted red.
14/10: Saisonabschluss Zolder: Lagodny; 16th OA.
04/11: Rheintal-Rennen, Hockenheimn: Lagodny; 1st.

1980:
07/04: Lorentzweiler (hillclimb): Lagodny; 1st.
13/04: Zittig (hillclimb): Lagodny; 1st.
27/04: La Roche (hillclimb); Lagodny; 3rd OA.
01/05: Rheingold-Bergrennen: Lagodny; 1st.
04/05: Course de la Cote de la Semois (hillclimb): Lagodny; 3rd OA, 1st in class.
19/05: Luxembourg-Trophy, Nürburgring: Lagodny; 1st.
26/05: Remerchen (hillclimb): Lagodny; 5th OA.

15/06: Abracheville (hillclimb): Lagodny; 5th OA.
22/06: Wissembourg (hillclimb): Lagodny; 3rd OA.
20/07: Nürburgring-Trophy, Nürburgring: Lagodny; 1st.
10/08: Mont Dore (EHC): Lagodny; 31st OA. 2nd in Group 5 class.
15/08: Heisdorf (hillclimb): Lagodny; 1st.
24/08: Wasserbillig (hillclimb): Lagodny; 1st OA.
31/08: Tys des Glandes (Hillclimb): Lagodny; 4th OA.
14/09: Cote de Rhouyet: Lagodny; 5th OA.
21/09: Luxembourg-Trophy, Nürburgring: Lagodny; 1st.
1981:
26/04: Zittig (hillclimb): Lagodny; 3rd OA.
01/05: Rheingold-Bergrennen: Lagodny; 1st.
08/06: Remerchen (hillclimb): Lagodny; 4th OA.
05/06: Wissembourg (hillclimb): Lagodny; 3rd OA.
28/07: Goesdorf (hillclimb): Lagodny; 3rd OA.
13/09: Zittig (hillclimb): Lagodny; 8th OA.
20/09: Bilstein-Supersprint, Nurbirgring DRM: Lagodny, #68; 15th.
Sold back to Kannacher.
Sold to Heinz-Jorgen Dahmen. Repainted a darker red.

Sold to Belgium and hillclimbed.
Sold to Bo Strandell.
1983: Raced by Anders Olofsson in the Swedish GT Championship.
Displayed in a museum.
1984: Sold to John Greasley.
2006: Sold to Pontus Wahlund, Sweden.Restored back to original paint scheme.
Sold to Klaes Wahlund. All body and chassis work completed, engine and gearbox overhauled by Stefan Roitmayer, Germany.
2007: Sold to Michael Foeveny, Germany.
2009: STPO.

Chassis No: 930 890 0017
Engine No: 698 0023.
Gearbox No: 798 0000.
Colour: Orange.

Raced first of all by Manfred Schurti for Max Moritz racing in the familiar "Jagermeister" colours, 0017 was sold at the end of 1978 to "Victor", (Vittorio Coggiola), in Italy and from then on won many races. What's more, "Victor" and the constantly updated 0017 kept on winning races right up until 1986!

Sold to Max Moritz of Reutlingen, Germany.

1978: Jaegermeister sponsored.
11/03: Bergischer Lowe Zolder (DRM): Schurti, #5; 11th.
02/04: Goodyear 300Km Nürburgring (DRM): Schurti, #5; DNF. (no oil pressure)
30/04: Eifelrennen Nürburgring (DRM): Schurti, #5; 8th.
21/05: Avus-Rennen (DRM):Schurti, #5; 2nd.
29/05: Nürburgring 1000Kms (WCM):J. Ickx/M. Schurti, #8; 2nd.
18/06: Mainz-Finthen (DRM): Schurti, #5; 4th.
02/07: Zandvoort Trophy (DRM):Schurti, #5; 13th. (wheel bearing)
16/07: Kassel-Calden (DRM): Schurti, #5; 5th.
29/07: G.P. von Deutschland, Hockenheim (DRM);Schurti, #5; 2nd.
20/08: Westfalen-Pokal Zolder (DRM): Schurti, #5; 1st.
17/09: Norisring: Schurti, #5; (DRM); 1st. 200 Miles; DNF. Oil smoke.
01/10: Supersprint, Nürburgring (DRM): Schurti, #5; 5th.
Sold to Vittorio Coggiola, ("Victor"), in Italy.
1979:
25/03: Monza (IC): Coggiola, #97; 1st OA.
16/04: Magione (IC): Coggiola, 1st OA.
22/04: Varano, Coppa Pro Loco (IC): Coggiola; 1st OA.
20/05: Magione (IC): Coggiola; 1st OA.
01/07: Mugello (IC): Coggiola, #166; 1st OA.
19/08: Magione (IC): Coggiola; 1st OA.
02/09: Monza, Coppa Intereuropa: Coggiola; 1st OA.
07/10: Monza, Coppa Carri (IC): Coggiola; 1st OA.

Winner of Csai Trophy.

1980: Fitted with Martini style 935-77 bodywork, painted silver.
Engine number 690 002, 3170 cc in use.
07/04: Magione (IC): Coggiola; 1st OA.
13/04: Mugello 6-Hours (WCM): Zorzi/Coggiola/ Schoen, #32; DNS.
27/04: Monza 6-Hours (WCM): Coggiola/Schoen, #19; 7th OA.
Fitted with 935/78 bodywork. Painted silver.
25/05: Mugello (IC): Coggiola, #166; 1st OA.
01/06: Vallelunga (IC): Coggiola; 1st OA.
15/06: Varano, Trofeo Cariplo (IC): Coggiola; 1st OA.
29/06: Pergusa, Coppa Florio (IC): Coggiola; 1st OA.
06/07: Varano (IC): Coggiola; 1st OA.
24/08: Magione (IC): Coggiola; 1st OA.
21/09: Pergusa, Coppa Citta di Enna (IC): Coggiola; 1st OA.

05/10: Monza, Coppa Carri (IC): Coggiola; 1st in class, 2nd OA.
12/10: Magione (IC): Coggiola, #152; 1st in class, 2nd OA.
03/11: Vallelunga, Trofeo Natale Nappi (IC): Coggiola; 1st in class, 2nd OA.
Winner of Italian Group 5 Trophy.

1981: Italian Championship.
22/03: Vallelunga, Trofeo Cristarga (IC): Coggiola; 1st OA.
20/04: Magione (IC): Coggiola; 3rd OA.
26/04: Mugello (IC): Coggiola, #104; 1st.
03/05: Giro dell'Umbria: Coggiola/"Cipi", 1st in class, 2nd OA.
24/05: Monza, Coppa Carri (IC): Coggiola; 1st OA.
31/05: Vallelunga (IC): Coggiola; DNF.
14/06: Varano, Trofeo Cariplo (IC): Coggiola; 1st in class, 2nd OA.
28/06: Magione (IC): Coggiola: 2nd in class.
13/07: Cesana-Sestriere: Coggiola; 1st in class, 5th OA.
22/08: Misano (IC): Coggiola; 1st in class.
25/08: Magione, Trofeo Urat (IC) Coggiola, #810; 1st OA.
20/09: Pergusa, Coppa Citta di Enna (IC): Coggiola; 1st OA
27/09: Varano (IC): Coggiola; 1st OA.
11/10: Magione (IC): Coggiola; 1st OA.
01/11: Vallelunga, Trofeo Natale Nappi (IC): Coggiola, 5; 1st OA.
Winner of Italian Champioship (Group 2-4-5).

1982:
18/04: Monza 1000Kms (WCM): Coggiola/Giuliani/Pallavicini, #85; DNF.
Note: "Victor" also raced a Porsche 934 in 1982.

1983:
06/03: Magione (IC): Coggiola; 1st OA..
25/04: Mugello (IC): Coggiola; 1st OA.
12/05: Mugello (IC): Coggiola; 1st OA.
29/05: Varano (IC): Coggiola; 1st OA.
17/06: Cesana-Sestriere: Coggiola; 1st in group 2-4-

5-B, 2nd OA.
10/07: Varano (IC): Coggiola; 1st OA.
30/08: Misano (IC): Coggiola; 2nd OA.
18/09: Vallelunga (IC): Coggiola; 1st OA.
09/10: Monza: Lap record on new circuit.

1984:
23/04: Monza 1000Kms (WCM): Coggiola/Facetti/Mussato, #131; DNF. Engine.
13/05: Silverstone1000Kms (WCM): Coggiola/Mussato/Giudici, #131; 1st in class, 22nd OA.
15/07: Nürburgring 1000Kms (WCM): Coggiola/Giudici/Pallavicini, #64; 2nd in class, 20th OA.
29/07: Brands Hatch1000Km (WCM): Coggiola/Giudici/Pallavicini, #131; 1st in class, 13th OA.
02/09: Spa-Francorchamps 1000Kms (WCM): Coggiola/Giudici/Pallavicini, #131; 1st in class, 11th OA.
16/09: Imola 1000Kms (WCM): Coggiola/Rebai/Pallavicini, #131; 1st in class. 12th OA.

1985: Painted white with red and blue stripes.
14/04: Mugello 1000Kms (WCM): Coggiola/Bertuzzi/Giudicci, #155; 1st in class,10th OA.
28/04: Monza 1000Kms (WCM): Coggiola/Giudicci/Bertuzzi, #171, 1st in class,14th OA.
12/05: Silverstone 1000Km: (WCM): Coggiola/Bertuzzi/Giudicci, #155; DNA.
14/07: Hockenheim 1000Km (WCM): Pallavicini/Taverna/Coggiola, #171: DNF. Engine.
01/09: Spa-Francorchamps 1000Kms (WCM): Coggiola/Palma/Taverna, #160; 1st in class, 20th OA.

1986:
20/04: Monza Supersprint: Coggiola/Palma, #181; 1st in class, 16th OA.

Chassis No: 930 890 0018
Engine No: 698 0028.
Gearbox No: 930 79 699.
Colour: White.

Peter Gregg dominated the IMSA Camel GT

Championship with this car in 1978, winning nine out of the fifteen races he entered. In 1979, he started the season using a new 1979 car with 0018 as a back-up. He then sold 0018 to Bruce Leven, driving it himself on one occasion to take a victory at Laguna Seca in October. After this, Bruce Leven shared the driving of the car with Hurley Haywood until 1980 when Leven sold 0018 to Bill Brooks in 1982 who in turn sold it to Kevin Jeannette in 1985 before Kevin sold 0018 back to Brumos. It has since been sold.

1978: Sold to Peter Gregg. IMSA Championship.
16/04: Road Atlanta: Gregg, #59; 1st OA.
30/04: Laguna Seca: Gregg; 3rd OA.
07/05: Hallett: Gregg; 13th NR.
29/05: Lime Rock Coca-Cola 300: Gregg; 1st OA.
18/06: Brainerd, Pepsi G.P: Gregg: 1st OA.
04/07: Daytona: Paul Revere 250/Pepsi 6-Hours: Gregg; 1st OA.
30/07: Sears Point: Mr Pibb's Camel GT Challenge: Gregg; 26th OA. (DNF).
06/08: Portland: G.I. Joe's G.P: Gregg; 1st OA.
27/08: Mid-Ohio: Gregg; 35th OA, (DNF).
04/09: Road Atlanta 6-Hours: Gregg; 1st OA.
26/11: Daytona Finale: Gregg; 1st OA.

1979: IMSA Races. Back-up car to 930 990 0030. Engine number 699 0056 installed.
Sold to Bruce Leven. IMSA races unless otherwise noted.
05/08: Portland: Haywood, #7; 2nd.
02/09: Road America: Gregg/Leven/Haywood, #86; 32nd NR.
23/09: Road Atlanta: Leven, #86; 10th.
14/10: Laguna Seca (Trans Am): Gregg, #86; 1st.

1980: Engine number 698 0028 re-installed.
22/03: Sebring 12-Hours: Gregg/Haywood/Leven, #86; 10th OA.
13/04: Road Atlanta: Haywood, #86; 2nd.
27/04: Riverside: Leven/Haywood, #86; 3rd OA.
04/05: Laguna Seca: Haywood, #86; DNS. Acc.
03/08: Portland: Haywood, #86; 3rd.

1981: IMSA Races.
16/08: Mosport: Haywood/Leven; DNS.
23/08: Road America, Elkhart Lake: Haywood/Leven; DNS
1982: Sold to Bill Brooks.
1985: Sold to Kevin Jeannette.
1986: Sold to Brumos.
2007: STPO.

Chassis No: 930 890 0019
Engine No: 699 0040.
Gearbox No: 799 0029.
Colour: Black.

One of the two 1978 cars raced by the Interscope team of Ted Field and Danny Ongais, this car raced through 1979 as the team then had a new 1979 car. In 1980, it was sold to a California collector, who later on sold it to Rick Rothenberger who, after eleven years of ownership, sold 0019 to Harry Bytzek of Canada in 2000. In 2006, your author sold this car to France. It has since been resold to the USA.

Sold to: VWoA. Sold to Interscope Racing
Race Number: "00"

1978: #00 car. IMSA Races.
16/04: Road Atlanta: Field, #00; 6th.
30/04: Laguna Seca: Field, #00; 10th OA.
07/05: Hallett: Field, #00; 17th OA.
29/05: Lime Rock. Coca-Cola 300: Field, #00; 6th OA.
04/07: Daytona. Paul Revere 250: Field/Ongais, #00: 36th OA NR.
04/09: Road Atlanta 6-Hours: Ongais, #00;27th NR. (Pole).
26/11: Daytona Finale: Field, #00; 6th.

1979: IMSA Races.
IMSA Championship.
03-04/2: Daytona 24-Hours: Field/Ongais/Henn, #00; 61stNR. (Henn-Acc.)
17/03: Sebring 12-Hours: Field/Ongais, #00; 35th,35th NR.
08/04: Road Atlanta: T. Field, #00; 14th.
22/04: Riverside 6-Hours WCM: Field/Minter, #00;34th NR.
29/04: Laguna Seca: Ongais, #00; 3rd. (Pole).
07/07: Watkins Glen 6-Hours WCM: Ongais/Field, #00; DNF, Acc.
15/07: Mid-Ohio: Field/Minter, #00; 4th.
29/07: Sears Point 100 Miles: Ongais, #00;34th NR.
26/08: Mid-Ohio: Field/Ongais/Minter, #00; 6th.
23/09: Road Atlanta 100 miles: Ongais, #00; 38th NR.
25/11: Daytona Finale: Ongais, #00; 47thNR.
Engine number 698 0032 from chassis number 930 890 0021 (Interscope Team car), installed.
1980. June: Sold to California collector.
1989: Sold to Rick Rothenberger. Engine Number: 699 0040.
2000: Sold to Harry Bytzek.
2006: Sold through John Starkey to Jean Guikas, GTC. France.
2010: Sold to Fred Kaimer, Texas, USA.
2015: "Rennsport Reunion", Laguna Seca.

Chassis No: 930 890 0020
Engine No: 698 0030.
Gearbox No: 798 0000.
Colour: Red.

The third of Georg Loos's 1978 935's, 0020 was driven mainly by Toine Hezemans and started off 1978 with two straight victories, aided by Hans Heyer and John Fitzpatrick at Mugello. Three more victories came its way in 1978.

For 1979, 0020 was fitted with long-tail bodywork with some slight differences in the front fenders also. The car won again at the Nürburgring in the Eifelrennen and at Silverstone.

At the end of 1979, 0020 was sold to Carlo Noce's "Sportwagen" team of Sassuolo, Italy and driven in World Championship races in 1980 by Henri Pescarolo and Jürgen Barth. The 935 took a second at Monza and victory at Dijon.

0020 was then sold to Bruce Spicer of Australia and he engaged John Latham who won the 1981 Australian Sports Car Championship with it. After this, it was sold to Rusty French. In 1983, the car was raced by Alan Browne.

Sold to Gelo Racing.

1978: German National Championship.
12/03: Bergischer Lowe Zolder DRM: Hezemans, #6; 1st.
19/03: Mugello 6-Hours WCM: Hezemans/Heyer/ Fitzpatrick, #12; 1st.
02/04: 300Km Nürburgring DRM: Hezemans, #6; 2nd.
16/04: Dijon 1000Km WCM: Hezemans/Ludwig, #6: DNF. (driveshaft)
30/04: Eifelrennen Nürburgring DRM: Hezemans, #6; 1st.
14/05: Silverstone 6-Hours WCM: Fitzpatrick/ Hezemans, #4; DNF.
21/05: Avus-Rennen DRM: Hezemans, #6; 1st.
28/05: Nürburgring 1000Km WCM: Hezemans/ Ludwig/Fitzpatrick, #1; DNF. (Acc.)

18/06: Mainz-Finthen DRM; Hezemans, #6; 5th.
02/07: Zandvoort Trophy DRM: Hezemans, #6; 2nd.
16/07: Kassel-Calden DRM: Hezemans, #6; 2nd.
29/07: G.P. von Deutschland Hockenheim DRM: Hezemans, #6; 3rd.
20/08: Westfalen-Pokal Zolder DRM: Hezemans, #6; 15th.
03/09: Vallelunga 6-Hours WCM: Hezemans/ Fitzpatrick/Heyer, #9;3rd.
17/09: Norisring Nurnberg DRM: Hezemans, #6;

DNF. Trophy race; 2nd.
1/10: Supersprint Nürburgring DRM: Hezemans, #6; 2nd.

1979: Fitted with "Long-tail" bodywork a la Works 935/77 cars and louvres in front fenders to extract pressurised air from the wheels.
03-04/02: Daytona 24-Hours WCM: Wollek/Schurti/ Fitzpatrick, #2; 50th NR.
11/03: Bergischer Lowe Zolder DRM: Wollek, #51; 7th.
18/03: Mugello 6-Hours: Wollek/Ickx/Schurti, #11; 2nd.
08/04: Jim Clark-Rennen, Hockenheim DRM: Wollek, #51; 5th.
22/04: Dijon 6-Hours WCM: Schurti/Fitzpatrick/ Wollek, #10; 13th
29/04: Eifelrennen, Nürburgring DRM: Wollek, #51;1st.
20/05: Bavaria Salzurgring DRM:Wollek, #51; 2nd .
NOTE: With 935/77 bodywork.
03/06: Nürburgring 1000Km WCM: Pescarolo/ Wollek, #9; 3rd.
17/06: Mainz-Finthen DRM:Wollek, #51; 3rd.
24/06: Norisring Nurnberg :Wollek, (DRM); 17th. (Trophy race 200 miles): 19th.
01/07: Zandvoort Trophy DRM: Wollek, #51; 2nd.
22/07: Diepholz DRM:Wollek, #51; 2nd.
19/08: Westfalenpokal Zolder DRM: Wollek, #51; 2nd.
02/09: Hessen-Cup Hockenheim (Kleiner Kurs) DRM: Wollek, #51; 5th.
23/09: Supersprint Nürburgring (Start-Ziel-Schleife) DRM:Wollek, #51; 2nd in both DRM and Group 5 race.

Sold to the "Sportwagen" Race team in Sassuolo, Italy. Carlos Noce.

1980:
27/04: Monza 6-Hours WCM: Barth/Pescarolo, #21; 2nd.
18/05: Mainz-Finthen DRM: Barth; 4th.
01/06: Kreutzritter-Rennen Spa DRM: Barth; DNF.

07/09: Vallelunga 6-Hours WCM: Barth/Pescarolo, #2; 7th.
28/09: Dijon 1000Km WCM: Barth/Pescarolo, #1; 1st.

Sold to Bruce Spicer in Australia.
3.2 liter engine fitted.
1981: Raced by John Latham.?/2: Sandown: Latham, #10; DNF.
E 930 670 0165.
Sold to Rusty French in Australia.

1982:
16/05: Winton: R. French; 5th OA.
06/06: Oran Park: R. French; 2nd.
20/06: Lakeside: R. French; 2nd OA.
04/07: Adelaide: R. French; 5th.
11/07: Wanneroo Park: R. French: 4th OA.
01/08: Calder: R. French; 2nd OA.
29/08: Surfers Paradise: R. French; 2nd OA.
19/09: Symmons Plains: R. French; 4th OA.
10/10: Baskerville: R. French; 5th OA.

1983: Raced by Alan Browne.
1983: Tested in the Australian magazine: "Racing" by Doug Hicks
2014-15: Restored.

Chassis No: 930 890 0021
Engine No: 698 0032.
Gearbox No: 798 0000.
Colour: Black.

The second 1978 935 of the Interscope Race team. At the end of the season, the car was sold to Preston Henn who previously had raced a Ferrari Daytona. Henn liked the 935 and shared it with the John Pauls in 1979, giving Junior his first victory.

In 1986, Monte Shelton bought the 935 and raced it in occasional vintage races. In 2006, your author brokered a sale to a very enthusiastic Portuguese racer. It has since been sold on.

Sold to VWoA.

Sold to Vasek Polak.
Sold to Interscope Racing.

1978: IMSA Races. Race #"0".
16/04: Road Atlanta: Ongais; 2nd.
30/04: Laguna Seca: Ongais; DNS. (half-Shaft).
04/07: Daytona; Field/Ongais, practice only.
30/07: Sears Point. Mr Pibb's GT Challenge: Field; 5th OA.
3-4/09: Road Atlanta 6-Hours: Field; 5th OA.
24-26/11: Daytona Finale: Ongais; 2nd OA.

1979: IMSA Races unless otherwise noted.
Sold to Preston Henn with engine number 698 0029 installed.
03-04/02: Daytona 24 Hours WCM: Henn, #00; 61st NR.
17/03: Sebring 12-Hours: Henn/Gregg/Haywood, #09; DNF. (Engine).
08/04: Road Atlanta 100 Miles: Henn, #09; 19th.
22/04: Riverside 6-Hours: Bondurant/Henn, #09; DNF.
29/04: Laguna Seca 100 Miles: Henn, #09; 7th.
28/05: Lime Rock 100 miles: Henn, #09; 11th.

17/06: Brainerd 100 miles: Henn, #09; 8th.
04/07: 250 miles of Daytona: J. Pauls, #09; 2nd.
07/07: Watkins 6-Hours WCM: R. Mears/Henn, #09; DNF. (Fire).
15/07: Mid-Ohio 250 Miles: Henn/O'Steen, #09; 37th NR.

05/08: Watkins Glen TA: P. Henn, #09; 6th.
19/08: Mosport TA: Henn, #09; 4th.
01/09: Trois Rivieres TA: Henn; 7th.
23/09: Road Atlanta 100 miles: Henn, #09; 11th.
25/11: Daytona 250 Miles: Henn, #09; 5th. Damaged
in accident.

1980: Converted to K3 specification by Chuck Gaa.
Engine No: 698 0029.
2-3/02: Daytona 24-Hours: Henn/Paul Sr./Holbert,
#09; 2nd.
22/03: Sebring 12-Hours: Henn/Paul Sr./Holbert,
#09; 4th.
13/04: 30 Min. Road Atlanta: Henn, #09; 24th NR.
27/04: 5 Hours of Riverside: John Paul, #09; DNF
04/05: Laguna Seca 100 Miles: Paul, #09; 3rd
26/05: Lime Rock 1Hr 30 Mins: John Paul Sr/J.Paul
Jr, #09; 1st.
17/08: Mosport 6-Hours WCM:Dale Whittington/P.
Henn/John Paul Sr., #09; 9th NR.
31/08: 500 Miles of Road America Elkhart Lake:
Henn/Dale Whittington, #09; 4th.
21/09: 50 Miles of Road Atlanta: John Paul Jr:, #09;
(1):4th. (2): 5th.
31/11: Daytona Finale: Henn, #09;57th NR.

1981:
31/1-1/02: Daytona 24-Hours: Henn/Bondurant, #09;
64th NR.
21/03: Sebring 12-Hours: Gunn/Henn/Belcher, #09;
48th NR
03/07: Daytona: P./B. Henn/R. Lanier, #51; 4th.
Traded by Preston Henn for the Andial 935: #930
890 0013.

1986: April: Sold to Monte Shelton. White with
black and orange stripes.

Portland, Rose Cup TA: Shelton; 1st OA.

1999: For sale.
2004: Sold by John Starkey to Portugal.
2015: Sold to Greece.

Chassis No: 930 890 0022
Engine No: 698 0031.
Gearbox No: 798 0000.
Colour: White.
Sold to the Kremer Brothers. Adolphe Lafont-
sponsored.

Driven mainly by Bob Wollek in 1978, 0022 had
a busy 1978 season, winning at Dijon and Misano,
(with Henri Pescarolo).
    For 1979, "John Winter" was the principal driver
and the 935 was converted to K3 bodywork. Sold
to Dudley Wood in 1980, the car raced in World
Championship races, scoring a best of a second
place at Monza in 1981. Your author did hear that
the car was so tractable that it was occasionally used
to take its owner to the pub!
    In 1983, Barry Robinson bought 0022 and com-
peted in the British "Thundersports" series with it.
In 1986, the 935 was sold to John Goate who raced
it in many British "clubbies" of the period.
    Nick Mason, the noted British rock drummer and
race car collector, bought the 935 during the 1990's.
It was then sold on to Michael Moore in England
and has been sold on again since.

1978:
04-05/02: Daytona 24-Hours: Wollek/Pescarolo,
#12, DNF. (engine).
19/03: Mugello 6-Hours WCM: Wollek/Pescarolo,
#9; DNF. (engine)
16/04: Dijon 6-Hours WCM: Wollek/Pescarolo, #2;
1st. (single turbo engine)
14/05: Silverstone 6-Hours WCM: Wollek/Pescarolo,
#8: 2nd
28/05: Nürburgring 1000Km WCM: Wollek/
Pescarolo, #4; 3rd.
9-10/06: Le Mans 24-Hours: Raymond/Wielemans/
Franey, #46; DNF. Ochre yellow, Fisons sponsored.
25/06: Misano 6-Hours WCM: Wollek/Pescarolo,
#2: 1st.
02/07: Zandvoort Trophy DRM: Winter, #4; DNS.
(Used to replace the crashed 007 0016).
16/07: Kassel-Calden DRM: Winter, #4; 8th.

29/07: G.P. von Deutschland Hockenheim DRM: Winter; DNF.

20/08: Westfalen-Pokal Zolder DRM: Winter, #4; 6th.

03/09: Vallelunga 6-Hours DRM: Wollek/Pescarolo, #3; 1st

17/09: Norisring Nurnberg: Winter, #4; (DRM); DNF. 200 Miles race; 10th.

01/10: Supersprint Nürburgring DRM: Winter, #4; 7th.

15/10: Zolder: Winter; 5th.
Track tested by Francois Rousselot in Belgian ,magazine AUTO Hebdo #150. (8-15/2/79).

1979: Minolta sponsored.
08/04: Jim Clark Rennen, Hockenheim DRM: Winter, #56; 8th.

20/05: Bavaria Salzburgring DRM: Winter, #56; DNF. (engine)

9-10/06: Le Mans 24 Hours: P. Gurdjian/A. Plankenhorn/"Winter", #45; 13th OA/5th Grp.V. K3 bodywork.

24/06: Norisring Nurnberg: Winter, #56; (DRM) 6th. 200 Miles: Winter; DNS. (Fitted with K3 bodywork).

01/07: Zandvoort DRM: Winter, #56; 6th.

22/07; Diepholz DRM: Winter, #56; DNF. (throttle linkage)

29/07: GP von Deutschland, Hockenheim DRM: Winter, #56; 2nd.

05/08: Brands Hatch 1000 km WCM: Plankenhorn/Ludwig, #27; 2nd OA

19/08: Westfalenpokal Zolder DRM: Winter, #56; 6th.

02/09: Hessen-Cup, Hockenheim: Plankenhorn, #55; 2nd.

23/09: Supersprint Nürburgring DRM: Winter, #56; 4th.

07/10: Hessenpreis, Kassel-Calden DRM: Winter, #56; 3rd.

14/10: Zolder: Winter; 3rd.

1980: Sold to Dudley Wood, England
16/03: Brands Hatch 1000 km WCM: Wood/Cooper/Lovett, #11; 5th OA.

11/05: Silverstone 6 hours WCM: Wood/Cooper/Lovett, #20; DNF.

14-15/06: Le Mans Race #44: Lovett/Wood/Cooper; DNF (engine).

06/07: Donington: Wood; 6th.

28/09: Dijon 1000 km WCM: Wood/Cooper, #20; 4th OA.

1981:
12/04: Mugello 6-Hours WCM: Wood/Cooper, #5; 2nd OA.

26/04: Monza 1000 km WCM: Wood/Cooper, #5; 11th OA.

10/05: Silverstone 6 hours WCM: Wood/Cooper, #21; DNF. (Acc.)

24/05: Nürburgring 1000Km WCM: Cooper/Wood, #23; 9th OA.

13-14/06: Le Mans 24-Hours Race No. 55: Cooper/Wood/Bourgoignie; 4th OA, 1st in Group 5.

27/09: Brands Hatch 1000 km WCM: Wood/Cooper, #25; 4th OA.

1982:
17/10: Brands Hatch 1000Km WCM: Wood/Jordan/Loxton, #20; DNF.

1983: Sold to Barry Robinson, raced in the Thundersports Championship.
04/04: Brands Hatch: Robinson/Wood; 6th.
02/05: Snetterton: Robinson/Wood; 6th.
30/05: Brands Hatch: Robinson/Wood; 8th.
25/06: Oulton Park; Robinson/Wood; 5th.
14/08: Donington: Robinson/Wood; 7th.
25/09: Brands Hatch: Robinson/Wood; ?
08/07: Thruxton: Robinson/Wood; 11th.

1986. September: Sold to John Goate.
Competed in 1987,1988,1989 and 1990 Modified Porsche Championship.

1994: June: Featured in "Thoroughbred and Classic Cars".
Sold to Nick Mason.
1998: Sold to Michael Moore.
2002: Sold on.
2004: For sale through Autofarm: £200,000.
2007: Sold to Peter Garrod. Raced in CER.
2008: Classic Le Mans. P. Garrod.
2010: Classic Le Mans: P. Garrod.
2012: Classic Le Mans: P. Garrod.
2014: Sold through John Starkey to USA.

Chassis No: 930 890 0023
Engine No: 698 0034.
Gearbox No: 798 0000.
Colour: Yellow.

Sold to the Whittington Brothers to start their Porsche racing careers, this car was raced in 1978 by Bill Whittington who scored victory at Mid-Ohio and a second plus one third place also.
    In 1979, it was hardly used, Bill Whittington concentrating on his new 1979 K3 and this car also was converted to K3 specification for 1980.

Sold to Volkswagen of America.
1978: Sold to the Whittington Brothers. IMSA Races.
02/04: Talladega 6-Hours: Bill Whittington/Don Whittington, #94; 2nd OA.

16/04: Road Atlanta: Bill Whittington, #94; 24th OA.
30/04: Laguna Seca: Bill Whittington, #94; 14th OA.
07/05: Hallett: Don Whittington, #94; 4th OA.
29/05: Lime Rock: BillWhittington, #94; 2nd OA.
18/06: Brainerd: Don Whittington, #94; 5th OA.
29/07: Sears Point 100 miles: Bill Whittington, #94; 14th.
06/08: Portland. G.I. Joe's GP: Bill Whittington, #94; 3rd OA.
27/08: Mid-Ohio: Bill Whittington/J. Busby, #94; 1st OA.
04/09: Road Atlanta 6-Hours: Bill Whittington, #94; 3rd OA.
26/11: Daytona Finale: Bill Whittington, #94;7th.

1979: IMSA Races.
23/09: Road Atlanta: Dale Whittington, #95;9th.
25/11: Daytona Finale: Dale Whittington, #95; 55th NR.

1980: IMSA Races. Engine number 698 0051 installed.

Built into K3 specification.
13/04: Road Atlanta: Bill Whittington, #95;1st.
21/09: Road Atlanta: Dale Whittington, #95; 2nd.
30/11: Daytona Finale: Dale Whittington, #95;35th NR.

1981: IMSA Championship.
12/04: Road Atlanta: Dale Whittington, #95; 5th.
27/09: Road Atlanta 50 Miles(1): Dale Whittington, #95; 2nd.
21/09: Road Atlanta 50 Miles(2): Dale Whittington, #95; 5th.
29/11: Daytona: Whittington/Lanier; 30th.

Chassis No: 930 890 0024
Engine No: 698 0035.
Gearbox No: 798 0000.
Colour: Guards Red.

Delivered in time for the 1978 Le Mans 24-Hour race to the Dick Barbour team, this 935 was driven there by Dick Barbour, Brian Redman and John Paul to place fifth overall and win the IMSA class, something the team made a habit of. At the following race, at Watkins Glen the car finished second.

In 1979, the 935 carried on racing with the Dick Barbour team. Thereafter, it was sold to John Paul, sold to Preston Henn and then back to Paul. It was sold to Robert Hendrickson shortly thereafter. The car is currently located in France.

Sold to Volkswagen of America.
1978: Sold to Dick Barbour Racing.
13-14/06: Le Mans 24-Hours: Barbour/Redman/Paul, #90; 5th OA, 1st in IMSA class.
07/07: Watkins Glen 6-Hours WCM: Stommelen/Schurti/Barbour, #90; 2nd OA
30/07: Sears Point IMSA: Bondurant: DNS. (Practice Acc.)

1979:
03-04/02: Daytona 24 Hours WCM WCM: Barbour/Redman/Newman, #6; 26th NR.
07/03: Sebring 12-Hours WCM: Stommelen/Barbour/Mears, #6; 4th OA.
22/04: Riverside 6-Hours WCM: Stommelen/Redman/Barbour, #6; 6th OA.
9-10/06: Le Mans 24-Hours: Akin/McFarlin/Woods, #71; DNF. Engine.
Talladega: DNF. Fire.

Sold to John Paul.
Sold to Preston Henn.

1980: Engine number 698 0085 installed
22/03: Sebring 12-Hours WCM: Marcus/Harmon/Hinze, #4; 60th NR. Yellow.
25/05: Nürburgring 1000Km WCM: Redman/Henn, #12; DNF.
8-9/06: Le Mans 24-Hours: Kirby/Harmon/Sherwin, #72; DNF. Acc.

Sold to John Paul.

1983: Advertised in Panorama from John Paul, Georgia.
1985: Sold to Robert P. Hendrikson. Restored by Gunnar Racing.
1998: Advertised for sale.
2006: For sale with the Blackhawk Collection.

Chassis No: 930 890 0025.
Engine No: 698 0033
Gearbox No: 798 0000.
Colour: White.
21/4/78: Sold to Vasek Polak. Damaged in transit.

Used but little, this was another of the 934/5's in the Vasek Polak collection. It was sold to Vasek Polak for George Follmer and Hurley Haywood to drive in the IMSA Championship. Since 1999, it has belonged to a very enthusiastic Porsche owner in Austria.
1978:
30/04: Laguna Seca IMSA: G. Follmer, #16; 1st.

1979:
22/04: Riverside 6-Hours: Follmer/Bell/Lunger, #16; 3rd OA.
29/07: Sears Point: Minter, #17; 4th.
05/08: Portland: Minter, #17; 4th.
16/10: Laguna Seca TA: M. Minter, #26; 2nd.

1980:
Tested at Mojave. Engine number 698 0033.

1998: With the Polak collection.
1999: Sold to Austria.

Chassis No: 930 890 0033
Engine No: 698 0033.
Gearbox No: 798 0000.
Colour: White
Ordered by Dick Barbour, this 935 was unusual
in being a 1978 customer car but arriving at Bob
Garretson's shop from the docks with a single, as
against the usual twin-turbo, engine. Effectively, it
was the prototype of the 1979 "Customer" 935. At
Daytona in February, 1978, the car placed second
overall and then took third place at Talladega and a
sixth at Laguna Seca.
0033 was badly damaged in an accident on the
Mulsanne straight at Le Mans in June, 1978 but later
on rebuilt.

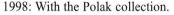

Sold to Volkswagen of America.
Sold to. Dick Barbour. Re-painted red by Dick
Barbour.

1978:
04-05/02: Daytona 24-Hours WCM: Barbour/
Schurti/Rutherford, #6; 2nd OA.
18/03: Sebring 12-Hours: Stommelen/Barbour/
Schurti, #6; DNF.
02/04: Talladega 6-Hours IMSA:Barbour/

Rutherford, #6; 3rd.
30/04: Laguna Seca IMSA: Barbour, #9; 6th.
10-11/06: Le Mans 24-Hours: Garretson/Akin/Earle,
#91; DNF. (Acc).
2007: STPO. USA.

Chassis No: 009 0044
Engine No: 698 0034.
Type: 930/78.
Gearbox No: 798 0000.
Colour: White
Bodyshell supplied to Bob Akin.

This 935 was built up on a factory competition
bodyshell by Franz Blam for Bob Akin and Charles
Mendez. After giving faithful service, it was
destroyed in a crash at the Nürburgring in 1981 after
it had left the road. The marshalls did not move it
and poor Herbert Muller was killed after he spun off
the track and hit it, both his 908 and the 935 catching fire. In later years the rights and a few parts were
sold, from Kremers and the car rebuilt.

1979:
07/07: Watkins Glen WCM: Akin/McFarlin/Woods,
#71; 3rd OA/1st in Trans Am class.
29/07: Sears Point IMSA: Akin, #71; 15th.
05/08: Portland IMSA: McFarlin, #71; 8th.
02/09: Road America 500 Miles IMSA: McFarlin/

Akin, #9; 5th OA.

1980:
2-3/02: Daytona 24-Hours WCM: Mendez/Redman/ Miller, #5; 39th NR. (Accident).
22/03: Sebring 12-Hours WCM: Mendez/Redman/ Miller, #5; DNF.
13/04: Road Atlanta IMSA: Akin, #5; 15th.
17/08: Mosport 6-Hours WCM: Akin/Miller/Nierop, #5; 6th.
31/08: Road America 500 IMSA: Akin/Redman/ Miller, #5; 5th.
21/09: Road Atlanta 50 Miles IMSA: Akin, #5;(1); 6th. (2); 17tth.
30/11: Daytona Finale IMSA: Akin, #5; DNF.

1981:
31/1-1/02: Daytona 24-Hours WCM: Akin/Bell/ Siebert, #5; 2nd.
21/03: Sebring 12-Hours WCM: Akin/Siebert/Bell, #5; DNF.
10/05: Silverstone 6-Hours WCM: Akin/Rahal/ Lovett, #39; 6th.
24/05: Nürburgring 1000Km WCM: Akin/Rahal, #25; DNF. Car hit by H. Muller and burnt. Wreck left in Germany.

1982: Car dismantled by Kremer Racing and rebuilt as an RSR.
Sold to UK.

Chassis No: 930 890 0035
Engine No: 698 0035.
Type: 930/78.
Gearbox No: 798 0000.
Colour: White

Sold to Vasek Polak, this 935 was stored by him until being sold to John Paul in 1980. Paul does not appear to have raced it, just used it in testing.

1983: Sold to John Sherwin. Crashed.
Stored.
2007: STPO. Under restoration.

Chassis No: 930 890 0037
Engine No: 698 0051.
Type: 930/78.
Gearbox No: 798 0000.
Colour: White

This is the rolling chassis which was supplied to Dick Barbour to rebuild 930 770 0953 which had been wrecked in the 1977 Daytona Finale and then bought by Dick Barbour.
It won the Sebring 12-Hour race in 1978 after which it was sold to the John Paul Racing team. The car was then further damaged by fire. Repaired, it did a few laps at the 1983 Daytona 24-Hours with Sr.

Sold to Volkswagen of America.
1978:
17/03: Sebring 12-Hours WCM: Redman/Garretson / Mendez, #9; 1st.
Sold to John Paul Snr.

02/04: Talladega 6-Hours IMSA: John Paul/B. Bondurant, #9; 18thNR. Fire.

John Paul then raced a Greenwood Corvette whilst this car was repaired.

1983:
Daytona 24-Hours: Paul Sr./P. Currin, #8; DNF. (15 laps).

See: JLP-1.

1978-1979: Seven customer 935's built with single/ twin turbochargers, big brakes and inverted ("upside down") transmissions.

Chassis No: 930 990 0026
Engine No: 699 0057
Gearbox No:
Colour: Yellow.

Bill Whittington's car of 1979. Don and Bill won

the Riverside six hours with it. The car was badly damaged in the big crash at the Daytona finale in 1979, despite being declared the winner! It was rebuilt in period.

Sold to: The Whittington Bros.

1979: IMSA Championship.
03-04/02: Daytona 24-Hours: Whittingtons./J.Barth, #94; 4th OA.
17/03: Sebring 12-Hours: Whittingtons, #94; 42nd NR.
08/04: Road Atlanta 100 Miles: Bill Whittington, #94; 13th.
22/04: Riverside 6-Hours: Don/Bill Whittington, #94; 1st.
29/04: Laguna Seca 100 Miles: Bill Whittington, #94; 23rd.
13/05: Hallett 100 miles: Bill Whittington, #94; DNF.
28/05: Lime Rock 100 miles: Bill Whittington, #94; DNF.
17/06: Brainerd 100 miles: Bill Whittington, #94; 7th.
15/07: Mid-Ohio 250 Miles: Don/Bill Whittington, #94; 2nd.

23/09: Road Atlanta 100 miles: Bill Whittington, #94; 16th.
Fitted with K3 bodywork.
25/11: Daytona 250 Miles: Bill Whittington, #94; 1st. Very badly damaged.

Chassis No: 930 990 0027
Engine No: 699 0042. Single turbo engine.
Gearbox No:
Colour: Blue.
Delivered: 1/79 to Vasek Polak.

This car apparently only ever did one race. It resides today with a well known Porsche enthusiast and race car collector.

Sold to: Otis Chandler.

1979:
22/04: L.A. Times GP at Riverside. Chandler/J. Thomas; 29th NR; (engine).

Single-turbo engine replaced with twin-turbo 3.2 litre engine.

Sold to David Hall.

STPO. Dark Blue with yellow/red/white stripes. Restored.
2000: 935 Challenge race at Daytona; D. Murry; 1st.

2001: STPO, USA.

Chassis No: 930 990 0028
Delivered to: VWoA.

Not much information known about this car but we do know that it was sold to the Whittington Brothers. 0028 was probably brought up to K3 specification for 1980.

1980: IMSA Championship.
02-03/02: Daytona 24-Hours: Bill Whittington/Plankenhorn, #94; 51st NR.
30/11: Daytona 250 Mile Finale: Bill Whittington, #94; DNF.
1981: IMSA championship.
31/1-1/02: Daytona 24-Hours: Whittington Bros, #94; DNF.
19/03: Sebring 12-Hours: Whittington Bros, #94; DNF.
12/04: Road Atlanta: Bill Whittington, #94; 13th.

Chassis No: 930 990 0029
Engine No: 699 0040.
Gearbox No: 799 0029.
Colour: Black.

Delivered: 1/79 to Vasek Polak.

Sold through VWoA, 0029 was delivered to Ted Field and Danny Ongais of Interscope racing and won the 1979 Daytona 24 Hours in 1979.

Later on in 1979, it was crashed in practice for the Daytona Finale and then sold to Vasek Polak where it remained in storage for the next eighteen years until bought by Jim Torres of Burbank Coach Works and restored. It has since been sold on twice.

Sold to Vasek Polak.
Sold to the Interscope Racing Team.
1979: IMSA championship unless otherwise noted.
3-4/02: Daytona 24 Hours WCM: Ongais/Haywood/Field, #0; 1st.
17/03: Sebring 12 Hours WCM: Ongais/Field, #0; DNS.
08/04: Road Atlanta 100 Miles: Ongais, #0;23rd NR.
29/04: Laguna Seca 100 Miles: Field, #0; 5th. Fastest lap.
13/05: Hallett 100 miles: Field, #0; 5th.
28/05: Lime Rock 100 miles: Field, #0; 4th.
17/06: Brainerd 100 miles: Field, #0; 3rd.
04/07: Daytona 250 miles: Field/Ongais, #0; 2nd.
07/07: Watkins Glen 6-Hours: Field/Ongais, #0; DNF. Accident.
29/07: Sears Point 100 miles: Field, #0; 2nd.
05/08: Portland 100 miles: Field, #0; 6th.

02/09: Road America 500 miles: Field/Minter, #0; 3rd.
23/09: Road Atlanta 100 miles: Field, #0; 7th.
25/11: Daytona Finale: Field; The car was damaged in a crash in practice with Engine No: 698 0063 installed.

1980: Sold to Vasek Polak .
1997: Sold to Jim Torres.
Restored.
1999: Sold to Bill Bachman. Vintage raced.
2004: Sold.
Sept: For sale, $225,000.
2005: STPO.

Chassis No: 930 990 0030.
Engine No: 699 0036 Single Turbo.
Gearbox No:
Colour: White.

This was Peter Gregg's 1979 IMSA Championship winner. Gregg kept the single-turbo set-up, giving him a weight advantage over the opposition, who all converted their single-turbo 1979 cars to twin-turbo set-up.

The car has 70,000 racing miles covered and is today with the Brumos collection

Sold to Peter Gregg.
1979: IMSA Championship.
08/04: Road Atlanta 100 Miles: Gregg, #59; 1st.
22/04: Riverside 6-Hours: Gregg/Ludwig, #59; 5th.
29/04: Laguna Seca 100 Miles: Gregg, #59; 1st.
13/05: Hallett 100 Miles: Gregg, #59; 2nd.
28/05: Lime Rock 100 miles: Gregg, #59; 1st.
17/06: Brainerd 100 miles: Gregg, #59; 1st.
04/07: Daytona 250 Miles: Gregg, #59; 3rd.
15/07: Mid-Ohio 250 Miles: Gregg/Haywood, #59; 1st..
21/07: Road America, Elkhart Lake TA: Gregg, #59; 1st.
29/07: Sears Point 100 miles: Gregg, #59; 1st.
05/08: Portland 100 Miles: Gregg, #59; 1st.
26/08: Mid-Ohio: Gregg/Haywood; 14th.

23/09: Road Atlanta 100 miles: Gregg, #59; 1st.
14/10: Laguna Seca: Gregg, #59; 1st.
25/11: Daytona 250 Miles: Gregg/Haywood, #59; 39th.
Gregg won the 1979 IMSA Championship, winning 9 out of 15 races.

1980: Now with 935/77 type bodywork.
2-3/02: Daytona 24 Hours WCM: Gregg/Haywood/ Leven, #59; 11th OA.
13/04: Road Atlanta 100 Miles: Gregg, #59;3rd.
27/04: Riverside 6-Hours: Gregg/Holbert; DNF.
04/05: Laguna Seca: Gregg; 2nd OA.
26/05: Lime Rock: Gregg, #59;14th NR.
04/07: Daytona 250 Miles: Gregg/Haywood, #59; 3rd.

With the Brumos collection.

Chassis No: 930 990 0031
Engine No: 699 0038
Gearbox No: 799 0031
Colour: White.
Sold to VWoA.

Originally sold to VWoA and then Vasek Polak for the Interscope team, this 935 was kept at Weissach and used for testing end development. It was raced at the Le Mans 24-Hours in 1979 and then went back to Weissach for more testing. At the end of

1979, it was finally delivered to Polak's where it spent the next ten years in storage before being sold to a collector.

1979
30/05: Invoiced to VWoA. $125, 535.
Sold to Vasek Polak.
Sent back to Weissach for development and testing.
9-10/06: Le Mans 24-Hours: Field/Minter/Morton, #68; DNF. (Engine).
More testing and development at Weissach. 935/77 bodywork fitted.
30/11: Sent to Polak.

1989: Mr Alain Kittler of France bought this 935 from Mr Polak and sent it to Paris to the auction of Palais des Congres in1990. At the auction this Porsche did not sell.

After the auction, Mr.Tomohiro Aono contacted Mr Kittler and bought this car.and sent it to Japan in

1990.
2002: STPO.
2007: Rennsport.
2015: In USA.

Chassis No: 930 990 0032
Engine No: 698 0051, Single-Turbo.
Gearbox No:
Colour: Red.

Sold to and raced by Dr Gianpiero Moretti in IMSA races in 1979, 0032 was converted to 935 "J" form by Joest with twin-turbo engine and 935/77 bodywork over the winter of 1979-1980. After the Daytona 24-Hours, 0032 became Moretti's back-up car for 1980 after he bought 930 890 0014 from Joest immediately after Daytona.

Moretti sold the car to Jim Busby at Laguna Seca in 1980. Busby needed to race to fulfill his sponsorship agreement and his BMW M1 had crashed in practice. Engine No: 698 0059 was installed and Jim Busby also had Dan McLoughlin of AIR later on install M16 bodywork. Jim Busby sold the "old" Joest 935/77 type bodywork to the Bayside Disposal team who used it on chassis number 000 0024.

In 1981, the car was sold to Pepe Romero and, in 1983, to Tico Almeida, who raced it through 1986. It then passed through several hands before winding up with Rick Rothenberger and has been restored by Gunnar Racing. It was later on sold to the present owner

Sold to G. Moretti via C. Vincentz.

1979: Converted to twin-turbo configuration.
Sold to G. Moretti. IMSA Single-turbo IMSA-specification engine fitted.
IMSA Races.
08/04: Road Atlanta 100 miles: Moretti; #30; 4th.
29/04: Laguna Seca: Moretti; #30; DNS, Fire over-night.
13/05: Hallett: Moretti; #30; 4th.
28/05: Lime Rock: Moretti; #30; 6th.
17/06: Brainerd: Moretti; #30;36th NR.
04/07: Daytona 250: Moretti; #30;36th NR.
29/07: Sears Point 100-Miles: Moretti, #30; 22nd.
05/08: Portland: Moretti; 24th NR.
23/09: Road Atlanta 100 Miles: Moretti, #30; 31st NR

20-25/10: Giro d'Italia: Moretti/Schon/Radaelli, #592; 1st.

To Reinhold Joest, converted to 935 'J' specification.

1980: IMSA Championship.
02-03/02: Daytona 24-Hours: Moretti/Cazzaniga/ Canepa, #30;59th NR.
Sold to Jim Busby Racing.
04/05: Laguna Seca: Red, Coors sponsored. Busby, #3; DNF.
05/07: Watkins Glen, WCM: Busby/Mears, #3; DNS. Engine.
27/07: Sonoma 100 Miles: Busby, #3; 6th.
03/08: Portland: Busby, #3; 6th . 3.1 litre engine.

1981:
22/01: Sold to J.R. & Hijos, S.A. (Pepe Romero). $130,000. Painted pink/maroon.

31/1-1/02: Daytona 24-Hours: Romero/Gonzales/ Mendez. #37; 52nd NR
16/08: Mosport: Romero/Febles, #17; 16th. (935J).
23/08: Road America, Elkhart Lake: Romero/Varde, #17; 43rd NR.
12/09: Crashed at Road Atlanta in practice.

1983: White.

5-6/02: Daytona 24-Hours: Rubino/Romero/Bundy/ Dale Whittington, #47; 11th.
27/02: Miami GP: Dale Whittington, #5; 14th.

Sold to Tico Almeida.
19/03: Sebring 12-Hours: Almeida/Soto, #05; 62nd NR. Accident.
10/04: Road Atlanta: Almeida/Soto, #05; 18th.
27/11: Daytona: Almeida/Morejohn, #05; 5th.

1984:
4-5/02: Daytona 24-Hours: Almeida/Morejon/ Garcia,/Gar; 26th.
24/03: Sebring 12-Hours: Almeida/Morejon, #05; 20th.
1985:
2-3/02: Daytona 24-Hours: Almeida/Morejon/Riano, #05; DNS.

1986:
1-2/02: Daytona 24-Hours: Almeida/Morejohn/ Varde, #06; 55th NR. Hi-Tech entry.

Sold to Gerry Sutterfield.
Sold to Rick Rothenberger
In restoration at Gunnar Porsche.
2006: With Vintage Racing Services.
2008: In Connecticut, partially restored.

Chassis No: 009 0029
Engine No: 698 0063.
Gearbox No:
Colour:

Sold to Bruce Canepa. Factory built. The last 1979 car. Just four races but in the top five at each race.

1979: IMSA Championship Races.
3-4/02: Daytona 24-Hours: Canepa/Mears/Shelton, #11; 3rd.
29/07: Sears Point 100 Miles: Canepa, #4; 5th.
05/08: Portland 100 Miles: Canepa, #11; 3rd.
16/10: Laguna Seca TA: Canepa, #111; 5th.

Kremer K1
Chassis No: 006 0019-K1
Engine Type: 930/72.
Gearbox Type: 930/25
Colour: White.

The Kremer Brothers entered this 935 built up in their dealership in 1976 in the WMC with slotted rear fenders. It is, effectively, the K1. They used a factory bodyshell, Chassis number: 006 0019, and factory parts. If the Works team faltered in 1976, this Kremer car was usually there as a back-up to the Porsche effort.

In 1977, this car was sold to Franz Konrad, another Porsche customer who had previously raced an RSR. In 1978, the car was sold to John Lagodny of Luxembourg who raced it many times in 1978 and 79, winning most of the time. At the Bolzano-Mendola hilllclimb in July, 1979, Lagodny crashed the 935 severely and rebuilt it around a 935 bodyshell, that of chassis number 930 890 0016, a twin-turbo 1978 car from Joest Racing.

Lagodny raced the 935 until 1981 and then sold it, via Jurgen Kannacher, to H.J. Dahmen. No further information is available.

1976: White.
21/03: Mugello 6-Hours WCM Heyer/Wollek, #5; 2nd OA.
04/04: Vallelunga 6-Hours WCM: Heyer/Wollek, #3; DNF.
09/05: Silverstone 6-Hours WCM: Heyer/Wollek, #10; 2nd OA.
30/05: Nürburgring 1000Km WCM: Heyer/Wollek, #2; DNF..
12-13/06: Le Mans 24-Hours: Bolanos/Heyer/Negrette/Sprowls, #47; DNF.
27/06: Austrian 1000Km, Osterreichring WCM: Bell/Schuppan, #2; 4th.
04/09: Dijon 6-Hours WCM: Heyer/Wollek, #5; 2nd.
17/10: Zolder: Krebs; 2nd.
31/10: Hockenheim, (EC-GT): Krebs, #51; 1st.
1977:
Sold to Franz Konrad.

German National Championship races unless otherwise noted.
13/03: Bergischer Lowe, Zolder: Konrad, #58; 4th.
27/03: Nürburgring: Konrad, #58; 8th.
01/05: Eifelrennen Nürburgring: Konrad, #59; 7th.
08/05: Kassel-Calden: Konrad, #59; DNF.
15/05: Silverstone 6-Hours WCM: Konrad,Hahnlein; 5th.
22/05: Mainz-Finthen: Konrad, #71; 6th.
29/05: Nürburgring 1000Km WCM: Konrad/Keller/Fitzpatrick, #5; 4th.
26/06: Zolder: Konrad; 1st.
03/07: Norisring, Nurnberg DRM: Konrad, #58; 5th. Trophy race; 5th.
24/07: Diepholz:Hahnlein, #71; 9th.
30/07: G.P. von Deutschland, Hockenheim:Hahnlein, #54; 6th.
14/08: Westfalen-Pokal, Zolder:Hahnlein, #72; 5th.
28/08: Nürburgring: Christman, #95; 2nd. (Konrad entry).
2/10: Supersprint Nürburgring:Hahnlein, #59; DNF.
9/10: Hockenheim 6-Hours: Konrad/Merl/Hahnlein, #16; 5th. Kremer entry.
16/10: Zolder: Hahnlein; DNF.

1978: Sold to John Lagodny.
12/03: Dudelange, (hillclimb): Lagodny; 11th OA, 1st in class.

19/03: Goodyear Trophy, Colmar: Lagodny; 1st.
27/03: Lorentzweiler, (hillclimb): Lagodny; 3rs OA, 1st in class.
02/04: Bekers van Belgie, Zandvoort: Lagodny; 4th.
09/04: Zittig (Hillclimb): Lagodny; 10th OA, 1st in class.
16/04: Krahbergrennen (hillclimb): Lagodny; 10th OA, 1st in class.
30/04: Remerchen (hillclimb): Lagodny; 3rd OA, 1st in class.
07/05: Goodyear-Trophy, Colmar: Lagodny; 1st.
21/05: Val d'Aisne (hillclimb): Lagodny; 4th OA, 1st in class.
28/05: Gorcy (hillclimb): Lagodny; 9th OA, 1st in class.
04/06: Heisforf (hillclimb): Lagodny; 2nd OA, 1st in class.
11/06: Bergpreis Freiburg-Schauinsland: Lagodny; 9th OA, 2nd in class.
02/07: Trierer Bergrennen: Lagodny; 2nd OA, 1st in class.
09/07: Goodyear-Trophy, Colmar: Lagodny; 1st.
18/07: Dudelange (hillclimb): Lagodny; 1st.
30/07: Coppa Carotti, Rieti-Terminillo: Lagodny; 19th OA, 2nd in class.
13/08: Mont Dore (EHC): Lagodny; 13th OA, 2nd in class.
20/08: Goodyear-Trophy, Colmar: Lagodny; 1st.
27/08: Wasserberg (hillclimb): Lagodny, 2nd OA, 1st in class.
01/10: EG-Trophy, Zolder: Lagodny; 2nd OA.

1979:
18/03: Dudelange, (hillclimb): Lagodny; 2nd OA, 1st in class.
25/03: Luxembourg-Trophy, Colmar: Lagodny; 1st OA.
01/04: Zolder: Lagodny; 2nd.
08/04: Zittig (Hillclimb): Lagodny; 2nd OA, 1st in class.
16/04: Lorentzweiler (hillclimb): Lagodny; 1st.
22/04: GP van Zolder: Lagodny; 2nd OA.
290/4: Coupes d'Ixelles: Lagodny; 2nd OA.
20/05: Goodyear-Trophy, Colmar: Lagodny; 2nd OA.

27/05: Coupe de Ixelles: Lagodny; 2nd.
10/06: Dobratsch (EHC): Lagodny; 8th OA.
24/06: Bolzano-Mendola (EHC): Lagodny; DNF. (accident).

Rebuilt around a 1978 935 bodyshell, chassis number 930 890 0016 bought from Jurgen Kannacher/ Joest Racing.
See: 930 890 0016.

Kremer 935/K2:
Chassis No: 007 0016
Colour: Vaillent green with yellow/red/mauve stripes.
Built up from a factory bodyshell in 1977 by the Kremer Brothers, this 935 was the second one to employ the Kremer Brothers ideas and became known as the "K2", the 1976 935 of the Kremers being simply called the "K".

Principally driven by Bob Wollek, K2 had a very good year and was sold, at the end of the season, to John Winter, who had it painted black. He then raced it, crashing it badly at Mainz-Finthen in 1978. Rebuilt, (probably around chassis number 007 0016), it was sold to Bo Strandell in 1992.

1977: German National Championship Races.
13/3: Bergischer Lowe Zolder DRM: Wollek, #51; 2nd.
27/3: 300Km Nürburgring DRM: Wollek, #51; 3rd.
01/5: Eifelrennen Nürburgring: Wollek, #51; 1st.
08/5: Kassel-Calden: Wollek, #51; 1st.
22/5: Mainz-Finthen: Wollek, #51; 2nd.
29/5: Nürburgring 1000Km: Wollek/Fitzpatrick, #1; 2nd OA.
03/7: Norisring, Nurnberg DRM: Wollek, #70; DNF. (Turbo).
23/7: Diepholz: Wollek, #51; 2nd.
31/7: GP von Deutschland, Hockenheim: Wollek, #51; 1st.
14/8: Westfalen-Pokal, Zolder: Wollek, #51; 1st.
2/10: Supersprint, Nürburgring: Wollek, #51; 2nd.
9/10: Hockenheim 6-Hours: (2x 3-Hours): Wollek/Fitzpatrick, #4; 1st.

1978:
4-5/2: Daytona 24 Hours: "Winter"/Schornstein/ Brambring, #14; 5th OA.
12/3: Bergischer Lowe Zolder DRM: Winter, #4; 9th; Black.
02/4: Nürburgring 300Km DRM:Winter, #4; 9th. NOTE: Black with pinstripes.
30/4: Nürburgring, Eifelrennen DRM: Winter, #4; DNF. White with blue stripes,
21/5: Avus-Rennen DRM: Winter, #4; DNF. (gearbox).
18/6: Mainz-Finthen DRM: Winter, #4; DNF, (acc.)
Repaired and rebuilt by Kremer Racing with K3 modifications?
1992: Sold to Bo Strandell.

Kremer K2:
Chassis No: 930 870 0652

This 935 K2 is one of 2 built by Kremer for VAILLANT. (other was DP935 911 660 9057).

All the engine parts came direct from Porsche Motorsport. Willi Rabl had the VAILLANT sponsorship for years in Austria.

The Car was built for Willi Rabl to compete in the European Hill Climb Championship. At first, it was built with 934 bodywork but later, it was rebuilt with 935 K2 bodywork, which it wears today. Using two 934/5s, Willi won 7 European titles

2007: Sold to J. Brodesser.
Restored by Kremer Racing/DP Motorsports, Cologne.
2008: Sold to Eric Charles.
2009: Swapped for Courage LMP1.
2009: Sold to Joel Riviera.
2010: Sold to Alex Valle, Italy.
2012: Swapped for Ferrari Challenge car.
2014: STPO.

1979: Kremer Brothers' 935 K3:
Chassis No: 009 0002
Colour: White, later blue.

The 935 K3 prototype. The "other" 1979 K3 of the 1979 Kremer team. This car won twelve out of fifteen German National Championship races plus two second places driven by Klaus Ludwig in 1979.

In 1980, it was sold to Claude Bourgoignie who, in turn, sold it to John Cooper or the Kremer Brothers in 1981/82? (Results for 1981 are missing as I write). Whatever, John Cooper bought it over the winter of 1981/2 and shared it in World Championship long-distance races with Paul Smith. Together with Claude Bourgoignie, the pair won the Group 5 class at Le Mans in 1982, placing eighth overall.

After this, Cooper amd Smith took the K3 to America and raced it in IMSA with decent results before a final class win at Brands Hatch in 1982.

At some time prior to John Cooper's ownership, the whole nose was tube-framed. Perhaps after Klaus Ludwig's accident at Hockenheim in September 1979? It then went into a museum in Wolverhampton, England. For many years it was in the capable hands of John Greasley in England. He restored it in 2003. In 2004, the author sold it to it's present owner in the USA. In 2006, it was sold again and stayed in the USA.

1979: German National Championship races. Race No: 54.

11/3: Bergischer Lowe Zolder: Ludwig; 1st.

08/4: Jim Clark Rennen Hockenheim: Ludwig; 1st.

29/4: Eifelrennen Nürburgring: Ludwig; 2nd.

20/5: Bavaria Salzburgring: Ludwig; 1st.

03/6: Nürburgring 1000Km WCM: Ludwig/Plankenhorn, #2; 2nd. (White/Green/yellow).

17/6: Mainz-Finthen: Ludwig; 1st.

24/6: Norisring Nurnberg: Ludwig; 1st. 200 Miles; 15th.

01/7: Zandvoort Trophy: Ludwig; 1st.

06/7: Donington: G. Edwards: 2nd. (Perhaps)

22/7: Diepholz: Ludwig; 1st.

19/8: Westfalen Zolder: Ludwig; 1st.

02/9: Hessen-Cup Hockenheim: Ludwig; DNF. Accident.

23/9: Supersprint Nürburgring: Ludwig; 1st. G5 race: 1st.

Sold to Team Willeme, Belgium.

14/10: Zolder: Bourgoignie; 1st.

1980: Track tested by Pierre Dieudonne in Belgian magazine AUTOhebdo #211 (04/80).

23/3: Bergischer Lowe Zolder DRM: Bourgoignie, #11; DNF.

01/6: Kreuzritter-Rennen, Spa DRM: Bourgoignie; 7th.

24/8: Westfalenpokal Zolder DRM: Bourgoignie, #18; 4th.

12/10: H.P. Joisten Trophy, Zolder: Bourgoignie; DNF.

Sold back to the Kremer Brothers?

1981: December: Sold to John Cooper.

1982:

04/4: Jim Clark Trophy, Hockenheim DRM: John Cooper; 5th.

Sold to Paul Smith.

18/4: Monza 1000Km WCM: Smith/Cooper, #88; DNF (Engine-Throttle stuck).

25/4: Eifelrennen, Nürburgring DRM: Smith, #23; DNF. (Acc.)

16/5: Silverstone1000Km WCM: Smith/Cooper, #60; DNF (engine).

30/5: Nürburgring 1000Km WCM: Smith/Cooper, #32; DNF. (Engine).

19-20/6: Le Mans 24-Hours: Ivey entry. Cooper, Smith, Bourgoigne, #60; 8th OA.

27/6: Norisring 200 Miles DRM: Cooper; DNF. (engine).

To USA. IMSA races:

15/8: Mosport: Cooper/Smith, #70; 6th

22/8: Road America, Cooper/Smith, #70; 7th.

05/9: Mid-Ohio. Cooper/Smith, #70; 5th.

12/9: Road Atlanta, Cooper/Smith, #70; 39th NR.

17/10: Brands Hatch 6-Hours: Smith/Cooper, #16; finished 12th. 1st in Group 5.

1983: In Wolverhampton museum.
1984: Engine sold to John Greasley.
Car sold to John Greasley. £28,000 inc. three engines. Restored.

11/99: For sale with 0-hours engine/gearbox.
2004: Sold through John Starkey to Ken Quintenz, USA.
2006: Sold through John Starkey to Richard Griot in the USA.
2010: STPO.

Chassis No: 009 0003
Kremer Brothers-built. K3.

As this is a 1979 chassis, I have to presume that this was the Kremer team's replacement for 009 0015, which they had sold to the Whittington Brothers, just before the Le Mans 24 Hours and which was shipped to America immediately after the race in mid-June, 1979. Sold to Werner Hermann, ("Weralit", the sponsor), on the 21st February, 1980, 0003 took part in the German Championship in 1980, 81 and 82, principally driven by Edgar Doren, sometimes with Jurgen Lassig sharing the driving. In 1983, 0003 was sold to Jurgen Lassig. In 1986, the car was sold to Willy Konig, the noted German tuner. He raced the car for many years at the Nürburgring before crashing it heavily.

John Greasley bought the damaged car and rebuilt it with right hand drive and then used it to win the British GT Championship in 1993. In 2005, John Starkey sold it to a German racer.

John Greasley also had a "twin" K3 built up for his team mate, Ross Hyett in 1992 on a 1978 930 chassis, 008 0038. This car was later on sold to Japan, re-sold to the USA in 2001 and auctioned at Monterey in 2002 to an American racer.

1979:
05/8: Brands Hatch 6 Hours: K. Ludwig/A.

Plankenhorn, #27; (2nd) A/1st Group 5.
1980: German National Championship. Race #4. White, Weralit/Elora-sponsored.
23/3: Bergischer Lowe Zolder: Doren; 4th.
16/3: Brands Hatch 6-Hours: Doren/Lassig, #9; DNF. (engine).
30/3: 300Km Nürburgring: Doren; DNF. (Acc).
13/4: Jim Clark-Rennen, Hockenheim: Lassig; DNF.
27/4: Eifelrennen Nürburgring: Doren; 5th.
11/5: Silverstone 6-Hours WCM: Doren/Holup/Lassig, #22; 6th.
18/5: Mainz-Finthen: Doren; 3rd.
25/5: Nürburgring 1000Km WCM: Doren/Lassig/Holup, #4; 11th.
01/6: Kreuzritter-Rennen Spa: Doren: 6th.
22/6: Norisring Nurnberg: Lassig; 3rd.
13/7: Bavaria Salzburgring: Lassig; 6th.
27/7: Diepholz: Doren; 10th.
24/8: Westfalenpokal Zolder: Doren; 3rd.
07/9: Vallelunga 6-Hours WCM: Doren/Lassig/Holup, #4; 5th.
21/9: Supersprint, Nürburgring: Doren; 4th.
12/10: H.P. Joisten Trophy Zolder: Holup; 9th.

1981: World Championship races unless otherwise noted. Black, WERA-sponsored.
22/3: Bergischer Lowe, Zolder DRM: Lassig, #54; 5th.
12/4: Mugello 6-Hours: Doren/Lassig, #4; 13th OA.
12/4: Monza 1000Km: Doren/Lassig/Holup, #3; 1st OA.
10/5: Silverstone 6-Hours: Doren/Lassig, #24; 5th OA.
24/5: Nürburgring 1000Km: Doren/Lassig, #19; 5th OA.
13-14/6: Le Mans: Wera Meissberg entry. Holup/Doren/Lassig. #61; DNF.
28/6: Norisring, Nurnberg: Lassig; RU.
01/8: Gold-Pokal, Hockenheim DRM: Lassig, #54; DNF. (engine).
27/9: Brands Hatch 6-Hours: Lassig/Doren, #23; DNS. (Acc.)
1982: World Championship races unless otherwise noted

04/4: Jim Clark Rennen, Hockenheim DRM: Lassig, #18; DNS.
18/4: Monza 1000Km: Doren/Lassig, #87; DNF.
16/5: Silverstone 6-Hours: Lassig/Doren, #64; 9th OA, 1st in Group 5 class.
30/5: Nürburgring 1000Km: Doren/Lassig/Duge, #34; DNF. (Acc.)
27/6: Norisring, Nurnberg DRM: Lassig; DNS.
05/9: Spa 1000Km: Lassig/Libert/Pilette, #62; 10th OA.

1983:
25/2: Sold to Jurgen Lassig.
1984-85: Used as a "Renntaxi". Edgar Doren drove guests around at the Nürburgring, Hockenheim, or Zolder.

1986:
26/8: Sold to Willy Konig.
4/10: DMV-Preis von Hockenheim: Konig; DNS.
08/11: Rheintal-Rundstreckrennen, Hockenheim: Konig; 2nd.
15/11: Preis der Stadt Heilbronn, Hockenheim: Konig; 3rd.

1987
29/3: Sportwagen-Festival, Hockenheim: Konig; 3rd
18/6: Mittelrhein-Cup, Nürburgring: Konig; 2nd.

03/5: Supersprint, Nürburgring; Konig; DNF.
05/7: H.P. Joisten Trophy, Nürburgring: Konig; DNF.
23/8: Alpentrophae Salzburgring: Konig; DNF.
16/9: Nürburgring: Konig; RU.
13/10: Munchen: Konig; RU.
18/10: Preis der Stadt Esslingen, Hockenheim: Konig; 1st.

1988
03/4: Bergischer Lowe, Zolder: Konig; DNS.
28/8: Alpentrophae Salzburgring: Konig;
02/9: Nürburgring: Konig; RU.
16/10: Preis der Stadt Esslingen, Hockenheim: Konig; 1st.
1989:
02/4: 100 Meilen von Hockenheim: Konig; 3rd.
14/5: Mainz-Finthen: Konig; 3rd.
04/6: Supersprint, Nürburgring: Konig; 3rd.
20/8:Rundsreckenrennen, Nürburgring: Konig; RU.
27/8: Siegerland Flughafenrennen: Konig; 3rd.
16/9: Grenzlandrennen, Nürburgring. Konig; RU.
1/10: DMV Preis von Hockenheim: Konig; RU.
15/10: Preis von Stadt Esslingen, Hockenheim: Konig; RU.

1990
25/3: 100 meilen von Hockenheim: Konig; 1st.
01/4: Bergischer Lowe, Zolder: Konig; 2nd.
06/5: Hungaroring:Konig; 1st.
01/7: Rundsreckenrennen Duren, Nürburgring: Konig: Konig; 1st.
08/7: Rundsreckenrennen, Nürburgring: Konig; 2nd.
15/7: Osterreichring/Zeltweg: Konig; 1st.
10/8: Most: Konig; 1st.
16/9: Zolder: Konig; 6th.
30/9: Super Sprint Nürburgring: Konig; 2nd.
14/10: Osterreichring: Konig; 2nd. Oster Meisterschaft; Konig; 1st.

Willy Konig was the overall winner of the "Spezial Tourenwagen Trophy"

1991:
After a crash at the Nürburgring, with Willy Konig,

when the car had a 962 engine and gearbox, this 935 was rebuilt with it's correct engine and gearbox by G-Force.

1993: Sold to John Greasley.
25/4: Donington: Greasley, #55; 1st.
09/5: Silverstone: Greasley, #55; 2nd.
12/6: Oulton Park: Greasley, #55; 2nd.
27/6: Donington: Greasley, #55; DNF.
15/8: Silverstone: Greasley, #55; 1st.
22/8: Silverstone: Greasley, #55; 1st.
12/9: Brands Hatch: Greasley, #55; 2nd.
3/10: Silverstone: Greasley, #55; 1st.

John Greasley won the 1993 BRDC British GT Championship.

2005: Sold to Gerald Fellner, Munich.
2006: Sold to U.K.
2007: STPO. UK.

Chassis number: 009 0005
Kremer Brothers K3.
Colour: Red, then black.

This is a re-shell of 930 770 0911. The previous number has a line through it with the present number

stamped beneath it. This probably happened after the accident at the 1979 Daytona Finale.

In 1980, the car was updated with a Kremer K3 kit. It raced under the "Racing Associates" banner. Coca-Cola sponsored.

1980: World Championship Races.
2-3/2: Daytona 24-Hours: Akin/Woods/Rahal, #05; 54th NR. (Engine).
22/3: Sebring 12-Hours: Akin/Woods/McKitterick, #05; 5th.
27/4: Riverside 5-Hours: Akin/Kent-Cooke/Woods, #05; 5th.
14-15/6: Le Mans 24-Hours: Mendez/Kent-Cooke/Akin.#: 69; DNF
05/7: Watkins Glen: Akin/Woods/Kent-Cooke, #69; 7th.
1981:
21/3: Sebring 12-Hours WCM: Kent-Cooke/Woods/McKitterick, #90; 2nd.
26/4: Riverside 6-Hours WCM: Garretson/Cooke-Woods, #90; 4th.

1982:
19-20/6: Le Mans 24-Hours: La Peyre/Snobeck/Servanin, #78; 5th/2nd. Black, yellow and green stripes, MALLARDEAU -sponsored.
3/10: Fuji 1000Km WCM: Kent-Cooke/Adams; 7th/2nd.

1983: Sold to Jim Torres.

1984:
29/4: L.A. Times GP, Riverside: J. Torres/J. Thomas, #33; 25th.

1985
28/4: LA Times GP, Riverside: J. Torres/M. Shelton, #39; 14th/2nd in GTO class.
28/7: Portland: Torres, #39; 33rd NR.:
25/8: Road America, Elkhart Lake: Torres/Shelton/Borlase, #39; 40th/12th in GTO class.

1986: As 930.

27/7: Portland: J. Torres, #39; 6th.
24/8: Road America: W. Frank/J. Torres, #39;
13th/3rd in GTO class.
5/10: Columbus: J. Torres, #39; 12th.
01/9: Lime Rock: J. Torres, #39; 17th.
20/9: Watkins Glen: J. Torres, #39; 24thNR.
Del Mar:
1987:
26/4: Riverside: J. Torres, #39; 12th.
24/10: Del Mar: J. Torres, #39; 18th.

Restored to 1982 935K3 specification..

2000: Sold to Ken Gold.
2001: STPO.

Chassis No: 009 0015
Colour: White.
Bodyshell sold to the Kremer Brothers. Built into a K3.

This, possibly the most famous of all the 935's, is notable for winning Le Mans in 1979 outright. The Whittington brothers, Don and Bill, purchased the car outright just hours before the start of the race and then, with Klaus Ludwig sharing the co-driving, went on to take victory from Dick Barbour's car.

Upon return to America, the Whittingtons raced it in some IMSA events before retiring it.

1979:
Sold to the Whittington Brothers.
9-10/6: Le Mans 24-Hours: Kremer entered. Klaus Ludwig/Whittington Brothers, #41;1st
07/7: Watkins Glen 6 Hours WCM: Whittington Bros/Klaus Ludwig, #94; 1st.
29/7: Sears Point 100 miles IMSA: Bill Whittington, #93; 14th.
23/9: Road Atlanta 100 miles IMSA: Don Whittington, #93; 5th.
25/11: Daytona 250 Miles IMSA: Don Whittington, #93; 2nd. Damaged in last-lap accident.

1980: Yellow; "Sun System" sponsorship.

03/2: Daytona 24-Hours WCM: Don/Dale/Bill Whittington, #93; 16th.
22/3: Sebring 12-Hours WCM: Bill/Dale/Don Whittington, #93; 3rd
13/4: Road Atlanta 30 Mins IMSA: Don Whittington, #93; DNS.
27/4: Riverside 5 Hours WCM: Don/Bill Whittington, #91;30th NR.
14-15/6: Le Mans 24-Hours: Don/Dale Whittington/H. Haywood, #85; DNF.

Displayed at the Indianapolis Museum.
2013: STPO, USA.

Chassis number: 009 0030
Known as "The Old Warhorse"/"Made in Mountain View special", this is the bodyshell used to rebuild 930 890 0033 after its accident at Le Mans in 1978

At Le Mans in 1979, Paul Newman, Dick Barbour and Rolf Stommelen drove the re-consti-tuted 935. Had it not been for a stuck wheel nut, they would almost certainly have won the race. As it was, they placed second overall.

In 1983, it was sold to Wayne Baker who turned it into a single-plug 934 and took part in the GTO class in IMSA. The "934" won the 1983 Sebring 12 Hours outright.

In 1985, Chet Vincentz bought it and raced it in GTO until 1987. In 2004, the car was sold to a noted

Porsche collector who had the car totally rebuilt by
Paul Willerson.

1979:
9-10/6: Le Mans 24-Hours: Barbour/Newman/
Stommelen, #70; 2nd. 1st in IMSA class.
17/7: Watkins Glen 6-Hours WCM: Stommelen/
Barbour/Newman, #70; 2nd OA.
02/9: Road America, Elkhart Lake IMSA: Barbour/
Redman/McKitterick, #6; 23rd NR.
Sold to Bob Garretson.

1980: World Championship races unless otherwise
noted
2-3/2: Daytona 24-Hours: Garretson/McKitterick/
Verney, #9; 9th.
Uprated to K3 specification.
22/3: Sebring 12-Hours: Garretson/Rahal/Nierop,
#9; 7th.
27/4: LA Times GP, Riverside: Garretson/Rahal, #9;
2nd.
14-15/6: Le Mans 24-Hours: Garretson/Rahal/
Moffat, #71; DNF. (engine). White, APPLE-
sponsored.
05/7: Watkins Glen 6-Hours WCM: Rahal/Garretson,
#71; DNF. (engine).
27/7: Golden State, Sonoma IMSA: Rahal, #9; 2nd.
17/8: Mosport 1000Km WCM: Rahal/Garretson,
#9;26th NR. (Acc.)
31/8: Road America 500: Rahal/Garretson, #9; 3rd.

1981. IMSA Championship races unless otherwise
noted. Modified by raising the rear suspension
pick-up points plus slight body modifications. Blue,
"STYLE AUTO" -Sponsored.
31/1-1/2: Daytona 24-Hours: Garretson/Rahal/
Redman, #9; 1st
21/3: Sebring 12-Hours: Garretson/Rahal/Redman,
#9; 17th. (roll-over.)
12/4: Road Atlanta: Rahal; 3rd.
26/4: LA Times GP, Riverside: Rahal/Redman, #9;
3rd.
03/5: Laguna Seca: Rahal, #9; 4th.
13-14/6: Le Mans 24-Hours: Verney/Garretson/

Cooke, #42; 6th OA/2nd in IMSA class. Black with
yellow and green stripes.
05/7: Daytona: Rahal/Garretson, #9; 18th.
12/7: Watkins Glen 6-Hours WCM: Garretson/
Mears/Rutherford, #9; 3rd. Black with red and yellow stripes.
26/7: Sears Point: Rahal, #9;18th NR. (engine).
02/8: Portland: Rahal, #9; 3rd.
23/8: Road America 500: Garretson/Gloy, #9; 4th.
27/9: Brands Hatch 6-Hours: Garretson/Rahal, #50;
2nd OA/1st in IMSA class.Yellow with blue and red
stripes.
29/11: Daytona Finale: Rahal/Garretson;17th.

Bob Garretson won the World Championship.

1982:
30-31/1: Daytona 24-Hours WCM: De Narvaez/
Wood/Garretson, #46; 3rd.
20/3: Sebring 12-Hours WCM: McKitterick/Ratcliff/
Clay, #9; 7th.
25/4: Riverside 6-Hours IMSA: Ratcliff/Clay, #9;
5th.
16/5: Charlotte IMSA: Ratcliff/Clay, #9; 4th.
19-20/6: Le Mans 24-Hours: Verney/Garretson/
Ratcliff, #77; 11th/ 5th in IMSA class. (lost cylinder). Black with red and yellow stripes.

Sold to Wayne Baker.
1983: IMSA Championship races. Converted to a

934. Prepared by Garretson Enterprises.
5-6/2: Daytona 24-Hours: Baker/Mullen, #9; 9th OA/9th in GTO.
27/2: Miami GP:Baker, #9; 25th NR in GTO race. (Acc.)
19/3: Sebring 12-Hours: Baker/Mullen/Nierop, #9; 1st OA
10/4: Road Atlanta: Baker/Mullen, #9; 7th/1st.
24/4: LA Times GP, Riverside: Baker/Mullen, #9; 5th/1st.
01/5: Laguna Seca: Baker, #9; 9th/5th.
15/5: Charlotte: Baker/Mullen, #9; 5th/1st.
30/5: Lime Rock: Baker/Mullen, #9; 5th/2nd.
19/6: Mid-Ohio: Baker/Mullen, #9; 24th/8th.
03/7: Daytona: Baker/Mullen, #9; 18th/7th.
10/7: Brainerd: Baker/Raub, #9; 10th/3rd.
24/7: Sears Point: Baker/Mullen, #18th/2nd.
31/7: Portland: Baker/Mullen, #9; 5th/3rd.
21/8: Road America: Baker/Muller/Nierop, #9; 18th/5th.
11/9: Pocono: Baker/Muller/Nierop, #9; 18th/5th.
27/11: Daytona Finale: Baker/Mullen/Blackaller, #9; 30th/6th.

1984: IMSA Championship Races.Changed back to K3 specification.
4-5/2: Daytona 24-Hours: Baker/Mullen/Blackaller, #9; 5th.
26/2: Miami GP: Baker/Blackaller, #9; 14th.
24/3: Sebring 12-Hours: Baker/Mullen/Blackaller, #9; 4th.
29/4: Riverside 6-Hours: Baker/Newsum, #9; 16th.
06/5: Laguna Seca: Blackaller, #9; 11th.

1985: IMSA Championship Races. Sold to Chet Vincentz. Changed back to 934 specification.
25/8: Road America: Vincentz/Nierop, #91;12th/2nd in GTO class.
08/9: Pocono: Vincentz/Nierop, #91; 26th/9th in GTO class.
29/9: Watkins Glen: Vincentz/Nierop, #91; 14th/3rd.
6/10: Columbus: Vincentz; 4th in GTO/GTU race.
1/12: Daytona Finale: Vincentz, #91;66th/22nd in GTO NR.

1986: IMSA Championship Races.
02/3: Miami GP: Vincentz; 33rd NR in GTO race.
06/4: Road Atlanta: Vincentz, #91; 2nd in GTO class.
As a 930S:
17/5: Charlotte: Vincentz, #91;DNF.
08/6: Mid-Ohio: Vincentz/Bauer; 20th NR.
22/6: West Palm Beach: Vincentz; 4th.
06/7: Watkins Glen: Vincentz/Bauer, #91;14th OA/3rd.
24/8: Road America, Road America, Elkhart Lake: Vincentz/Bauer; 38th/9th.
01/9: Lime Rock: Vincentz/Hutchings, #91; 6th.
20/9: Watkins Glen: Vincentz/Bauer, #91; 6th.
5/10: Columbus: Vincentz; 9th.

1987: IMSA Championship Races.
01/3: Miami GP: Vincentz, #91; DNF.
07/6: Mid-Ohio: Vincentz/Bauer, #91; 16th.
20/6: West Palm Beach: Vincentz/Bauer, #91; 5th.
28/6: Road Atlanta: Vincentz/Bauer, #91; 12th.
12/7: Summit Point: Vincentz/Bauer, #91; 9th.
16/8: Road America: Vincentz/Bauer, #91; 34th/9th.
27/9: Watkins Glen: Vincentz/Bauer, #91; 7th.

2004: STPO.
2007: March 11: Amelia Island. Restored back to 1979 configuration by Paul Willaston.
2015: Sold to Adam Corolla, USA.

Chassis No: 009 0044
935K3 built up for Bob Akin in 1980. #05 car.
1981: Destroyed at Nürburgring 1000Kms.

1980: 935's built by Race teams with competition 930 bodyshells supplied from the Factory.

Chassis No: 000 0009
Kremer Brothers built. K3.

Sold to Dick Barbour for the first half of the IMSA season, 0009 was dominant in the hands of John Fitzpatrick, winning the Championship in conjuction with another K3, (see: 000 0023). After its first sea-

son, it was sold to Preston Henn and raced by him until 1983.

1980: Delivered to the Kremer Brothers. K3/80.
2-3/2: Daytona 24-Hours: Fitzpatrick/Schurti/ Barbour, #6; 29th. (Acc.)
22/3: Sebring 12-Hours: Fitzpatrick/Barbour, #6; 1st.
13/4: Road Atlanta 30 Mins: Fitzpatrick, #6; DNF.
27/4: Riverside 5 Hours: Fitzpatrick/Barbour, #6; 1st.
04/5: Laguna Seca 100 Miles: Fitzpatrick, #6; 1st.
25/5: Nürburgring 1000Km: Fitzpatrick/Barbour/ Plankenhorn, #6; 1st OA.
22/6: Norisring Nurnberg: Fitzpatrick, #8; 1st.
04/7: Daytona 250: Fitzpatrick, #6; 1st.
05/7: Watkins Glen 6-Hours WCM: Barth/Merl, #4; 5th OA.
03/8: Portland: McKitterick; DNF. (Gearbox).
17/8: Mosport 6-Hours: McKitterick/Mears, #4; 5th OA.
Sold to Preston Henn.

1981: White, T-BIRD SWAP SHOP sponsored.
31/1-1/2: Daytona 24-Hours: Henn/Bondurant/Dale Whittington, #09; 64thNR.
21/3: Sebring 12-Hours: Henn/Gunn/Belcher, #09; 48th NR
26/4: Riverside: Henn/Hinze/Belcher, #08; 45thNR.
24/5: Nürburgring 1000Km; Wollek/Henn/Yates-

Smith, #27; 3rd (race stopped.)
13-14/6: Le Mans 24-Hours: Henn/Chandler/Mignot, #41; DNF.
16/8: Mosport: Henn/Doren, #09; 3rd.
23/8: Road America, Elkhart Lake: Doren/ Sullivan#09; 36thNR.
29/11: Daytona: P./B. Henn, #09' 49thNR.
1982:
03/7: Daytona: B. Henn, #09; 35thNR.
15/8: Mosport: P. Henn, #09; 30thNR.
22/8: Road America, Elkhart Lake: P/B.Henn/D. Wilson, #09; 41stNR.
05/9: Mid-Ohio 2: P. Henn, #09; 37thNR.
12/9: Road Atlanta 2: P. Henn/Bundy, #09; 2nd.
28/11: Daytona: Bell/Lanier, #09; 2nd.

1983:
Miami GP: Don Whittington, #09; 6th.
Crashed by Hurley Haywood at Mosport.
Rebuilt.

Chassis No: 000 0010
Kremer Brothers built. K3.
Sold to the Interscope Team.

This K3, built to the K3/80 specification, was sold to Ted Field and driven by Danny Ongais. Race No: "0". After Field and Ongais switched to Lola T600's, this 935 was sold. It has re-appeared in Europe in storage.

1980:
13/4: Road Atlanta: Field, #00; 14th.
04/5: Laguna Seca 100 Miles, Ongais, #00; DNF.
NOTE: Numbers changed to "0"
27/7: Golden State 100 Miles, Sonoma; Ongais, #0; 18th. Pole position.
21/9: Road Atlanta: (1) Ongais, #0; 33rdNR. (2) Ongais, #0;22nd.
30/11:Daytona 250 Miles Finale: Field, #0; 49th NR.

1981:
31/1-1/2: Daytona 24-Hours: Field/Ongais/Minter, #0; 39thNR.

21/3: Sebring 12-Hours: Ongais/Field, #0; DNS.
12/4: Road Atlanta: Field, #0; 7th.
26/4: Riverside 6-Hours: Field/Ongais, #0; DNS.
03/5: Laguna Seca: Field, #0; 7th.
25/5: Lime Rock: Field/Rahal, #0; 2nd.
31/5: Mid-Ohio: Field/B. Whittington, #0; 6th.
10-11/6: Le Mans 24-Hours: D/B. Whittingtons/
Field, #42; DNF. (engine).
04/7: Daytona: Field/Whittington, #0; 7th.
12/7: Watkins Glen 6-Hours: Field/B. Whittington,
#0; DNF. (Engine).
26/7: Sears Point: Field, #0; 19th NR.
02/8: Portland: Field, #0; 5th.
16/8: Mosport: Field/Whittington, #0; 3rd..
23/8: Road America, Elkhart Lake: Field/
Whittington, #0;7th.
13/9: Road Atlanta: Field, #0; 2nd.
27/9: Pocono: Field/B. Whittington, #0; 27thNR.

1982:
30-31/1: Daytona 24-Hours: Field/Ongais, #0; 62nd
NR.
(Interscope then used Lola T600-Chevrolets).

Sold to Al Lager, Spokane, WA.

1983:Re-painted silver/red.
24/4: Riverside 6-Hours: G. Dyer, #50; DNF.
10/7: Brainerd: G. Pusey/K. Rude, #50; DNF. (Acc.)

Parts sold to Kevin Jeannette, FL. Car rebuilt.

1985: Perhaps:
2-3/2: Daytona 24-Hours: F. Baker/D. Silver/D.
Herman, #20; 66th NR.
23/3: Sebring 12-Hours: F. Baker/D. Silver/D.
Herman, #20; 23rd.
09/6: Mid-Ohio: F. Baker/D. Silver/D. Herman, #00;
15th.
6/10: Columbus: D. Silver/J. Varde, #00; 17th.

Sold to Europe.

Chassis No: 000 0011
Kremer Brothers built. K3.

This K3/80 was a Kremer team car. In 1981, it
was sold to John Fitzpatrick for use in the IMSA
Championship. It was enthusiastically raced by its
owner in Vintage events in the USA up till about
2002, after which it was sold back to Europe.

1980: Jagermeister-sponsored. Race #2.
23/3: Zolder: Plankenhorn: 4th.
30/3: Nürburgring 300Km: Plankenhorn; DNF.
(Acc.)
13/4: Hockenheim: Plankenhorn: 2nd.
27/4: Eifelrennen, Nürburgring: Plankenhorn; 6th.
11/5: Silverstone 6-Hours: Fitzpatrick/Edwards/
Plankenhorn, #19; DNF. (engine)
18/5: Mainz-Finthen: Plankenhorn; DNF. (Acc.)
25/5: Nürburgring 1000Km: Fitzpatrick/
Plankenhorn/Barbour,#6; 2nd.
01/6: Kreutzritter-Rennen, Spa: Fitzpatrick; 2nd.
15/6: Le Mans 24-Hours: Field/Ongais/Lafosse, #41;
DNF. Interscope/Kremer entry.
22/6: Norisring, Nurnberg: Mass; DNF. (engine).
13/7: Bavaria Salzburg: Fitzpatrick; 2nd.
27/7: Diepholz: Stommelen; 6th.
24/8: Westfalenpokal Zolder: Fitzpatrick; 1st.
07/9: Hessen-Cup, Hockenheim: Fitzpatrick; 2nd.

21/9: Supersprint Nürburgring: Stommelen; DNF.
28/9: Preis von Baden-Wurttemberg, Hockenheim: Fitzpatrick; 1st.

1981:
31/1-1/2: Daytona 24-Hours: Fitzpatrick/Busby/Wollek, #1; 48th NR.
20-21/3: Sebring 12-Hours: Fitzpatrick/Busby, #1; 41st NR.
12/4: Road Atlanta: Fitzpatrick, #1; 1st.
26/4: Riverside 6-Hours: Fitzpatrick/Busby, #1; 1st.
03/5: Laguna Seca: Fitzpatrick, #1; 3rd.
25/5: Lime Rock: Fitzpatrick, #1; 22nd NR.
31/5: Mid-Ohio: Fitzpatrick, #1; 4th.
14/6: Brainerd: Fitzpatrick, #1; 3rd.
26/7: Sears Point: Fitzpatrick, #1; 22ndNR.
02/8: Portland: Fitzpatrick, #1; DNS.
16/8: Mosport 1000Km: Fitzpatrick/Busby, #1; 6th.
23/8: Road America, Elkhart Lake: Fitzpatrick/Busby, #1; 6th.
30/8: Mid-Ohio: Fitzpatrick/Busby, #1; 2nd.
13/9: Road Atlanta: Fitzpatrick, #1; 21st NR.
27/9: Pocono: Fitzpatrick/Busby, #1; 3rd.
20/10: Daytona Finale: Fitzpatrick, #1; 2nd.
1982:

30-31/1: Daytona 24-Hours: Fitzpatrick,#2; 61st NR.
20/3: Sebring 12-Hours: Fitzpatrick/Busby, #2; 65th NR.
04/4: Road Atlanta: Fitzpatrick, #22; 6th.
25/4: Riverside 6-Hours: J. Busby/V. Schuppan, #12; 37th NR.
02/5: Laguna Seca: D. Hobbs, #12; 6th.

1984: Sold to A. Pilla.
2003: Under restoration.
Sold to Sweden. Repainted in Jagermeister colors.
2005: Brands Hatch Group C race.
2007: Restored by Gunnar Racing.

Chassis No: 000 0013
Delivered to the Kremer Brothers.
Porsche 935 K3/80. Kremer team car
Colour: Yellow.

There is some doubt about the 1980 race results of 0013. What is certain is that it was driven by Bob Wollek in the first part of 1981 to score two first and two second places before being sold to Bob Akin to replace his car which had been destoyed at the Nürburgring. The Kremer Brothers sold the car to Akin without an engine; this went into their K4.

Bob Akin did well with 0013 before selling it to Chuck Kendall in 1984. Chuck did a few races with it before putting it into storage as he had bought a Lola T600.

In 1998, the 935 K3 was sold to a great enthusiast, Said Marouf of San Diego who planned to restore and race it. However, Marouf later on sold the car to another American, still unrestored, in 2005. It has since been restored.

1980:
14-15/6: Le Mans 24-Hours: Verney/Lapeyre/Trintignant, #43; DNF.
27/7: Diepholz: Winter, #3; DNF.
07/9: Hessen-Cup Hockenheim: Soldeck, #3; 11th.
21/9: Supersprint Nürburgring: Korten, #11; 5th.
28/9: Preis von Baden-Wurttemburg, Hockenheim: Korten, #3; 3rd.

1981: Colour: Orange. Sponsored by Jagermeister. Driven by Bob Wollek in German National Championship races.

22/3: Bergischer Lowe, Zolder: Wollek, #52; 2nd.
29/3: Nürburgring 300Km: Wollek, #52; 1st.
05/4: Jim Clark Trophy, Hockenheim: Wollek, #52; 2nd.
26/4: Eifelrennen, Nürburgring DRM: Wollek, #52; 2nd.
17/5: Mainz-Finthen: Wollek, #52; 1st.

Sold to the Hudson Wire Company in June, 1981. Coca-Cola sponsored. Red.

13-14/6: Le Mans 24-Hours 24-Hours: Akin/ Miller/ Craig Siebert; retired in 24th hour when lying 10th with electrical fault. Shipped to USA by Akin. Mallardeau-sponsored.

Driven by Akin for the IMSA season.

16/8: Mosport 1000Km: Bob Akin/Skeeter McKitterick, #5; 12th/8th in GTX class.
23/8: Road Atlanta: Akin/McKitterick;33rd NR; (Engine).
29/11: Daytona 250 miles: Akin; 11th OA, 8th in GTX class.

1982: Cola-Cola sponsored.
30-31/1: Daytona 24-Hours: Bob Akin/Derek Bell/ Craig Siebert, #5; 2nd OA.
20/3: Sebring 12-Hours: Akin/D.Bell/C. Siebert, #5; 12th OA.
25/4: Riverside 6 Hours: Akin/D.Bell/C. Siebert; 4th OA.
16/5: Charlotte 500 Km: Akin/D.Bell/C. Siebert; 3rd OA.
15/8: Mosport 6-Hours: Akin/Bell; 4th OA.
22/8: Road America 500Km: Akin/Bell; 33rd NR.

1983:
27/2: Miami GP: Dale Whittington, #5; 14th OA.
19/3: Sebring 12-Hours: Bob Akin/Dale Whittington/

John O'Steen; 2nd OA, 1st in GT class.
24/4: Riverside 6-Hours: Akin/Whittington; 7th OA, 5th in GTX.
30/5: Lime Rock 3-Hours: Akin/O'Steen; 2nd OA.
19/6: Mid-Ohio 6-Hours: Akin/O'Steen; 2nd OA.
03/7: Daytona 250Miles: Akin/O'Steen; 3rd OA.
10/7: Brainerd 500Km: Akin/D.Aase; 4th OA.
11/9: Pocono 500Km: Akin/O'Steen; 4th OA.

Akin 3rd in the IMSA Championship.

1984:
Sold to Chuck Kendall.

1985:
5-6/2: Daytona 24-Hours:C. Kendall/ J. Hotchkiss/P. Fitzgerald, #11; 21st OA. (burnt piston).
21/3: Sebring 12-Hours: C. Kendall/J. Hotchkiss/R. Kirby, #11; 8th OA and 6th in GTP.

Engine rebuilt. Stored.
1999: Sold to Said Marouf, San Diego through John Starkey.
2005: Jan: Sold through Mark Osborne of Bonhams to present owner.
2007: Rennsport 111. Restored back to Jagermeister sponsored spec.

NOTE: Another 0013 is in existence. According to the last English owner, he bought it from Manfred Freisinger, who in turn bought it from Bo strandell, who bought it directly from Erwin Kremer! A mystery. Your author sold the ex-Akin car in 1998 and has to say that this car looked exactly as a tired old 935 should look. Certainly, this was Akin's 935 from 1981 on and had the original chassis number correctly stamped in the front compartment.
2006: Sold to Europe.

Chassis No: 000 0017
Engine No: 676 2025.
Gearbox No:
Colour: Black.
Delivered to the Kremer Brothers. K3/80.

Sold to Ted Field, of the Interscope Team, 00017 had a good 1980, placing well in nearly all the races it took part in. At the Daytona Finale, Danny Ongais put it on pole and set the fastest lap but then had a "coming together" with Bill Whittington which put both cars out of the race.

In 1982, John Klug bought the K3/80 and had Dennis Lymann rebuild it for him and paint it white. After 1986, the car was stored until rebuilt in 1998. Your author bought the car in 2000 and sold it to a Porsche race car collector who raced it enthusiastically in HSR events.

1980:
2-3/2:Daytona 24-Hours: Field/Ongais/Minter, #0; 3rd.
18/3: Sebring 12-Hours: Field/Ongais, #0; 2nd.
13/4: Road Atlanta 30 Mins: Ongais, #0; 5th.
27/4: Riverside 6-Hours: Field/Ongais, #0; DNF. Engine.
04/5: Laguna Seca 100 Miles: Field, #0; 4th. Fastest lap.
Note: Car numbers switched over for the rest of the season.
26/5: Lime Rock: Field, #00; 2nd.
04/7: Watkins Glen 6-Hours: Field/Ongais, #00; 4th.
05/7: Watkins Glen 6-Hours: Field/Ongais, #00; 4th.

27/7: Golden State, Sonoma: Field, #00; 3rd.
03/8: Portland: Field, #00; 5th.
17/8: Mosport: Field/Ongais, #00; 3rd. Fastest lap.
27/7: Golden State 100Miles, Sonoma; Ongais,#0; 18th.
21/9: Road Atlanta: Ongais: Heat 1: 33rdNR. Heat 2: 22nd NR. Fastest lap.
30/11: Daytona 250 Miles: Ongais, #00; 36th NR. (Acc.) Pole position. Fastest lap.

1982: Interscope then swapped to using Lola T600-Chevrolets.
Sold to John Klug, restored.

1983: As a 930 "S".
13/6: Portland: Klug; 19th.
18/7: Mid Ohio: J.Klug; 17th.
01/8: Road America: Klug;27th.
25/9: Riverside: Klug; 22nd.

1984: IMSA races as a 934.
29/4: Riverside: J.Klug/Lindley, #80; 24th/7th GTO.
03/6: Sears Point TA: 16th.
16/6: Portland TA: Klug; 18th.
29/7: Portland:J. Klug/Lindley, #90; 17th/4th GTO.
05/8: Sears Point: J.Klug, #90; 20th/7th GTO.
11/11: Riverside 3-Hours SCCA: Klug/Sell; 2nd
1985: 935 K3/80 bodywork re-fitted. Andial engine No: 181 fitted.

14/4: Road Atlanta: J.Klug/L.Sell, #90; DNF.
28/4: Riverside: J.Klug/L.Sell, #90; 40th NR.
27/7: Portland:J. Klug, #90; 15th/1st in class.

1986:
Riverside TA: Klug; 21st.
Stored.
2000: Sold to Carlos de Quesada by John Starkey..
2001: Sold to Steve Goldin, Miami.
2006: Sold to Bruce Canepa.
2014: Sold to Fred Kaimer, USA.
2015: "Rennsport Reunion:, Laguna Seca.

Chassis No: 000 0018
Built up for Walter Wolf by the Kremer brothers.
Roadgoing only. Blue. Road-registered in Alberta,
Canada.

1986: Featured in "*Auto Motor und Sport*", #13.
Sold to Angelo Pallavicini in Switzerland.

Chassis No: 000 0023
Delivered to the Kremer Brothers. K3/80.
Sold to Dick Barbour.

This was the second "Sachs" sponsored car for John
Fitzpatrick to take the IMSA Championship with in
1980. The Barbour Team took delivery of the car in
June at Le Mans

1980:
14-15/6: Le Mans 24-Hours: Barbour/Fitzpatrick/
Redman, #70: 5th OA. 1st in the IMSA class.
05/7: Watkins Glen 6-Hours: Barbour/Fitzpatrick/
Redman, #6; 3rd OA.
27/7: Sears Point: Fitzpatrick, #6; 1st.
03/8: Portland: Fitzpatrick, #6; 1st.
17/8: Mosport1000Km: Fitzpatrick/Redman, #6: 1st
OA.
31/8: Road America: Fitzpatrick/Barbour, #6; 2nd.
21/9: Road Atlanta: Fitzpatrick, #6; (1);1st. (2); 2nd.
Sold to Fantasy Junction.
Sold on.

1999:Restored and for sale by Bruce Canepa.
2000: STPO.
2005: Monterey Historics, Laguna Seca.
2015: With Charles Nearburg, USA.
2015: "Rennsport Reunion", Laguna Seca.

Chassis No: 000 0027
Delivered to the Kremer Brothers. K3/80.
Colour: Black.
Sold to the Interscope Racing Team.

0027 was the the car bought to replace 000 0017
which had been damaged at the 1980 Daytona
Finale. Danny Ongais kept the K3 until selling it
to Kevin Jeannette, who in turn sold it to an owner
who raced it enthusiastically in HSR events. Sold
again in 2004.

1981:Race No: "00".
12/4: Road Atlanta: Ongais, #00; 4th.
03/5: Laguna Seca: Ongais, #00; 5th.
05/7: Daytona: B. Whittington, #00; 33rd NR.
29/8: Suzuka 1000Km: Field/B. Whittington, #00;
DNF. (Acc.)
29/11: Daytona: Field/B.Whittington, #00; 5th.

1982:
20/3: Sebring 12-Hours: Field/Ongais, #00; 18th NR.
04/4: Road Atlanta: Ongais, #00; 2nd.
25/4: Riverside: B. Whittington, #00; 45th NR

1983:
5-6/2: Daytona 24-Hours: Run in practice only. Lola T600 used in race.

Stored since 1984.
1999: Sold to Jay Policastro.
Has 1983 IMSA Daytona sticker on the rollcage. Vintage raced.
2000: Daytona: Policastro; 2nd.
2003: STPO.
2005: For sale. $350,000. Ken Gold. 3.2 engine freshened.
2006: Sold to Ray Hartman.
2006: Sold to Peter Garrod, UK.
2012: Le Mans Classic: P. Garrod.
2014: Sold via Prescott Kelly and John Starkey/Phil Bagley to Jeroen Bleekemolen.
2015: Rennsport Reunion. David McNeil.

1981: 930 Competition bodyshell supplied by the Factory.

Chassis No: 001 0020
Colour: White/Pink.
A K3-81 built up by the Kremer Brothers, with some K4 features. Usually driven by "John Winter".
Afterwards displayed in the Rosso Bianco col-

lection, Germany, until 1999 when sold to America. In 2004, your author sold it back to Europe where its enthusiastic owner had it mechanically restored, using all original parts.
1981:
13-14/6: Le Mans 24-Hours: Don/Bill Whittington/Ted Field, #59; DNF. (Engine).
21/6: Wunstorf: Winter, #66; 7th.
28/6: Norisring, Nurnberg: Winter, #62; DNF. (Eng.)
05/7: G.P. von Tourenwagen, Nürburgring: Winter, #56; 3rd.
12/7: Bavaria-Rennen, Salzburgring: Winter; DNS. (Car parts used in Wollek's car).
01/8: AvD Gold Pokal, Hockenheim: Winter, #72; 5th.
23/8: Westfalen-Pokal Zolder: Winter, #57; DNF. (Eng.)
06/9: Hessen-Cup Hockenheim: Winter, #57; DNF. (Suspension).
20/9: Supersprint Nürburgring; "Winter", #57; 13th

1982:
18/4: Monza 1000Kms WCM: Rolf Stommelen/Ted Field: 2nd OA/Class win Grp 5 .
19-20/6: Le Mans 24-Hours: K3. E.Doren/B. Sprowls/A.Contreras, #64; DNF. (out of fuel).
27/6: Norisring, Nurnberg: Winter; 13th.

1999: Sold to Phil Bagley, Klub Sport, USA. STPO

2003: Engine rebuilt.

2004: STPO, Europe by John Starkey.

2006: Monza CER: M. Devis; DNF whilst leading, (engine).

1981: Kremer Brothers-built K4. Their version of the 935/78 "Moby Dick"

935 K4:
Chassis No: K4/01. Kremer Team car, Tube Framed

Driven with success by Bob Wollek, this car was sold to John Fitzpatrick Racing in San Diego at the end of the 1981 season. Continuously developed by the team, it suffered from overheating until the air intakes for the intercooler were placed into the tops of the front fenders. Thereafter, the K4 ran very well.

John Fitzpatrick took the car to Australia where it was tried out by Alan Jones but a sale did not materialize. In 1983, the car raced again in the USA and was then sold to Brian de Vries. The car has been sold on since.

1981:

21/6: Wunstorf: Wollek, #52; 5th.

28/6: Norisring 200 Miles DRM: Wollek, #52; (DRM);6th, 1st. 200 Miles race:6th.

05/7: G.P von Tourenwagen, Nürburgring: Wollek, #52; 1st.

12/7: ADAC Bavaria - Rennen, Salzburgring: Wollek, #52; 2nd.

01/8: AvD Gold Pokal, Hockenheim: Wollek, #52; DNF. (gearbox).

23/8: Westfalen-Pokal, Zolder, #52: 2nd.

06/9: Hessen-Cup, Hockenheim: Wollek, #52; 2nd.

20/9: ADAC-Bilstein Super Sprint, Nürburgring: Wollek, #52; 2nd.

07/81: Featured in: "Rallye and Racing".

12/81: Track test in: "Rallye and Racing".

Sold to John Fitzpatrick.

1982:

30-31/1: Daytona 24-Hours: Fitzpatrick/Hobbs/ Baker, #2;61st NR.

20/3: Sebring 12-Hours: Fitzpatrick/Hobbs, #2; 65th NR. Acc.

25/4: Riverside: Fitzpatrick/Hobbs; 34th.

02/5: Laguna Seca 100-Miles: Fitzpatrick, #2; 3rd.

16/5: Silverstone 6-Hours: Fitzpatrick, #79; DNA.

23/5: Mid-Ohio 100-Miles: Fitzpatrick, #2; 1st.

31/5: Lime Rock: Fitzpatrick, #2; 1st.

27/6: Nurnberg 200, Norisring: Fitzpatrick, #2; DNF..

11/7: Brainerd 200Km: Fitzpatrick, #2; 21st.

25/7: Sears Point 100 Miles: Fitzpatrick, #2; 4th.

01/8: Portland 100 Miles: Fitzpatrick, #2; 19th NR.

22/8: Road America 500 Miles: Fitzpatrick/Hobbs, #2; 1st.

05/9: Mid Ohio 6-Hours: Fitzpatrick/Hobbs, #2; 1st.

12/9: Road Atlanta 500 Km: Fitzpatrick/Hobbs, #2; 31st NR.

17/10: Brands Hatch 1000Km: Fitzpatrick/Hobbs, #22; 3rd.

9/11: Kyalami 9-Hours: Fitzpatrick/Wilson; DNF. (engine).

28/11: Daytona 3-Hours Finale: Fitzpatrick/Wollek; 2nd.

1983:

24/4: Riverside 6-Hours: Fitzpatrick/Hobbs/Bell, #2; 1st.

27/2: Miami GP: Fitzpatrick; 4th.

Sent to Australia for Alan Jones to race in the Australian Sports Sedan and GT series. Probably one race only before being returned to America.

?/11: Calder Park: Jones; 1st.

1984:

24/3: Sebring 12-Hours: Graham/Gralia/Henn/ Wollek/Holbert, #14; 6th OA.

1985: Sold through Kerry Morse to Mike Hagen.

1988: Sold to Brian de Vries

1999: Sold on.

2000:
04/2: Practiced at the Daytona Enduro.
06/3: Sebring HSR event.
2006: Sold to Rob Walton, USA.
2014: For sale with Bruce Canepa.

Chassis No: K4/02. Kremer built, Tube framed. Interscope Team car.
Colour: Black.

Never raced. Bought by Ted Field for DM350,000. Practiced at Road Atlanta.

1983: Sold for $75,000. Stored with the Vasek Polak collection.

1997: Sold to M. Lauer. 962-engined.
1998-9: Raced in HSR events.
2000: STPO. (Marshall Field Much work carried out.
2001: Raced at Watkins Glen and Lime Rock by Bob Akin.
2003: Sold at Auction.
2015: In USA.

1979: Bodyshells supplied to various Race Teams to build up their own versions of the 935
Chassis No: 009 0001
Engine Type: 930/81. 3160cc.
Gearbox Type: 930/60.
Colour: White.

This bodyshell, number 009 0001, was sold to Reinhold Joest and built up by his team as a 935J for 1979. It is noted as a 935/78 in the documentation with the car. Driven by the irrepressible Rolf Stommelen, it won at the Norisring.

For 1980, it was further modified by the team and used by Volkert Merl in the German Championship. It was also raced by Jochen Mass. Sold to the Swiss collector, Albert Obrist, it was then sold to that noted motorsport entrepreneur, Bernie Ecclestone. It has since been bought and sold again several times.

1979: German National Championship.
11/03: Bergischer Lowe Zolder: Stommelen, #66; 2nd,
08/04: Jim Clark-Rennen, Hockenheim: Stommelen, #66; 4th.
29/04: Eifelrennen, Nürburgring: Stommelen, #66; 3rd.

20/05: Bavaria Salzurgring: Stommelen, #66; 5th.
17/06: Mainz-Finthen: Stommelen, #66; 2nd. (Used modified rear tail).
24/06: Norisring Nurnberg: Stommelen, #66;14th.
200 Miles:Stommelen; 1st.
01/07: Zandvoort Trophy: Stommelen, #66; DNF. (brakes)
22/07: Diepholz: Stommelen, #66; 3rd.
19/08: Westfalenpokal Zolder: Stommelen, #66; 5th.
26/08: Ulm-Mengen G5 + 2000: Joest; 5th.
02/09: Hessen-Cup Hockenheim (Kleiner Kurs): Stommelen, #66; 8th.
23/09: Supersprint Nürburgring (Start-Ziel-Schleife): Stommelen,#66; DNF. (engine)

Reconstructed to Type 935J/80 at Joest Racing by Porsche Weissach mechanics.

1980: German Championship unless otherwise noted. Liqui-Moly-sponsored.
23/03: Zolder: Merl, #7; DNS.
30/03: 300Km Nürburgring: Merl, #7; 1st.
13/04: Jim Clark Rennen Hockenheim: Merl, #7; 3rd.
27/04: Eifelrennen, Nürburgring: Merl, #7; 10th.
18/05: Mainz-Finthen: Merl, #7; 2nd.
01/06: Kreuzritter-Rennen Spa: Merl, #7; 5th.
22/06: Norisring Nurnberg: Merl, #7; (DRM) 2nd. (200 miles); 6th.
13/07: Bavaria Salzurgring: Merl, #7; 4th.
27/07: Diepholz: Merl, #7; 5th. (modified tail section).
24/08: Westfalenpokal Zolder: Merl, #7; 5th.
07/09: Hessen-Cup Hockenheim: Merl, #7; 5th.
21/09: Supersprint Nürburgring: Merl, #7; 3rd.
28/09: Preis von Baden-Wurttemburg, Hockenheim: Merl, #7; 2nd.
30/11: Daytona Finale IMSA: Merl/De Narvaez, #46; 3rd.

1981: German Championship unless otherwise noted.
Spot oil sponsored. #67 in the DRM.
22/03: Zolder: Merl; 6th.

29/03: Nürburgring 300 Km: Merl; 4th.
05/04: Hockenheim: Merl; DNF. (3.2 litre engine).
17/05: Mainz-Finthen: Merl; 3rd.
28/06: Norisring, Nurnberg DRM: Mass, #66; DNF.
(engine).
01/08:AvD Gold-Pokal, Hockenheim: Merl; 4th.
06/09: Hessen-Cup, Hockenheim: Merl; 4th.
20/09: Super Sprint, Nürburgring: Merl; 3rd.
27/09: Sauerland-Bergpreis: Mass; 1st in class.
11/10: Zolder: Mass; 2nd OA.
08/11: Kyalami 9-Hours: Bell/De Narvaez; 3rd OA.

1984: Sold to Albert Obrist.
1997: Sold to Bernie Ecclestone.
2005: Sold to David Mohlman.
2005: Sold to Bruce Canepa.
2008: Sold to Jamie Mazotta.
2009: Sold to Richard Harris.

Chassis No: 000 0016
Engine Type: 930/80.
Gearbox Type: 930/60.
Colour: White/Blue/Red.
Delivered to Joest Racing Team. Used to build up a
935J.

Reinhold Joest built/modified at least one car in
1980/81 with tube-frame fronts and rear. Raced with
success by Rolf Stommelen in 1980, it was sold to
Dieter Schornstein in part-exchange for his 1978
935, chassis number 930 890 0012.

At the Le Mans practice days of 1982, Harald
Grohs was driving the 935 when it left the road at
very high speed on the Mulsanne straight. He was
lucky to escape but the 935J was all but destroyed.
Rebuilt by Siggi Brunn, it was sold to Pat Jennings
in 2000. It has since been sold on again through
Stephan Roitmayer of Germany.

1980: Race #6.
23/03: Bergischer Lowe: Stommelen; 1st.
30/03: Nürburgring 300Km: Stommelen; 2nd.
13/04: Jim Clark-Rennen, Hockenheim: Stommelen;
DNF.
27/04: Eifelrennen, Nürburgring: Stommelen; 4th.
18/05: Mainz-Finthen: Stommelen; DNF.
01/06: Kreuzritter-Rennen Spa: Stommelen; 3rd.
22/06: Norisring Nurnberg: Stommelen;DNF. (Acc.)
13/07: Bavaria Salzburgring: Winkelhock; 1st.
27/07: Diepholz: Winkelhock; 3rd.
24/08: Westfalenpokal, Zolder; Winkelhock;DNF.
07/09: Hessen-Cup, Hockenheim: Winkelhock; 3rd.
21/09: Supersprint Nürburgring: Winkelhock; 1st.
28/09: Preis von Baden/Wurttemburg: Winkelhock;
DNS. (Eng.)
05/10: Sauerland-Bergpreis: Barth; 1st in class.

1981:
22/03: Bergischer Lowe, Zolder: Schornstein, #53;
12th.
29/03: Nürburgring 300Km: Schornstein, #53; 5th.
05/04: Jim Clark Trophy, Hockenheim: Schornstein,
#53; 4th.
26/04: Monza 1000Km: Schornstein/Grohs, #4;
DNF. (Acc.)
10/05: Silverstone 6-hours: Schornstein/Grohs;/
Rohrl, #22; 1st.
17/05: Mainz-Finthen; Schornstein, #53; 4th.
24/05: Nürburgring 1000Km: Schornstein/Grohs/
Rohrl, #20; 7th OA.
13-14/06: Le Mans 24-Hours: Schornstein/Grohs/
von Tschirnhaus, #60; 10th OA.
21/06: Wunstorf: Schornstein, #53; 4th.
28/06: Norisring: Grohs; 4th. (Money race).
(DRM);DNF. (Eng.)

05/07: G.P. von Tourenwagen, Nürburgring, #53: Schornstein; 4th.

01/08: AvD Gold Pokal, Hockenheim: Schornstein, #53; 7th.

23/08: Westfalen-Pokal, Zolder; Schornstein, #53; 5th.

06/09: Hessen Cup, Hockenheim: Schornstein, #53; 8th.

27/09: Brands Hatch 6-Hours: Schornstein, #26; 6th OA.

08/11: Kyalami 9-Hours: Schornstein/Wilson; DNF.

1982: (As a Joest entered 2.8 "J").

21/03: Bergischer Lowe, Zolder: Schornstein, #7; 5th.

28/03: Nürburgring: Heyer; DNF. (Turbocharger).

04/04: Jim Clark Trophy, Hockenheim: Schornstein, #7; 7th.

18/04: Monza 1000 Km WCM: Merl/Schornstein/Wollek, #86; 4th OA.

25/04: Eifelrennen, Nürburgring, #7: Schornstein; DNS. (Crash in warm-up).

09/05: Mainz-Finthen: Schornstein, #7; 8th.

16/05: Silverstone 6-Hours WCM: Schornstein/Grohs, #63; 12th.

23/05: Bavaria-Rennen, Salzburgring DRM: Schornstein, #7; 5th.

06/06: Wunstorf DRM: Schornstein, #7; DNF. (Engine).

18/06: Reported as "destroyed" at the Le Mans 24-Hours practice when driven by Harald Grohs;

1984: Remains sold to Siggy Brun; restored.
1987: Sold to Hein Gericke.
2000: Sold to Pat Jennings, South Africa.
2004: Sold to Stephan Reutmayer.
2005: Sold to Dario Afonso.
Latest 3.2 liter twin-turbo engine w/ air-to-air cooler fitted.
2005: Sold to George Nuenas. Portugal.
2008: STPO.

Chassis No: 935.81. J.R.001
Colour: White.

The first Joest-built "Moby Dick" replica was raced by Jochen Mass for the Joest Racing Team in 1981 before being leased and then sold to Joest's customer, Dr. Gianpiero Moretti.

Moretti raced the car in IMSA events in 1981 and then, with Mauro Baldi, undertook some World and German National Championship races in 1982 with some good results. In 1983, Moretti raced the car again in U.S. IMSA races and then retired it, having taken delivery of a March 82G.

1981: German National Championship:
22/03: Zolder: Mass, #66; 3rd.
29/03: 300Km Nürburgring: Mass, #66; 2nd.
05/04: Hockenheim: Mass, #66; 1st.

Leased, sold to G. Moretti. Repainted red. "Momo" sponsorship.

26/04: Riverside; Los Angeles Times GP: Moretti/Mass, #30; 14th.
03/05: Laguna Seca: Moretti, #30; 8th.
25/05: Lime Rock: Moretti/Holbert, #30; 4th.
31/05: Mid-Ohio: Moretti/Rahal, #30; 2nd.
14/06: Brainerd: Moretti, #30; 22nd.
28/06: Norisring: Moretti, #70; 2nd in DRM, 5th in

200 Miles.

12/07: Watkins Glen 6-Hours: Moretti/Rahal, #30; 6th.

26/07: Sears Point: Moretti, #30; 4th.

02/08: Portland: Moretti, #30; 2nd.

16/08: Mosport: Moretti/Rahal, #30; 26th NR.

23/08: Road America: Moretti/Rahal, #30; 5th.

13/09: Road Atlanta: Moretti, #30; 22nd NR.

1982:

16/05: Silverstone 6-Hours: Moretti/Baldi, #78; 7th OA.

23/05: ADAC Salzburgring: Moretti, #16; 4th.

06/06: ADAC Wunstorf: Moretti, #16; 5th.

27/07: Nurnberg 200, Norisring: Moretti; DNF. (Acc.)

07/08: G.P. von Deutschland, Hockenheim: Moretti; DNF. (Acc.)

05/09: Spa 1000Km: Moretti/Baldi, #60; 7th OA.

19/09: Mugello: Moretti/Baldi, #3; 8th OA.

06/11: Kyalami 9-Hours: Moretti/Baldi/van der Merwe, #7; 5th.

1983:

10/04: Road Atlanta: Moretti/Van der Merwe, #30; 3rd.

24/04: Riverside 6-Hours: Wollek/de Narvaez, #46; 3rd.

24/07: Sears Point: Moretti/Van der Merwe, #30; 7th.

31/07: Portland: Moretti/Van der Merwe, #30; 22ndNR.

11/09: Pocono: Moretti/Van der Merwe, #30; 2nd.

27/11: Daytona finale: Moretti/Van der Merwe, #30; 7th.

Sent to Australia, not allowed to be raced by CAMS regulations, returned to America.

1993:

Sold through Rick Cole.

Sold to Angelo Pallavicini.

2000: Sold through John Starkey

2001: For sale.

2002: Sold to Wayne Jackson.

Sold to Chris Cox.

Sold to Roger Brown.

2005: RM Auction, Monterey. Sold, $340,000.

2007: RM Auction, Amelia Island: STPO.

Chassis No: 935.81.J.R.002

Tube framed 935/78.

Engine: 930/79.

Gearbox Type: 930/60.

Colour: White/Blue.

The second Joest built "Moby Dick" replica with air-cooled engine. Built for the long distance races and sold to John Fitzpatrick Racing. It won it's class, placing 4th overall, at Le Mans in 1982. Sadly, Rolf Stommelen was killed in it at Riverside when the tail flew off at a fast part of the track.

The remains were stored and the car later on rebuilt.

1982:

19-20/06: Le Mans: Fitzpatrick entry. J.Fitzpatrick/ Hobbs, #:79; 4th OA, 1st in class.

06/11: Kyalami 9-Hours: J.Fitzpatrick/D. Wilson, #10; DNF.

1983:

24/04: Riverside 6-Hours: R.Stommelen/D.Bell, #12.; DNF, Accident. Car badly damaged.

2007: Sold in USA.

2011: STPO, France.

Chassis No: 000 0012
Color: White.
A Joest built 935J.

When Moretti bought 930 890 0014 in February, 1980, he also ordered this car, (000 0012). The car was sold to Mauricio de Narvaez, and was looked after by Franz Blam's shop in Atlanta, Georgia in 1981. In the next two years, it was raced by Mauricio de Narvaez in IMSA events.

It has the distinction of being the last 935 to win a major International race, (Sebring 12-Hours, 1984).

1980: Delivered to Gianpiero Moretti.
05/07: Watkins Glen: Joest/Moretti/Ploe, #30; DNF. Pole position.
30/10-6/11: Giro d'Italia: Moretti/Schon/Radaelli; DNF. (Engine).

1981:
31/1-1/02: Daytona 24-Hours: Merl/Mass/Joest, #6; 59th NR. (Acc).
Repaired and leased to De Narvaez.
26/04: Riverside: Akin/McKitterick/deNarvaez, #46; 23rd OA.
03/05: Laguna Seca: De Narvaez, #46; 11th OA.
05/07: Daytona 250 Miles: De Narvaez/Haywood, #46; 1st OA .

26/07: Sears Point 100 Miles: De Narvaez, #46; 5th OA.
02/08: Portland 100 Miles: De Narvaez, #46; 7th OA.
16/08: Mosport 1000 Kms: De Narvaez/Garretson, #46; 7th OA.
23/08: Road America 500 Miles: De Narvaez/Bell, #46; 27th OA.
13/09: Road Atlanta 150 Miles: De Narvaez, #46; 3rd OA.
07/11: Kyalami 9-Hours: Bell/de Narvaez/Martin, #3; 3rd OA.
29/11: Daytona 250 Miles: De Narvaez, #46; 4th OA.

1982: Returned to Joest Racing. Stored.

1983:
27/02: Miami GP: De Narvaez, #46; 15th.

The car has an Andial-built engine fitted, (originally from Moretti's March 82G).

1984:
25-26/02: Miami GP: De Narvaez/Heyer, #46; DNF.

1985:
24/02: Miami GP: De Narvaez/"Winter", #48; 14th.
23/03: Sebring 12-Hours: De Narvaez/Cowart/ Miller, #43; DNF.

Sold to Andre Bauer of Guatamala.
Sold to Roy Bauer.

1987?: Sold to Kevin Jeannette. Engine #: Andial 183 installed.
1988:Sold to Burkhard von Schenk. White, In Vegla colours.
1999: Sold to Kerry Morse and Jim Oppenheimer.
2000: Sold to Morespeed, CA.
2004: Sold again. (Kerry Morse).

Chassis No: 000 0022
Delivered to Gelo Racing Team.

Colour: White.
935/77 type rear bodywork.
This 935 was built by the factory mechanics for Georg Loos and raced by Bob Wollek in 1980 with success. It was sold to Alan Hamilton of Australia afterwards and raced there by Alan Jones and Rusty French.

Alan Jones won the 1982 Australian GT Championship and Rusty French won the 1983 Australian GT Championship with it.

1980:
23/03: Bergische Lowe Zolder: Wollek, #16; 3rd.
30/03: Nürburgring 300Km: Wollek, #16; DNF. (Acc).
13/04: Jim Clark-Rennen Hockenheim: Wollek, #9; 4th.
27/04: Eifelrennen Nürburgring: Wollek, #9; 2nd.
18/05: Mainz-Finthen: Wollek, #9; 1st.
01/06: Kreutzritter-Rennen Spa: Wollek, #9; 4th. Painted black with red and white stripes and sponsored by Krause.
14-15/06: Le Mans 24-Hours: Wollek/Kelleners, #45; DNF. (Engine).
22/06: Norisring Nurnberg: Wollek, #9; DNF. (Acc).
13/07: Bavaria-Rennen Salzburgring: Wollek, #9; 3rd.
27/07: Diepholz: Wollek, #9; 2nd.
24/08: Westfalen-Pokal Zolder: Wollek, #9; 2nd. Repainted in white, sponsored by Kastle.
07/09: Hessen-Cup Hockenheim: Wollek, #9; 4th.

21/09: Supersprint Nürburgring: Wollek, #9; 6th.
28/09: Preis von Baden-Wurtemburg Hockenheim: Wollek, #9; DNF. (engine).

Rebuilt by the factory.
1981: Sold to Alan Hamilton, Australia.

1982: Raced by Alan Jones to win the 1982 Australian GT Championship. Won 16 out of 17 races entered.
16/05: Winton: A. Jones; 1st OA.
16/06: Oran Park: A. Jones; 1st OA.
20/06: Lakeside: A. Jones; 1st OA.
04/07: Adelaide: A. Jones; 1st OA.
11/07: Wanneroo Park: A. Jones; 1st OA.
01/08: Calder: A. Jones; 1st OA.
29/08: Surfers Paradise: A. Jones; 1st OA.
19/09: Symmons Plains: A. Jones 1st OA.
10/10: Baskerville: A. Jones; 1st OA.

1983: Sold to Rusty French.
Australian GT Champion won by French.

Chassis No: 000 0024
Supplied to Brumos to be built up by Jack Atkinson.
Colour: White.

Sold to Bruce Leven and raced by him and Hurley Haywood, 00024's main claim to fame was winning the Sebring 12 Hour race in 1981. At this event, 0024 wore the Joest 935/77 style bodywork taken off 930 990 0032, the Moretti/Jim Busby 935 of 1979. Sadly, Hurley Haywood had a hub break on him at practice at Sears Point in July and the car went off course. Although little damaged, the hot turbochargers set fire to the dry grass and the car was burnt out.

Leven bought chassis #000 0028 from Brumos to replace the #000 0024 car. He later on sold the old bodyshell.

1980:
22/03: Sebring 12-Hours: Gregg/Haywood/Leven, #86; 10th OA.

27/04: Riverside: Leven/Haywood; 3rd OA.
17/08: Mosport 6-Hours: Haywood/Leven, #86; 14th OA.
31/08: Road America, Elkhart Lake: Haywood/Leven; DNF.

1981:
31/1-1/02: Daytona 24-Hours: Leven/Haywood/Barth, #86; 42nd NR.
21/03: Sebring 12-Hours: Leven/Holbert/Haywood, #86; 1st.
12/04: Road Atlanta: Haywood, #86; 6th.
26/04: Riverside 6-Hours: Haywood/Leven, #86; 5th.
03/05: Laguna Seca: Haywood, #86; 9th.
31/05: Mid-Ohio: Leven, #86; 31st NR.
14/06: Brainerd: Leven, #86; 4th.
26/07: Sears Point: Haywood, #86; DNS. (Acc.)
Car crashed and burned in practice.

Chassis No: 000 0025
Sold to the John Pauls, not assembled until the 1990s.

1999/2000: Raced in HSR events.

Chassis No: 000 0026
Engine number: 698 0054.
Colour: White/Blue.

This 935 appears as if it is a re-shell of an earler, possibly 1977 car. Sold to the Swiss privateer, Antoine Salamin in 1980. It has 1978/79 factory bodywork, upright gearbox and a twin-turbo 930/78 engine.
    Sold to Germany in the 90s and sold to America in 2000.

All Swiss Championship Races:

1981: (First result overall, second result is in class)
22/03: Hockenheim: Salamin; 1st.
12/04: Hockenheim: Salamin; 6th/3rd.
19/04: Dijon: Salamin: 6th/2nd.

10/05: Dijon: Salamin; 6th/2nd.
07/06: Misano: Salamin; 4th/2nd.
12/07: Hockenheim: Salamin; 8th/3rd.
09/08: Ayent-Anzere: Salamin; 8th/2nd.
23/08: St. Ursannes: Salamon; 3rd in class
06/09: Laroche - La Berra: Salamin; 4th/1st.
13/09: Gurnigel: Salamin; 7th/3rd.
11/10: Hockenheim 3-Hours: Salamin/Vanoli; 2nd OA.

1982:
21/03: Hockenheim: Salamin; 2nd.
31/05: Zeltweg: Salamin; 1st/1st.
11/07: Hockenheim: Salamin; 10th/6th.
25/07: Hockenheim: Salamin; 4th/4th.
01/08: Ayent-Anzere: Salamin; 10th/6th.
10/10: Hockenheim 3-Hours: Salamin/P. Schaerer; 1st OA.

1983:
03/04: Dijon: Salamin: 2nd.
17/04: Hockenheim: Salamin; 2nd/1st.
01/05: Monza: Salaminl; 16th, 1st in class.
15/05: Dijon: Salamin;16th, 1st in class.

03/07: Hockenheim: Salamin; 4th, 2nd in class.
31/07: Ayent-Anzere: Salamin; 6th, 1st in class.
28/08: Oberhallau: Salamin; 3rd, 1st in class.
11/09: Gurnigel: Salamin; 9th, 1st in class.
18/09: Bergrennen Kalter Wangen: Salamin; 1st in class.

1984:
22/04: Dijon: Salamin: 5th, 1st in class.
06/05: Hockenheim: Salamin; 3rd, 1st in class.
10/06: Zeltweg: Salamin; 3rd, 2nd in class.
08/07: Hockenheim: Salamin; 9th, 2nd in class.
19/08: Oberhallau: Salamin; 7th, 2nd in class.
26/08: St. Ursanne: Salamin; 28th, 1st in class.
16/09: Bergrennen Kalter Wangen: Salamin; 1st.

1985:
07/04: Dijon: Salamin: 3rd, 1st in class.
12/05: Hockenheim: Salamin; 3rd, 1st in class.
26/05: Misano: Salamin; 2nd, 1st in class.
23/06: Magny Cours: Salamin; 4th, 2nd in class.
07/07: Hockenheim: Salamin; 5th, 1st in class.
21/07: Eggbergrennen: Salamin; 1st.
11/08: Ayent-Anzere: Salamin; 6th, 3rd in class
18/08: St. Ursanne: Salamin; 24th, 1st in class.
01/09: Laroche La Berra: Salamin; 6th, 1st in class.

1986:
12/01: Hockenheim 3 hours: Salamin; 5th/3rd.
13/04: Dijon: Salamin: 7th, 1st in class.
11/05: Hockenheim: Salamin; 5th, 1st in class.
18/05: Varano: Salamin; 4th.1st in class.
08/06: Varano: Salamin; 1st in class.
22/06: Magny Cours: Salamin; 4th, 1st in class.
13/07: Hockenheim: Salamin; 1st.
17/08: St. Ursanne-Les Rangiers: Salamin; 1st in class.
24/08; Vuiteboeuf; Salamin; 4th. 2nd in class.
31/08: Oberhallau: Salamin; 10th, 1st in class.
07/09: Laroche La Berra: Salamin; 7th, 1st in class.
14/09: Gurnigel: Salamin; 7th, 1st in class.

Sold to Hubertus von Donhoff. Engine number 698 0954 installed.

2000: Sold to Kerry Morse.
2005: STPO.

Chassis No: 000 0028
Colour: White/Red/Blue.
Built up by Jack Atkinson of Brumos with factory-supplied bodyshell, six inches wider front track, "Moby Dick" type nose, 935/77 bodywork and air to air intercooler. Delivered to Peter Gregg in 1980 and, in December, tested by him at Daytona. Not raced.

In late 1981, after his other 935 had been burnt out at Sears Point, it was sold to Bruce Leven who, with Hurley Haywood, raced it until 1984.

1980:
December: Tested at Daytona.

1981: Sold to B. Leven.
13/09· Road Atlanta: Leven/Haywood, #86; 19thNR.
27/09: Pocono: Leven/Haywood, #86; 6th.
29/11: Daytona: Haywood, #86; 3rd.

1982:
30-31/01: Daytona 24-Hours: Leven/Haywood/Holbert, #86; 13th.
20/03: Sebring 12-Hours: Leven/Haywood/Holbert, #86; 4th.
01/08: Portland: Haywood, #85; 21st NR.
28/11: Daytona: Holbert/Bundy/Henn, #6; 4th.

1983:
5-6/02: Daytona 24-Hours: Leven/Haywood/Holbert, #86; 16th.
19/03: Sebring 12-Hours: Haywood/Holbert, #86; 3rd.

1984:
4-5/02: Daytona 24-Hours: Leven/Haywood/Holbert, #86; 4th.
24/03: Sebring 12-Hours: Ballot-Lena/Haywood/Holbert, #86; 44th NR.
Sold to a Toyota dealer in Chicago. (Werner).
30/09: Watkins Glen: Frank/D. White, #83; 6th/1st. (as a 935?)
25/11: Daytona: Frank/White;52nd NR.

1985:
19/5: Charlotte: Frank/White, (935); 10th/6th.

1986: Sold to Dennis de Franceski.
1999: Sold to Phil Bagley.

2000: 03/6: Exchanged for 934, uprated to 935, chassis number 930 670 0152 at Watkins Glen HSR meeting. (Paul Reisman).
2004: STPO.

Chassis No: 000 0029
1980 Competition shell sold to Alan Hamilton.
Built up by Hamilton with Kremer K3 bodywork & 3.2 engine.
1984: Sold to Rusty French.
1984/5: Raced by French in Australia and Britain.
1989: Won the British G.T. Championship.

Chassis No: 911 660 9057
This 1976 Bodyshell was ordered from Porsche-Kremer/DP-Motorsport by Gabriel Schon and was built up as a 935. Schon did a few races with the car and then sold it to the German team of Altenbach-Oppermann. (1976 chassis).
Altenbach-Oppermann raced this car for one year and won the German Endurance title.

The team bought from the Factory an 2,994 ccm twin turbo IMSA engine type 962-78, giving 805 horsepower. (Porsche built just one of these engines).
Willi Rabl bought the car via Ekkehard Zimmermann of DP-Motorsport from Mr Otto Altenbach.
He used it in the European Hill Climb Championship and won 2 titles. Afterwards, Willi Rabl kept the car for many years, before selling it to America.

Chassis No: 935-84
Colour: Red.

A tube frame car built for Bob Akin; "the last 935" was a success, although appearing just too late to make a significant mark. 3.2 engine giving 836 BHP.

1984:
4-5/02: Daytona 24 Hours WCM: Akin/O'Steen/Rahal, #5; 56thNR.
20/02: Miami G.P: Akin/O'Steen, #05;22ndNR.
28/05: Lime Rock: Akin/O'Steen, #05; 7th.

1985:

2-3/2: Daytona 24 Hours WCM: Mullen/Nierop/
McIntyre, #7: 5th OA.
1997:
Sold to Steve Southard.
Raced in HSR events.
2006: Sold to Van Zannis.
2007: STPO. (James Edwards)
2015: "Rennsport Reunion", Laguna Seca. Patrick
Long driving.

**Chassis No: JLP-1: See: Chassis No: 930 770
0953/930 890 0037**
Engine Type: 930/78.
Gearbox Type: 930/25.
Color: Blue w/yellow stripes.

After Dick Barbour's damaged 934 1/2, chassis
number 930 770 0953 had been stripped of parts,
Barbour used chassis number 930 890 0037 to build
up another car. That car was sold to John Paul who
raced it until it was destroyed at the 1979 Daytona
Finale. Along the way, John Paul Sr. racked up
some good results.

1978:

27/08: Mid-Ohio: Paul Sr/Haywood, #18; 12thNR.
26/11: Daytona: Paul Sr, #18; 3rd.
1979:
3-4/02: Daytona 24 Hours WCM: Paul Sr/Holbert/
Keyser, #18;65th NR.
17/03: Sebring 12 Hours WCM: Paul Sr/Holbert,
#18;24th NR.
22/04: Riverside 6-Hours: Paul Sr/Holbert, #18; 2nd
OA.
09/05: Mexico City TA: J. Paul Sr; 1st.
03/06: Westwood TA: J. Paul Sr; 1st.
10/06: Portland TA: J. Paul Sr; 1st.
07/07: Watkins Glen 6-Hours: Paul Sr/Holbert, #18;
6th OA.
21/07: Road America, Elkhart Lake TA: J. Paul Sr;
4th.
05/08: Watkins Glen TA: J. Paul Sr; 1st.
19/08: Mosport: J. Paul Sr; 1st.
31/08: Road America 500 Miles: Pauls, #18; 1st.
01/09:Trois Rivieres TA: J. Paul Sr; 1st.
23/09: Road Atlanta: Paul Sr, #18; 2nd.
16/10: Laguna Seca: J. Paul, #18; 14th.
25/11: Daytona 250 Mile Finale: Paul/Miller,
#18;4th. Wrecked in last-lap accident.

Chassis No: JLP-2
Chassis No: 009 0043
Engine Type: 930/80

Gearbox Type: 930/60.
Color: Blue w/yellow stripes.
A competition chassis bought from the factory, 009 0043 was built to Kremer K3 specification for John Paul Sr; painted blue and yellow. With it, he won the 1980 Endurance Driver's Championship, for the best results obtained in Europe and America. Sold to Marty Speer in 1982 and continued racing with him and Terry Wolters until 1984.

1980:
13/04: Road Atlanta 30 Minutes: Paul, #18; 6th.
27/04: L.A. Times GP, Riverside 5-Hours: Paul Sr, #18; DNF. (Engine).
11/05: Silverstone 6-Hours: J.Paul Sr./Redman, #18; 3rd OA.
18/05: Nürburgring 1000Kms: Redman/Henn/Paul, #12; DNF.
12-13/06: Le Mans 24-Hours: Paul/Edwards/Paul, #73; 9th OA, 2nd in IMSA class.
05/07: Watkins Glen 6 Hours: J. Paul Sr/J.Paul Jr/P. Henn, #73; 14th OA.
27/07: Golden State 100 Miles: Paul Sr, #18; 5th.
03/08: Portland 100 Miles: J.Paul Sr, #18; 4th.
17/08: Mosport: J. Paul Sr/J.Paul Jr, #18; 2nd OA.
31/08: Road America 500 Miles: J. Paul Sr/J.Paul Jr, #18; 1st OA.
21/09: Road Atlanta 50 Miles: J. Paul Sr., #18; (1):

3rd OA. (2): 3rd OA.
30/11: Daytona 250 Miles Finale: J. Paul Sr/J.Paul Jr, #18; 2nd OA.

1981:
31/1-1/2: Daytona 24-Hours: Paul/Paul/Smiley, #18; 60th NR.
20-21/3: Sebring 12 Hours: J.Paul Sr/J. Paul Jr, #8; DNF.
26/04: L.A. Times GP, Riverside 6-Hours: Moran/ Erstad, #18; 10th.
12/07: Watkins Glen 6-Hours: J. Paul Sr/J.Paul Jr, #18; DNF.
39/08: Mid-Ohio: R. /M.L. Speer, #18; 9th.
29/11: Daytona Finale: J. Garza, #8; 6th.

1982:
30-31/1: Daytona 24-Hours: J. Paul Sr, #18; DNS.

Sold to Marty Speer.
20/03: Sebring 12-Hours: Speer/Wolters/Mendez, #8;3rd OA.
25/04: L.A. Times GP, Riverside: Speer/Wolters; 3rd OA.
16/05: Charlotte: Speer/Wolters; 5th OA.
04/07: Daytona: Speer/Wolters; 2nd OA.
15/08: Mosport: Speer/Wolters; 5th OA.
22/08: Road America: Speer/Wolters; 8th OA.
05/09: Mid-Ohio: Speer/Wolters: 7th OA.
12/09: Road Atlanta: Speer/Wolters; 4th OA.
26/09: Pocono: Speer/Wolters; 11th OA.
28/11: Daytona Finale: Speer/Wolters; 9th OA.

1983:
5-6/02: Daytona 24-Hours:Speer/Madren/Ratcliff, #24; 4th OA.
21/03: Sebring 12-Hours: Speer/Madren/Ratcliff, #24; 44thNR.
10/04: Road Atlanta: Speer/Madren; 25th OA.
24/04: L.A. Times GP, Riverside: Speer/Madren; 49thNR.
15/05: Charlotte; Speer/Madren; 4th OA.
19/06: Mid-Ohio: Madren/Speer; 9th OA.
03/07: Daytona: Speer/Pickering; 5th OA.

14/08: Mosport: Speer/Madren/Pickering; 9th OA.
21/08: Road America, Elkhart Lake: Madren; 48th NR.
27/11: Daytona: Lanier/Varde;43rd NR.

1984:
5-6/02: Daytona 24 Hours: B. Hefner/J. Griffin/H. Gralia, #24; 19th OA.
24/03: Sebring 12 Hours: M.L. Speer/J. Griffin, #24; 50thNR.
08/05: L.A. Times GP, Riverside: M.L. Speer/J. Griffin, #24; 12th OA.
26/08: Road America, Elkhart Lake: Speer/Griffin; 38thNR

1985:
23/03: Sebring 12 Hours: M. Hinze/M. Minter/A. Yarosh, #16; 50thNR.

1986:
23/03: Sebring 12 Hours: M. Hinze/J. Newsum/T. Blackaller, #16; 15th OA.

1988: Sold to Dick Silva.

1994/5: Restored by Andial. 8-Hours time since rebuild. Zytec injection installed plus 17 inch rear wheels fitted.
1995: Raced in vintage events by Bruce Dandrew.
1999: Sold to James Floyd, Houston, Texas. $175,000. One test at Texas Speedway. Engine rebuilt by Andial.
2006: Sold to Present owner.
2013: Bodywork renovated, repainted. New FIA fuel cell.

Chassis No: JLP-3
Chassis number: ??
Engine Type: 930/80.
Gearbox Type: 930/60.
Color: blue w/yellow stripes.

A space Frame car built by GAACO in Norcross, Georgia. The roof and cabin were from a 1972

911T. John Paul Jr. was the IMSA Camel GT Champion of 1982 using this car and a Lola T600.
1981:
21/03: Sebring 12-Hours: J.Pauls, #8;66th NR.
12/04: Road Atlanta: J. Paul Jr;, #8; 8th NR.
26/04: Riverside 6-Hours: John Pauls, #8; 2nd.
03/05: Laguna Seca: J. Paul Jr, #8; 2nd.
25/05: Lime Rock: J. Paul Jr, #18; 6th.
31/05 Mid-Ohio: J. Paul Jr, #18; 3rd.
14/06: Brainerd: J. Paul Sr;, #18 3rd.
04/07: Daytona: J. Paul Jr, #18; 3rd.
16/08: Mosport 6-Hours: Pauls/Bell; 30th NR. (Acc.)
23/08: Road America, Elkhart Lake: Pauls, #18; 13th NR.
30/08: Mid-Ohio: Ratcliff/Speer, #18; 9th.
13/09: Road Atlanta: Paul Sr, #18; 27th NR.
27/09: Pocono: Paul/Paul, #18; 1st.
29/11: Daytona Finale: Paul Jr, #18; 1st.

1982:
30-31/01: Daytona 24-Hours: John Pauls/ Stommelen, #18; 1st OA.
20/3: Sebring 12-Hours: John Paul Sr/Paul Jr, #18; 1st OA.
04/04: Road Atlanta: Paul Jr, #18; 1st.
25/04: Riverside 6-Hours: John Pauls; 1st.

16/05: Charlotte: Paul Jr/Paul Sr, #18; 1st.
03/07: Daytona: Paul Jr, #18; 18th NR.
25/07: Sears Point: Paul Jr, #18;20th NR.
15/08: Mosport: Pauls, #46; 1st.
22/08: Road America: Paul Jr./De Narvaez, #46; 2nd.
05/09: Mid-Ohio: Paul Jr, #46; 41st NR.
12/09: Road Atlanta: Pauls, #46; 1st.
26/09: Pocono: John Paul Jr, #46; 2nd.

1983:
5-6/02: Daytona 24-Hours: Paul, Sr; 76th NR.

1985: Sold to Dick Silva.
2-3/02: Daytona 24-Hours: F. Baker/D. Silver/D. Herman, #20; 66th NR.
23/03: Sebring 12-Hours: F. Baker/D. Silver/D. Herman, #20; 23rd.
09/06: Mid-Ohio: F. Baker/D. Silver/D. Herman, #00; 15th.
06/10: Columbus: D. Silver/J. Varde, #00; 17th.

2005: Sold to Wayne Jackson
2006: Sold to Chris Cox.
2007: RM Auction, Amelia Island: Bid to $680,000. No sale.
2008: Sold to Eric Endeholm. USA.
2009: Sold to Steve Goldin, USA.
2012: Sold to Europe.

Chassis No: JLP-4
Colour: Blue/Yellow, later red/white.

1982:
11/07: Brainerd: John Paul Jr.,,#18; 1st.
25/07: Sears Point: John Paul, #18; 20th NR.
01/08: Portland: John Paul Jr #18; 1st.
22/08: J. Paul Sr/H. Haywood, #18; 9th.
Crashed at Road Atlanta in testing; rebuilt.
28/11: Daytona Finale: J. Paul Jr, #1; 51st NR. (transmission).

1983:
10/04: Road Atlanta: John Paul Jr; 6th.

Sold to an attorney.
Stored in a museum.

1998: For sale with Grand Prix Classics.
1998: Sold to R. Tornello.
Daytona Enduro: DNF (Turbo).

1999:
05/03: Sebring Enduro: Tornello; DNF, (acc).
07/11: Daytona Finale: Tornello/Starkey; 2nd in class.

2004: Rennsport, Daytona: Totally rebuilt.
2008: Sold to Mauro Borella, Italy.
2017: STPO.

Chassis No: 935.81. J.R.001
Engine Type: 930/79.
Gearbox Type: 930/60.
Colour: White.

The first Joest-built "Moby Dick" replica was raced by Jochen Mass for the Joest Racing Team in 1981 before being leased and then sold to Joest's customer, Dr. Gianpiero Moretti.

Moretti raced the car in IMSA events in 1981 and then, with Mauro Baldi, undertook some World

and German National Championship races in 1982 with some good results. In 1983, Moretti raced the car again in U.S. IMSA races and then retired it, having taken delivery of a March 82G.

1981: German National Championship:
22/03: Zolder: Mass, #66; 3rd.
29/03: 300Km Nürburgring: Mass, #66; 2nd.
05/04: Hockenheim: Mass, #66; 1st.

Leased, sold to G. Moretti. Repainted red.

26/04: Riverside; Los Angeles Times GP: Moretti/Mass, #30; 14th.
03/05: Laguna Seca: Moretti, #30; 8th.
25/05: Lime Rock: Moretti/Holbert, #30; 4th.
31/05: Mid-Ohio: Moretti/Rahal, #30; 2nd.
14/06: Brainerd: Moretti, #30; 22nd.
28/06: Norisring: Moretti, #70; 2nd in DRM, 5th in 200 Miles.
12/07: Watkins Glen 6-Hours: Moretti/Rahal, #30; 6th.
26/07: Sears Point: Moretti, #30; 4th.
02/08: Portland: Moretti, #30; 2nd.
16/08: Mosport: Moretti/Rahal, #30; 26th NR.
23/08: Road America: Moretti/Rahal, #30; 5th.
13/09: Road Atlanta: Moretti, #30; 22nd NR.

1982:
16/05: Silverstone 6-Hours: Moretti/Baldi, #78; 7th OA.

23/05: ADAC Salzburgring: Moretti, #16; 4th.
06/06: ADAC Wunstorf: Moretti, #16; 5th.
27/07: Nurnberg 200, Norisring: Moretti; DNF. (Acc.)
07/08: G.P. von Deutschland, Hockenheim: Moretti; DNF. (Acc.)
05/09: Spa 1000Km: Moretti/Baldi, #60; 7th OA.
19/09: Mugello: Moretti/Baldi, #3; 8th OA.
06/11: Kyalami 9-Hours: Moretti/Baldi/van der Merwe, #7; 5th.

1983:
10/04: Road Atlanta: Moretti/Van der Merwe, #30; 3rd.
24/04: Riverside 6-Hours: Wollek/de Narvaez, #46; 3rd.
24/07: Sears Point: Moretti/Van der Merwe, #30; 7th.
31/07: Portland: Moretti/Van der Merwe, #30; 22ndNR.
11/09: Pocono: Moretti/Van der Merwe, #30; 2nd.
27/11: Daytona finale: Moretti/Van der Merwe, #30; 7th.
Sent to Australia, not allowed to be raced by CAMS regulations, returned to America.

1993:
Sold through Rick Cole.

Sold to Angelo Pallavicini.
2000: Sold through John Starkey.
2001: For sale.
2002: Sold to Wayne Jackson.
Sold to Chris Cox.
Sold to Roger Brown.
2005: RM Auction, Monterey. Sold, $340,000.
2007: RM Auction, Amelia Island: STPO.

Chassis No: 935.81.J.R.002
Tube framed 935/78.
Engine: 930/79.
Gearbox Type: 930/60.
Colour: White/Blue.

The second Joest built "Moby Dick" replica with air-cooled engine. Built for the long distance races and sold to John Fitzpatrick Racing. It won it's class, placing 4th overall, at Le Mans in 1982. Sadly, Rolf Stommelen was killed in it at Riverside when the tail flew off at a fast part of the track.

The remains were stored and the car later rebuilt.

1982:
19-20/06: Le Mans: Fitzpatrick entry. Fitzpatrick/Hobbs, #79; 4th OA, 1st in class.
06/11: Kyalami 9-Hours: Fitzpatrick/D. Wilson, #10; DNF.

1983:
24/04: Riverside 6-Hours: R.Stommelen/D.Bell, #12; DNF, Accident. Car badly damaged.

2007: Sold in USA.
2011: STPO, France.

Chassis No: 935 L
Engine Type: 930/80.
Gearbox Type: 930/60.
Colour: White.

Preston Henn's "Swap Shop" car. A tubeframe car built by Andial along "Moby Dick" lines. The car won the Daytona 24-Hours in 1983 with a notable crew of drivers!

1982:
25/04: LA Times GP, Riverside: A.Holbert/H.Grohs, #3; 2nd.

1983:
1-2/02: Daytona 24 Hours WCM: Henn/Wollek/Foyt/Ballot-Lena, #6; 1st.
27/02: Miami: Wollek, #09; 9th.
19/03: Sebring 12-Hours: Bell/Andretti/Paul, #09; DNF.
24/04: Riverside 6-Hours: Andretti/Henn/Foyt; 20th NR.
03/07: Paul Revere 250, Daytona: Foyt/Haywood; 1st.
14/08: Mosport: Graham/Haywood/Wachs, #6; 10th.
21/08: Road America: Henn/Paul Jr; 33rd NR.

1984:
4-5/02: Daytona 24 Hours WCM: Race No: 6. Foyt/Wollek/Bell, #6; 2nd O.A.
26/02: Miami GP: Foyt/Wollek, #6; 4th.
24/03: Sebring 12 Hours WCM: Bell/Foyt/Wollek, #6; 3rd OA.

1985:
2-3/02: Daytona 24 Hours WCM: Grohs/Brun/
Schlesser, #16;74th NR.
23/03: Sebring 12-Hours: Wollek/Whittington/Henn,
#7; DNF.

In the Harrah collection.

Chassis No: 935-LT1
Engine Type: 930/80.
Gearbox Type: 930/60.
Colour: Red.

A Monocoque-chassised car built up by Chuck Gaa
in Atlanta for Bob Akin. The car always suffered
from handling problems although being very fast in
a straight line.

1982: Coca-Cola sponsored.
19-20/06: Le Mans 24-Hours: Akin entry. Akin/
Cowart/Miller. #76. DNF.
22/08: Road America: Akin/Bell, #5; 33rd NR.
05/09: Mid-Ohio 2: Akin/Haywood, #5; 4th.
12/09: Road Atlanta 2: Akin/Bell, #5; 7th.
26/09: Pocono: Akin/Bell; DNF.
28/11: Damaged at the Daytona Finale.
1999: Restored by Jacques Rivard.
07/11: Daytona: Rivard; DNF.

2000: STPO.
2001: Lime Rock: N. Guarriello.
2006: Sold through John Starkey to Bruce Canepa.
2006: Sold.
2007: For sale again.

Chassis No: 935 L-1
A Tubeframe car built for the 1980 German DRM
Championship by Swede Jan Lundgardh, and Josef
Zierkelbach and Porsche Engineer Eberhard Braun,
both German, to run in the under 2.0 L Class of
the DRM. It used one of the only two 1.4 L Turbo
engines built by the factory in 1977 (the factory built
Baby car won the 1977 Season final at Hockenheim
using the other 1.4 L engine).

This car then raced in the 1980-1981 German
DRM Championship, the World Endurance
Championship as well as at the 24H of Le Mans in
1981. This car was very light, weighing just 817
Kg at the 1981 Le Mans 24H scrutineering. A 3L
Turbo engine was then installed for the 1982 season
and the car was entered in a further four races of the
World Endurance Championship until retiring from
Racing in 1984.

1984: In storage with Kremer Racing.
1986: Sold to Austria.
1999: Sold to USA.
2003: STPO.

PORSCHE

ERSATZTEILEKATALOG
Nachtrag 1979

turbo

TYP 935

MODELL 1979

DR. ING. h. c. F. PORSCHE AG
STUTTGART-ZUFFENHAUSEN

APPENDIX II – THE ENGINES

All Engines: Flat Six

Car/Engine Type	Displacement (cc) Bore x Stroke (mm)	Compression Ratio	Power in DIN hp @ rpm + boost	Torque in lb. ft. @ rpm.
1974 **RSR Turbo Carrera** Type number: 911/76	2,143 cc 83 x 66 mm	6.5:1	480 @ 8,000 1.4 bar	340 @ 5,900

1976 **934** Type number: 930/71	Chassis numbers: 930 670 0151-0180 + 0540			
	2,994 cc 95 x 70.4 mm	6.5:1	530 @ 7,000 1.35 bar	434 @ 5,400
1976 **935** Type number: 930/72	Chassis numbers: 930 570 0002 + 001-002			
	2,856 cc 92.8 x 70.4 mm	6.5:1	590 @ 7,900 1.45 bar	438 @ 5,400

1977
934 and a half   Chassis numbers: 930 770 0951-0960
Type number: 930/73   2,994 cc   6.5:1   590 @   438 @
                        95 x 70.4 mm   7,500   5,400
                                                         1.45 bar

(Engine number: 677 2811-777 2820)

1977
935   Chassis numbers: 930 770 0901-0912 + 0956
Type number: 930/72   2,994 cc   6.5:1   630 @   60 mkg
                        95 x 70.4 mm   8,000   @ 5,400
                                                         1.45 bar

(Engine number: 677 2901-777 2913)

Car/Engine Type	Displacement (cc) Bore x Stroke (mm)	Compression Ratio	Power in DIN hp @ rpm + boost	Torque in lb. ft. @ rpm.
1977 **935 "Baby"** Type number: 911/79	Chassis number: 935 2 001 1,425 cc 71 x 60 mm	6.5:1	370 @ 8,000 1.4 bar	

1978
935/78
Type number: 930/78   2,994 cc   6.5:1   720 @
                        95 x 70.4 mm   7,800
                                                         1.4 bar

(Engine number: 698 0021-698 0035)

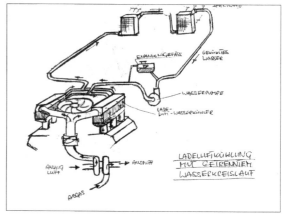

*Original factory drawing of the 1976 934's water-cooling
system to cool the engine intercoolers.*

Type number: 935/71   3,211 cc   7.0:1   750 @
95.7 x74.4 mm   8,200
1.4 bar

1979
IMSA Single-Turbo
Type number: 930/79   3,122 cc   6.5:1   715 @
97 x 70.4 mm   7,800
1.4 bar

1980
Twin-Turbo
Type number: 930/80   3,164 cc   7.2:1   760 @
95 x 74.4 mm   7,800
1.4 bar

(Engine number: 930 990 00)

1981
Twin-Turbo
Type number: 930/81   3,164 cc   7.2:1   750 @
95 x 74.4 mm   8,200
1.4 bar

1986
959/Group B   2,849 cc   8.0:1   450 @   369 @
95 x 67 mm   6,500   5,500

APPENDIX III – SPECIFICATIONS

(All linear measurements are metric unless noted otherwise.)

	1976 935	**1977 935-77**	**1978 935-78**	**1979 935K3**
ENGINE				
Cylinders	Flat 6	Flat 6	Flat 6	Flat 6
Capacity	2,856 cc	2,856 cc	3,211 cc	2,994 cc/3,162 cc
Bore/stroke	92.8 x 70.4	92,8 x 70.4	95.7 x 74.4	95 x 70.4 / 97 x 74.4 mm
Compression Ratio	6.5:1	6.5:1	7.0:1	6.5:1 / 6.8:1
Turbocharger	1 x KKK	1 x KKK	2 x KKK	2 x KKK
Injection System (all)	Bosch plunger pump			
Max Power	(see Appendix B)			

TRANSMISSION
Clutch (all) Fichtel & Sachs single-plate
Gearbox (all) Porsche 4-speed with spool
NOTE: 1977 "Baby" had Type 915, 5-speed gearbox with spool.

CHASSIS
Bodyshell As per 911 production with roll cage and strengthening.
GRP bodywork except 935 K3, which used Kevlar bodywork (prototype).
Wheels (all) 11 x 16 front (inches)
15 x 19 rear (inches)
Brakes (mm, diameter) Porsche ventilated

	332	332	332	Discs, 300 mm, perforated
DIMENSIONS				
Wheelbase	2,271 mm	2,271	2,273	2,273
Track, front	1,502 mm	1,502	1,630	1,502
Track, rear	1,560 mm	1,560	1,575	1,560
Overall Length	4,655 mm	4,680	4,890	4,790
Width	1,998 mm	1,998	1,990	1,998
Height	1,270 mm	1,265	1,200	1,230
Fuel capacity (all)	114 liter			
Weight (kg, unladen)	970	970	1,025	1,032

PORSCHE

BETRIEBSANLEITUNG

turbo

TYP 934

DR. ING. h. c. F. PORSCHE AG

STUTTGART-ZUFFENHAUSEN

EPILOGUE

It seems strange, in 2018, to have written an epilogue for a car that was so recently still in production. However, whilst the road-going turbo has gone from strength to strength, the 934s and 935s had, of course, disappeared from the modern motor racing scene. Happily, they're back! Whilst a few stalwarts, such as John Greasley and Rusty French, kept on racing them in Porsche Club competition during the 1980s, that seemed to be the end of the line for the flame-spitting behemoths.

All that changed with the upsurge of enthusiasm that accompanied the formation of, first of all, HSR (Historic Sports Racing) in America in the 1990s. This organization, headed in 2000 by the then tireless Joe and Carol Pendergast, can claim to be an historic version of the late-lamented "IMSA" series. Now one can attend HSR meetings at such classic venues as Daytona, Sebring and Road Atlanta to see the monsters in action again.

And then came, in Europe, C.E.R., or "Classic Endurance Racing", run by Frenchman Patrick Peters' organization, Peter Auto. Via the "Tour Auto", Peter Auto has come to dominate historic/vintage Motor Sport in Europe, promoting races at such iconic circuits as Spa, Monza, and latterly putting on the bi-yearly "Classic Le Mans". If you want to win in your class, you need a 934 or 935 to win this one ...

I can't leave this subject without paying tribute to the "behind the scenes" people who keep the cars running. People such as Marc de Siebenthal in Switzerland; Stefan Roitmayer of Germany; Chris Fisher of Powerhaus II in Iowa; Kevin Jeannette of Gunnar Racing in West Palm Beach, Florida; Franz Blam in Atlanta, Georgia; Phil Bagley of "Klub Sport", also in Florida; Jacques Rivard in Canada; and Jim Torres of Burbank Coachworks in Burbank, California. All enthusiastically support the racers in the USA with parts and dedicated service. Keep it up fellas! We need to enjoy these cars for as long as possible. ❏

PORSCHE

BETRIEBSANLEITUNG

TYP 934

DR. ING. h. c. F. PORSCHE AG

STUTTGART-ZUFFENHAUSEN

Also from Veloce Publishing

Follows Porsche's year-by-year progress in top flight racing, and looks in detail at the pure competition cars which brought the German marque such immense success and worldwide acclaim on the tracks. This particular volume starts with the story of the giant-killing 550 Spyders of 1953 vintage, and takes the reader, car-by-car, through all of the subsequent racing models.

ISBN: 978-1-904788-44-7
Hardback • 25x25cm • 272 pages
• 610 colour and b&w pictures

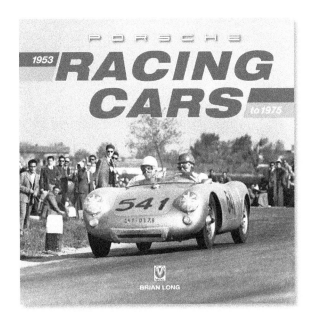

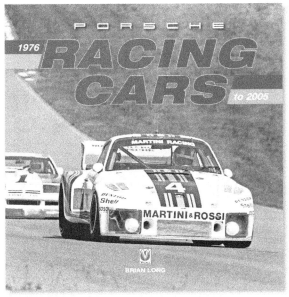

This follow-up volume begins with the story of the pure racers of 1976 vintage, and takes the reader, car-by-car, through all of the subsequent racing models, including the glorious 956 and 962, up to 2005.

ISBN: 978-1-904788-45-4
Hardback • 25x25cm • 272 pages
• 629 colour and b&w pictures

For more information and price details, visit our website at www.veloce.co.uk • email: info@veloce.co.uk
• Tel: +44(0)1305 260068

Also from Veloce Publishing

This work is a comprehensive account of the racing cars that were powered by Porsche engines, but where the chassis and development of the car was done by others. The first book on the subject, it is illustrated with many previously unpublished photos, and answers many questions for the enthusiast and newcomer alike.

ISBN: 978-1-845849-90-0
Hardback • 25x25cm • 468 pages • 799 pictures

For more information and price details, visit our website at www.veloce.co.uk • email: info@veloce.co.uk
• Tel: +44(0)1305 260068

Also from Veloce Publishing

A limited edition of 1500 copies. The 924 Carrera was a homologation model built to qualify the 924 model to race in Group 4. One of the great supercars of the 1980s, the 924 Carrera was considered by many to have better handling characteristics than Porsche's flagship 911. The book features interviews with many of those involved with the car at the time together with race stories, statistics, and a unique exposé of component failures during racing.

ISBN: 978-1-845846-45-9
Hardback • 25x25cm • 320 pages • 408 pictures

For more information and price details, visit our website at www.veloce.co.uk • email: info@veloce.co.uk
• Tel: +44(0)1305 260068

Also from Veloce Publishing

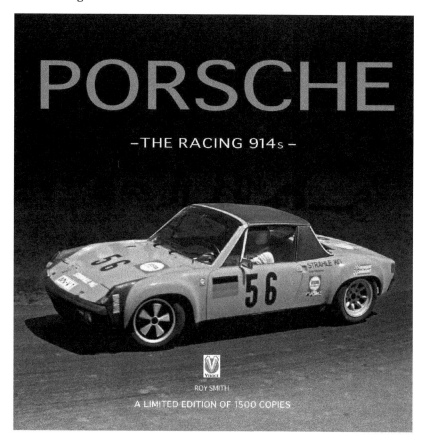

Detailed study of a remarkable little car that, when it appeared in 1969, was considered a mish-mash of ideas, and not a 'proper' Porsche. It's also the story of the 'little' guys ... the privateers and dealer teams who did most of the development that turned the 914 into great little racer.

ISBN: 978-1-845848-59-0
Hardback • 24.8x24.8cm • 320 pages • 452 colour and b&w pictures

For more information and price details, visit our website at www.veloce.co.uk • email: info@veloce.co.uk
• Tel: +44(0)1305 260068

VISIT VELOCE ON THE WEB – WWW.VELOCE.CO.UK
All current books • New book news • Special offers • Gift vouchers • Forum